The Homosexual
and Society

THE HOMOSEXUAL AND SOCIETY

An Annotated Bibliography

Compiled by
ROBERT B. MARKS RIDINGER

Bibliographies and Indexes in Sociology, Number 18

GREENWOOD PRESS
New York • Westport, Connecticut • London

Library of Congress Cataloging-in-Publication Data

Ridinger, Robert B. Marks.
    The homosexual and society : an annotated bibliography / compiled
by Robert B. Marks Ridinger.
        p. cm.—(Bibliographies and indexes in sociology, ISSN
0742-6895 ; no. 18)
    Includes bibliographical references.
    ISBN 0-313-25357-9 (alk. paper)
    1. Homosexuality—Bibliography. I. Title. II. Series.
Z7164.S42R5   1990
[HQ76.25]
016.30676'6—dc20   90-31738

British Library Cataloguing in Publication Data is available.

Library of Congress Catalog Card Number: 90-31738
ISBN: 0-313-25357-9
ISSN: 0742-6895

First published in 1990

Greenwood Press, 88 Post Road West, Westport, CT 06881
An imprint of Greenwood Publishing Group, Inc.

Printed in the United States of America

The paper used in this book complies with the
Permanent Paper Standard issued by the National
Information Standards Organization (Z39.48-1984).

10 9 8 7 6 5 4 3 2 1

Contents

Preface

In 1972, a book appeared under the title *Society and the Healthy Homosexual* from psychotherapist Dr. George Weinberg. It would have been dismissed as merely another treatment of the subject except for its focus on "a phobia--an irrational revulsion so widespread that it had gone unrecognized by most people." Weinberg's volume gave a formal name to what had been an attitude present in Western civilizations beginning with the writing of certain verses in the Book of Leviticus condemning homosexuality. In the two thousand years since those first texts were written, discrimination against homosexual men and women has taken many forms, ranging from social ostracism and the belief that killing "queers" was condoned because they had no value to society, to more extreme reactions such as drowning, hanging and the death camps of the Third Reich. Researchers interested in exploring the history of society's relationship with its homosexual members thus face a gigantic amount of literature expressing all points of view.

With the rise of the contemporary gay and lesbian liberation effort since the Stonewall Riots of 1969 came a parallel creation of bibliographies and indexes to the gay and lesbian press, opening up this body of literature for examination. In the main, however, such bibliographies have attempted to order the information into fairly broad categories. The present work takes as its subject seven areas where homophobia has been expressed in coherent form: adoption and foster care, child custody, the military establishment, employment discrimination, censorship, religion and police attitudes and actions.

Five sources of information have been consulted to obtain the entries listed: three mainstream journals of the American homosexual community--*The ADVOCATE, The Ladder* and *The Mattachine Review*, the literature of the legal profession, and popular periodicals such as *Time* and *Newsweek*. In addition, monographs dealing with any of the indicated topics, whether from an historical or contemporary viewpoint, have been included. This latter category includes such standard texts as Malcolm Boyd's *Take Off The Masks* and personal accounts by gay and lesbian professionals. With several exceptions, items issued after December, 1987 have not been entered. The time span covered comprises some two thousand years of time. Researchers wishing to place their findings in a convenient historical context will use it as a reference point.

Literature dealing with the reaction of the public towards the homosexual community as a result of the AIDS pandemic has not been included, as AIDSphobia, while usually directed at homosexuals, has since been generalized to members of other social groups.

Terms utilized in the index have been drawn from the texts of the articles and books entered. Names of specific military installations have not been used, as their designations are in the main unfamiliar to persons outside their immediate geographical regions. With regard to court cases and court decisions, researchers should be aware that each case has been entered under the personal names of the people involved, as well as under its formal title from the legal literature, e.g., *Schuster v. Schuster*. Slang terms from the gay and lesbian subculture have been referred to their standard equivalents.

In the course of every project, certain individuals are of great importance to its success without realizing it. I would like to acknowledge the advice and criticism of H. Robert Malinowsky, Stan Huntington of the Henry Gerber and Pearl M. Hart Library and Archives in Chicago, Professor Gary Klein, University Libraries, University of Toledo and Mr. Roland Hansen, Library, School of the Art Institute of Chicago. The work is dedicated to the late Joseph Gregg, Director of the Gerber-Hart Library, whose death from AIDS in November, 1987 ended a lifetime interest in the preservation and collection of the history of the gay and lesbian community of the Midwest and the United States in general. His encouragement to the original discussions on the idea of this book is gratefully remembered.

The Homosexual
and Society

Adoption/Foster Care

1. "Adopting a Lover." TIME, 98 (6 September, 1971), 50.

    This article reports the decision by a Minneapolis
    judge to permit James McConnell, 29, to legally adopt
    his roommate and lover, Jack Baker. The Gay Activists
    Alliance, a local organization, stated that this was
    believed to be the first such ruling in the United
    States permitting two homosexual men to legalize their
    relationship. Inheritance rights and university
    tuition were also discussed.

2. "Saddest of All: The Gay Kids Whom No One Wants." THE
    ADVOCATE, 102 (7 January, 1973), 7.

    The treatment accorded to gay teenagers who became
    wards of state and city governments is explored through
    interviews with Sidney Abbott (a founding member of New
    York City's Identity House), Dr. Bernice Goodman, and
    Steve Hochman of the New York Department of Child
    Welfare. Foster parent selection processes and the
    foster care system in New York State are also
    reviewed.

3. "'I' House Places Unwanted Teen." THE ADVOCATE, 103 (17
    January, 1973), 8.

The case of a black gay teenager successfully placed in a foster home through the efforts of the Identity House counselling center, New York City, is reviewed. Ms. Sidney Abbott and Dr. Bernice Goodman, both professional social workers on the center's staff, discuss their work with two other placement cases and liaison negotiations under way with the Bureau of Child Welfare, and the Department of Mental Health and Social Services of New York City.

4.   "Agency Reveals Kids Placed with Gay Couples." THE ADVOCATE, 118 (15 August, 1973), 2.

Dr. Jerome Miller, Head of Illinois' Department of Children and Family Services revealed in a newspaper interview in Chicago that his agency had placed children with homosexual tendencies in the homes of gay foster parents. Such placement was viewed as an alternative when all other efforts at foster care had failed. Miller stated that all such plans thus far submitted had been processed through the DCFS Northern District offices in Chicago. Tom Kmetko, the district director, pointed out that one of the chief problems was locating suitable homosexual couples willing to serve as foster parents. DCFS officials estimate that about a sixth of the 30,000 or so young people who are wards of the state would exhibit homosexual behavior. Carl Franklin, president of Mattachine Midwest, signalled his group's readiness to assist DCFS programs as necessary.

5.   "Gay Ban Claimed in Chicago Child Placement." THE ADVOCATE, 119 (29 August, 1973), 22.

Chicago attorney Paul Goldman, responding to statements made by Illinois Department of Children and Family Services director Dr. Jerome Miller that gay teenagers were being (or had been) placed in homosexual foster homes, charged that Miller had issued a directive banning the practice. The present article consists of interviews with Dr. Miller, who referred to the traditional approach "not to intrude on a casework decision," while admitting their personal preference for liberal heterosexuals as foster parents. Goldman cited an alleged case of placement blocked by Miller and stated that a suit had been prepared to challenge DCFS policies.

6. "Foster Teen Can't Go to Caseworker's Lover." THE
    ADVOCATE, 135 (10 April, 1974), 135.

    In 1971, Wanda Adams of Seattle left her husband and
    children, later developing a lesbian relationship with
    Pat Cull, a social worker involved in the placement of
    foster children in suitable homes. One fifteen-year-
    old girl under consideration for placement informed
    Cull that she did not want to be placed in a tradition-
    al family situation. Judging Adams (a licensed foster
    parent) to be a positive influence, Cull recommended
    that the girl be placed with her. Preliminary visits
    had been completed and preparations for receiving the
    foster child were under way when Dale Swenson, Cull's
    supervisor in the Department of Social and Health
    Services, rescinded permission. Reasons given were
    that social workers should not become emotionally
    involved with individual cases, and "the placement of a
    heterosexual girl in a lesbian home." Adams appealed
    the DSHS decision, but was informed foster parents had
    no right to a hearing. After being refused a second
    appeal at an administrative hearing, the case was taken
    to Superior Court.

7. "Seek to Block Gay Foster Homes." THE ADVOCATE, 138 (22
    May, 1974), 8.

    A series of proposed revisions in foster parent licens-
    ing regulations for the state of Washington which
    addressed the fitness of gays and lesbians to serve as
    foster homes is presented and discussed. The Isaacson-
    Schuster case is cited as legal precedent for grounds
    of fitness. Public hearings held in Olympia were
    attended by members of Action Children's Coalition (an
    organization opposing the regulations). Petition
    drives by ACC and supporters of the measure led to a
    decision to postpone a final decision until the end of
    May.

8. "Judge Places Boy in Lesbian Foster Parent's Home." THE
    ADVOCATE, 138 (22 May, 1974), 8.

    A lesbian couple in Philadelphia, Pennsylvania were
    awarded custody of a fifteen-year-old transvestite male
    with the full knowledge and assistance of the state
    agency involved. The child had a long history of
    unsuitable placement in traditional family settings,
    and was initially located through the prison ministry

of Rev. Dennis Foster of the local Metropolitan Community Church.

9. "New Row Over Gay Foster Homes." THE ADVOCATE, 141 (3 July, 1974), 6.

Following presentation of a paper entitled "Gay Men and Foster Care" to the National Conference on Social Welfare in Cincinnati, Rev. David Sindt of Chicago was accused of breaching confidentiality by citing three such placements in Illinois. Sindt discusses the accusation and reviews the history of this issue within the Department of Child and Family Services.

10. "Gay Concerns Urged for Social Workers." THE ADVOCATE, 141 (2 July, 1974), 6.

On the last day of a five-day National Conference on Social Welfare held in Cincinnati, Ohio in May, 1974, three openly gay professionals addressed the issues of acceptance, self-image, and child custody in foster parenting. David Sindt and George Alexander of Chicago and Barbara Bryant of Sacramento were the featured speakers, with Sindt specifically exploring the issue of gays as foster parents.

11. "Married Males Apply for a Child." THE ADVOCATE, 141 (3 July, 1974), 12.

The efforts of activist Jack Baker and his partner, Michael McConnell, to adopt a child are profiled. Of three agencies applied to in the Minneapolis-St. Paul area, only one, Lutheran Social Services, had so far responded to their inquiry. An interview with Patricia Eldridge, an adoption supervisor with the agency, discussed the general picture of adoption in the United States in 1974. Background on both the agency and the couple is included.

12. "Ban on Gay Foster Care Scratched from Guide." THE ADVOCATE, 142 (17 July, 1974), 11.

After three months of protest by Action Childcare Coalition (ACC) and gay activists, the State of Washington Department of Social and Health Services dropped a section of its proposed foster home guidelines prohibiting gay persons from being licensed as foster parents for placement.

13. "Agency Backs Down on Foster Children." THE ADVOCATE, 142 (17 July, 1974), 22.

Cleighton Penwell, director of Oregon's Department of Human Resources, issued an order "not to allow any children under state supervision to be knowingly placed in the foster care of gay families" (p. 22). This move was occasioned by a recommendation from a social worker that a fourteen-year-old boy be placed in a gay foster home. Penwell's order supersedes an earlier ruling by Don Miller, head of the Children's Services Division, stating that he would support such placements when they would be beneficial to the children involved.

14. "Families by Adoption - A Gay Reality." THE ADVOCATE, 145 (28 August, 1974), 1.

Under the laws governing adoption in the state of California, single men and women may adopt children whose problems make placement in a traditional home setting inadvisable. Examples of gay men who have successfully used this means to become parents are offered, chiefly from northern California, and the general future of such placements assessed.

15. "Complaint Hits Adoption Bias." THE ADVOCATE, 147 (25 September, 1974), 22.

A discrimination complaint was filed against the Minneapolis United Way on September 27, 1974 by Jack Baker and his partner, Michael McConnell, stating that the organization financially supports an agency which refused their adoption request solely because they are homosexuals. Legal grounds for the complaint lie in a civil rights ordinance passed in April, 1974 which prohibited discrimination in public services. An investigation into the charges was ordered in keeping with the legislation.

16. "Lover's Adoption Fight Continues." THE ADVOCATE, 149, (23 October, 1974), 16.

On September 27, 1974, a complaint was filed in St. Paul, Minnesota against the Children's Home Society of Minnesota by Jack Baker, contending that a letter asking whether he and his partner had ever applied to any other agency was clearly discriminatory. Gerald Williams of the Society responded by saying that refusal of multiple applicants is routine policy. Baker was advised to file the complaint anew in St. Paul by officials of the Minneapolis Civil Rights Department.

17. "Complaint to be Cured." THE ADVOCATE, 160 (26 March, 1975), 6.

The St. Paul, Minnesota Department of Human Rights ruled that "reasonable grounds" exist to support the suit by Jack Baker and Michael McConnell of discrimination in the refusal of their application to adopt a child. However, the agency stresses that its finding does not address the issue of whether the couple is legally entitled to adopt. Baker and McConnell are on record as protesting the department's intention to limit the scope of the complaint.

18. "Adoption Reform Proposed." THE ADVOCATE, 163 (7 May, 1975), 11.

A bill was introduced into the California House of Assembly by James Keepar (D–San Fernando) proposing a change in the state's single-parent adoption policies and procedures. The new system would require licensed private and public agencies to accept such applications on an equal basis with two-parent couples. As previously written, California law permits such applications only when an insufficient number of two-parent couples is available.

19. "Ruling Due in Parents Test Case." THE ADVOCATE, 173 (24 September, 1975), 10.

An upcoming hearing in Vancouver, Washington over the placement of Pat Davis, a juvenile with "homosexual tendencies," in the foster home of Gary McQuiston and John Clark, is discussed. Case history from 1973 is reviewed and Rick Blumburg, the attorney handling Davis' presentation, is interviewed. A decision in late August by the Juvenile Parole Center in Everett,

Washington upheld an earlier decision by the State Department of Social and Health Services in favor of the placement.

20. "Alternative Parenthood." THE ADVOCATE, 175 (22 October, 1975), 28.

The issue of gay foster parents is discussed in general, with the example of the Pat Davis case in Vancouver, Washington offered as illustration.

21. "Foster Homes for Gay Children: Justice or Prejudice?" THE ADVOCATE, 179 (17 December, 1975), 11-13.

The history of the placement case of Pat Davis in Vancouver, Washington is presented using pseudonyms as required by that state's law. On October 10, the presiding justice ruled Davis should be removed from the Clark-McQuiston household because "neither the court nor the state's institutions should be used to promote highly questionable lifestyles" (p. 13). An appeal is planned.

22. "No Evidence Gay Parents Unsuitable." THE ADVOCATE, 188 (21 April, 1976), 12-13.

Results of a year-long study by the Massachusetts Department of Public Welfare into abuse and exploitation of foster children in that state were released in early April, 1976. Among the final recommendations offered by the report was that "homosexuality per se is not evidence of unsuitability as a foster parent" (p. 13).

23. "Gay Foster Homes Approved." THE ADVOCATE, 193 (30 June, 1976), 11.

A new policy decision by the California State Health Department permits gay persons with no police record to operate state-financed child care facilities. The policy was writen after the regional office in San Francisco received a licensure application from a homosexual male with an unsatisfactory background. Specific classes for denial are former inmates of state mental hospitals, convicted offenders and those with a history of child molestation.

24. "L.A. Adoption Seeks Single Parents." THE ADVOCATE, 194 (14 July, 1976), 10.

> An appeal has been issued by the Los Angeles County Department of Adoption for single men as adoptive fathers. No restrictions were placed on the candidates' qualifications due to an unusually large number of boys over nine needing homes.

25. Survey: Between Gay Parent and Child." THE ADVOCATE, 215 (4 May, 1977), 13.

> This questionnaire explores issues facing gay and lesbian parents, including custody; legal history (if applicable); attitudes towards sexuality and sex education; relationships between life partners and children; and the possible role of outside agencies. National discussion of child abuse prompted this study, because "it does seem clear that society and parents alike could learn much from gay people's approaches in child raising" (p. 13).

26. "Children of Gays: Sexually 'Normal'." SCIENCE NEWS, 113 (17 June, 1978), 389.

> A research study originally reported in the June, 1978 *American Journal of Psychiatry* on the children being raised by homosexual and transsexual parents is reviewed. Dr. Richard Green of SUNY-Stony Brook evaluated the thirty-seven children on game preferences, peer group composition, clothing preferences, fantasy roles and vocational choices. Results indicated that thirty-six of the children had responses which suggested a heterosexual orientation: such findings accord with accepted psychoanalytic theory.

27. "Gay Couple Granted Adoption of Child." THE ADVOCATE, 262 (8 March, 1979), 12.

> The Superior Court of Los Angeles County granted custody of a twenty-three-month-old infant to the Rev. Jim N. Dykes, pastor of the Metropolitan Community Church of San Francisco, and his physician partner. It is believed to the first time such an adoption has occurred.

28. "Arizona Body OK's Antigay Adoption Bill." THE ADVOCATE, 265 (5 April, 1979), 9.

   On February 2, 1979, the Judiciary Committee of the Arizona legislature voted 8-0 to approve an amendment to an adoption procedures bill precluding "homosexuals and bisexuals from adopting children." Rep. Marge Olson (D-San Manuel), who sponsored the amendment, admitted she knew of no cases in Arizona where such adoption had been requested, "but we need to have it in law so that there will be no potential for this to happen."

29. "OK to Adopt Lover, NY Court Decides." THE ADVOCATE, 313 (19 March, 1981), 11.

   Judge Leon Deutsch of the Family Court of New York ruled that the adoption of one adult male homosexual by another was legal. In part, the ruling stated that "the fact that the parties were involved in a homosexual relationship was not sufficient in itself to prevent the adoption" (p. 11). Legal precedent was provided by the opinion of the New York Court of Appeals in *People vs. Onofre.*

30. "NY Court OK's Adoption of Man by His Lover." THE ADVOCATE, 350 (September 2, 1982), 10.

   On July 8, 1982, the Appellate Division of the New York State Supreme Court voted 4-1 to revise a family court decision that the adoption of one man by another was illegal. The original case stemmed from an attempt by a couple to avoid eviction from their apartment. Writing for the majority, Justice Sidney Asch stated that "the realities of present-day family life allow many types of nontraditional families" (p. 10).

31. "Riverside, California, Gay Man Sues to Adopt 17-Year-Old Youth." THE ADVOCATE, 359 (6 January, 1983), 63.

   David Fraser, a systems analyst, applied to the Riverside County adoption authorities for permission to adopt his foster son Kevin, resident with him since 1980. Authorities responded to Fraser by stating that they would neither approve nor deny his request. This was viewed by legal counsel as an attempt to delay matters until Kevin reached his majority at eighteen, when permission would no longer necessary. A suit was filed against the county on November 23, 1982.

32. "Expanding the Parent Pool: Adoption and Gay Men Who Wish to Father." THE ADVOCATE, 372 (21 July, 1983), 25-26.

The general problems encountered by homosexual men are presented and discussed from the viewpoints of both the applicant and the agency. A case is presented from New York City (James Thomason-Bergner) as illustration.

33. "N.Y. Court Rules Man Cannot Adopt Longtime Lover." THE ADVO-CATE, 408 (27 November, 1984), 18.

The New York State Court of Appeals ruled 4-2 against a petition by an established gay couple of twenty-five years standing to permit adoption of the younger partner by the elder. Reasons cited in support of the adoption included emotional ties and financial obligations. The majority opinion admitted that there were no restrictions on adult adoptions but refused to permit lovers of any sort to utilize adoption as a method of legalizing relationships. The Lambda Legal Defense and Education Fund indicated that such an approach to legitimization has not been widely used in the United States.

34. "Boston Gay Couple Appeals Removal of Foster Children." THE ADVOCATE, 422 (11 June, 1985), 15.

The removal of their foster sons from the home of Donald Babets and David Jean of Boston by the Massachusetts Department of Social Services, and subsequent media and legal action, is reviewed. Grounds for the removal originated with an article in the Boston *Globe* focusing on neighbors' objections to the placement, although the natural mother of the children had given her consent. The opinions of David Scondras, city councilman of Boston and Marie Matwa, DSS director, are included. Governor Michael Dukakis requested the agency to create a policy regarding placement of children in gay households.

35. "Massachusetts Acts to Prevent Placement with Gays: Foster Furor Erupts." THE ADVOCATE, 424 (9 July, 1985), 8-9.

The series of events subsequent to the removal from the household of a Boston homosexual couple of their two foster sons by the Department of Social Services is presented. These include, a) passage by the Massachusetts House of Representatives of an item "barring lesbians and gay men from becoming foster parents or adoptive parents," using as grounds the position that "a homosexual preference shall be considered a threat to the psychological and physical well-being of a child"; b) issuance of an order by the state secretary of human services prohibiting any further placement of foster children with gays or lesbians; and c) increased debate over a statewide gay rights bill for Massachusetts. Community leaders David Scondras and Steve Tierney are interviewed.

36. "Lutherans Plan Foster-Care System for Gay Youths in Philadelphia." THE ADVOCATE, 424 (9 July, 1985), 10.

With the closing in 1983 of the Eromin Center, a gay agency which ran a group home for gay children, Philadelphia city officials approached Lutheran Children and Family Services of Eastern Pennsylvania for aid. Allan Goldby, a social worker with the agency, designed a program combining small group residential environments with individual placement in gay and lesbian households. The foster care controversy in Massachusetts was not viewed as related to this development. A. Damien Martin, director of the I.C.P.G.Y. agency in New York, is also interviewed on this issue.

37. "Mass. Government Refuses to Change Policy Banning Gay Foster Parents." THE ADVOCATE, 426 (6 August, 1985), 10-11.

After a wave of protests and demonstrations, Governor Michael Dukakis of Massachusetts met on June 20, 1985 with fourteen opponents of his administration's policy banning placement of foster children with gay people. David Jean and Don Babets, the couple who lost their children in May, were among those participating. A meeting sponsored by the Massachusetts Association for Mental Health saw some forty-one organizations criticizing the policy. Despite such criticism, Dukakis stated that "he believed the policy was based on sound evidence" (p. 11), but could not cite evidence when pressed. Details of statewide preparations to oppose the enactment of the policy at both legislative and agency levels complete the article.

38.   "Massachusetts Foster Care: Dukakis Policy Called Antigay, Antichild." THE ADVOCATE, 430 (1 October, 1985), 11.

An August 22 hearing in Worcester, Massachusettts, sponsored by the State Department of Social Services, resulted in the majority of the seventy speakers over-whelmingly opposing the proposed policy barring gay persons from serving as foster parents. Criticisms included reduction of the already inadequate number of potential foster homes available in the state, discrim-ination in favor of "traditional" families, and subse-quent violence to children through inappropriate placement. A statement issued by the Gay and Lesbian Defense Committee noted that the Jean-Babets foster children had been moved five times since their removal from the gay couple in May. Further protests are planned.

39.   "N.H. Considering Ban on Gays As Foster Parents." THE ADVOCATE, 433 (12 November, 1985), 17-18.

A policy establishing a priority list for foster child placement (with relatives and two-parent families given preference) is being considered in New Hampshire. Shortly after the June, 1985 controversy over a similar policy appeared in Massachusetts, David Bond, Director of Children and Youth Services, issued a memorandum specifically prohibiting placement of children with "practicing homosexuals" (p. 17). This was consequent to a series of articles in a local newspaper about a gay couple who had served as foster parents for some fifteen years. The conservative political climate and absence of gay organizations in the state are noted as factors affecting these events.

40.   "Donald Loveland: Barred from Foster Parenting." THE ADVOCATE, 441 (4 March, 1986), 47.

An interview with Donald Loveland of Woburn, Massachu-setts, a gay man whose fifteen-year-old foster son was removed from his care. Subsequent to the announcement of a policy barring homosexuals from serving as foster parents in Massachusetts on May 24, 1985, Loveland was removed as a candidate. A brief outline of legal actions taken by the homosexual community against the policy is also provided.

41. "N.H. House of Reps Defeats Antigay Bill." THE ADVOCATE,
     442 (18 March, 1986), 16.

     On February 12, 1986 a bill aimed at prohibiting homo-
     sexuals from becoming foster parents or adopting child-
     ren was defeated 205-195 in the New Hampshire
     legislature. The history of the effort to pass (and
     defeat) the proposed measure and a related policy in
     Massachusetts is briefly reviewed.

42. "Two Dads and A Mom: Reinventing the Rules of Gay
     Parenting." THE ADVOCATE, 443 (1 April, 1986), 29-31.

     This article is an interview with Joy Schulenberg of
     San Francisco, author of *Gay Parenting*. Issues of
     traditional family structure, possibilities of alterna-
     tive home styles, and the moral questions these pose
     for participants are discussed.

43. "New Hampshire Proposes Nondiscriminatory Foster Parent
     Guidelines." THE ADVOCATE, 454 (2 September, 1986), 16-
     17.

     Following a one year study, the Division for Children
     and Youth Services of New Hampshire proposed guidelines
     for the selection of foster parents emphasizing ability
     to provide "a safe, nurturing and stable environment"
     (p. 16). A brief review of the legislative controversy
     over homosexual foster parents and interviews with
     local activists on both sides are included.

44. "Judge Refuses to Dismiss Mass. Foster Parent Policy
     Lawsuit." THE ADVOCATE, 458 (28 October, 1986), 14.

     Chief Justice Thomas Marse of the Massachusetts
     Superior Court refused to dismiss a lawsuit brought
     against the state by a coalition of professional and
     gay organizations opposing Governor Michael Dukakis'
     policy on foster parents. This ruling ensured that the
     case would come to trial. A brief history of prior
     developments is provided as background. Justice Marse
     did, however, uphold the right of the state to inquire
     into the sexual preference of a foster parent candi-
     date.

Child Custody

45. Gregory, Sasha. "Gay Mother Wins Children's Custody."
THE ADVOCATE, 90 (19 July, 1972), 6.

> A detailed analysis of the custody case filed and won
> by Camille Mitchell of San Jose, California, with
> regard to her three children. The full legal history
> of the case is presented and testimony from Mitchell's
> former spouse dissected. Santa Clara County Superior
> Judge Gerald Chargin awarded Mitchell custody under
> conditions which effectively prevent her from contin-
> uing her relationship with her partner. This is the
> first such case on record in California.

46. "Return of the Amazon Mother." MS, 1 (September, 1972),
90-93.

> An essay by *Village Voice* columnist Jill Johnston
> reflecting on the traditional and feminist philosophies
> of motherhood and the lesbian's relationship to them.
> An appearance at a panel on lesbian motherhood in New
> York City in February, 1972 is used as the point of
> departure. The 1971 statement of the National Organi-
> zation for Women which acknowledged lesbianism as a
> feminist issue is quoted.

47.   Cordova, Jeanne. "Judge's Advice to Gay Parents: Don't Admit it." THE ADVOCATE, 99 (22 November, 1972), 16.

A discussion panel on "Medical Testimony in Family Cases" held at the Beverly Hills Hotel and sponsored by the Beverly Hills Bar Association and Academy of Medicine is covered. The bulk of the article is an interview with Los Angeles Superior Court Judge William P. Hogsboom centered on the relevance of homosexuality to custody awards. Reference is made to the Camille Mitchell case as precedent. Justice Hogsboom stressed that while "this is a numerically relatively rare situation," the chief consideration would be the influence of the relationship on the children.

48.   "Court Upholds Gay Father's Right to Visit." THE ADVOCATE, 99 (22 November, 1972), 16.

On October 19, 1972, Judge Benjamin Schwartz of the Philadelphia Domestic Relations Court ruled that Anthony Messina's admitted homosexuality was irrelevant to his rights of visitation to his children. A brief history of the case is provided. Judge Schwartz stated that "private sexual tastes, which would not jeopardize the health or well-being of the children," do not qualify "as sufficient cause to deny the parental right."

49.   "Gay Mothers Win Children But Lose Each Other." THE ADVOCATE, 103 (17 January, 1973), 10.

A profile of a case decided in Seattle by the Superior Court on a custody battle between two lesbians and their former husbands. James Noe, the presiding judge, requested psychiatric evaluation of all parties involved before rendering an opinion. Final decision was that the women would be awarded custody but would have to separate to keep the children. Sandra Schuster and Madeleine Isaacson plan to appeal.

50.   Laurence, Leo. "Gay Mothers Tour West Coast With Kids, Film About Court Case." THE ADVOCATE, 119 (29 August, 1973), 13.

Sandra Schuster and Madeleine Isaacson, awarded custody of their children in a recent custody decision in Seattle, are touring Los Angeles, San Diego and San

Francisco to raise funds to pay four thousand dollars in court costs. Their efforts are assisted by a half-hour color film produced via the University of Washington visual arts department by a faculty pediatrician familiar with the case. Film treatment includes reactions of the probation caseworker assigned to the couple and has been televised in Los Angeles and Burbank.

51. Armanno, Benna F. "The Lesbian Mother: The Right to Child Custody." GOLDEN GATE LAW REVIEW, 4, 1 (Fall, 1973), 1-18.

A survey article examining "child custody law and practice and their application to cases in which the mothers petitioning for custody are homosexuals" (p. 2). The author's aim is to call into question the relevance of sexual orientation as a factor in custody and to eliminate the special category of "homosexual mothers" so that all petitioners in such cases may be judged by a uniform set of standards. While the focus here is specifically on custodial statutes of the state of California, general issues of lesbian mothers and their rights are also considered. Specific attention is given to the discretionary powers of judges presiding in such cases. Armanno calls for increased education of members of both the bar and judiciary as to the real facts concerning homosexuality and the development of information on "what type of adult a child who lives with his or her lesbian mother will grow up to be" (p. 10). A review of constitutional arguments which can be used in custody cases (such as due process, equal protection, etc.) completes the article.

52. "Lesbian As Mother." NEWSWEEK, 82 (24 September, 1973), 75-76.

A general article on the concept of lesbian mothers and their households. Interviews with a lesbian mother from Los Angeles, a couple and Dr. Judd Marmor are included as illustrations of varying viewpoints on this issue.

53. Sarpp, Doug. "Gay Father Wages Uphill Battle Just to See Sons." THE ADVOCATE, 125 (21 November, 1973), 5, 15.

This article summarizes a two-year court battle between Jerry Purpura of Hackensack, New Jersey and his wife over visitation rights with their two sons. Details of the successive court decisions and psychiatric testing ordered for the defendant are included. The case was initiated in July, 1971. At the time this article was written, Purpura had been granted four hours each Sunday afternoon. A brief interview is included.

54. "Court Says Lesbian Pair Not 'Depraved', Return Kids." THE ADVOCATE, 126 (5 December, 1973), 5.

The Supreme Court of the State of Michigan has ruled that "being gay, in and of itself, does not constitute 'moral depravity'." This opinion was rendered as part of a decision dismissing charges against Eunice Brown and Arlene Smith and restoring custody of their eight children to them. A brief legal history of the case, which lasted from 1970 to December, 1973, is provided.

55. "ACLU Enters Court Custody Battle." THE ADVOCATE, 130 (30 January, 1974), 13.

The American Civil Liberties Union has provided Sally Hall of Newark, Ohio with legal counsel in a suit by her former husband demanding custody of her five-year-old daughter. The suit is based entirely on Hall's lesbianism. The article notes that the "case marks the first time the ACLU, long involved in visitation cases, has entered a child custody battle in behalf of an admitted lesbian." Counsel has obtained a continuance until December, 1974.

56. "One Loses Job, Another Her Daughters." THE ADVOCATE, 131 (13 February, 1974), 2.

A brief summary of two cases being handled by the legal committee of the Lesbian Tide Collective of Los Angeles. One involves employment discrimination while the second is a custody battle between parent and grandparents over two children. In the latter, Lynda Chaffin's parents went to an Idaho court in 1969 following her revelation of lesbianism to them to request transfer of custody to them from their divorced mother. Chaffin did not learn of the decision until 1973, when she planned to have the daughters resume residence with her. A California judge in Torrance declared Chaffin "unfit to keep the children because of her sexual activities," but the girls refuse to leave. An appeal is planned.

57. "Denies Lesbian Relationship, Gets Child Custody Grant." THE ADVOCATE, 133 (13 March, 1974), 11.

At a two-day hearing in Madisonville, Kentucky, a Hopkins County judge has ruled that Mary Adkins may retain custody of her two daughters. The custody dispute was initiated by Adkins' ex-husband, who claimed she was in a lesbian relationship with another woman presently staying at her home. Both women denied there was any such relationship.

58. "Women's Group Seeking Legal Aid for Lesbian Mothers." THE ADVOCATE, 140 (19 June, 1974), 4.

Women in Transition, a Philadelphia feminist collective, has begun investigating the legal problems of lesbian mothers seeking to acquire or retain custody and visitation rights. While the group has had complaints with regard to Pennsylvania's child custody laws, data on the general state of such matters is solicited for an updated edition of their local information manual.

59. "Legal Fight Forces Mom and Kids Underground." THE ADVOCATE, 141 (3 July, 1974), A-2.

A review of two cases involving lesbians currently being funded by the Women's Defense Committee of Los Angeles. The custody decision involving her two daughters rendered to Lynda Chaffin resulted in an effort to obtain a court order permitting them to retain residence with her while the appeal is filed. This was denied, and the family is now in hiding. Information on the security clearance case of Anna Marie Nunes is also provided.

60. "Lesbian Gets Her Children and Still Keeps Her Lover." THE ADVOCATE, 141 (3 July, 1974), A-20.

Judge William LaVeque of Tacoma issued a decision granting full custody of her three children to Nancy Driber in a case involving questions of the fitness of an open lesbian as a parent. Of particular note is the absence of any condition that Driber terminate her present relationship. Suit was brought by the defendant's ex-husband solely on the ground of her sexual orientation. A brief summary of the witnesses called is included.

61. "Ex-Husband Steals Kids from Lesbian." THE ADVO-CATE, 146 (11 September, 1974), 20.

A summary of a court case in Saskatoon, Saskatchewan in which a woman who entered a lesbian relationship following the granting of custody of her two children in a divorce settlement faces charges of unfitness by her former spouse. The latter has already refused to return their daughter. This is believed to be the first case in Canadian courts where the sexual orientation alone has been challenged as sufficient grounds for custody denial. Reference is made to a similar case in California.

62. "An Enlightened Judge OK's Lesbian Family." THE ADVO-CATE, 141 (11 September, 1974), 20.

Justice Roger Bright of Lee Supreme Court of Australia granted custody to a twenty-five-year-old woman of her two children, stating that "the days are gone when courts will disqualify a woman from the role of parent merely because she has engaged or is engaging in some form of extramarital sex." The defendant originally filed for divorce on grounds that her husband had repeatedly threatened and struck her.

63. "Lesbian Appeals Custody Case for Lack of 'Reason'." ADVOCATE, 149 (23 October, 1974), 9.

In a brief to the Second District Court of Appeals of California, attorney Al Gordon is seeking a reversal of the decision issued by Judge William Kennedy in Los Angeles on December 12, 1973. This decision granted custody of the children of Lynda Chaffin to her parents. Gordon's brief is based upon the provisions of the California Family Law Act, which mandates that before custody is awarded, the court must state its grounds for preferring the designated custodian. The Act was passed in 1969 as an amendment of then-current legislation which involved the vague concept of "the best interest of the child." Extensive background information on this legal point is included.

64. "Custody Defense Fund Launched." THE ADVOCATE, 151 (20 November, 1974), 6.

An announcement of the creation of the Lesbian Mother's National Defense Fund in Seattle. Organization goals are stated as serving as a resource and information center for lesbians engaged in custody battles by providing guidelines on preparing for court appearances and the distribution of copies of prior decisions, attorney's briefs and transcripts.

65. "Mother Surrenders to Judge, Returns Kids." THE ADVOCATE, 154 (1 January, 1975), 19.

After eight months in hiding in Arizona, Nevada and California in an attempt to evade a California Superior Court ruling transferring custody to her parents, Lynda Chaffin sent her daughters to their grandparents in Idaho. She then presented herself to Judge William Kennedy in Torrance, California. At that time charges were dropped. A new court case is pending in Washington to prevent a "registration of foreign judgment," transferring an earlier custody decision to Washington jurisdiction.

66. "Gay Father Wins Visiting Rights." THE ADVOCATE, 157 (12 February, 1975), 26.

Full unsupervised visitation privileges were restored to Troy Turner by Judge Mary Caloff of the California Supreme Court in mid-January, 1975. This decision followed the results of court-ordered psychological testing. Caloff "rejected the implication that a father, just because he is gay, constitutes a moral danger to children." Turner's ex-wife and her husband were admonished by the court.

67. "A Display of Homophobia in Appeals Court." THE ADVOCATE, 159 (12 March, 1975), 6.

Writing for the three-man panel, Justice Macklin Fleming of the Los Angeles Second District State Court of Appeals upheld a superior court order granting

custody of the children of Lynda Chaffin to their out-
of-state grandparents. The bulk of this article is an
exposition of the reasons why homosexuality should be
considered as a possible factor in custody decisions.

68. "Custody Test Due." THE ADVOCATE, 161 (9 April, 1975),
11.

A family court judge in western New York state denied
custody of her three children to a lesbian mother
despite two full days of testimony by clergy and psychologists in her behalf. Counter-arguments were
presented by the ex-husband that the mother's lesbianism would exert an "unhealthy influence" on the
children. Legal counsel states that the decision will
be appealed. At present, no appellate case exists in
New York regarding the rights of gay parents of either
sex.

69. "Mother Gets Custody." THE ADVOCATE, 166 (18 June, 1975),
7.

Lynda Chaffin was awarded custody of her two daughters
by Superior Court Judge A. Garenfeld upon a request for
modification of the original court decision granting
custody to her parents. The request was occasioned by
the girls running away from their grandparents' home in
Seattle to rejoin their mother. Counsel for the grandparents decided not to contest the decision.

70. Cordova, Jeanne. "For Lesbian Mothers, the Battle Is in
the Courtroom." MAJORITY REPORT, 5 (28 June, 1975), 6-7.

The various types of problems facing a lesbian mother
suing for custody from spouses, judges, social workers,
in-laws and state laws are illustrated through the
successful case of Lynda Chaffin in California. Much
of this article is an extensive interview with Cheryl
Bratman, Chaffin's lawyer. Topics addressed include
types of testimony required, courtroom strategies, and
"that child custody battles are never really over."

71. "Orgasm Means More to Them." THE ADVOCATE, 167 (2 July,
1975), 6.

Portage County Ohio Common Pleas Court Judge Albert Caris reluctantly awarded custody of the children of Lorraine Townend to the children's grandmother; this decision ended Townends's interim custody of her children. In his opinion, Caris noted that if Townend had been willing to "abandon her lesbianism," the court might have "experimented" by permitting her to retain the children. Counsel for Townend indicated the appeal procedures have been initiated.

72. Saten, Tom. "Child Custody--Some Ups, Some Downs." THE ADVOCATE, 168 (16 July, 1975), 5.

An opinion piece summarizing five custody cases heard between 1973 and July, 1974 involving favorable decisions to lesbian mothers and gay fathers. The author notes that "because homosexuality is taboo in our society," most custody cases involving gay parents go unreported in "the media as well as legal publications." References to each case and relevant legal literature are included.

73. Graham, Linda. "Education Is Working in The East." THE ADVOCATE, 168 (16 July, 1975), 7.

A profile of court cases involving custody requests of lesbian mothers heard in the state of Massachusetts. The article title refers to a program of consciousness raising done for the court social work staff in a related case in southern Massachusetts which was never taken to court. State resources for such cases are available via the Women's Law Collective in Cambridge.

74. Carnier, J. M. "Custody Study Under Way." THE ADVOCATE, 170 (13 August, 1975), 8.

Speaking at the convention of the American Psychiatric Association and the Western Psychological Association in Los Angeles, UCLA researchers Katharine Smith and Martha Kirkpatrick reported on their cooperative study of children raised by lesbian mothers. Initiated on September, 1974, its aim is to provide precedent upon which courts may base decisions in custody cases which, they note, have increased in recent years. A detailed summary of the structural and control population used in the research design is provided.

24

75. Shilts, Randy. "Sandy And Madeleine: Lovers with a Houseful of Kids." THE ADVOCATE, 175 (22 October, 1975), 26, 30.

   An interview with Madeleine Isaacson and Sandy Schuster of Seattle. The discussion explores their relationship and the ongoing legal efforts to retain custody of their six children.

76. Gengle, Dean. "G.F.U.--A Solution for Some." THE ADVOCATE, 175 (22 October, 1975), 31.

   An interview with B. A. Aiken of San Francisco, founder of Gay Fathers Unlimited, a support group formed in August, 1975. The goals of the organization and problems of gay fathers in general, including custody, are discussed.

77. Knutson, Don. "Justice for Gay Parents." THE ADVOCATE, 175 (22 October, 1975), 31-32.

   An investigative essay reporting on the current legal opinions in custody cases involving gay fathers and lesbian mothers. Knutson notes that "the courts have routinely . . . based their decisions on three generally unstated assumptions: 1) that a child would be sexually abused by a gay parent; 2) that a child's sexual orientation would be influenced by observation of a gay parent's lifestyle; and 3) that a child would be rejected because of the parents' gay lifestyle" (p. 31-32). The validity of these assumptions is examined.

78. Maves, Karl. "Help Us Out!" THE ADVOCATE, 175 (22 October, 1975), 33.

   An interview with Pat Norman, counselor at San Francisco's Center for Special Problems and active member of Lesbian Mothers and Friends. The discussion covers community reaction to lesbian mothers in general, legal obstacles and attitudes.

79. Shilts, Randy. "L.M.D.F.'s 'Apple Pie' Battles." THE ADVOCATE, 175 (22 October, 1975), 33-34.

An interview with Geraldine Cole of the Lesbian Mothers' National Defense Fund, headquartered in Seattle. The activities of the group in offering legal courses and financial assistance are discussed.

80. "Kidnapped Child." THE ADVOCATE, 179 (17 December, 1975), 10.

A news report regarding legal proceedings against an Austin, Texas father who abducted his daughter to keep her away from her mother, an admitted lesbian. Custody had been awarded to the mother by the Texas courts.

81. "Risher To Pay Child Support." THE ADVOCATE, 184 (25 February, 1976), 15.

A brief survey of the child support payments placed upon Mary Jo Risher's custody case in Dallas. Full details of this case may be found in the account *By Her Own Admission,* which is based upon the trial transcripts.

82. "Court Custody Fight." THE ADVOCATE, 186 (24 March, 1976), 9.

New York State Supreme Court Justice Edward McLaughlin found that custody of a ten-year-old daughter should be restored to the divorced husband of a lesbian mother. This decision is believed to be the first such case in which a member of the New York judiciary based an opinion on the mother's homosexuality. An appeal is planned.

83. "Advice for Mothers." THE ADVOCATE, 189 (5 May, 1976), 8, 42.

A report on the speech given by Nancy Polikoff of the Catholic University of America Law School at the seventh national conference on Women and the Law held at Temple University in March, 1976. Her position included advice on management strategies for child custody cases, preferring out-of-court settlements and legal counsel at the earliest possible time.

84. "New Twist in Custody." THE ADVOCATE, 193 (30 June, 1976), 12.

> A summary of legal action being considered against Cynthia Forcier of Orange County, California. Plaintiffs are the current foster parents of Forcier's daughter, who have claimed that she sexually molested the child during Christmas vacation, 1975. The daughter is eight years old.

85. "Welfare League Hears Custody Speakers." THE ADVOCATE, 193 (30 June, 1976), 45.

> A panel of gay professionals presented a program on the history of parental custody rights at the annual convention of the Child Welfare League of America in Reno, Nevada in April, 1976. Increased public awareness of the existence of gay parents was noted.

86. "Mother Disallowed New Trial." THE ADVOCATE, 194 (14 July, 1976), 9.

> A Dallas justice rejected the request for a new trial by Mary Jo Risher in her continuing attempt to gain custody of her nine-year-old son. Risher lost custody in December, 1975 following a widely-publicized court battle.

87. "Good News for Gay Parents." THE ADVOCATE, 195 (28 July, 1976), 21.

> On June 28, 1976 the City Council of the District of Columbia passed unanimously a resolution removing sexually discriminatory language from the legal code and providing that sexual orientation "shall not be a conclusive consideration" in determining custody and visitation rights. Passage followed lobbying by feminists, gay and civil liberties groups.

88. "Maine Lesbian Mother Wins." THE ADVOCATE, 197 (25 August, 1976), 8.

> Maine Superior Court Justice Harry Glassman awarded unconditional custody of two children to their openly lesbian mother in late June, 1976. This decision in favor of Carol Whitehead marks the first time the state

legal system has considered gay parental rights of custody.

89.   "APA Approves Child Custody." THE ADVOCATE, 200 (6 October, 1976), 11.

On September 5, 1976, the governing council of the American Psychological Association unanimously adopted a resolution recommending that parental sexual orientation "should not be the sole or primary variable considered" in cases involving foster children or child custody. An interview with Hal Kooden of Cumberland Hospital, New York City, a member of the gay and lesbian caucus steering committee, provides background information on this event.

90.   "Lesbian Mother Study Slated." THE ADVOCATE, 202 (3 November, 1976), 13.

A joint research project of the Long Island Institute and the Department of Psychiatry, SUNY-Stony Brook is profiled. Objective of the study is to "compare lesbian and non-gay mothers and their children's adjustments." Contact information for volunteers is provided.

91.   "Seattle Lesbian Mom Case Goes to Court, Again." THE ADVOCATE, 203 (17 November, 1976), 9.

The 1974 decision of a Washington state court awarding custody to Madeleine Isaacson and Sandra Schuster is being challenged in that state's Supreme Court. The fathers of the children have initiated the appeal and both sides have indicated appeals will be filed with the U.S. Supreme Court regardless of the outcome of present litigation.

92.   Gibson, Gifford Buy and Mary Jo Risher. BY HER OWN ADMISSION: A LESBIAN MOTHER'S FIGHT TO KEEP HER SON. Garden City, NY: Doubleday & Company, 1977.

On December 16, 1975 in Dallas, Texas, the first known jury trial involving the custody rights of a homosexual parent began. Mary Jo Risher and her lover, Ann Foreman, worked with Gibson to create this account of a divorced father's successful efforts to remove his children from living in a lesbian relationship. Trial transcripts are included in the text where appropriate. On December 23, 1975, the Dallas Domestic Relations Court transferred custody of her son Richard to his father Douglas. An appeal to the Fifth Civil Court of Appeals was dismissed for want of jurisdiction. As an historical document illustrating the beginnings of lesbian custody battles, this volume is invaluable.

93.   Wyland, Francie. MOTHERHOOD, LESBIANISM AND CHILD CUSTODY. Bristol, England: Falling Wall Press, 1977.

Written in 1977 by the Toronto, Ontario chapter of Wages Due Lesbians as part of the international Wages for Housework campaign, this short volume discusses the problems facing women in general and lesbian mothers in specific. Its orientation is clearly lesbian feminist, with several American and Canadian custody trials briefly summarized. References to materials for further study on the subject complete the contents. Researchers should use this as a distinctly secondary source.

94.   Gregory-Lewis, Sasha. "Custody Travail: New D.C. Law May Be Flawed." THE ADVOCATE, 209 (9 February, 1977), 11.

A review of the history of the recent revision of District of Columbia custody legislation barring sexual orientation as the conclusive factor. Interviews with Washington lawyer Nancy Polikoff and activist Frank Kameny are included.

95.   "Lesbians Win in 2 Key Rulings." THE ADVOCATE, 221 (10 August, 1977), 10, 41.

A news report covering two custody decisions in Colorado and Michigan. The Colorado case resulted in an award of custody to the lover of a deceased lesbian; the Wayne County (Michigan) ruling in June, 1977 was decided in favor of joint custody.

96.   Engle, Dean. "All in the Gay Family." THE ADVOCATE, 224 (21 September, 1977), 33.

This article reports on the results of a survey questionnaire printed in the May 4, 1977 issue of *The*

ADVOCATE involving relationships with children in gay and lesbian family settings.

97.   "Going Public with a Private Hell: One Lesbian Mother's Custody Battle." THE ADVOCATE, 224 (21 September, 1977), 34-35.

An interview with Jean Jullion discusses her battle for custody of her two sons and her reactions to legal questions regarding her lesbianism. At the time of the interview, a third hearing was pending. Researchers interested in the complete record of the Jullion case should consult her account *Long Way Home.*

98.   "Lesbian Mother Wins Custody Fight." THE ADVOCATE, 232 (11 January, 1978), 12.

Lynn Ransom of Oakland, California was awarded custody of her two children in the Alameda Superior Court on November 10, 1977. A brief history of the case and principals is provided. Court debts will be retired through film showings in the Bay Area.

99.   "Jullion Regains Custody." THE ADVOCATE, 237 (22 March, 1978), 13.

Alameda Court Judge Robert Kroninger split custody of her two sons between Jeanne Jullion and her estranged husband. No evidence relating to sexual preference was admitted.

100.   "Gay Father Gets Custody." THE ADVOCATE, 240 (3 May, 1978), 9-10.

A report on a ruling by Judge Eleanor Smith on a custody dispute involving a gay man and his separated wife. Full custody was awarded to the father. Background on the case provided, which is "according to the presiding judge and several legal experts . . . the first time a gay man has won a custody battle in Canada."

101.   Payne, Anne T. "The Law and the Problem Parent: Custody and Parental Rights of Homosexual, Mentally Retarded,

Mentally Ill and Incarcerated Patients." JOURNAL OF FAMILY LAW, 16 (August, 1978), 797-818.

A note examining treatment and judicial attitudes (as evidenced in extant case law) with regard to four categories of parents who deviate "in a highly noticeable way from society's norms" (p. 797). The four conditions--mental retardation, mental illness and prisoner status, as well as homosexuality--are seen as placing the individuals involved under distinct legal disabilities. Payne notes that custody battles involving homosexuality usually involve either a lesbian mother who desires custody or a mother who possesses custody and who adopts a homosexual lifestyle. Cases examained are *Chaffin vs. Frye* (California, 1975), *Townend vs. Townend* (Ohio, 1975), and the Maine case of *Whitehead vs. Black* (1976). Comparison of judicial attitudes towards the four groups finds the mentally retarded as the least understood, although "homosexual parents not only get relatively poor results in the courts, they are subjected to frequent lectures from the judiciary on what judges consider to be the unacceptability and unpopularity of their behavior" (p. 817). Favoring the heterosexual parent in custody decisions is viewed as defensible in that it spares the child potential prejudice, abuse and ridicule: however, decisions based on inaccurate information may also lead to awards of custody to third parties whose qualifications are doubtful.

102. "Lesbian Mothers Keep Custody." THE ADVOCATE, 255 (29 November, 1978), 8.

The Supreme Court of the State of Washington, through a lack of a majority, has reaffirmed the custody award made to lesbian mothers Sandra Schuster and Madeleine Isaacson. Results of a public poll taken by the Dorian Group are also reviewed.

103. Hitchens, Donna and Barbara Price. "Trials Strategy in Lesbian Mother Custody: The Use of Expert Testimony." GOLDEN GATE UNIVERSITY LAW REVIEW, 9 (1978/ 1979), 451-479.

The applicability of psychological testimony by expert witnesses in cases involving lesbians and custody is reviewed. Three topics are addressed: the prejudices most often encountered in such cases, types of social scientific and psychological evidence which are acceptable to courts, and the selection and management of said testimony. The first includes attitudes towards sexual behavior of lesbians, effects of homosexual parenting and possible social stigmatization of the child. Emphasis is placed upon rebutting common prejudices so as to provide the presiding judge with information to correct possible biases. The tactic of seeking a ruling that the mother's sexual preference is irrelevant is opposed on ground that counsel for the parent will then be barred from presenting as evidence popular myths which may be raised during the case.

104.   "Woman Loses Children in Custody Battle." THE ADVOCATE, 260 (8 February, 1979), 7.

A review of a decision of a Denver court in December, 1978 refusing custody to Kathryn Stover of that city and her lover. Grounds were lack of fitness and interest in being a mother, with sexuality not central to the finding.

105.   "Lesbian Gets Custody of Daughter." THE ADVOCATE, 262 (8 March, 1979), 8-9.

The Supreme Court of the State of Michigan on January 17, 1979 reversed a lower-court decision, restoring custody of Jillian Miller to her mother Margaret. The decision concludes two and one-half years of litigation and "is believed to be the first time a state supreme court has ruled in a gay parent's favor when the contest was between parents."

106.   Goodman, Ellen. "Homosexuality of a Parent: A New Issue in Custody Disputes." MONASH UNIVERSITY LAW REVIEW, 5 (June, 1979), 305-315.

Four cases involving awarding of custody to homosexual parents heard before the Family Court of Australia between 1974 and 1979 are reviewed and approaches taken by lower courts evaluated. Beginning with the Family Law Act of Australia, the cases examined are *In the Marriage of N, In the Marriage of Spring, In the Marriage of O'Reilly,* and *In the Marriage of Brook.* While holding that "homosexuality per se does not render a mother unfit to have custody of her child" (p. 311), most Australian decisions have involved possible

harmful consequences to the children. Two such consequences are analyzed: possibilities of adverse effects
on children reared in an environment where homosexuality is open and acceptable behavior, and concern that a
child so reared will develop into a homosexual. Both
assumptions are seen to be of doubtful validity.
Judgment of each individual case on its merits and
following the precedent set in *In the Marriage of
O'Reilly* by not requiring special conditions of the
mother are regarded as the preferred approach for the
judiciary in such cases. Researchers will find this
article useful for the comparative perspective provided
between Australian and American legal systems on this
issue.

107. "Lesbian/Woman/Mother." THE ADVOCATE, 269 (14 June,
1979), 19.

An interview with Denise Steele of the Lesbian and Gay
Parents Project Center in Boston. Founded in 1977 as
an offshoot of the National Lawyers' Guilds' Committee
Against Sexism, its purposes and services are reviewed.
A profile of a lesbian mother in Boston is included as
an illustrative case study.

108. "Lesbian's Daughters Awarded to Father." THE ADVOCATE,
271 (12 July, 1979), 7-8.

Custody of her three daughters was transferred from
Susan Joffee to her ex-husband, whose residence is
Seattle. In making this ruling, Justice R. A. Green of
Florida was "relying on evidence that society condemns
homosexuality." The decision's logic has been ques-
tioned and an appeal is planned.

109. "Lesbian in Virginia Fights to Keep Son." THE ADVOCATE,
275 (6 September, 1979), 11-12.

The American Civil Liberties Union has filed a suit on
behalf of an Ohio lesbian whose son was taken to
Virginia by her ex-husband and his new wife. Goal of
the suit will be to block a proposed adoption on the
grounds that "the defendant's lesbianism has not been
shown relevant to the custody of her child" (p. 12).

110. Leitch, Patricia. "Custody: Lesbian Mothers in the Courts." GONZAGA LAW REVIEW, 16 (1980), 147-170.

A comment exploring both child custody cases in general and lesbian custody cases in specific as they affected legal precedent within the state of Washington. Centering upon the 1978 case of *Schuster vs. Schuster* and *Isaacson vs. Isaacson,* eight prior cases involving homosexual custody or fitness under law are reviewed. The effect of the decision in *Schuster vs. Schuster* (where the children were granted to their lesbian mothers) on Washington law is examined. Special care is seen as necessary for the courts to state clearly how each individual custody award was determined. Leitch concludes that "child custody disputes involving a lesbian parent have . . . been afforded inadequate treatment based on inconsistent legal standards" (p. 169).

111. Brownstone, Harvey. "The Homosexual Parent in Custody Disputes." QUEEN'S LAW JOURNAL, 5 (1980), 199-240.

A general survey article comparing the treatment of heterosexual parents deemed "immoral" and that of homosexual parents as regards determination of parental fitness in child custody disputes. Following a lengthy detailed review of the case records in these areas within both American and Canadian jurisdictions, the author concludes that "when the issue of a parent's homosexuality arises in a custody dispute, the alleging party ought to bear the burden of proving its relevance" (p. 237). Canadian cases of custody involving homosexual parents begin with the 1974 *Case vs. Case* decision in Saskatchewan, and include the Alberta *K vs. K* decision in 1976 and the Ontario case of *D vs. D* in 1978. Most of the cited cases are from the case record of the states of Washington, New Jersey, Ohio and New York. Researchers will find this article a useful comparison of the Canadian and American legal approaches to homosexual custody questions. An appendix lists fifty-nine custody-related cases with full citations to the legal literature.

112. "Arizona Lesbians Get Custody of Daughters." THE ADVOCATE, 293 (29 May, 1980), 10.

A report on a decision by a Phoenix, Arizona judge awarding custody of her son to a lesbian currently living in a racially mixed relationship. Testing from a clinical psychologist on the effects of being raised in a homosexual household on a child was admitted.

113. "Colorado Judge Rules Mother's Lesbianism Is Bar to Good Parenting." THE ADVOCATE, 294 (12 June, 1980), 12-13.

A review of the decision by Golden, Colorado Justice Winston Wolvington removing custody from Carol Mueller of Lakeland, due to the adverse effect of the mother's lesbianism on her son and daughter. An appeal is planned.

114. Smart, Barbara A. "Bezio VS Patenaude (Mass.) 410 N E 2d 1207): The 'Coming Out' Controversy of Lesbian Mothers in Court." NEW ENGLAND LAW REVIEW, 16 (1980/1981), 331-365.

The Massachusetts case of *Bezio vs. Patenaude* is reviewed along with its implications for lesbian custody cases in general. The facts and holding of the decision are presented, followed by a detailed examination of standards to be applied in such disputes, with special attention given to the role of the trial judge. Impact of the decision (in which the Supreme Judicial Court of Massachusetts held that lesbianism was not a bar to custody unless it could be established that "a nexus existed between the mother's homosexuality and her fitness as a parent" (p. 333) on Massachusetts law completes the article. The ruling is seen to expand the protection of lesbian mothers.

115. "Massachusetts Lesbian Regains Two Daughters." THE ADVOCATE, 313 (19 March, 1981), 13.

Judge Sanford Keedy of the Franklin County, Massachusetts probate court has ruled that custody of her two daughters be returned to Brenda Bezio King, denied same in 1979. This decision follows a finding of the Supreme Court of Massachusetts in December, 1980 that "being a lesbian did not automatically preclude a woman's being a good mother." King will receive custody in June, 1981.

116. "Study Says Lesbians' Children Like Others." THE ADVOCATE, 315 (16 April, 1981), 9.

A report of the results of a survey of children aged seven to twelve living in lesbian households conducted by three social workers at the University of Southern California. Done as part of master's degree work, their findings indicate such children cope well with the traumas of divorce and feel themselves less to blame for their parents' separation.

117.   "Supreme Court Balks at Custody Ruling." THE ADVOCATE, 319 (11 June, 1981), 9.

On April 20, 1981, the United States Supreme Court declined to accept a custody case from the state of Kentucky involving a lesbian mother. The Kentucky Court of Appeals ruling denying Luanne Stevenson her daughter was permitted to stand. The decision was viewed as indicating reluctance to involve the court in custody matters *per se*.

118.   "Sexuality Not Valid Issue in Custody, Indiana Court Rules." THE ADVOCATE, 319 (11 June, 1981), 14.

On March 10, 1981, an Indiana Court of Appeals ruled that "homosexuality standing alone without evidence of any adverse effect upon the welfare of the child doesn't render the homosexual parent unfit as a matter of law to have custody of the child." In the case under review, custody was given to the children's father on other grounds.

119.   "Iowa Custody Case Could Set Precedent." THE ADVOCATE, 332 (10 December, 1981), 14, 50.

A review of the request of Sheila King to the Iowa Supreme Court "to rule that a parent's sexual orientation does not automatically make him or her a bad parent and should not be a bar to child custody in divorce cases." While King has had actual custody of her children since February, 1980, this is the first time this legal issue has reached Iowa's highest court. Ten other states have faced similar cases, but no legal consensus had been established.

120.   Hanscombe, Gillian E. and Jackie Forster. ROCKING THE CRADLE. LESBIAN MOTHERS: A CHALLENGE IN FAMILY LIVING. Boston: Alyson Publications, Inc., 1982.

Gillian Hanscombe and Jackie Forster have compiled the first general work on lesbian mothers which is not exclusively the story of a specific court case. In the summer of 1978, they traveled through England and Wales, meeting lesbian mothers and their families. The result of that journey is a straightforward discussion of such topics as artificial insemination, the personal and social implications of mothering as lesbians, child custody and child rearing. Chapter 3, "Courts of Flaw," provides an interesting view of the British legal approach to lesbian mothers. Researchers will find a comparison with Jeanne Jullion's *Long Way Home* illuminating.

121.   Evans, Marie Weston. "Parent and Child: M.J.P. VS J.G.P. (640 P 2d 966 Okla.): An Analysis of the Relevance of Parental Homosexuality in Child Custody Determinations." OKLAHOMA LAW REVIEW, 35 (Summer, 1982), 633-658.

"The main focus of this note is on the need for a reevaluation of the 'Best interests of the child' standard as it is applied in custody decisions" (p. 633). A 1982 decision of the Oklahoma Supreme Court removing a two-and-one-half-year-old from the custody of his mother is examined. The record indicates that, while espousing the requirement that a nexus should exist between parental homosexuality and detriment to the child, "both the trial court and the Supreme Court evidenced bias, prejudice and predisposition" (p. 635). The concept of the "nexus requirement" (as established in the Massachusetts case of *Bezio vs. Patenaude*) is explained and compared with traditional standards of evaluation in such cases.

122.   Cardwell, Gary R. "Doe v. Doe: Destroying the Assumption that Homosexual Parents Are Unfit--The New Burden of Proof." UNIVERSITY OF RICHMOND LAW REVIEW, 16 (Summer, 1982), 851-866.

In 1981, the Virginia Supreme Court, in a decision concerning adoption, "decided to hold that every lesbian mother or homosexual father is *per se* an unfit parent" (p. 851). This decision places *Doe vs. Doe* within the extant body of case law addressing the rights of homosexual parents. Cardwell assesses the value of this decision as a precedent for similar cases through analysis of older decisions which did not demand a factual demonstration that the parent in question was unfit--the facts of *Doe vs. Doe* are then presented. Although the Virginia Supreme Court did not deal with the constitutional issues involved in the case, it did impose the nexus test to deal with a presumption deemed irrebuttable, that being the innate unfitness of any homosexual parent. Cardwell notes that "the United States Supreme Court has consistently disfavored irrebuttable presumptions and found them to violate the Due Process Clause" (p. 858). A trend is seen in lesbian and gay custody decisions towards increasing demand for substantive proof of homosexuality being a detriment to "the best interests of the child." Such a trend begins to provide "constitutional protection for the parental rights of homosexual parents" (p. 862). Related cases and their findings are summarized, with emphasis on the broad discretionary powers of the court as a factor in future decisions.

123. "Missouri Gay Father Wants Son to Visit." THE ADVOCATE, 351 (16 September, 1982), 58-59.

The Missouri Court of Appeals in Kansas City had as part of its caseload a suit involving the prohibition of overnight visits by the son of a noncustodial gay father. The positions of both defense and prosecution counsels are presented. The father attacked the restrictions as unconstitutional because they were based on a single factor.

124. "'Uneasy' English Judge Grants Custody of Child to Lesbian Mum." THE ADVOCATE, 352 (30 September, 1982), 10.

An appeals court decision of the British bar granting custody of a five-year-old girl to her lesbian mother is reviewed. Custody was granted in response to the attempt of the biological father to place the child with local welfare services. Future application of this precedent are discussed.

125. "Okla. Supreme Court Awards Gay Father Custody of Twin Sons." THE ADVOCATE, 355 (11 November, 1982), 11.

On September 21, 1982, the Oklahoma Supreme Court, by a vote of four to two, returned custody of his twin eleven-year-old sons to their admittedly gay father. The case is contrasted with a similar decision earlier wherein a lesbian mother was denied custody. The decisive factor in both was stated to be the best interests of the children.

126. "Child Custody Denied to N.Y. Gay Father for 'Unusual Sexual Identity.'" THE ADVOCATE, 357 (9 December, 1982), 13-14.

Richard Gottlieb of New York City was denied custody of his daughter and his rights of visitation sharply limited in a ruling by Acting State Supreme Court Justice Henry Williams. Grounds for the decision focused on Gottlieb's sexual identity, which Williams characterized as "made up of hostile homosexual and heterosexual drives of almost equal strength which are constantly warring with each other." The response of the Gay Fathers' Forum of Greater New York is also noted. An appeal is under consideration.

127. Miller, Suzanne. "The Rights of Homosexual Parents." JOURNAL OF JUVENILE LAW, 7 (1983), 155-159.

A review article examining recent custody decisions involving the rights of homosexual parents and the relationship between homosexuality and "the best interests of the child." Cases from Oklahoma *(M.J.P. vs. J.G.P.)*, North Dakota *(Jacobson vs. Jacobson)*, Tennessee *(Dailey vs. Dailey)* and Virginia *(Doe vs. Doe)* are presented. Five elements are seen of emerging impact: peer pressure and possible social stigma for the child, absence of same-sex role models, current social values, presence or absence of lifestyle and the relationship between parent and child.

128. Dolce, Joe. "Gay Daddies Shatter Stereotypes." THE ADVOCATE, 359 (6 January, 1983), 25-27.

A general article on the emotional and legal situation facing openly gay fathers in 1982 and the organizations founded to provide support and counseling.

129. "Gay California Man Wins Custody of 17-Year-Old." THE ADVOCATE, 360 (3 February, 1983), 87.

On December 9, 1982, the California courts ruled against the Riverside County Department of Adoption in the suit brought by David Frates. At issue was Frates' custody of the seventeen-year-old who has lived in temporary custody in his household for the past two and one-half years. The department had refused to grant final approval to Frates despite certificates of eligibility to adopt.

130. "Boy Placed Away from Both Gay Dad, Fundamentalist Mom." THE ADVOCATE, 395 (29 May, 1984), 11-12.

A review of the custody case involving twelve-year-old Brian Batey, placed in a San Diego juvenile unit by a federal judge in Denver to permit both parents visitation privileges. The case has become a cause celebré to the Pentecostal church and right-wing groups. Brian's openly gay father has filed a five million dollar suit against the church for its alleged role in helping his wife hide their son from him.

131. Torno, Lynn. "In re Marriage of Cabalquinto: Protection of the Visitation Rights of Homosexual Parents." WILLAMETTE LAW REVIEW, 20 (Summer, 1984), 598-605.

A brief note analyzing the decision in *In re Marriage of Cabalquinto* permitting a gay father to retain visitation rights with his son. The opinions of both the plurality and dissenting members of the Washington Supreme Court are examined. Torno notes that this decision, which held "that homosexuality is not per se a bar to child custody and visitation rights" (p. 598), does not address the application of the "nexus" concept of demonstrable harm. This latter would compel a trial court to make a specific finding, on the basis of court records, that a child would suffer physical, mental or emotional harm by being exposed to a homosexual environment, before restricting visitation rights.

132. Clemens, Margaret A. "In the 'Best Interests of the Child' and the Lesbian Mother: A Proposal for Legislative Change." ALBANY LAW REVIEW, 48 (Summer, 1984), 1021-1044.

A comment on the child custody laws of New York State as they were in 1984 which includes the attitude towards homosexual rights and proposes "a legislative amendment to the current law that would limit the use of information regarding the sexual conduct of the

parent in a child custody case" (p. 1024). An historical review of the concept of the "best interests of the
child" is followed by considerations of parental fitness, standards of proof, lesbian mothers and the
constitutional right to privacy, the role played by
homophobia in custody decisions, and legal precedent.
Clemens notes that the dimensions of the problems posed
by lesbian custodial decisions are difficult to determine, due to a) the question of identification as
lesbians; b) the discretion of the presiding judge to
seal court records to thwart publicity; and c) the
infrequency of appeals in such cases.

133. Bagnall, Robert C., Patrick C. Gallagher and Toni L.
Goldstein. "Burdens of Gay Litigants and Bias in the
Court System: Homosexual Panic, Child Custody and
Anonymous Parties." HARVARD CIVIL RIGHTS-CIVIL
LIBERTIES LAW REVIEW, 19 (Summer, 1984), 497-559.

This comment states two conclusions: "first, that our
judicial system is not unaffected by social prejudices
and stereotyped; second, that such prejudices and
stereotypes can be overcome--or at least alleviated"
(p. 559). Three specific points of law are examined:
the "homosexual panic" defense, restrictions on
parental rights as evinced in custody decisions, and
the ability of gay litigants to proceed anonymously.
Case law and litigation on each point is provided.

134. "Gay Dads Claim Rightful Place As Part of Families." THE
ADVOCATE, 400 (7 August, 1984), 14.

A report on the June 2, 1984 conference of the Gay
Fathers' Coalition International at Riverside Church
in New York City. A chief topic of panel discussion
was "the discrimination many of them suffer from the
legislatures and the courts in such areas as custody
and child visitation." Interviews with members and
their children are included.

135. Maclean, Judy. "Lesbian's Visitation Rights Acknowledged
by Calif. Court." THE ADVOCATE, 407 (13 November, 1984),
11.

Judge Demetrius Agreletis of the Alameda County
Superior Court issued a ruling permitting visitation
rights to a lesbian whose relationship with her partner

had terminated. In the opinion of counsel, this decision is significant in its treatment of a lesbian couple as equivalent to a heterosexual couple. Background on the case is also provided.

136. Jullion, Jeanne. LONG WAY HOME: THE ODYSSEY OF A LESBIAN MOTHER AND HER CHILDREN. San Francisco: Cleis Press, 1985.

In 1977, Jeanne Jullion, mother of two boys, lost custody of her sons to her ex-husband. The trial, occurring as it did at a high tide of gay political activity in the Bay Area, received wide publicity. The children were taken by Ms. Jullion's ex-husband to their grandparents' home in Italy, where they were kept under close supervision. Their mother was only permitted to see them under certain limited conditions. As this violated the original custody ruling, it was eventually decided to have Jeanne Jullion "kidnap" her youngest son out of Italy. Trial transcripts are interspersed with a clear and vivid account of the abuses, frustrations, outrages and joys suffered by a lesbian mother as seen from the inside.

137. Susoeff, Steve. "Assessing Children's Best Interests When a Parent Is Gay or Lesbian: Toward a Rational Custody Standard." UCLA LAW REVIEW, 32 (April, 1985), 852-903.

Focusing on the laws of California as they existed in 1985, this commentary notes that, in most custody claims by "acknowledged gay and lesbian parents" (p. 807), courts have considered parental sexual orientation relevant to the proceeding. Denial is often based on the possibility of harm to the child. Factors cited include the "alleged 'mental instability' of gays and lesbians" (p. 808), influence on the sexual development of the child, and peer harassment. Research in the disciplines of psychiatry and psychology has to some extent vitiated these factors. Where courts have not required a gay or lesbian parent to prove fitness, joint custody has proven a common option. A model amendment to the child custody law of California is the proposal which "would protect the rights of gay and lesbian parents and parents who belong to other groups traditionally subjected to irrational prejudice and arbitrary discrimination" (p. 903).

138. "News Briefs." THE ADVOCATE, 423 (25 June, 1985), 24-25.

In a review of the case of Richard Gottlieb, a New York State Appeals Court removed a number of severe restrictions regarding visitation rights imposed by Judge Henry Williams in the original custody decision.

139. Walter, Dave. "They're Taking Our Children." THE ADVOCATE, 427 (20 August, 1985), 18-19.

A news article surveying four recent court cases and decisions from Virginia, Pennsylvania and Colorado involving gay and lesbian parents and custodial matters. Two of the principals are interviewed under pseudonyms, and representatives of the Lambda Legal Defense and Education Fund and similar groups comment on the general legal situation. First part of a two-part article.

140. "Gay Father Gives Up Custody Fight: Cites Son's Welfare." THE ADVOCATE, 428 (3 September, 1985), 20-21.

On July 10, 1985, Frank Batey of San Diego filed a forty-four-page document stating his intention to cease to obtain custody of his son, Brian. A detailed history of the case is provided, along with an interview with Batey and his lover Craig Corbett.

141. Freiberg, Peter. "Gay Father Ordered to Take HTLV-3 Test: Chicago Judge Makes AIDS a Custody Issue." THE ADVOCATE, 448 (10 June, 1986), 15.

A survey article on the possible role of AIDS as a factor in disputes involving child custody and visitation rights. While such use has been infrequent, due in part to education of involved parties by counsel, a Chicago case is on record where the HTLV-3 test was mandated as a preliminary for visitation. Interviews with Roberta Achtenberg of the Lesbian Rights Project of San Francisco and lawyers in Michigan and New York with experience in the matter are also included as background.

142. Walter, Dave. "Gay Father Awarded Custody of Son: Pentecostal Mother May Face Child Stealing Charges." THE ADVOCATE, 450 (8 July, 1986), 13-14.

In May, 1986, Frank Batey was awarded custody of his son Brian by a San Diego County judge, ending the boy's two-year placement in a succession of foster homes. Batey's ex-wife may face possible reinstatement of charges of child-stealing. Legal background of the case is presented.

143.   "News Briefs." THE ADVOCATE, 450 (8 July, 1986), 26.

Judge John Beatty of the Cook County (Illinois) bar has disqualified himself from presiding in the case of a Chicago gay father ordered to take the HTLV-3 test as a precondition for visitation "because of the man's lifestyle."

The Military

144. "Under Honorable Conditions." THE MATTACHINE REVIEW, 1, 3 (May-June, 1955), 6-9, 39-42.

> James Barr Fugate relates his experiences with homo-phobic persecution in the U.S. Navy during re-enlist-ment in the Korean War. His authorship of a novel, *Quatrefoil,* concerning gays, and subsequent actions were seen as sufficient grounds for discharge. This is one of the earliest accounts of U.S. Navy discrimination after World War II, and is valuable for the de-tails given of typical attitudes and procedures applied in such matters.

145. "The Homosexual Veteran." THE MATTACHINE REVIEW, 1, 4 (July-August, 1955), 29-31.

> This is an excellent overview of the laws pertaining to veterans' benefits and their respective emendations from 1933 to 1954. Sections dealing with undesirable discharges for homosexuality are given in full. A trend towards harsher penalties and reduced benefits is clear for the period covered.

146. "Mattachine Salutes Rep. Torbert H. MacDonald." THE MATTACHINE REVIEW, 3, 6 (June, 1957), 3.

This entry consists of an excerpt from the *Congressional Record* for 18 April, 1957. On that date, Representative MacDonald proposed legislation providing for a review of all "undesirable" military discharges when the person involved could show a three-year record of good conduct in civilian life. The figure of 69,323 such discharges is given for the period of July 1, 1950 to June 30, 1955.

147. "Move Afoot to Review Undesirable Discharges." THE LADDER, 1, 9 (June, 1957), 18.

H.R. 1108, introduced by Congressman Clyde Doyle of California, was debated in public hearings by the House Armed Services Subcommittee. This bill (along with forty others identical in nature) would provide for a more equitable review procedure for undesirable discharges. This is the type of discharge usually granted to open homosexuals in all cases so far adjudicated.

148. "A Review by the Army of Risk Discharges." THE MATTACHINE REVIEW, 4, 2 (February, 1958), 13.

This item reports on a review by the U.S. Army of all soldiers discharged in the period 1948-1955 as security risks. Many homosexual individuals were so separated, and this program offered an opportunity to remove the stigma such an event placed on their employment history.

149. "Punishment for Homosexuals in Service." THE MATTACHINE REVIEW, 4, 8 (August, 1958), 20.

This article is composed of a letter which appeared in the *London Observer* questioning the Wolfenden Commissions' stance that, while civil laws on homosexuality should be liberalized, military laws should remain unchanged. A call is issued for reform in these areas as well.

150. Asprey, Robert B. THE PANTHER'S FEAST. New York: G. P. Putnam's Sons, 1959.

On May 24, 1913, Colonel Alfred Redl, member of the General Staff of the Royal and Imperial Austro-Hungarian Army, committed suicide. He had been black-mailed for several years agents of the Imperial Russian intelligence service, who had learned of his homosexuality. During this time, Redl passed extremely valuable military secrets (including troop deployment) to the enemies of Austria-Hungary. It is the Redl case which provided justification for the view that homosexuals are unfit for military service because they are security risks and can be forced to betray their country. This attitude has resulted in uncounted anguish for great numbers of capable men and women. An understanding of this case is vital to comprehending the history of military homophobia.

151. "Homosexuals in Uniform." THE LADDER, 3, 9 (June, 1959), 17-20.

This excellent, if brief, article reviews the attitudes of the United States armed forces towards homosexuals from 1943-1959. Citing evidence ranging from the Kinsey Report to sample ROTC induction questions, the official position is protested as a violation of basic civil rights. An interesting feature is the three grounds upon which military discrimination has been based.

152. "One Soldier in Twenty-Five?" NEWSWEEK, 15 May, 1961, 92-93.

A review of addresses given by two speakers at a symposium on homosexuality held at the Armed Forces Institute of Pathology in early May, 1961. Lt. Col. Van H. Tanner, commander of the Washington, D.C. area military police noted that "in 1960, of the one hundred military arrests for sexual offenses in Washington, half were for homosexuality," double the 1959 statistic. Col. Tanner regards most of these persons as latent homosexuals forced into the open by the pressures of an all-male military environment. In contrast, Dr. Ben Karpna, chief psychotherapist at St. Elizabeth's Hospital, termed these individuals as "sick and in need of treatment," claiming that latent homosexuals could be detected as early as seven years of age.

153. "Boxed In: Homosexual's Exclusion from Military Service." NEW REPUBLIC, 154 (21 May, 1966), 8-9.

In several sections of the United States, demonstrations against the restrictions imposed upon homosexuals in the armed services were planned for May 21, 1966, Armed Forces Day. This article summarizes regulations (including questions on pre-induction screening forms) prohibiting homosexuals from service and outlines procedures used in eliminating them once detected. Of particular interest is a section of text from a letter of resignation provided to many homosexuals who wish to avoid further legal action. Groups involved in the planned protests include The Janus Society and the Washington, D.C. chapter of the ACLU. Opinions of their effects on this issue are included.

154. "Mattachine Tests Security Oust." THE ADVOCATE, 2, 3 (March, 1968), 3.

A review of the case of Benning Wentworth, an electronics technician whose seven-year secret security clearance was revoked following accusations of homosexuality by a member of the U.S. Air Force. He has requested the assistance of the Mattachine Society of Washington, D.C. This will be a test case under a 1967 Defense Department directive giving accused homosexuals the right to answer charges. If the case is litigated it will provide a test of whether homosexuality is a valid basis for deprivation of security clearances in federal employment.

155. "Benefits for Homosexual Veterans." THE LADDER, 12, 7 (May-June, 1968), 21-23.

Gordon Elliot and Joseph Murray of the Veterans Administration spoke at the May 3, 1968 meeting of the Council on Religion and Homosexuality in San Francisco, and provided a brief but clear summary of the rights and redress procedures available to gay and lesbian veterans. Title 30A of the U.S. Code states that all veterans with other than dishonorable discharges are eligible for full benefits. "Other than dishonorable" is defined by Federal regulations as inclusive of homosexual acts. Prior to 1962, the phrase used was "homosexual tendencies," eliminated in that year as being too vague. However, "it is believed that during World War II and the Korean Police Action that many homosexuals, particularly lesbians, were drummed out of the service for homosexual tendencies or associations."

Formation of a gay/lesbian veterans organization to lobby for change was also discussed.

156. "NLDF to Aid in Defense of WACS Facing Discharge." THE ADVOCATE, 3, 1 (January, 1969), 1.

The National Legal Defense Fund of San Francisco has contributed $500 toward court costs in the appeal cases of seven members of the Women's Army Corps. All have been charged with lesbian activity and face dishonorable discharges.

157. "Homosexuals in the Military." FORDHAM LAW REVIEW, 37 (March, 1969), 465-476.

The text of this legal comment discusses "some of the problems and inequities in the military treatment of the homosexual" (p. 476), for the period from the beginning with World War II to date. Detailed presentation is made of the development of then-current regulations (establishing three classes of homosexual persons subject to discharge) and their interpretation under article 125 of the Uniform Code of Military Justice. Cases cited include *Clackum vs. United States* and *Grant vs. United States*. Class II homosexuals--the bulk of those discharged from the services--and the consequences of their discharge upon civilian life are the chief topic of discussion. A re-evaluation of military approaches to this issue is called for.

158. "Army Doesn't Want Gays, But Sandy Doesn't Look Gay." THE ADVOCATE, 3, 3 (March, 1969), 7.

A summary of a case presently under appeal involving an inductee who admitted his homosexuality on the Selective Service questionnaire but was not believed. Following appeal of his classification as 1-A, a warrant was issued for his arrest. A lengthy interview with Don Slater of the Committee to Fight Exclusion of Homosexuals from the Armed Forces commenting upon the present legal status of homosexuals in the military is included. Under a 1966 Defense Department regulation, homosexuals can only fulfill their obligation to military service by denial of their identities, and therefore commit perjury.

159. "Cross-Currents." THE LADDER, 13, 9-10 (June-July, 1969), 39-44.

In the news items in this column is the report of ten members of the Women's Army Corps (WACS) at Fort McClellan, Alabama, charged with being homosexuals and facing undesirable discharges.

160. "'How Gay Is My Marine,' Snoop Asks." THE ADVOCATE, 3, 7 (August, 1969), 3.

A personal account of an attempt by an investigator from the Office of Naval Intelligence to establish the homosexual identity of a serviceman via contact tracing.

161. "WACS Prevail Over Army." THE LADDER, 13, 11-12 (August-September, 1969), 7-9.

Written by Franklin Kameny, a leading gay activist of Washington, D.C., this article reports on the outcome of the case involving ten members of the Women's Army Corps at Fort McClellan, Alabama. In the autumn of 1968, a "purge" of homosexuals was taking place throughout all WAC units. Detailed summaries of two individual cases are included: security clearances for the women involved were later restored.

162. "Cross-Currents." THE LADDER, 13, 11-12 (August-September, 1969), 44-48.

The formation of the Committee to Fight Exclusion of Homosexuals from the Armed Forces in Los Angeles and its objectives are briefly reported.

163. "Gay Discharges May Get Review." THE ADVOCATE, 3, 8 (September, 1969), 23.

One of the final decisions of the U.S. Supreme Court under Chief Justice Earl Warren limited the jurisdiction of military authorities to offenses committed "within the scope of military service." This means that personnel can no longer be penalized by courts-martial for activities occurring off-base. One implication of this ruling is that all discharges given for such conduct must now be re-evaluated. Homosexuals who were dishonorably discharged and wish to clear their names and records are instructed to contact the Judge Advocate General of the specific branch of service for information on application procedures.

164. "Undesirable Discharges from the Air Force." THE MATTACHINE REVIEW, 5, 9 (September, 1969), 18-20.

With the passage of the Unification Act on April 15, 1959, all branches of the U.S. military service came under the aegis of the Department of Defense. In an effort to standardize variant approaches to all issues, the Department issued new rules, among them being a policy on homosexuality. Three basic categories-- latent, association with known homosexuals, and overt-- were drawn up. Persons in the first two classes are to be given general or honorable discharges depending on their service records. Active homosexuals are still to be discharged as undesirables. The author--an officer in the Air Force--also presents statistical information on the rates of discharge for the various services, with the Air Force ranking at the top with almost ten percent of all discharges falling into its category.

165. "An American Tragedy: He Served Well, But . . ." THE ADVOCATE, 3, 10 (November, 1969), 1.

A reprint of a letter sent to The ADVOCATE by a subscriber. The author is a twenty-year-old soldier stationed at Cam Ranh Bay in Viet Nam presently facing expulsion.

166. "Kameny, Scourge of Federals, Continues on Government, Military Bias." THE ADVOCATE, 4, 2 (February, 1970), 3, 5.

A news article covering the activities of Dr. Franklin Kameny of the Mattachine Society of Washington, D.C. in opposition to federal standards excluding homosexuals from government positions. Extensive quotations from statements made at the hearing of the Benning Wentworth security clearance case are included. Brief summations of other cases in which Mattachine is involved are also provided.

167. "AF Sergeant Names 200-250 Men, Sets Off Homosexual Witchhunt." THE ADVOCATE, 4, 4 (April, 1970), 1.

A twenty-four-year-old sergeant stationed at Offutt Air Force Base, Omaha, Nebraska was discovered to be homosexual in August, 1969. Between that time and his administrative discharge in February, 1970, he implicated some two hundred and fifty other individuals as being homosexuals. As a result of these investigations, sixteen servicemen have been discharged at Offutt and three others face expulsion. Data on other branches of the services has been forwarded to the appropriate judicial officers.

168. "WACS Seek Honorable Discharge After AWOL." THE ADVOCATE, 4, 4 (April, 1970), 3.

Two members of the Women's Army Corps, harassed for a lesbian relationship, went on leave to Los Angeles and requested assistance from Tangents, a homosexual organization. Following counseling, they decided to return to base and apply for discharges. The individuals involved are Sandra Hagen and Antoinetta Garland.

169. "Two Gay WACS Get Discharges - Others May Follow." THE ADVOCATE, 4, 5 (May, 1970), 2.

Antoinetta Garland and Sandra Hagen of the Women's Army Corps returned to Fort McClellan, Alabama after their period of being AWOL and received honorable discharges. Following the conclusion of this nationally publicized case, twenty-seven other WACS at McClellan have applied for similar discharges or requested assistance in challenging the Army's policies against lesbians.

170. "AF Man Names Sgt. X in Suit, Fights Discharge." THE ADVOCATE, 4, 5 (29 April-12 May, 1970), 7.

Air Force Staff Sgt. Scott F. Benson, one of the 270 persons named as homosexuals by Sgt. Richard G. Burchill, has filed suit against the U.S. Air Force to block his expulsion with an undesirable discharge. Details of the military and civilian legal options open to Benson are summarized. Sergeant Burchill was given an honorable discharge on January 30, 1970 following his testimony against fellow airmen at Offutt Air Force Base, Omaha and elsewhere.

171. "Editorial: The Uniform Dilemma." THE ADVOCATE, 4, 5 (May, 1970), 22.

> An editorial from *The ADVOCATE* criticizing the treat-ment of homosexuals by the armed services and calling for the removal of sex laws from the Uniform Code of Military Justice to end the practice of investigative "witchhunts." The Burchill scandal at Omaha's Offutt Air Force Base is used as an illustration of the present conditions.

172. "Air Force Used Threats, Promises, Then Broke Its Word: Sgt. X." THE ADVOCATE, 4, 6 (13-26 May, 1970), 1, 7.

> An interview with former Air Force Sgt. Richard Burchill regarding his role in the homosexual scandal at Offutt Air Force Base. He stated that he had been assured of continued retention in the service following the discovery by the OSI of a letter marking him as gay. Rather than the 270 names quoted by Air Force sources, Burchill testified that he provided officials with only thirty. Once his information was received, he was shipped to Lackland Air Force Base for dis-charge. He declined to testify in any of the upcoming trials of other individuals involved. Contacts at Offutt indicate that the investigations initiated through Burchill's questioning are continuing.

173. "Wentworth Hassle Nears End in Pentagon: Court Battle May Follow." THE ADVOCATE, 4, 6 (13-26 May, 1970), 5.

> On March 30, 1970, a hearing was held regarding the August, 1969 decision of the Eastern Field Board in the case of Benning Wentworth. The 1969 finding placed Wentworth in a class of individuals known to be vulner-able to blackmail--homosexuals--as grounds for his dismissal from his position. The language of the decision implied the need for a higher level of conduct for homosexuals than for heterosexuals in similar situations. Wentworth has stated his intention to carry the case as far as necessary to obtain restora-tion of his status. At this time, no case involving a homosexual and his security clearance had yet been accepted by the U.S. Supreme Court, most being stopped at the district court or Court of Appeals levels by unfavorable decisions for the plaintiffs.

174. "Cross-Currents." THE LADDER, 14, 9-10 (June-July, 1970), 33-40.

> Among the news stories reported here is that of Antoinetta Garland, age twenty-three, and Sandy Hagen, age twenty. Both women enlisted in the WACS on September 30, 1969. Having established a relationship, they took leave together and arrived in Los Angeles. Through the efforts of the Los Angeles Metropolitan Community Church and local activist Morris Kight, arrangements were made for their return to the U.S. Army for a promised honorable discharge, due on March 18, 1970.

175. "Military Policies on Gays Make No Sense." THE ADVOCATE, 4, 10 (8-21 July, 1970), 7, 10, 17.

> A general review of the military's policies regarding both induction and separation from the service of homosexuals. Specific U.S. Army regulations and relevant sections of the Uniform Code of Military Justice are quoted and explained. Two current cases involving Lawrence Ostroff and Richard Burchill are summarized. Of interest is the admission by the Air Force that an increasing number of inductees are claiming homosexual status to avoid service in Viet Nam. Don Slater of Los Angeles' Homosexual Information Center provides advice on how to cope effectively with these issues.

176. Williams, Colin J. and Martin S. Weinberg. HOMOSEXUALS AND THE MILITARY. New York: Harper & Row, 1971.

> Colin Williams' and Martin Weinberg's volume is a report on the results of a study of two groups of gay men, one of whose members received honorable discharges from military service and one where dishonorable expulsion occurred. Official military policies (of all branches of service) are presented and analyzed. While intended as a study of the social consequences of being "labeled," it provides a detailed examination of the rationale and environment behind the American military's attitudes towards gay and lesbian individuals.

177. "Demonstrators Seek Airman Discharge." THE ADVOCATE, 4, 23 (6-19 January, 1971), 7.

The Los Angeles Gay Liberation Front held a demonstration at Edwards Air Force Base during the week of December 18, 1970 to support the request for discharge of security policeman Jeffery Orth. Even though he had admitted his sexual orientation, no specific action had been taken against Orth as of January, 1971. Officials would only state that the case was under investigation, a claim challenged by the military counsel for the Gay Liberation Front.

178. "Gay Airman Aided by GLF May Get Quick Discharge." THE ADVOCATE, 4, 24 (20 January-2 February, 1971), 3.

Following a demonstration by the gay liberation movement of Los Angeles at Edwards Air Force Base on behalf of Jeffery Orth, he was reassigned to office duty and scheduled for psychiatric evaluation. As Orth has no other complaint on his service record, an honorable discharge is seen as likely.

179. "Airman's Discharge: Is It Yes, No or Maybe?" THE ADVOCATE, 43 (27 February-2 March, 1971), 5, 14.

Following psychiatric evaluation at March Air Force Base on December 19, 1970, it was recommended that security policeman Jeffery Orth be retained by the Air Force despite his homosexuality. On January 26, 1971 Orth's commanding officer notified him of initiation of action recommending granting him a general discharge.

180. "GLF/L.A. Seeks Aid on Military Counseling." THE ADVOCATE, 54 (3-16 March, 1971), 2.

A request from the Gay Liberation Front of Los Angeles for assistance from licensed psychologists and psychiatrists to provide professional testing and interviews for gay servicemen desiring separation with honorable discharges.

181. "Orth Honorably Discharged." THE ADVOCATE, 56 (31 March-April 13, 1971), 7, 35.

On March 2, 1971, Jeffery Orth was separated from the U.S. Air Force with an honorable discharge after some four months of effort. Background information on the case is provided.

182. "Gay Army or No, Draft Case Dismissed." THE ADVOCATE, 57 (14-27 April, 1971), 14.

> A report on the disposition of the case of Bob McIvery, a Los Angeles activist facing charges of failure to report for induction. Having been quite frank with officials at all levels as to his sexual preferences, he was acquitted under Regulation 40-501, which prohibits induction of homosexuals.

183. "Army Won't Believe He's Gay." THE ADVOCATE, 57 (14-27 April, 1971), 14.

> Terry Barnard of San Francisco was drafted into the U.S. Army despite his admission of homosexuality. A psychiatrist at San Francisco General Hospital refused to defer him on grounds that he did not exhibit effeminate characteristics. His case is presently under consideration by the Army's Civilian Investigation Division.

184. "Lover, Lawyer Finally Convince Army He's Gay." THE ADVOCATE, 58 (28 April-11 May, 1971), 9.

> An honorable discharge was granted to Terry Barnard after his lover signed a statement for the U.S. Army confirming Barnard's statements regarding sexual relations. Background data on the case is provided.

185. "Gay Life Is There, Vietnam GI Says, But You Have to Be Careful." THE ADVOCATE, 60 (26 May-8 June, 1971), 10, 19.

> An anonymous interview with a gay GI serving in Viet Nam describing the homosexual subculture there in the military establishment.

186. "The Big Question Dropped from Military Forms." THE ADVOCATE, 62 (23 June-6 July, 1971), 18.

> Following expressions of concern over the privacy rights of inductees by Sen. Sam Ervin, a number of questions have been eliminated from the Public Health Services' medical history forms signed by all draftees.

Among them is one inquiring as to the sexual history of the individual and whether he had ever exhibited homosexual tendencies. Service physicians expressed disapproval of the alterations, saying that many of the questions were legitimate portions of a coherent medical record needed to assess fitness for service.

187. "GLF Advises Gays to Write in the Truth." THE ADVOCATE, 62 (23 June-6 July, 1971), 8.

Military counselors at the Los Angeles Gay Liberation Front reacted to the news of the deletion of the question on homosexuality from draft forms by urging all inductees to declare themselves frankly in another section of the form used for additional comments.

188. "SIR Quietly Recruits GIs." THE ADVOCATE, 65 (4-17 August, 1971), 1.

The Society for Individual Rights of San Francisco is attempting to contact homosexuals presently serving in the armed services for the purposes of setting up discreet meetings where the problems occasioned by current regulations can be discussed. Attendance will be limited to currently enlisted servicemen and officers.

189. "Military Court Forbids Fraternization in the Ranks." THE ADVOCATE, 65 (4-17 August, 1971), 3.

A ruling of the U.S. Council of Military Justice, Washington, D.C. has cleared Navy Lt. Carl Pitasi of sodomy charges, but convicted him of fraternizing with an able seaman of lower rank. The history of this prohibition is explored. Under this ruling, Pitasi may still face expulsion from the service.

190. "Sociologists Slam Military Policy on Gays." THE ADVOCATE, 66 (18-31 August, 1971), 25-26.

A summary of the findings of a four-year study of U.S. military policy towards homosexuals by Drs. Martin Weinberg and Colin Williams of the Kinsey Institute. Recently published under the title *Homosexuals and the Military*, it details policies of intimidation and coercion which are deemed "unwise, unjust and essentially unenforceable." Researchers should consult the full text of this document.

191.   "Rejected Lover's Prank Leads Annapolis Sailor, Navy to Battle." THE ADVOCATE, 69 (29 September-12 October, 1971), 5.

Dental technician Ronald Stinson, USN, is currently seeking an honorable discharge from the service. His career was interrupted when a former partner sent incriminating photographs and an anonymous letter to the Navy in July, 1971. Details of the legal proceedings are included.

192.   "D.C. Post Backs Top Discharge for Navy Gay." THE ADVOCATE, 70 (13 October, 1971), 11.

An editorial in the September 11, 1971 *Washington Post* supported the request of Ronald Stinson for an honorable discharge from the Navy on grounds of homosexuality. It was the opinion of the staff that "the Navy should want to pursue the man for its error, should seek to humiliate and injure him because it disapproves of his sexual preference seems to us beyond comprehension."

193.   "Gays in Uniform: All Those Ratings Wouldn't Mean a Thing." THE ADVOCATE, 70 (13 October, 1971), 30, 34.

"The United States is the only nation in the world which makes heterosexuality a formal prerequisite of military service." With this statement, a general treatment of why many gay men lie to fulfill their felt obligations for service and the tensions this creates for them while in the service is presented. Punishment can range from immediate discharges to harassment and isolation. Personal testimony is included from three individuals.

194.   "Navy Kicks Out Stinson: Lawyer Readies Own Kick." THE ADVOCATE, 71 (27 October, 1971), 14.

On October 7, 1971, Ronald Stinson received a general discharge from the United States Navy. ACLU counsel for the plaintiff plans to file suit in district court to request an honorable discharge, as general discharges pose problems with civilian employers since the codes are not limited to military matters for causes of separation.

195. "Navy Discharges: Drugs Up, Gays Down." THE ADVOCATE, 72 (10 November, 1971), 26.

A statistical report issued by the U.S. Navy indicates that in 1971 a greater number of individuals were separated from the service for drug-related reasons than for homosexual activities. This is viewed as a possible response to a Department of Defense crackdown on drugs in all branches.

196. "Sailor Facing Discharge Seeks Info on Straight Trade in USN." THE ADVOCATE, 77 (19 January, 1972), 9.

Seaman Robert A. Martin, facing discharge in Naples, Italy on ground of "suspected homosexuality" has requested testimony from former servicemen as to the prevalence of same-sex activity in the Navy. His approach in legal proceedings will use this data to put his actions in perspective within the subculture of naval life. A hearing in the case is scheduled for January 26, 1971.

197. "Major Test Being Sought on Navy Homosexuality." THE ADVOCATE, 79 (16 February, 1972), 11.

Naval radioman Robert Martin has received counsel and assistance from several gay liberation groups and will be represented by counsel from the American Civil Liberties Union at the Naval Discharge Board Hearing in March.

198. "International Support Helping Sailor Fight Navy." THE ADVOCATE, 80 (1 March, 1972), 7.

The case of Robert Martin, USN, is receiving widespread attention from the media and from organizations concerned with obtaining fair treatment for homosexuals. Among them are the Society for Individual Rights in San Francisco, Dr. Franklin Kameny and the Mattachine Society of Washington, D.C. and Morris Kight in Los Angeles. Martin's requested formal administrative hearing before a discharge board has not yet been held.

199. "Abzug Aids 'The Ram.'" THE ADVOCATE, 81 (15 March, 1972), 1.

    Congresswoman Bella Abzug has urged that the U.S. Navy either provide radioman Robert Martin with sea orders or an honorable discharge. His defense is planned to be to challenge Naval Regulation 1900.9 of 20 April, 1964 making homosexuality grounds for refusing an applicant for induction. Abzug has also contacted Sen. Sam Ervin's subcommittee on constitutional rights, which has been studying administrative discharges for some time.

200. "Major Legal Confrontation Shaping Up In Gay Case." THE ADVOCATE, 82 (29 March, 1972), 16.

    The case of radioman Robert A. Martin has expanded beyond the original group of persons and organizations, with support received from the Metropolitan Community Church. Efforts to obtain an honorable discharge through Congressional means have failed. Martin has been ordered to Norfolk, Virginia from his previous posting at Naples, Italy. The legal positions of both parties are profiled, with hearings scheduled for March 23, 1972.

201. "Naval Board Gives Martin General Discharge: Appeal Set." THE ADVOCATE, 83 (12 April, 1972), 4.

    A naval board in Naples, Italy has recommended that Robert Martin be separated from the service under a general discharge following repudiation of the original statement by the accuser. Coercion by the Naval Intelligence Service is alleged. The decision will now be referred to the Bureau of Naval Personnel, which has the power to modify it.

202. "Abzug Calls Martin Case 'Witchhunt.'" THE ADVOCATE, 83 (12 April, 1972), 4.

    In a personal letter to Secretary of the Navy John H. Chafee, Congresswoman Bella Abzug called upon him to intervene in the discharge case of radioman Robert Martin. She described the ongoing effort as "a gross denial of due process" without proof or opportunity for the accused to cross-examine. An administrative discharge hearing has been set for March 23, 1972.

203. "Marine's Discharge Draws Protests." THE ADVOCATE, 83 (12 April, 1972), 4.

> A review of the case of Lance Corporal Anthony Dunbar. On March 21, 1972, an administrative discharge board unanimously voted an undesirable discharge for him despite an unblemished service record. Dunbar has admitted his homosexuality following an attempt at suicide occasioned by unmanageable stress. The Mattachine Society of Washington, D.C. has become involved, with Dr. Franklin Kameny expressing a willingness to take the Marine Corps to court.

204. "Lawmakers Eye Marine Discharge." THE ADVOCATE, 84 (26 April, 1972), 3.

> Several members of Congress, including Senators Edward Kennedy and Jacob Javits and Rep. Edward Koch have expressed concern about the undesirable discharge recommended for Marine corporal Anthony Dunbar. The Gay Activist Alliance of Washington, D.C. has also charged the Marine Corps with inserting pre-dated derogatory materials into Dunbar's service file. The question of the propriety of the discharge has also been raised in an editorial in the *Washington Post*.

205. "Major Test Seen in Navy Case." THE ADVOCATE, 84 (26 April, 1972), 3, 10.

> The decision of the administrative discharge board in Naples to recommend a general discharge for seaman Robert Martin on grounds of unfitness for military service is examined. Detailed coverage of the arguments of both defense and prosecution is included. Lawyers for the American Civil Liberties Union stated that they would attempt to halt implementation of the board's order.

206. "Pentagon Holds to Antigay Stand." THE ADVOCATE, 86 (24 May, 1972), 3.

> A report on a series of letters exchanged between Rep. Edward Koch of New York and Pentagon officials on the issue of military policies requiring automatic expulsion for homosexuals in the armed services. Koch raises the issue of gratuitous punishment, using the case of radioman Robert Martin as example.

207. "RAM's 'Unfit' Discharge Sticks." THE ADVOCATE, 87 (7 June, 1972), 2.

> The Department of the Navy has upheld a recommendation that R. A. Martin be separated from the service under a general discharge. Counsel for Martin stated that a post-discharge lawsuit has not been ruled out. Processing will take place in Brooklyn after May 23, 1972.

208. "VFW Meet Hits Gay Lib." THE ADVOCATE, 87 (7 June, 1972), 17.

> At the Seventh District Convention of the Veterans of Foreign Wars meeting in Minneapolis on April 30, 1972, delegates adopted a resolution condemning the gay liberation movement as "dangerous to the morals and well-being of the nation."

209. "Restore Wentworth Clearance, Says Judge." THE ADVOCATE, 88 (21 June, 1972), 1.

> On May 26, 1972, U.S. District Judge Pratt of the District of Columbia ordered the Defense Department to restore the security clearance of Benning Wentworth, as the present policy "effectively deprives the plaintiff of his right to a fair and impartial hearing and restricted his constitutional right of due process." Use of intimate questions as to Wentworth's sexual life was also condemned. This decision is seen to effectively neutralize the existing sodomy legislation of the District of Columbia as it applies to consenting adults.

210. "'RAM' Back in U.S." THE ADVOCATE, 89 (5 July, 1972), 17.

> Seaman Robert Martin was processed for a general discharge at the Brooklyn Naval Station in a record four hours, undergoing an intensive search of his personal effects. Immediate plans were to file for unemployment and to attend a Quaker conference in Ithaca, New York.

211. "Marines Give Cpl. Dunbar 'Undesirable.'" THE ADVOCATE, 90 (19 July, 1972), 14.

Despite efforts from the Gay Activist Alliance of
Washington, D.C. and Dr. Franklin Kameny of the Mattachine Society, the undesirable discharge recommended
for Corporal J. Arthur Dunbar of the Marine Corps was
confirmed by Commander Robert E. Cushman. Actions
taken by the GAA included a demonstration at the Marine
base at Quantico, Virginia.

212. "Stinson Won't Press Navy Discharge Suit." THE ADVOCATE,
      97 (25 October, 1972), 12.

      R. L. Stinson has decided to withdraw a planned suit to
      compel the U.S. Navy to grant him a full honorable
      discharge due to fear of adverse publicity which might
      harm his elderly parents. Dr. Franklin Kameny of the
      Washington, D.C. Mattachine Society is seeking other
      servicemen who may be willing to challenge naval regu-
      lations on homosexuality.

213. "Sex Arrest Brings Suicide of U.S. Official." THE
      ADVOCATE, 98 (8 November, 1972), 11.

      A survey of the facts behind the suicide on August 30,
      1972 of the assistant deputy for program control, U.S.
      Naval Air Systems Command. Following entrapment and
      arrest by police in Atlantic City, he was released on
      bond, returned to his residence in Virginia, and hanged
      himself. A protest is planned by the Washington gay
      community to commemorate his death.

214. "WACS Getting Army Boot After Wedding." THE ADVOCATE,
      107 (14 March, 1973), 18.

      Rev. Ray Broshears of San Francisco joined two members
      of the Women's Army Corps on February 3, 1973. Both
      were stationed at Fort Ord, California and presently
      face undesirable discharges. Mishandling of the case
      by local military law counselors is blamed for the rank
      of discharge being advocated.

215. "Love Conquers All: WACS Ride Out Storm Caused by
      Marriage." THE ADVOCATE, 108 (28 March, 1973), 1.

      A detailed summary of the events leading to the expul-
      sion from the Women's Army Corps of Pvt. Gail Bates and
      Pvt. Valerie Randolph, including their marriage by

Reverend Broshears and subsequent news conference. Randolph received an honorable discharge but had her papers coded to indicate separation due to homosexuality.

216. "Bill Would Halt Disclosure of Military Discharge Facts." THE ADVOCATE, 124 (7 November, 1973), 16.

A bill has been introduced in Congress by Sen. George McGovern and Reps. Les Aspin and Edward Koch which would forbid military services from indicating reasons for discharge on separation papers. At this time some five hundred and thirty numerical codes were in use, with the recipients having no chance to establish evidence or file appeals against them. Employers conversant with the system are enabled to ascertain the cause of termination.

217. "Solons Hear Vets Protest Stigma of Discharge Labels." THE ADVOCATE, 125 (21 November, 1973), 22.

An informal amnesty committee of Congress heard testimony by both heterosexual and homosexual veterans on October 8, 1973 attacking the military power to brand veterans with undesirable discharges. Consequences for eligibility for veterans' benefits and civilian employment were expressed. Committee members were Reps. Bella Abzug and John Conyers.

218. "Help of Veterans Asked for Lawsuit." THE ADVOCATE, 128 (2 January, 1974), 3.

The Gay Students Association and the Veterans Affairs Commission of the University of Washington are exploring the possibility of a class-action suit against the Veterans Administration on behalf of veterans whose benefits have been denied on grounds of less-than-honorable discharges. Homosexual veterans are urged to contact the groups for testimony.

219. "Gay WAC Defies Army, Tries to Force Test." THE ADVOCATE, 128 (2 January, 1974), 21.

A profile of the efforts made by Dierdre Green, a WAC supply clerk at Fort Sam Houston, San Antonio, Texas to force the U.S. Army to deal with her homosexuality.

Despite two trips to Washington, D.C. resulting in time AWOL, no formal charges have been levied against her. She plans to use her AWOL hearing as a forum to raise the issue. Counsel has been retained from the American Civil Liberties Union.

220. "Army Says Gay GI Can Serve." THE ADVOCATE, 131 (13 February, 1974), 20.

An administrative review board in Frankfurt, West Germany decided that a G.I. who has admitted his homosexuality may be allowed to complete the final six months of his enlistment in the hope that this time will serve to "rehabilitate" him. This decision is subject to review by both Fifth Army Headquarters and the Department of Defense.

221. "WAC Gets Court Martial, But Not Because She's Gay." THE ADVOCATE, 132 (27 February, 1974), 10.

Sp/4 Dierdre Green of the Women's Army Corps is facing court-martial for her period of being AWOL in October, 1973. This was a deliberate effort on Green's part to permit her to file suit against the Department of Defense for its policies against homosexuals. Complaints against her commanding officer are also recorded.

222. "Court Says All Veterans Must Get Equal Treatment." THE ADVOCATE, 132 (27 February, 1974), 14.

Ruling in the case of a veteran who received an undesirable discharge for refusal to go to Viet Nam on conscientious objector grounds, the Fifth Circuit Court of Appeals in New Orleans unanimously struck down a city ordinance barring persons in this class from municipal employment. This decision is viewed as part of a continuing effort to challenge the military discharge system. ACLU counsel noted that less-than-honorable discharges can be granted without a trial before a court-martial, which is seen as a violation of due process and equal protection rights. Homosexual veterans with such discharges typically encounter problems finding adequate civilian employment.

223. "'Those Queers Think They're Human Beings Like the Rest of Us.'" THE ADVOCATE, 132 (27 February, 1974), 28, 32.

   A satirical essay on the military mentality towards homosexuals reflecting attitudes held in the early 1970s.

224. "Army Will Quit Discharge Coding." THE ADVOCATE, 136 (24 April, 1974), 5.

   In a letter to Rep. R. Edwards Hebert, Chair of the House Armed Services Committee, Secretary of Defense James Schlesinger stated that the practice of numerically coding all discharge papers will be discontinued as of March 27, 1974. In the past, employers familiar with the system could discern the reasons for discharge and refuse to employ otherwise qualified individuals. Among the reasons for such discharges is homosexuality. This action is seen as the culmination of pressures from both the public and members of Congress.

225. "Gays Still Marked in the Pentagon." THE ADVOCATE, 137 (8 May, 1974), 5.

   Rep. John Seiberling (D-Ohio) has proposed that the separation program numbers used as a system of coding, which have been deleted from public records of service discharges, be removed from internal Pentagon documents as well. If the internal usage is retained, veterans with anything less than an honorable discharge could be pressured by prospective employers into authorizing the release of this potentially prejudicial information. Statistics on these discharges and the codes used to mark the various types of homosexual veterans are listed.

226. "Swedes Protest Army Policy: Are Gays Partially Accepted?" THE ADVOCATE, 138 (22 May, 1974), 22.

   The Swedish Federation for Sexual Equality has protested an army policy of excusing admitted homosexuals from their obligatory military service. Officials stated that they have no objections to homosexuals serving in the ranks, but opposed their presence in officer corps positions. This protest was occasioned by an incident in southern Sweden where a gay man's request to serve his full time was refused.

227. "How to Get 'Spin' Code Off Discharge." THE ADVOCATE, 140 (19 June, 1974), 16.

An informational article providing veterans with contact addresses to enable them to have the numerical "spin" codes removed from their discharge papers. This new system will be in effect as of May 1, 1974.

228. "Navy Hounds Its Gay Sailors." THE ADVOCATE, 142 (17 July, 1974), 18.

The cases of radarman Alonzo Bradley and personnel officer Carol Spears are used as illustrations of the official policy of the U.S. Navy towards homosexuals. Much of the article is a detailed interview with Mike Manning, a counselor at the Los Angeles Gay Community Services Center who is advising both parties. Relevant naval regulations are quoted.

229. "A Lesbian Purge." THE ADVOCATE, 160 (26 March, 1975), 10.

A report on a recent three-month investigation of suspected lesbian activity in the Woman's Marine Corps contingent stationed at Camp Elmore, Virginia.

230. "Homosexual Sergeant." TIME, 105 (9 June, 1975), 18-19.

An interview with Technical Sgt. Leonard Matlovich covering personal history, evolution of his identity as homosexual and his decision to fight the decision of the U.S. Air Force to expel him despite exemplary service reviews and ratings. The Pentagon intends to enforce existing prohibitions in the matter.

231. "Rep. Koch (NY) Writes." THE ADVOCATE, 167 (2 July, 1975), 9.

The full text of a letter from Rep. Edward Koch of New York to James Schlesinger, Secretary of Defense, supporting the right of Sgt. Leonard Matlovich to remain in the United States Air Force as an open homosexual.

232. "ADVOCATE Special Report: Gay People and the Military." THE ADVOCATE, 167 (2 July, 1975), 19-29.

A group of eleven articles reviewing policies in the military towards homosexuals as they were in 1975. Each entry has been entered under its individual title in the present bibliography.

233. "ADVOCATE Special Report: A Question of Banners." THE ADVOCATE, 167 (2 July, 1975), 19-20.

A column reflecting on the "polite amnesia" suffered by the gay liberation movement with regard to homosexuals in the military and their status, calling for recognition of their rights.

234. "ADVOCATE Special Report: How to Get Help." THE ADVOCATE, 167 (2 July, 1975), 20-21.

A review of the harassment problems facing homosexuals in the military, the types of discharge procedures available, and the role a civilian counselor conversant with military law can play in assisting such efforts. An interesting point raised is the origin of the military's resistance to accepting claims of gay identity in the widespread use of this tactic by draft resisters in the late 1960s and early 1970s.

235. "ADVOCATE Special Report: One Woman's Viewpoint." THE ADVOCATE, 167 (2 July, 1975), 21.

A personal account by a lesbian member of the Coast Guard reserve of the attitudes of sexism and homophobia present in that branch of the service.

236. "ADVOCATE Special Report: A Perfect Test Case." THE ADVOCATE, 167 (2 July, 1975), 22.

A frank interview with Sgt. Leonard Matlovich, discussing his decision to come out as a member of the U.S. Air Force and challenge the official policies of discharge for homosexuals.

237. "ADVOCATE Special Report: How Uncle Sam Brought Me Out." THE ADVOCATE, 167 (2 July, 1975), 23.

A personal account by a former member of the U.S. Air Force of the atmosphere of anti-gay attitudes as he experienced them. Of particular interest is an attempt by members of the Office of Special Investigations to force him to incriminate himself following successful completion of service and an honorable discharge.

238. "ADVOCATE Special Report: The Enemy Sleeps in the Next Bunk." THE ADVOCATE, 167 (2 July, 1975), 24-25.

A consideration of the ways in which American films stereotype desirable attitudes, with particular reference to "showing what happens to the less-than-men who try to become men by joining the army." The film *The Gay Deceivers* is used as an example of the negative image.

239. "ADVOCATE Special Report: It's As Old As the Greeks." THE ADVOCATE, 167 (2 July, 1975), 26.

Homosexual activity in the military is placed within an historical context through quotations from sections of *The Iliad* dealing with the grief of Achilles over the killing of Patroklos.

240. "ADVOCATE Special Report: ACLU Attorneys Publish Upgrade Book." THE ADVOCATE, 167 (2 July, 1975), 27.

Attorneys Susan Hewman and David Addlestone of the American Civil Liberties Union's Military Law Project have written a manual of procedures for those veterans desiring to upgrade their discharge papers. Options available for changing military attitudes on homosexuality are reviewed.

241. "ADVOCATE Special Report: Matlovich--First Step in Battle." THE ADVOCATE, 167 (2 July, 1975), 28.

An interview with Dr. Franklin Kameny of the Mattachine Society and David Addlestone of the ACLU on the potential for change represented by the case of Sgt. Leonard Matlovich against the U.S. Air Force.

242. "ADVOCATE Special Report: 22-Year Reservist Unwelcome Now." THE ADVOCATE, 167 (2 July, 1975), 28.

A brief summary of the facts in the case of Gary Hess, a member of the Naval Reserve who has decided to challenge official policies on the discharge of homosexuals. Hess has served in exemplary fashion and the challenge is seen as an opportunity to make significant changes within that branch of service.

243.   "ADVOCATE Special Report: Honor Platoon WACS Fighting Discharge." THE ADVOCATE, 167 (2 July, 1975), 29.

Two members of the Army Security Agency at Fort Devens in Ayer, Massachusetts have been placed on security hold and assigned menial labor following their disclosure as lesbians. Separation is to be carried out under Army Regulation 635-200. Barbara Randolph and Debbie Watson are being assisted by the ACLU and the Legal In Service Project of the Unitarian Universalist Association.

244.   "Hess Loses Round One in Court." THE ADVOCATE, 169 (30 July, 1975), 5.

U.S. District Judge Manuel Real of Los Angeles denied the request of Naval Reserve Commander Gary Hess for a restraining order to prevent a naval hearing on his fitness to serve, stating that such an action would be premature in that no formal action has yet been taken against him. Hess is under consideration for discharge following disclosure of his homosexuality.

245.   "Lesbians Ousted from Marine Corps." THE ADVOCATE, 169 (30 July, 1975), 5.

Approximately ten percent of a Marine corps of eighty-seven officers and enlisted women at Camp Elmore have either been discharged, released or investigated on grounds of lesbianism. Five women have received honorable discharges while two more are under investigation.

246.   "Honorably Discharged." THE ADVOCATE, 169 (30 July, 1975), 6.

Following a four-hour administrative hearing at the Jacksonville Naval Air Station, a three-man panel recommended that Naval Reserve Commander Lawrence Leonard Heisel be given an honorable discharge from the service. Heisel, a seventeen-year veteran and pilot, was exposed by his former wife upon learning of his possible assignment to the town where she was living.

247. "Navy Board 'Powerless to Change Policy.'" THE ADVOCATE, 170 (13 August, 1975), 5.

A naval hearing board in San Diego recommended the Commander Gary Hess be granted an honorable discharge, stating that it was unable to alter official policy on the discharge of homosexuals. Hess has obtained a court order prohibiting action on the discharge until a hearing scheduled for August 22, 1975 at the San Diego District Court.

248. "Second Sergeant Comes Out." THE ADVOCATE, 170 (13 August, 1975), 9.

A review of the case of U.S. Air Force Sgt. Rudolf Keith and the consequences of his decision to admit his homosexuality. Excerpts from an interview with Keith are included. He is stationed at the Dover Air Force Base in Delaware.

249. "Veterans Asking Help." THE ADVOCATE, 170 (13 August, 1975), 9.

The Veterans Committee of the National Gay Task Force has requested assistance from lesbian and gay veterans in gathering materials to be used in several cases pending involving official military policies against homosexuals. Information being requested includes time served, branch of service, awards and medals received, rank held and opinions as to service effectiveness and the probability of blackmail. Cases involved with these submissions will be those of Leonard Matlovich, Rudolf Keith, Debbie Watson and Barbara Randolph.

250. "'Unfit' WACS Going to Court." THE ADVOCATE, 170 (13 August, 1975), 9.

A review of the hearing at Ayer, Massachusetts in the cases of Barbara Randolph and Debbie Watson of the Women's Army Corps. Both have been recommended for discharges despite efforts of defense counsel to use their case as a general test of military policies against homosexuals. Challenge will continue in civilian court. An interesting feature noted is that all related cases cited by the defense were dismissed as irrelevant.

251. "APA Gets on Military's Case." THE ADVOCATE, 171 (27 August, 1975), 5.

The National Gay Task Force is in receipt of a letter from Dr. Judd Marmor, president of the American Psychological Association, which affirms the right of gay persons to serve in the military forces. An APA resolution on the absence of impact of homosexuality on ability to function is quoted.

252. "Lobbying Blitz Moves Military." THE ADVOCATE, 171 (27 August, 1975), 7.

The National Gay Task Force mounted a lobbying effort to inform members of the House and Senate of the shift in the hearing date for Sgt. Leonard Matlovich from September to July 22. Grounds of protest were that this left insufficient time to prepare an adequate brief. Under pressure, the Air Force rescheduled the hearing for September 8, 1975.

253. "Bay State Solons Ask Military Changes." THE ADVOCATE, 171 (27 August, 1975), 7.

Sixteen members of the Massachusetts state legislature sent a letter to President Ford requesting that the provisions of the U.S. Code relating to service by homosexual persons in the military be changed. Brigadier General Phillip Kaplan, Director of Military Personnel Management, replied that "the homosexual person is considered unacceptable for military service and is not permitted to serve in . . . any capacity," citing the "unique character" of the military environment as a limiting factor. Among the signatories of the letter were Reps. Elaine Noble and Barney Frank.

254. "Corpsman Plans Fight." THE ADVOCATE, 172 (10 September, 1975), 8.

Naval Corpsman John W. Fortner of Jacksonville has retained counsel to fight the general discharge awarded to him on grounds of homosexuality in a hearing on

April 28, 1975. In a related development, a group of servicemen in Pensacola has formed the American Armed Forces Association to oppose anti-gay bias in the military.

255. "Lesbian Military Purge Uncovered in Florida." THE ADVOCATE, 173 (24 September, 1975), 9.

A profile of efforts currently underway at the Boca Chica Naval Air Station in Key West to remove suspected lesbians from the two hundred women stationed there. Tactics being used by the Naval Investigative Service are given in detail.

256. "Run-Around." THE ADVOCATE, 173 (24 September, 1975), 11.

Commander Gary Hess, USNR, was denied access to the transcript of his administrative discharge hearing and to the testimony of two witnesses who were unable to be present at the original determination. Hearings to review these matters were set for September, 1975.

257. "No to Matlovich." TIME, 106 (29 September, 1975), 32.

In late September, 1975, a three-officer panel at Virginia's Langley Air Force Base unanimously recommended that T/Sgt. Leonard Matlovich be separated from the U.S. Air Force on grounds of homosexuality. Arguments used by the prosecution were that Matlovich's conduct would interfere with his ability to perform military service. A review of final arbitration in this case lies with the Secretary of the Air Force John McLucas.

258. "Discharged: Honorably." THE ADVOCATE, 174 (8 October, 1975), 13.

Sgt. Rudolf Keith, USAF, was given an honorable discharge following a hearing on his case at Dover Air Force Base. This article summarizes the testimony and arguments of that hearing. Of particular interest is the argument by the defense counsel that this case should not deal with regulations prohibiting gay persons from military service, but whether they were applicable in the instant case.

259. "Matlovich Appeal Readied." THE ADVOCATE, 175 (22
      October, 1975), 9, 51.

          Sgt. Leonard Matlovich was granted an honorable dis-
          charge by the commander of Langley Air Force Base, who
          upgraded the initial suggestion of a discharge panel
          that he be separated with a general discharge. A
          detailed summary of testimony is provided. ACLU
          counsel indicated plans to appeal the case through both
          military and civilian systems of justice.

260. "Senator Brooke Blasts DOD." THE ADVOCATE, 176 (5
      November, 1975), 9.

          The text of a statement issued by the office of Sen.
          Edward W. Brooke terming the present policy of exclud-
          ing qualified homosexuals from military services
          "benighted, self-defeating and not in the best
          interests of the United States."

261. "Hess Suit Dismissed." THE ADVOCATE, 176 (5 November,
      1975), 9.

          U.S. District Judge Gordon Thompson of San Diego dis-
          missed the suit brought by Commander Gary Hess seeking
          to enjoin the Navy from discharging him on grounds of
          sexual orientation. The court stated that such action
          was premature. The dismissal with prejudice leaves
          open the possibility of further legal action if
          desired.

262. "Guest Editorial: Sgt. Leonard Matlovich." THE ADVOCATE,
      176 (5 November, 1975), 41.

          An editorial by Leonard Matlovich calling upon the gay
          community to support passage of the Equal Rights Amend-
          ment as an asset to the expansion of the legal grounds
          for gay rights.

263. "The Case of the Gay Sergeant." NEW YORK TIMES
      MAGAZINE, 9 November, 1975, 16-17, 58, 60, 64-71.
      Discussion, 28 December, 1975, 19.

          Written by an historian with an interest in attitudes
          toward sexual behavior who was present at the initial
          hearings for Sergeant Leonard Matlovich at Langley Air

Force Base, this article reflects on the testimony offered on homosexuality as a mirror of American social consciousness on sexuality. Specific issues addressed were causal factors relating to homosexuality, gender identification, sexual orientation and psychological attempts to redirect homosexuals to heterosexuality. Witnesses quoted were psychologist Dr. John Money and Dr. Wardell Pomeroy of the Kinsey Institute. The accompanying letter section contains an exchange between the author and Dr. Irving Bieber as well as a summation of testimony prepared by Karen DeCrow, president of the National Organization for Women.

264. "Matlovich--Fighting Racism." THE ADVOCATE, 177 (19 November, 1975), 18.

A news report on the appearance of Sgt. Leonard Matlovich at the National Student Coalition Against Racism conference at Northeastern University in Boston on October 10-12, 1975. The expanded role of gay persons in this organization at both programming and policy levels is noted.

265. "Cannibalization of a Hero." THE ADVOCATE, 180 (31 December, 1975), 7.

An interview with Leonard Matlovich criticizing the manner in which the organized gay movement has both supported his case against the Air Force and attempted to co-opt him as a media figure. Background on the case is provided.

266. "Protest in the Military." THE ADVOCATE, 180 (31 December, 1975), 14-15.

A general survey of the protest cases against military discharges on grounds of homosexuality filed in 1975 by members of the Air Force, Navy and Army. Individuals involved are Vernon Berg, Leonard Matlovich, Rudolf Keith, John Fortner, Richard Hicks, Gary Hess and Lawrence Heisel.

267. "Gay--A Media Fad." THE ADVOCATE, 180 (31 December, 1975), 20-21.

A review of the presentation of gay people in the American mass media in 1975. The coverage of the Leonard Matlovich case provided by *Time* magazine is analyzed.

268. "Military Update." THE ADVOCATE, 181 (14 January, 1976), 37.

Two news stories covering the discharge of naval personnel Carmen Banos and Patricia Veldon and the complaint filed with San Diego State University activity board by the campus gay association requesting that military recruiters be barred from the campus under a provision of university regulations opposing discrimination on grounds of sexual orientation.

269. "Meteorologist Will Fight Navy." THE ADVOCATE, 181 (14 January, 1976), 37.

A news report on the decision of Dennis Beller, a naval meteorologist stationed in Monterey, California, to fight the service's decision to expel him. While an administrative hearing board has recommended an honorable discharge, the base commander has yet to take action on the case.

270. "Marine Corps Not Immune." THE ADVOCATE, 181 (14 January, 1976), 37.

S. Sgt. Robert LeBlanc has threatened to sue the U.S. Marine Corps following charges of "homosexual tendencies." Marine headquarters in Washington, D.C. ordered a postponement of the discharge pending a review of the case.

271. "Lesbian Suit Filed in Massachusetts." THE ADVOCATE, 181 (14 January, 1976), 37.

A suit has been filed in Massachusetts Federal District Court on behalf of two lesbians, Barbara Randolph and Debbie Watson, discharged from the U.S. Army, by the Civil Liberties Union of Massachusetts. The plaintiffs are charging a violation of their constitutional rights based solely "on the basis of their affectional and sexual preference."

272. "Navy Cover-Up Exposed." THE ADVOCATE, 182 (28 January, 1976), 7.

> A detailed report on the efforts of the U.S. Navy to discharge meteorologist Dennis Beller, including a review of all legal procedures initiated against him. These include denial of access to counsel and timing of proceedings to prevent publicity. Attorney Roland Fox plans a defense based upon invasion of privacy and denial of due process.

273. "Sergeant Ben Shalom--Woman Fighting the Army." THE ADVOCATE, 184 (25 February, 1976), 8-9.

> An interview with Sgt. Miriam benShalom discussing her legal contest with the U.S. Army over her right to serve. Proceedings against her were initiated following her graduation from Drill Instruction school in Milwaukee on December 1, 1975.

274. "Shalom Foundation." THE ADVOCATE, 184 (25 February, 1976), 9.

> A corporate foundation has been founded to raise funds to pay court costs and attorney's fees in the case of Miriam benShalom. Structure and address of the organization are provided.

275. "Matlovich Court Order Delayed." THE ADVOCATE, 184 (25 February, 1976), 11.

> The request of Air Force Sgt. Leonard Matlovich for a court order forcing his readmission to the service has been delayed until early May to permit legal counsel to file an appeal with the Air Force Board for Military Corrections. Said action was taken to prevent government arguments that all possible military avenues of redress in the case had not been exhausted. Grant of the appeal would vitiate the court proceedings presently before Judge Gerhard Gesell in U.S. District Court.

276. "Annapolis Graduate Decides to Fight." THE ADVOCATE, 184 (25 February, 1976), 11-12.

> A summary account of the decision by Ensign Vernon Berg III to initiate legal action against the U.S. Navy's

"less than honorable discharge" given to him due to his homosexuality. A brief precis of Berg's naval career is provided. Researchers should consult *Get Off My Ship* for a full treatment.

277. "Military Purge in Montana." THE ADVOCATE, 186 (24 March, 1976), 9.

A report on Air Force investigations of "suspected gay activity" among personnel stationed at the Malmstrom Air Force Base at Great Falls, Montana which have been underway since February, 1976. Some thirty or forty individuals are involved. A suicide attempt is believed to have been the incident that occasioned the beginning of the probe.

278. "Two Receive Discharges." THE ADVOCATE, 187 (7 April, 1976), 10.

Carmen Banos and Patricia Veldon, personnel stationed at the Naval Air Station at Key West, have been discharged on the basis of having a suspected lesbian affair. Banos is a communications expert in Spanish and Russian and Veldon is a petty officer.

279. "Discharge Temporarily Prohibited." THE ADVOCATE, 190 (19 May, 1976), 8.

U.S. District Judge Walter Nixon, ruling in Biloxi, Mississippi, issued an order temporarily prohibiting the U.S. Air Force from discharging Sgt. Julius T. Robinson on grounds of homosexuality. Background on the case is provided.

280. "Injunction Denied." THE ADVOCATE, 190 (19 May, 1976), 9.

Meteorologist Dennis Beller, USN, was denied a preliminary injunction against the Navy to prevent his separation with an honorable discharge by Judge George Harris. Arguments by the plaintiff that the term "homosexual" was unconstitutionally vague were not accepted.

281. "Matlovich Case Moving to Court." THE ADVOCATE, 191 (2 June, 1976), 11-12.

The Air Force Board for Correction of Military Records refused to overturn a decision to discharge Sgt. Leonard Matlovich due to homosexuality, stating that it would not rule on the constitutionality of banning homosexuals and that Matlovich's exemplary record did not qualify him for the legally permitted exemption.

282. "Navy Discharge Overturned." THE ADVOCATE, 192 (16 June, 1976), 6.

The Bureau of Naval Personnel in May, 1976, overturned a finding by an administrative board at the Key West Naval Air Station recommending the discharge of Petty Officer Patricia Veldon. Grounds used were the ruling of the Secretary of the Navy that discharge was not mandatory for homosexual personnel.

283. "Recruiting Bans Challenged." THE ADVOCATE, 192 (16 June, 1976), 7.

A review of efforts by student governments at the University of Nebraska and San Diego State University to bar military recruiters from their facilities because of the policies of discrimination against homosexuals.

284. "Military Counselling Manual Published." THE ADVOCATE, 193 (30 June, 1976), 14.

A manual outlining techniques for avoiding discharge from the military due to charges of "homosexual tendencies" has been produced by the community center in San Diego. Forms and copies of pertinent military laws are included.

285. "Hathaway vs. U.S. Army." THE ADVOCATE, 194 (14 July, 1976), 7.

Former First Lieutenant Joseph Hathaway, U.S. Army, filed suit in the Court of Military Review against the sections of the Uniform Code of Military Justice with the aim of having them declared unconstitutional. Grounds for the argument will be violation of the right of privacy and equal protection via selective enforcement. The case will be heard in September, 1976.

286. "Berg vs. U.S. Navy." THE ADVOCATE, 194 (14 July, 1976), 7.

Judge Gerhard Gesell has agreed to hear the appeal case of Lt. Vernon Berg, USN, who was dismissed on June 3, 1976 on grounds of admission of homosexuality. The goal of the appeal is both reinstatement and examination of constitutional issues relating to the instant case and general Navy policy.

287. "LeBlanc vs. U.S. Marine Corps." THE ADVOCATE, 194 (14 July, 1976), 7.

A restraining order has been issued by the Ninth Circuit Court of Appeals in San Francisco prohibiting the U.S. Marine Corps from discharging Sgt. Robert LeBlanc on grounds of homosexuality. This is the first such order issued in this area since 1965. LeBlanc has denied homosexuality and been both exonerated and condemned by internal Marine procedures.

288. "Matlovich Loses First Round in U.S. District Court." THE ADVOCATE, 196 (11 August, 1976), 11.

On July 16, 1976, Judge Gerhard Gesell, after hearing arguments from both plaintiff and defense, ruled that Sgt. Leonard Matlovich had failed to meet the legal test required before a civilian court could judge an action by the military. Defense counsel had argued that incomplete instructions to the administrative hearing panel had invalidated the procedures in Matlovich's initial hearing. The bulk of the article is Gesell's opinions on current military policies and their future.

289. "ROTC Under Fire for Anti-Gay Policy." THE ADVOCATE, 197 (25 August, 1976), 9.

The gay student organization of Northeastern University in Boston plans to lodge a formal complaint against the policies of the ROTC department regarding homosexuals in the faculty senate in September, 1976. The body has previously gone on record as opposing the discrimination against gay faculty members.

290. "Still, No Gay Sailors." THE ADVOCATE, 198 (8 September, 1976), 8.

Naval Chief of Personnel Vice Admiral James Watkins in a recent statement confirmed that the U.S. Navy "could not be effective with gay personnel."

291. "Man Discharged for Using Gay Jargon." THE ADVOCATE, 203 (17 November, 1976), 9.

Sgt. Jack Tyler, USAF, has been recommended for an honorable discharge by a hearing board at Ohio's Wright-Patterson Air Force Base. Ground for this claim are letters which allegedly use homosexual jargon. Tyler is a twelve-year veteran with four children.

292. "Ought to Be in Pictures." THE ADVOCATE, 204 (1 December, 1976), 10.

NBC television plans a two-hour drama on the struggle by Sgt. Leonard Matlovich to remain in the United States Air Force.

293. "Randomly Noting . . . On Law and Justice." THE ADVOCATE, 209 (9 February, 1977), 8.

The possibility that the pardon plan recently discussed by President Carter would include a clause upgrading less-than-honorable discharges of homosexual personnel was not mentioned in a recent meeting of ACLU counsel David Addlestone and other amnesty activists with Carter aide Charles Kirbo.

294. "Randomly Noting . . . The Media." THE ADVOCATE, 209 (9 February, 1977), 8.

A West Virginia Christian publication, *Parson's Advocate,* has attacked the proposal for a documentary drama on the case of Leonard Matlovich planned by NBC, calling it an assault on decency and morality.

295. "Mary Saal vs. U.S. Navy: Navy Appeals Ruling." THE ADVOCATE, 216 (1 June, 1977), 9, 45.

   The United States Navy has notified the Ninth Circuit Court of Appeals in San Francisco that it will contest a February, 1977 decision of Judge William Schwarzer. Ruling in the case of air traffic controller Mary Saal's request for re-enlistment, the court stated that Naval personnel policies "should be free of any policy of mandatory exclusion," enjoining the Navy to consider Saal's qualifications alone when deciding on her re-enlistment status. Arguments advanced by both defense and prosecution are summarized.

296. Gibson, E. Lawrence and Vernon E. Berg III. "A Personal View of the Pentagon's Homophobia." THE ADVOCATE, 217 (15 June, 1977), 6-7, 43.

   A statement by Ens. Vernon Berg on his expulsion and that of instructor Lawrence Gibson from the United States Navy. Details of the tactics used by the Naval Investigative Service and court proceedings are given in full, as are the texts of Naval regulations relating to the case.

297. "Navy Homophobia: Out of the Files and into the Courts." THE ADVOCATE, 217 (15 June, 1977), 7.

   As part of the litigation in the case of *Berg vs. Claytor,* the Justice Department has released the text of a report commissioned by the U.S. Navy on March 15, 1957 "for the revision of policies, procedures and directives dealing with homosexuals." Chaired by Capt. S. H. Crittenden, this body issued a report citing fourteen points relative to the matter, among them that "the concept that homosexuals necessarily pose a security risk is unsupported by any factual data." In its conclusions, the Crittenden commission states that the best interests of the military would not be served if it took a leadership position in liberalizing treatment of homosexuals when such treatment was not mirrored by attitudes in civilian society.

298. "Copy Berg's Naval Battle." THE ADVOCATE, 217 (15 June, 1977), 17.

On April 27, 1977, W. Graham Claytor, Secretary of the Navy, upgraded the discharge granted to Ens. Vernon Berg to an honorable one. While this action is applauded, this editorial comment notes that the central issue of excluding homosexuals from military service was not addressed. Berg plans an appeal in federal court.

299. "New Gay Military Cases." THE ADVOCATE, 219 (13 July, 1977), 43.

A review of two legal cases filed by the U.S. Army against specialists Roger Rich and Marie Sode on grounds of homosexuality.

300. "Berg Loses Round." THE ADVOCATE, 220 (27 July, 1977), 14.

Ens. Vernon Berg will appeal a ruling of Judge Gerhard Gesell denying his request for reinstatement in the U.S. Navy. In his remarks, Gesell noted that personnel policies should be updated to take scientific knowledge and social changes into account.

301. "Army Discharges Gay Man (Again)." THE ADVOCATE, 220 (27 July, 1977), 15.

Specialist/4 Roger Rich is appealing his honorable discharge from the U.S. Army. Grounds used by the Army were that Rich had denied his homosexuality on a re-enlistment form and could therefore be separated under rules governing fraudulent enlistment.

302. "Fighting for their Jobs." THE ADVOCATE, 223 (7 September, 1977), 10.

A review of the cases of Commander Gary Hess and computer engineer Roy Fultin. Hess has filed a one million dollar suit against the United States Navy and eight individuals, demanding to be restored to his rank as commander in the Naval Reserve. Details of Hess' efforts to obtain materials under the Freedom of Information Act are provided.

303. "Navy Upgrades Discharge." THE ADVOCATE, 229 (30 November, 1977), 13.

> In late September, 1977, a Navy Department review board voted unanimously to upgrade the 1971 general discharge granted to radioman Robert A. Martin to honorable. This occurred under a request for review filed as part of President Carter's discharge review program.

304. Gibson, E. Lawrence. GET OFF MY SHIP: ENSIGN BERG VS. THE U.S. NAVY. New York: Avon Publishers, 1978.

> In 1975, Ens. Vernon E. Berg became the first naval officer to openly challenge the United States Navy's policy of immediate termination of homosexuals. This volume is a full account of the first two years of Berg's efforts at fighting for his constitutional rights, and is the only monograph telling about a case of military homophobia from the viewpoint of the victim. Five appendixes include a chronology of the case, personal evaluations of Ensign Berg and of the Navy's policies of discrimination, a copy of the official U.S. Navy policy with regard to homosexuality, the policy of the Veterans Administration on homosexuality, a review of suppressed studies of homosexuality in the military, and a bibliography of magazine and newspaper coverage of the case.

305. "Court Stops Navy from Discharging Sailor." THE ADVOCATE, 232 (11 January, 1978), 13.

> U.S. District Court Judge Cecil Poole has issued a preliminary injunction to stop the Navy from discharging a sailor accused of being gay. Ruling in *Martinez vs. Brown*, his opinion was that blanket exclusionary policies deny due process. Although already cleared of the charges by an internal board, Martinez was ordered discharged by the chief of naval personnel. A hearing is scheduled for January 20, 1978.

306. "Military Policies." THE ADVOCATE, 232 (11 January, 1978), 13-15.

> The stabbing deaths of two gay men in Great Britain by members of the elite Coldstream Guards has led to an investigation of their stateside training programs. An

example is included stressing homophobic attitudes and brutality.

307. "Bill Threatens Gay Activism." THE ADVOCATE, 235 (22 February, 1978), 6.

A profile of S.274/HR.120, a bill which forbids members of any branch of the armed services from joining an organization whose purpose is negotiation with the government on conditions of service. While originally targeted at unionization efforts in the military, the definition of "labor organization" in the text is so general as to preclude assistance to personnel by any external group, including gay activist agencies involved with discrimination cases.

308. "Judge Stops Navy." THE ADVOCATE, 236 (8 March, 1978), 11-12.

U.S. District Court Judge Cecil Poole has ordered the Navy to halt all proceedings and discharge processing for sailors who are being expelled on grounds of suspicion of homosexuality. Poole based his order on the grounds that, since Naval regulations provide only mandatory discharge for the resolution of such cases, this action constitutes arbitrary and capricious punishment and is therefore unconstitutional. This ruling was made in the case of *Martinez vs. Brown*, in which Robert Martinez was ordered to be permitted to re-enlist. An appeal is expected.

309. "Vandenberg Air Base Ousts Men." THE ADVOCATE, 237 (22 March, 1978), 11.

Between January and March, 1978, twelve members of the U.S. Air Force stationed at Vandenberg Air Force Base were dismissed on grounds of homosexual behavior. This article provides a brief summary of the actions taken by both the Office of Special Investigations and the various personnel involved. Sgt. James Jacobs, a base career adviser and six-year veteran, has retained civilian counsel to contest his expulsion.

310. "Navy Changes Policy." THE ADVOCATE, 239 (19 April, 1978), 8.

A new regulation has been issued by the United States
Navy eliminating a previous provision which called for
mandatory discharge for discovered gay personnel.
Under the new 1900.9C, while separation is called for,
provisions for retention are also included. This
development follows upon the decision by Judge Cecil
Poole in *Martinez vs. Brown* that such mandatory
exclusion was unconstitutional and a violation of due
process rights.

311. "Judge Refuses Navy." THE ADVOCATE, 242 (31 May, 1978),
11.

Judge Cecil Poole has refused a request by the U.S.
Navy to dismiss *Martinez vs. Brown*, the case which
resulted in his decision that mandatory discharges were
unconstitutional and violated certain rights of gay
people. While acknowledging that Martinez had been re-
enlisted and that a new and clarified naval regulation
was in place, Poole stated that it was not the number
of homosexual incidents uncovered (as stipulated in the
new regulations) which was relevant to an individual,
but that person's fitness for duty.

312. "Prime Time for Sergeants." THE ADVOCATE, 249 (6
September, 1978), 34-35, 37.

A review of the NBC film *Matlovich* scheduled to be
shown on national television August 21, 1978.
Criticism is leveled at both the factual content and
style of presentation.

313. "Matlovich--The Movie and After." THE ADVOCATE, 251 (4
October, 1978), 7.

An interview with Leonard Matlovich on the making and
value of the documentary film aired by NBC in 1978 on
his case. Personal reflections on his life since
coming out and future plans are reviewed.

314. "Gay Vets Can Upgrade Discharges." THE ADVOCATE, 251 (4
October, 1978), 8.

On August 20, 1978, the Department of Defense announced
that homosexual veterans who received less-than-honorable discharges may apply to have them upgraded until

January 1, 1980. The process will be based on service records and will not include those persons separated under misconduct discharges. This action is seen as a possible reaction to the findings in *Martinez vs. Brown.*

315. "Sergeant in Full Drag Discharged." THE ADVOCATE, 252 (18 October, 1978), 7.

Master Sgt. William Douglas, USAF, walked into the mess hall at Fort Carson in Colorado Springs in full women's dress as a tactic to force the service to grant his request for a discharge.

316. "Vet Counseling Is Key, Upgrade Expert Says." THE ADVOCATE, 253 (1 November, 1978), 7.

R. Charles Johnson of Marin Military Counseling recommends that all veterans considering utilizing the upgrade opportunity presently being offered by the Department of Defense obtain professional advice prior to the actual filing of their cases.

317. "Key Ruling in Matlovich Appeal Suit." THE ADVOCATE, 258 (11 January, 1979), 14.

On December 6, 1978, the U.S. Court of Appeals in Washington, D.C. ruled unanimously that the Pentagon cannot discharge persons from military service without specifying reasons in addition to their homosexuality. This ruling overturns a lower court finding upholding the discharges of Sgt. Leonard Matlovich and Ens. Vernon Berg. The court held that although justification of discharges might be possible, in neither case had it been given "reasoned explanation . . . which . . . permits meaningful judicial review." Contacted in San Francisco, Matlovich expressed the opinion that significant change would take years.

318. "Naval Battles and New Maneuvers: Berg and Gibson Begin Again." THE ADVOCATE, 263 (22 March, 1979), 27-28.

An interview with Lawrence Gibson and Vernon Berg discussing the publication of *Get Off My Ship*, Gibson's account of the details of the naval effort directed at expelling Berg as a case study in homophobia. Gibson stated that "what is represented in the Berg case is not just homophobia . . . it represents to an infinite degree a whole legal system which is not legal." The effect of the case upon their lives is discussed in terms of employment.

319. "Gay Court Martial Suit Filed by ACLU." THE ADVOCATE, 265 (19 April, 1979), 8.

On March 6, 1979, the American Civil Liberties Union filed a complaint in U.S. District Court in San Francisco calling for reversal of a court-martial conviction in the case of Army Lt. Joseph Hathaway, who had received a discharge on grounds of sexual misconduct. The unconstitutionality of the unequal enforcement of military laws against heterosexuals is viewed as violation of due process and the equal protection clause. Illegal surveillance is also alleged.

320. "The Long Gay Look at the Long Gray Line." THE ADVOCATE, 266 (3 May, 1979), 41-42.

An interview with Lucian Truscott IV, author of *Dress Gray,* a novel involving the murder of a homosexual plebe at West Point. Truscott comments upon the writing of the novel and the attitudes instilled into cadets at the academy with regard to homosexuality.

321. "Denver Judge to Hear Antigay Army Case." THE ADVOCATE, 270 (28 June, 1979), 12.

October 17-19, 1979 has been set by Judge Richard Matsch for the hearing of the case of nurse Roger W. Rich against the U.S. Army. Rich was discharged in 1977 following his admission of homosexuality and is seeking reinstatement with pay, punitive damages for career damage and removal of anti-gay strictures in the military.

322. "A Gay Vet? Here's How to Upgrade Your Discharge." THE ADVOCATE, 274 (23 August, 1979), 10.

An article by attorney R. Charles Johnson of Marin Military Counseling providing details on the process of upgrading general and dishonorable discharges. The system of discharge review boards is explained.

323. Duban, Patricia Dodge. "Administrative Law and Procedure --Armed Services--Military Discharge--Matlovich vs. Secretary of the Air Force. 591 F.2d 852 (D.C. Cir. 1978)." DUQUESNE LAW REVIEW, 18 (Fall, 1979), 151-160.

This article presents an analysis of the actions taken by the United States Court of Appeals for the District of Columbia in the case of *Matlovich vs. Secretary of the Air Force*. A brief summary of the history of the case is presented, followed by an examination of the judicial precedents utilized. Duban notes that the appeals court did not focus upon the constitutional issues involved in "discharging a serviceman who has admitted to homosexual acts in violation of service regulations" (p. 160). The administrative law cases which led the court to require the Air Force to provide "a meaningful explanation" (p. 158) of its action are seen as of doubtful value, and thus diminishing the effect of the findings in the case.

324. "Air Force Captain Fights for Rights." THE ADVOCATE, 279 (1 November, 1979), 13.

Capt. Robert Coronado, USAF, has decided to fight charges of forcible sexual assault of an enlisted man. Details of the case are not given.

325. "Army Boots Out Gay Soldier." THE ADVOCATE, 280 (15 November, 1979), 8-9.

A profile of the discharge case of Pfc. Roger Cutsinger. Details of his discharge hearing on October 4, 1979 at Fort Lewis, Washington are included.

326. "Air Force Dismisses Gay Officer." THE ADVOCATE, 281 (29 November, 1979), 10.

A court-martial at Pope Air Force Base in North Carolina found Capt. Robert Coronado guilty of sexual misconduct with an enlisted man. Coronado plans to appeal, challenging the right of the Air Force to control the private lives of its personnel.

327. "U.S. Airmen Dismissed from British Base." THE ADVOCATE, 284 (10 January, 1980), 10-11.

A reprint of a story from London's *Gay News* on the dismissal of two members of the U.S. Air Force from the base at Hitchin, Herts. Both of the men expelled held high-level security clearances.

328. "More Time for Vets to Change Discharges." THE ADVOCATE, 286 (21 February, 1980), 8.

The deadline for filing requests for changing status of discharges for persons with undesirable documentation has been extended to April 1, 1981. Since the beginning of the review period, some thirty-five hundred cases have been seen, with fifty-six hundred more awaiting resolution.

329. "VA Liberalizes Gay Veterans Benefits." THE ADVOCATE, 293 (29 May, 1980), 8.

The Veterans Administration has liberalized a subsection of Paragraph 1012 of its compensation and pension rules permitting homosexual veterans to qualify for certain benefits. As of December 31, 1979, homosexuality will be considered adequate for denial of benefits only when there are additional aggravating circumstances such as use of force or fraternization between ranks.

330. "Lesbian Sergeant Wins Battle for Retention." THE ADVOCATE, 295 (26 June, 1980), 7.

U.S. District Judge Terrence Givens of Milwaukee has ordered the U.S. Army to reinstate Sgt. Miriam benShalom, dismissed in 1976 following admission of lesbian identity. The opinion states that the Army had failed to respond adequately to charges of violation of First Amendment rights of freedom of speech and association.

331. "Navy Probe of Lesbians Termed 'Witch-Hunt.'" THE ADVOCATE, 297 (24 July, 1980), 10.

A review of the investigation of alleged lesbian activity aboard the USS Norton Sound, presently docked at Long Beach. Sixteen of the sixty-one crew members are reportedly involved and administrative discharge procedures have been instituted against several of them.

332. "8 Women Sailors Charged in Probe of Lesbianism." THE ADVOCATE, 298 (7 August, 1980), 7.

Eight women stationed aboard the USS Norton Sound have been charged with lesbianism. Their options are immediate discharge or review of the charges by an administrative board.

333. "Trials of Eight Alleged Lesbian Sailors Begin." THE ADVOCATE, 301 (18 September, 1980), 7.

Two of the eight women originally charged with lesbian activity from the complement of the USS Norton Sound have been cleared of the charges. Naval Investigative Service tactics are discussed. In a related case, three servicewomen stationed at the secret Skagg Island Naval Security base north of San Francisco have been discharged for lesbianism.

334. "Navy Drops Charges Against Four Sailors." THE ADVOCATE, 302 (2 October, 1980), 10-11.

The U.S. Navy has dropped charges against four of the eight women involved in the lesbian case aboard the USS Norton Sound. An interview with ACLU counsel Ramona Ripston provides details of the progress of the case.

335. "Ed Asner Condemns Navy, Supports Gay Rights." THE ADVOCATE, 302 (2 October, 1980), 10.

Appearing at a fund-raiser for the "Norton Sound Eight," actor Edward Asner urged continued support for the ACLU and condemned the actions of the Navy in this matter. Asner has previously supported gay rights in Dade County, Florida and was a vocal opponent of California's Proposition 6 initiative against gay teachers.

336. "Five Years Later, Matlovich Wins Reinstatement, Back Pay." THE ADVOCATE, 303 (16 October, 1980), 9.

On September 9, 1980, U.S. District Judge Gerhard Gesell ruled that the U.S. Air Force had failed to comply adequately with a 1978 court order by the U.S. Appeals Court requiring it to clarify the conditions under which homosexuals would be retained in that branch of the service. Although several briefs had been filed, Gesell ruled that their contents did not sufficiently address the question. On these grounds, he ordered that Sgt. Leonard Matlovich be reinstated with full back pay and restoration of rank.

337. "Montanans Protest Firing of Gay Airmen." THE ADVOCATE, 305 (13 November, 1980), 15.

Three gay organizations in the state of Montana have begun circulating petitions protesting the recent discharge of eight men at Malmstrom Air Force Base for homosexual activity. Calling the action "a scandalous betrayal of thousands of gay veterans and currently enlisted persons," the groups plan to send their petitions to President Carter.

338. "California Sailors Vow to Fight Navy Purge." THE ADVOCATE, 306 (27 November, 1980), 10.

Two naval enlisted men at the Defense Language Institute in Monterey, California are opposing attempts to discharge them from the service. They are part of a group of between twenty-five and thirty-five people under investigation for alleged homosexual acts at the school. Four civilian liberties organizations are involved and the Justice Department has agreed to meet all parties to negotiate a settlement. Both servicemen have excellent records.

339. "Military Court Upholds Ban on Gays." THE ADVOCATE, 307 (11 December, 1980), 7.

The U.S. Ninth Circuit Court of Appeals in San Francisco ruled in a majority decision that the U.S. Navy may legally discharge sailors who engage in homosexual conduct, citing "the necessity to protect the fabric of military life." Activist opinions from the Harvey Milk Democratic Club and the Gay Rights Activists of San Francisco are cited.

340.   "U.S. Army Pays $10,000 in Discrimination Case." THE
        ADVOCATE, 308 (25 December, 1980), 7.

        The case of Warren Preston, a civilian graphic designer
        employed at a California firm under defense contract,
        has been settled out of court. In 1979, Preston was
        stripped of his security clearance on grounds of homo-
        sexuality. Following legal action in March, 1980, the
        U.S. Army agreed to restore his clearance and "would
        formulate regulations insuring that civilian employees
        would not be discriminated against on the basis of
        their sexual orientation alone." Legal counsel
        stressed that the civilian nature of Preston's employ-
        ment was crucial in this decision.

341.   Heilman, John. "The Constitutionality of Discharging
        Homosexual Military Personnel." COLUMBIA HUMAN
        RIGHTS LAW REVIEW, 12 (Fall/Winter, 1980/1981), 191-204.

        "Each year at least 2,000 men and women are discharged
        under less than honorable terms for reasons relating to
        homosexuality" (p. 192). Beginning with this state-
        ment, the author examines the conflicting statements
        and findings of then-current legislation. Of particu-
        lar interest is his analysis of the claim often
        advanced by the armed services that "the plaintiff must
        have first exhausted any available administrative
        remedies" before a court can legitimately consider
        constitutionality. Minority opinions recognizing that
        exceptions to this regulation may be made are also
        noted. Constitutional grounds upon which discharges
        from the various branches of service have been chal-
        lenged (violation of the First Amendment rights of free
        speech and association, privacy, procedural due pro-
        cess, substantive due process, and deprivation of
        liberty) are then reviewed, together with extracts from
        the relevant cases. The author concludes that,
        especially on constitutional grounds, military policy
        towards homosexuality "is irrational to some extent,
        unnecessary to some extent, and unwise in toto" (p.
        204).

342.   "USAF Pays Matlovich Not to Re-Enlist." THE ADVOCATE,
        309 (8 January, 1981), 7-8.

        In an out-of-court settlement, the U.S. Air Force
        agreed to pay $160,000 to former Sgt. Leonard Matlovich
        on condition that he agree not to attempt re-enlist-

ment. Taken on the advice of legal counsel, this action leaves intact a 1978 Court of Appeal ruling requiring the military to explain conditions of retention for homosexual personnel.

343. "Gay Sailor Appeals to Supreme Court." THE ADVOCATE, 310 (22 January, 1981), 7.

Dennis Beller, former U.S. Navy weatherman discharged in 1976, has decided to appeal to the U.S. Supreme Court to overturn his dismissal. Civil rights lawyers note that the conservative nature of the court has discouraged similar efforts in the gay rights field in recent years. If the court agrees to hear the case, it will mark the first time that a gay-related case has reached this level of the American judicial system.

344. Seidenberg, Faith. "Military Justice Is to Justice . . ." CRIMINAL LAW BULLETIN, 17 (January-February, 1981), 45-59.

A philosophical analysis of the case of Lt. "Carlos Rodrigues" against the U.S. Air Force written by the counsel for the defense. Seidenberg presents the construction of her strategy in detail as an illustration of the factors to be considered when presenting a case as a civilian lawyer before a military court. Extensive quotations from cross-examinations and the complete "statement of reasons" issued against the defendant by the Air Force are included. The defendant was acquitted of charges of "being a homosexual," a decision later upheld by the Secretary of the Air Force.

345. "Out But Not Down, Sgt. Bryant Fights On." THE ADVOCATE, 311 (19 February, 1981), 8.

An administrative hearing board at MacDill Air Force Base in Tampa, Florida has recommended that Sgt. Harold Bryant be separated from the service with an undesirable discharge. Details of the hearing testimony and subsequent legal action are included.

346. "Military Move Will Exclude All Gays." THE ADVOCATE, 312 (5 March, 1981), 8.

A directive from the Department of Defense, dated January 16, 1981, requires a mandatory discharge for all personnel "who have engaged in, attempted to engage in, or solicited another" for homosexual purposes. This document is seen as a response to recent court decisions demanding clarification of conditions for retention of homosexual personnel. Under the new directive, homosexuals may only serve in the military in limited capacities in time of war or when national security is otherwise threatened. The action will also prevent further cash payments such as the $160,000 settlement in the Matlovich case.

347. "Booted by Navy, Sailor Will Appeal." THE ADVOCATE, 312 (5 March, 1981), 11-12.

An administrative hearing board at the Treasure Island Naval Station in San Francisco has recommended that an enlisted man be separated with a general discharge. The anonymous sailor was a student at the Defense Language Institute in Monterey and the only one of a group recently investigated for homosexual actions to contest the charges. Background on the case is provided.

348. "U.S. Navy Will Pay Cash to Ousted Berg." THE ADVOCATE, 313 (19 March, 1981), 10.

Ens. Vernon Berg III has agreed to accept a cash settlement from the U.S. Navy, on condition that he agree not to attempt to re-enlist. By doing so, Berg leaves intact a 1978 ruling in his case by a federal court of appeals that inadequate explanation of its procedures had been provided by the military. A recent directive prohibits service by homosexuals "except in time of war."

349. "Sailor's Case Filed at Supreme Court." THE ADVOCATE, 314 (2 April, 1981), 10.

Navy meteorologist Dennis Beller's petition to overturn his 1980 separation from the service on grounds of homosexuality has been filed with the United States Supreme Court. The petition requests the court to "resolve the conflict between the Beller case and *Matlovich vs. Secretary of the Air Force.*" Relevant Department of Defense regulations are cited.

350. "Navy 1, Sailor 0 in Retention Fight." THE ADVOCATE, 319 (11 June, 1981), 9.

> In Washington, D.C., U.S. District Court Judge Aubrey Robinson refused to issue a temporary restraining order against the U.S. Navy to permit Petty Officer James Dronenburg to remain in the service. A former student at the Defense Language Institute, Dronenburg was dismissed on grounds of homosexuality.

351. "U.S. Supreme Court Lets Stand Sailor's Ouster." THE ADVOCATE, 321 (9 July, 1981), 10.

> On June 1, 1981, the Supreme Court of the United States refused to hear the appeal of Navy meteorologist Dennis Beller, leaving intact his dismissal from the service on homosexual grounds. Filing the case were lawyers from Gay Rights Advocates, a San Francisco public interest law firm. Officials of the organization noted that, with the increase in gay-related precedents in recent years, the high court would be forced to rule on such a matter eventually.

352. "English Army Ejects Suspected Lesbians." THE ADVOCATE, 326 (17 September, 1981), 8.

> Two women under scrutiny by the Special Investigative Division at Wilton Park, Bucks, have been cleared of charges of lesbian conduct. Despite this, they will be separated from the service.

353. "ACLU Aids Discharged Colorado Soldier." THE ADVOCATE, 327 (1 October, 1981), 10.

> A review of the appeal filed by the American Civil Liberties Union in U.S. Circuit Court of Appeals challenging the decision of a district judge upholding the authority of the Army's discharge policy in the case of Roger W. Rich.

354. "Gay Sailor Loses First Round with Navy." THE ADVOCATE, 328 (15 October, 1981), 10.

> A summary of the current status of the case of Melvin Dahl, a Navy enlisted man stationed at the Great Lakes Naval Training Center near Chicago. Following the

recommendation of a board of officers that he be discharged on grounds of admission of homosexuality, Dahl
plans legal action. Prior to the hearing, he held a
secret level security clearance.

355. Berube, Alan. "Marching to a Different Drummer: Gay and
Lesbian GI's in World War II." THE ADVOCATE, 328 (15
October, 1981), 20-24.

An historical essay exploring the legal and social
status of homosexual men and women in the Armed
Services during World War II. Berube notes that the
Surgeon General, in a 1944 circular, stated that "homosexual relationships should be tolerated" unless they
interfered with unit functioning.

356. "Gay Soldier Sues to Stop Ouster." THE ADVOCATE, 329 (29
October, 1981), 9.

Sgt. Perry Watkins, U.S. Army, filed suit in U.S.
District Court August 31, 1981 seeking reinstatement to
the service and restoration of his security clearance.
This last was removed on grounds that homosexuality
makes Watkins a security risk.

357. Deiter, Lawrence R. "Employment Discrimination for the
Armed Services - An Analysis of Recent Decisions Affecting
Sexual   Preference   Discrimination   for   the   Military."
VILLANOVA LAW REVIEW, 271 (January, 1982), 351-373.

This comment on employment discrimination against
homosexuals by the armed services reviews three cases
decided in 1980 whose findings bear on the issue.
These cases are *Beller vs. Middendorf, benShalom vs.
Secretary of the Army* and *Matlovich vs. Secretary of
the Air Force.* Details of the logic of each case are
presented, with emphasis placed on the *benShalom* case
as being the only one to address "the issue of discharge for homosexual status" (p. 362). The other
cases reviewed were seen to have avoided or evaded the
question of the constitutionality of the military
policies in question. A general principle of applying
the "nexus test"--requiring the branch of service
involved to "demonstrate that sexual preference has an
adverse effect on military capabilities of performance"
(p. 365)--as was done in benShalom, to cases of this
type is recommended, as is replacement of existing

regulations with policy modeled upon the Civil Service Commission's suitability guidelines. The author notes that "the contradictory state of the law has arisen primarily because none of the cases have resolved, or even reached, the issue of whether private consensual homosexual activity between adults is protected by the Constitution" (p. 371).

358. "Illinois Gay Sailor Tests New Guidelines." THE ADVOCATE, 338 (18 March, 1982), 15.

The Illinois chapter of the American Civil Liberties Union has filed suit in federal court in Chicago on behalf of seaman Melvin Dahl as a challenge to new naval regulations which stipulate conditions under which homosexuals may be retained in the service. As an admitted homosexual, Dahl's discharge has already been approved by the chief of naval personnel.

359. Canepa, Theresa J. "The Aftermath of Saal Vs. Middendorf: Does Homosexuality Preclude Military Fitness?" SANTA CLARA LAW REVIEW, 22 (Spring, 1982), 491-511.

This article explores "the problem of balancing government interests against an individual's right to freely choose a sexual preference" (p. 510) and using the 1973 case of Mary Roseann Saal as example. Her case against the automatic discharge required by U.S. Naval regulations resulted in the promulgation of a new regulation providing for "*limited* retention of homosexuals" (p. 493). The fitness issue is examined on the constitutional grounds of protectable liberty and property interests, equal protection of the law, and the right to privacy. Canepa notes that "even though the Navy has had the opportunity to retain known homosexuals in the ranks, in no instance has it done so: thus the Navy has no basis for its current claims that such sexual orientation would be disruptive" (p. 509). Parallels are drawn between treatment accorded to homosexuals and the Navy's position on women. The new regulations are viewed as inadequate, as it does not address the constitutional questions involved nor provide guidelines for assessing fitness. Revision of guidelines is seen as possible by incorporating the concept of fitness for duty or by research studies demonstrating that the posited disruption occasioned by retention of homosexual personnel does in fact occur.

360. "British Army Told to Ease Up on Gays." THE ADVOCATE, 339 (1 April, 1982), 11.

The English Ministry of Defense has issued a memorandum order to commanding officers recommending that homosexuals be separated from the service with an administrative discharge. The present system of disgraceful or dishonorable classification is seen as both unwieldy and ineffective.

361. "Lesbian Wins Pentagon Security Clearance." THE ADVOCATE, 346 (8 July, 1982), 10.

A summary of the case of Betty Anderson, a Pentagon secretary ordered to undergo a psychology exam to ascertain whether she was suffering from "ego-dystonic homosexuality" prior to the granting of a security clearance. The concept was ruled to be self-diagnostic and not requiring the attention of a professional. Anderson was granted the clearance after some two years of effort.

362. "U.S. Army Must Retain Seattle Gay Soldier." THE ADVOCATE, 346 (8 July, 1982), 10.

A review of the May 19, 1982 decision of Seattle District Judge Barbara Rothstein in the case of Sgt. Perry Watkins requiring that the U.S. Army re-examine the removal of his security clearance on grounds of homosexuality. The decision did not address the question of the plaintiff's right to re-enlist.

363. "Lesbian Loses Case Against U.S. Army." THE ADVOCATE, 349 (19 August, 1982), 13.

The challenge of a lesbian to her discharge from the U.S. Army has been denied on constitutional grounds. The court ruling stated that Sylvia Pedraza could be legally discharged under military law covering false enlistment, as she had denied being homosexual on her initial application for service.

364. "Air Force Officer Bucks Military Policy on Gays." THE ADVOCATE, 352 (30 September, 1982), 10.

Staff Sgt. Lawrence O. Salcedo, an eighteen-year veteran of the U.S. Air Force, has filed suit in Oklahoma City challenging his attempted discharge for homosexuality on constitutional grounds. Salcedo's orientation was disclosed to his superiors following medical treatment for hepatitis.

365. "NGRA Seeks Favorable Military Policy with Dronenburg Case." THE ADVOCATE, 357 (9 December, 1982), 8.

Following an October 5 decision upholding the right of the Navy to discipline homosexuals on grounds of maintaining order in the ranks, the case of Petty Officer James Dronenburg will be filed with the U.S. Court of Appeals in Washington, D.C. Counsel for the National Gay Rights Advocates, which is representing Dronenburg, explained that the ruling sought will be one to "establish a favorable federal court precedent on the rights of gay military personnel."

366. "Gay Seattle Soldier Re-Enlists, But Fight Not Over." THE ADVOCATE, 358 (23 December, 1982), 10.

Following two court decisions in October, 1982, Sgt. Perry Watkins was permitted to re-enlist in the Army for a further six-year term. Judge Barbara Rothstein's rulings in the case are expected to be appealed.

367. Loda, Gifford. "Homosexual Conduct in the Military: No Faggots in Military Woodpiles." ARIZONA STATE LAW JOURNAL, 1 (1983), 79-112.

In this analysis of military judicial treatment of homosexual persons, the author examines the bases used in recent decisions. While acknowledging the armed services' right to curtail certain constitutional rights of its personnel under "exigent circumstances peculiar to the military" (p. 80), Loda argues that the issue of procedural due process has not been adequately considered in legal decisions thus far rendered. Detailed consideration is then given to the legal attacks presented against regulations of this type within the area of due process. The cases of *United States Navy vs. Mary Saal* and *Beller vs. Middendorf* are offered as examples of recent cases where this issue has been raised. The author concludes that "the tenets of regulatory construction and both procedural and substantive due process should compel the military services to adopt regulations requiring them to show a rational connection between homosexual conduct and diminished quality of service. Only then should discharge of homosexual personnel take place" (p. 112).

368.   "Uncle Sam Doesn't Want You: Soldiers of Misfortune Past and Present." THE ADVOCATE, 367 (12 May, 1983), 20-21.

A research study entitled *The Evolution and Impact of Federal Antihomosexual Policies* commissioned by the National Gay Task Force states that between forty and fifty thousand individuals were separated from the military between 1950 and 1970 on homosexual grounds. The cases currently being pursued of Capt. Dusty Pruitt, Sgt. Perry Watkins, seaman Melvin Dahl and linguist James Dronenburg are reviewed.

369.   "Uncle Sam Doesn't Want You: Renewed Discrimination Against Gays." THE ADVOCATE, 367 (12 May, 1983), 57-59.

An article by a specialist in military law examining forty years of military attitudes toward gay and lesbian individuals, including the 1978 memorandum by the Secretary of the Navy and the 1981 expansion of culpable conduct and behavior relating to homosexuality through Directive 1332-14. This last mandates discharge for all gay personnel. Court decisions summarized are *Saal vs. Middendorf, Beller vs. Middendorf* and the Miriam benShalom case.

370.   "Air Force Paroles Lesbian Jailed on Sodomy, Drug Charges." THE ADVOCATE, 377 (29 September, 1983), 8-9.

Joann Nowak, an Air Force Lieutenant serving a three-year sentence at Fort Leavenworth, Kansas on charges of sodomy and drug-related offenses, was paroled on August 17, 1983 following agreement to enter rehabilitation. A brief summary of the case is included.

371.   "Our Standards Are Different." NEWSWEEK, 102, 48 (12 December, 1983), 48.

A news report covering the trial and conviction of naval commander Gerald Michael Vanderwier for engaging in homosexual conduct with a hospital corpsman under his authority. Recent trends in the military to tighten standards against homosexuality are noted and specifics from the court martial given. The position taken by the Naval authorities was that Vanderwier was dismissed more for violating the rule prohibiting fraternization between the ranks than for his homosexual activities.

372. "A Gay Soldier's Right to Serve." NEWSWEEK, 103, 15 (23 January, 1984), 15.

A news report on the continuing case of Diane Matthews to be reinstated in the Reserve Officer Training Corps program at the University of Maine at Orono. After admitting her identity as a lesbian, the Army forced her to undergo psychological testing and remove her from the program. Suit was brought on her behalf by the Maine ACLU on grounds of violation of Matthews' constitutional protected rights of free speech and privacy. The Army takes the position that homosexuals cannot be soldiers because they adversely affect morale and discipline. No decision has yet been reached in the case.

373. "General Unease." TIME, 123 (23 January, 1984), 23.

The accusations leveled against NATO deputy commander Gunter Kiessling have eroded with the discovery of a soldier frequenting the bars of Cologne who bears a marked resemblance to him. Kiessling's relations with Defense Minister Manfred Warner indicate a possible political motive for said accusations.

374. "Der Skandal." NEW REPUBLIC, 190 (6 February, 1984), 9-10.

A short article considering two current upsets in domestic West German politics, one of which is the Kiessling affair involving accusations of homosexuality against a NATO general.

375. "Bonn's Cage Aux Folles." NEWSWEEK, 103, 38 (6 February, 1984), 38.

A summary article covering the suspension of General Gunter Kiessling by West German Defense Minister

Manfred Warner on grounds of suspected homosexuality. The reliability of eyewitness accounts from gay bar patrons in Cologne and testimony of the publisher of *Du und Ich,* a Swiss gay magazine, is regarded as highly questionable.

376. "Restoring a General's Honor." MACCLEANS, 97, 36 (13 February, 1984), 36.

A review of the evidence and events involved in the accusation and dismissal of General Gunter Kiessling on grounds of alleged homosexual behavior. Of particular interest is the role played by the Militarische Abschirmsdienst, the West German counterintelligence service.

377. "Kohl Cleans Up a Messy Affair." NEWSWEEK, 103, 38 (13 February, 1984), 38.

Calling reports used by West Germany's Defense Minister to suspend General Gunter Kiessling "unfounded assertions," Chancellor Helmut Kohl reinstated him to normal duty and responsibility. Heavy criticism and calls for the resignation of the Defense Minister were raised by members of the Bundestag.

378. "Legal Right to Overturn Military's Gay Policy: Is Victory Impossible?" THE ADVOCATE, 388 (21 February, 1984), 10-11.

Recent legal decisions affecting gay and lesbian military personnel are reviewed, including the necessity of re-evaluating strategies for changes. Activists are now seen as shifting from attempting to obtain court decisions declaring military homophobic policies unconstitutional to using Congress and the political process as an arena to promote armed service changes. Interviews with Steve Smith of the Gay Activists Alliance of Washington, D.C. and Joseph Schuman, a Chicago lawyer familiar with extant court cases are appended.

379. "Maine Federal Judge Tells Army to Reinstate Lesbian in ROTC." THE ADVOCATE, 393 (1 May, 1984), 9.

U.S. Magistrate Brock Hornby has ordered the reinstatement of Diane Matthews to her ROTC unit, considering

that discrimination "simply on the basis of acknowledged homosexual identity was unconstitutional." A
brief history of the case is provided.

380. "Mondale in N.Y. Says He Opposes Antigay Bias in the
Military." THE ADVOCATE, 393 (1 may, 1984), 12-13.

On April 3, 1984, two days before the New York state
primary elections, Democratic presidential candidate
Walter Mondale told a group of prominent New York City
women supporters that sexual orientation *per se*
should not be a reason for dismissal from the military.
Campaign officials were unable later to formally
restate this view. Background on the participation of
gay people in the 1984 election is provided.

381. "Sgt. Perry Watkins Loses Appeal to Stay in Army." THE
ADVOCATE, 396 (12 June, 1984), 13.

The Ninth Circuit Court of Appeals in San Francisco on
May 8, 1984 refused to rehear the case of Sgt. Perry
Watkins and returned the case to Judge Barbara
Rothstein so that the constitutional issues which were
not addressed in the initial proceedings could be dealt
with.

382. "News Briefs." THE ADVOCATE, 399 (24 July, 1984), 11.

A suit has been filed in U.S. District Court in
Washington, D.C. by eight gay veterans, the National
Gay Task Force and Vietnam Veterans of America. The
class-action charges the military with illegally discharging gay people under less than honorable conditions. If successful, it would force the military to
upgrade the discharges of the plaintiffs as well as
obliging reconsideration of similar cases already
heard.

383. "Court Rules Gays Have No Right to Privacy." THE
ADVOCATE, 403 (18 September, 1984), 10.

Ruling in the case of Petty Officer James Dronenburg's
discharge appeal against the United States Navy, a
three-judge panel of the Court of Appeals for the
District of Columbia stated on August 17, 1984 that
constitutional guarantees of rights of privacy and

equal protection did not extend to private homosexual conduct. Writing for the panel, Judge Robert Bork expressed an unwillingness to place "all private sexual behavior" within the concept of ordered liberty. An appeal is planned to the full court.

384.   Jones, Andrew Berrien. *"Dronenburg Vs. Zech*: Judicial Restraint Or Judicial Prejudice?" YALE LAW AND PUBLIC POLICY REVIEW, 3 (Fall, 1984), 245-262.

A comment on the decision rendered by the U.S. Court of Appeals for the District of Columbia in the case of *Dronenburg vs. Zech*. The decision is challenged on two grounds: the finding that a rational nexus exists between naval regulations proscribing homosexuals and "legitimate government purposes" (p. 245); and application of the rational basis test instead of strict scrutiny analysis. Such analysis is predicated upon the ideas that homosexuals are a class of individuals eligible for special protection from discrimination or that the right to privacy doctrine extends to cover homosexual activity, thus rendering it immune from government regulation. The author views the decision as relying "on traditional misconceptions about homosexuality to justify repression of nonconformist behavior" (p. 261). Limiting Supreme Court cases to their facts, as this decision does, permits courts to evade or avoid obligations with regard to fundamental constitutional rights. Jones concludes by noting that "unless courts are willing to fulfill their obligation to deliberate seriously such issues when presented to them, members of the homosexual minority . . . appear to have nowhere left to turn for recognition of their fundamental right as autonomous individuals" (p. 262).

385.   "Legion Denies Charter for S.F. Gay Vets." THE ADVOCATE, 407 (13 November, 1984), 12.

The Alexander Hamilton Veterans Organization, a group of gay veterans, has filed a complaint with the San Francisco Human Rights Commission charging that the denial of chapter charter by the American Legion violates two city ordinances covering anti-gay discrimination in public accommodations and contract business with the city. Legion officials denied the charges.

386.   "Military Spends Millions to Exclude Gays." THE ADVOCATE,
        408 (27 November, 1984), 8.

        A report on a study requested by seven members of
        Congress on eighteen questions regarding discrimination
        in the armed services against gay and lesbian personnel
        between 1974 and 1984. The annual cost of processing
        was estimated at twenty-three million dollars, covering
        recruitment, training and discharge of affected person-
        nel. Financial costs in both money and expertise are
        reviewed.

387.   "Lesbian Sues Over Ouster from Guard." THE ADVOCATE, 408
        (27 November, 1984), 9.

        A summary of the case of Julie Johnson, a lesbian
        lieutenant in the California Air National Guard ex-
        pelled in August 1984 following three years of service.
        ACLU counsel claimed this action violated an executive
        order of Governor Edmund Brown prohibiting discrimina-
        tion in state agencies as well as laws protecting
        political acts. Attorneys for the Air Force are
        expected to argue that federal law takes precedence
        over state in areas of dual jurisdiction.

388.   "Copy Berg: Courage of an Original." THE ADVOCATE, 408
        (27 November, 1984), 22, 25.

        An interview with Vernon Berg reflecting on his strug-
        gle with the U.S. Navy and subsequent civilian career.

389.   "Dronenburg Loses Bid for New Hearing in Battle with
        Navy." THE ADVOCATE, 411 (8 January, 1985), 9.

        A request for a hearing *en banc* in the appellate case
        of James Dronenburg was denied on November 15, 1984 by
        a majority of the district court in Washington, D.C.
        The consequences of Judge Robert Bork's dicta and of
        the conclusions in *Dronenburg vs. Zech* for subsequent
        litigation involving gay people and the military is
        discussed.

390.   Allen, Katherine M. *"Dronenburg Vs. Zech*: The Wrong
        Case for Asserting a Right of Privacy for Homosexuals."
        NORTH CAROLINA LAW REVIEW, 63 (April, 1985), 749-
        766.

This comment analyzes the conduct of the United States
Circuit Court for the District of Columbia and offers
criticism on three grounds: a) its selection of precedent cases from the Supreme Court was limited to findings protecting rights within marriage or traditional
family settings; b) its disregard of the separate
community doctrine as a framework of analysis; and
c) inattention to the facts of the case. Disregard of
recent lower court precedent in the area of homosexual
rights, beginning with the 1969 *Norton vs. Macy*
decision, is also noted. The basic arguments of
Dronenburg are reviewed against the court's actions
in light of the legal history of the right of privacy
as established by the Supreme Court and extended in
subsequent lower court findings. Allen sees the
District court's decision (which "would find it impossible to conclude that a right to homosexual conduct is
'fundamental' or 'implicit' in the concept of ordered
liberty" [p. 753]) as "the most restrictive decision in
the recent development of case law concerning the
rights of homosexuals" (p. 765). The case is not seen
as the proper venue for establishing right-of-privacy
protections for homosexual activity as the plaintiff
attempted to do.

391. "Homosexuals in the Military: They Would Rather Fight Than
Switch." JOHN MARSHALL LAW REVIEW, 18, 4 (Summer,
1985), 937-968.

This is a clearly written exploration of the military
policy of excluding homosexuals from service. Over
fifteen thousand people have been discharged on these
grounds between 1975 and 1985. The author addresses
the practice on the basis of three constitutional
rights: "Freedom of association or the right to be
homosexual, personal autonomy or the right to partici-
pate in private consensual sex, and the right to be let
alone" (p. 938). An historical treatment of United
States military policy begins by presenting current
regulations (courts-martial and administrative discharges) and their purposes as stated by the Department
of Defense. Other topics discussed are the right to
privacy and the homosexual soldier, with specific court
cases related to each constitutional right as required.
The author concludes that, in the absence of a Supreme
Court decision on the constitutionality of consensual
sexual relationships, confusion will continue to exist
in the courts. However, the military policy is clearly
at odds with attitudes towards homosexuality in society

as a whole. Service personnel who are homosexuals should be evaluated on a performance basis rather than under a blanket set of regulations which infringe personal rights.

392. Winn, Jeffrey Michael. "*Dronenburg Vs. Zech*: Sexual Preference Discrimination Sanctioned in the Name of Judicial Restraint." PACE LAW REVIEW, 5 (Summer, 1985), 847-878.

A note reviewing the 1984 case of *Dronenburg vs. Zech* (involving the discharge of a naval petty officer) in the context of legal decisions regarding the constitutionally protected right to privacy. Topics addressed in the five sections include applicable military regulations, rulings of the Supreme Court on the right to privacy, a summary of the facts of *Dronenburg vs. Zech*, and the opinion of the circuit court. The latter, written by Judge Robert Bork, "asserts that the Supreme Court's privacy cases, linked by no unifying principle, are to be confined strictly to their facts" (p. 877). The author concludes private consensual sexual conduct is subsumed under the privacy right as defined through the cases extant in the Supreme Court record.

393. McQuown, Richard C. "*Dronenburg Vs. Zech*: The Right to Privacy and Its Future." CAPITAL UNIVERSITY LAW REVIEW, 14 (Winter, 1985), 313-326.

"The propriety of legislating morality and the extent to which morality may be legislated is at the very core of the controversy surrounding the right of privacy and homosexual conduct" (p. 325). This note examines the decision of the U.S. Court of Appeals for the District of Columbia in the case of *Dronenburg vs. Zech*. In the original decision, the policy of the U.S. Navy of mandatory discharge for homosexual persons was upheld. In the appeal, Dronenburg challenged this policy on three grounds: violation of a constitutionally protected right to privacy, traditional constitutional theory, and equal protection. Resolution of the appeal for equal protection was based upon the premise that the U.S. Supreme Court, in a series of cases beginning with the 1965 *Griswold vs. Connecticut*, had developed a constitutional right of privacy which included "intimate personal decisions" (p. 315). Justice Robert Bork "found no cases where the right of privacy had been defined broadly enough to include homosexual conduct" (p. 316). Dronenburg's dismissal from the service was upheld. The bulk of this note is an analysis of the history of the idea of a right to privacy, with the negative decision in Dronenburg viewed as a "judicial response to society's conservative shift" (p. 326). Clarification of the question of whether homosexual conduct is protected will, in McQuown's opinion, only be obtained through a precise legal definition of the boundaries of privacy.

394.   Carbetta-Scandy, Kelly. "The Armed Services Continued Degradation and Expulsion of their Homosexual Members: *Dronenburg Vs. Zech,* 741 F.2d. 1388 (D.C. Dir. 1984)." UNIVERSITY OF CINCINNATI LAW REVIEW, 54, 3 (1986), 1055-1067.

On April 21, 1981, petty officer James L. Dronenburg was discharged by the United States Navy after having admitted to engaging in homosexual relations on the naval base. His appeal to the Secretary of the Navy failing, the case was filed in the U.S. District Court for the District of Columbia. At issue were the Navy's discharge policy, a request to vacate the discharge and a request to issue an order for immediate re-instatement. The district court found for the U.S. Navy. Dronenburg had used the argument that the official Navy policy was an unconstitutional invasion of the right to privacy. This article reviews this argument through the examination of related cases, these being *Griswold vs. Connecticut* (1965), *Eisenstadt vs. Bird* (1972) and the *Roe vs. Wade* decision of the U.S. Supreme Court. Cases specifically related to homosexuality and privacy are then dealt with. These are: *Doe vs. Commonwealth Attorney for Richmond* (1976), *benShalom vs. Secretary of the Army* (1980), *Saal vs. Middendorf* (1977) and *Matlovich vs. Secretary of the Air Force* (1978). In only one cases, that of Miriam benShalom, was a homosexual plaintiff able to obtain a ruling that discharge on grounds of homosexuality infringes on an individual's right to privacy. The decision in *Dronenburg vs. Zech* is analyzed and found wanting in that it is based on a one-word summary given by the Supreme Court in *Doe vs. Commonwealth* indicating homosexuality is not constitutionally protected by the right of privacy. Such affirmations only settle specific litigations and should not be used as the basis of judicial principles. Even if the Supreme Court were to rule eventually that homosexuality does fall within the right of privacy, no change in the military attitude of exclusion for the best interests of the service is seen. *Dronenburg vs. Zech* is therefore seen as a setback for gay rights as regards the armed services.

395. "Gay Air Force Captain Forced to Resign: Claims Gestapo-Like Tactics Used in Antigay Witchhunt." THE ADVOCATE, 440 (18 February, 1986), 13.

A summary of the case of U.S. Air Force Capt. David Marier, one of five men charged with homosexuality and separated from the service at Wurtsmith Air Force base in Michigan. The suit seeks an upgrade of the general discharge granted to Marier to an honorable one.

396. "Lesbian Wins: U.S. Army Must Do Things Miriam's Way." THE ADVOCATE, 442 (18 March, 1986), 15.

Federal Judge Terence Evans on January 28, 1986 again ordered that Sgt. Miriam benShalom be reinstated to her rank in the Army Reserve by March 1. A brief history of past litigation in the case is given, covering some ten years.

397. "Lesbian Lieutenant Fights Discharge from Air National Guard." THE ADVOCATE, 451 (22 July, 1986), 15.

A review of the case of Lieutenant Ellen Nesbitt of the New York Air National Guard, presently under consideration for discharge on grounds of lesbian activity. Legal counsel is being provided by Citizen Soldier, a veterans' advocacy group in New York City.

398. "News Briefs--West Point, New York." THE ADVOCATE, 459 (11 November, 1986), 27.

Eight military policewomen stationed at the U.S. Military Academy have been discharged honorably under grounds of lesbian conduct. Several claimed they had been intimidated into incriminating other members of the unit.

399.   Murphy, Lawrence R. PERVERTS BY OFFICIAL ORDER: THE
       CAMPAIGN AGAINST HOMOSEXUALS BY THE UNITED
       STATES NAVY. New York: Harrington Park Press, 1988.

A detailed historical account of the activities carried
out by the United States Navy following World War I
directed to the detection and expulsion of homosexual
men from the ranks. The focus of the work is the
massive scandal which erupted in 1919 at the Newport,
Rhode Island Naval Training Station. Extensive detail
on both the community of Newport at this period and the
expansion of a local investigative effort to all the
northeast is provided. As Section A within the office
of the Assistant Secretary of the Navy, this regional
effort to pursue "homosexuals within the Navy" was next
expanded to include civilians as well. The political
implications for the then-incumbent of that office,
Franklin Delano Roosevelt, are also set out in detail,
including the hearings on the matter in the U.S. Senate
in 1920. Researchers should be aware that material on
the Newport scandal is also contained in *Government
vs. Homosexuals.* An extensive bibliography of sources,
including manuscripts and government documents, completes the work.

Employment Discrimination

400. "Investigations. Files on Parade." TIME, 61 (16 February, 1953), 26.

> Coverage of testimony given before Sen. Joseph McCarthy's investigative committee as to the presence of information on homosexuals in the personnel files of the U.S. State Department. The atmosphere and attitudes surrounding federal workers known or suspected to be homosexual in the early 1950s is conveyed through interviews with two staff members.

401. "The Invert and His Job." THE MATTACHINE REVIEW, 1, 3 (May-June, 1955), 15-16.

> A series of discussions on the role of homosexuality in employment was held by the Chicago chapter of the Mattachine Society and is summarized here. Topics touched upon include the types of professions homosexuals enter (and their respective degrees of tolerance), importance of social contacts and the pressures to conform.

402. "Fair Employment Practices and the Homosexual." THE MATTACHINE REVIEW, 2, 2 (April, 1956), 41-42.

> Robert Kirk presents a brief critique of employers' efforts at identifying and expelling homosexual employ-

ees. An interesting note is the origin of the federal practice of considering homosexuals to be threats to national security. During the early twentieth century, an official of the Austro-Hungarian Empire was black-mailed by Tsarist agents, who threatened to expose his homosexuality if he did not comply with their demands for state papers. The article closes with a call for an end to such practices.

403. "You're Fired." THE MATTACHINE REVIEW, 2, 3 (June, 1956), 27.

This short article illustrates graphically the atti-tudes of American society in the 1950s which made conviction for a sex offense so damning. Several specific cases are cited, ranging from a military officer with fourteen years' service to the registra-tion of a sex offender in California. Practices such as being required to inform one's employer upon arrest for a sex offense come under heavy criticism.

404. "Job-Hunting Doesn't Need to Be a Problem." THE LADDER, 1, 6 (March, 1957), 5-7.

This article presents the results of a panel discussion held on February 26, 1957 on "Employment and the Homosexual." Basic principles of employer-employee relations are stated. One case of lesbians keeping aloof from other workers is cited as a negative example of practical coping behaviors for the workplace.

405. "Bread and Butter Tips: Homosexuals Can Get Jobs--And Keep Them!" THE LADDER, 2, 3 (December, 1957), 17-18.

A presentation on employment problems and strategies for gays and lesbians at the December, 1957 meeting of the Mattachine Society in Los Angeles is reviewed. Points emphasized included self-image and the difficul-ty of civil service employment with an undesirable discharge.

406. "Employment for the Social Variant." THE LADDER, 6, 7 (April, 1962), 12.

An address given by Mr. Charles Davis to the Hollywood Assistance League is summarized. Frequent change of employment, emotional instability and alcoholism were cited as problems of homosexuals seeking employment.

407. "Homosexuals in Government: Can We Afford the Manpower Waste and Human Tragedy Resulting from Our Double Standard of Morals?" THE MATTACHINE REVIEW, 3, 11 (November, 1962), 13-26.

This documented report covers the subject of federal attitudes towards employment of homosexuals and includes a listing of seven cases filed between 1957 and 1962. A comparative study of sanctioned prostitution and bathroom hieroglyphics indicates a distinctly double standard of morality, with the question being raised as to why the government is involved in regulating morality at all.

408. "Cross Currents." THE LADDER, 7, 11 (August, 1963), 19-20.

The featured story in this news column is the suit brought by Bruce Scott against the United States Civil Service Commission. After successfully passing several qualifying examinations, Scott was told that the CSC had evidence he was a homosexual, and was barred from employment due to "immoral conduct." The lawsuit challenges the CSC authority to characterize homosexuality as immoral, to use immorality as a criterion for federal employment, and to use homosexual conduct as grounds for unsuitability for government positions.

409. "Cross Currents." THE LADDER, 9, 2 (November, 1964), 21-23.

Federal employment discrimination against homosexuals was the target of censure by the National Capital Area Civil Liberties Union in August of 1964. That body issued a resolution calling for an end to such practices, addressing what is called "the three principal arguments given by the government that homosexuals are unsuitable as employees." These were: 1) that the presence of a homosexual in an office is detrimental to morale and efficiency; 2) homosexuality is immoral and hence grounds for disqualification; and 3) homosexuals have greater susceptibility to coercion through blackmail. Immorality is the argument most frequently used as grounds for separation. A similar resolution is stated to be under consideration by the general body of the ACLU.

410. "The Charge of Immorality." NEW REPUBLIC, 153 (3 July, 1965), 6-7.

A review of the decision made by the U.S. Court of Appeals for the District of Columbia in the case of an unnamed federal employee discharged in 1962 on "vague, unspecified charges of homosexual conduct." Said majority decision required the Civil Service Commission to specify objectionable conduct and relate it to employment fitness. Simple imposition of "the stigma of 'immoral conduct'" was not held to be a valid basis for termination.

411. "Rusk Probed on Picketing." THE LADDER, 10, 1 (October, 1965), 18.

Exclusion of qualified homosexuals and lesbians from employment by the United States State Department provoked a demonstration on August 28, 1965 in Washington, D.C. Secretary of State Dean Rusk, in a press conference held on August 27, was queried as to official department policy; his response cited the potential for blackmail and personal instability as bases for such discrimination. In their literature, the demonstrators responded that it was federal policy which created security risks of this nature.

412. "U.S. Government Clings to Prejudice." THE LADDER, 10, 4 (January, 1966), 22-24.

The case of Bruce Scott, a federal employee denied eligibility for re-hiring due to being a homosexual, is presented in detail. After being defeated in the U.S. District Court for the District of Columbia, Scott appealed to the U.S. Court of Appeals. On June 16, 1965, following a period of six months' deliberation, the court reversed Scott's denial of eligibility, on the grounds that vague charges of "immoral conduct" were insufficient. In early October, 1965, he received notification that his original rating had been restored, but that the Civil Service Commission was "compelled by information available to us, to initiate action pending your suitability for employment." That decision effectively negated all legal action taken to that point.

413. "Security Clearances for Homosexuals." THE LADDER, 10, 6 (March, 1966), 19-20.

The issue of whether or not homosexuals should be given security clearances in federal employment was addressed by the Mattachine Society of Washington, D.C. Beginning with correspondence from the office of the Vice-President suggesting the Justice Department as the proper agency for such an issue, officials of the Society met with representatives of the Department's Internal Security Division. Homosexuality as a valid ground for discrimination was challenged, with questions raised as to how current policies could be changed. It emerged that there existed no central body coordinating security policy. Federal employees were under the jurisdiction of the Civil Service Commission, with individual agencies setting their own procedures and guidelines. Thus, no consensus on this problem could be reached.

414. "U.S. Government Hides Behind Immoral Mores." THE LADDER, 10, 9 (June, 1966), 17-20.

The Civil Service Commission's discriminatory employment policies toward homosexuals and efforts of the Mattachine Society of Washington, D.C. to oppose them are reviewed. After two years of fruitless correspondence, a demonstration was held at the CSC building in June, 1965. In response, a meeting with two officials representing the commissioners took place on September 8, 1965. At that time, a seventeen-page statement entitled "Federal Employment of Homosexual Citizens," as well as four other pieces of supporting documentation, were given to the CSC personnel. On February 25, 1966, Mr. John Macy, chairman of the Commission, issued a rebuttal. To quote the Mattachine Society, "this reply first denies the existence of a homosexual per se, and then re-invokes his existence by calling him a sexual deviate, and then denies his existence again by claiming in effect that sexual tendencies do not exist, only acts." As an arm of the government, the Civil Service Commission believed it must concur with and uphold social mores. This was the first instance where a rationale for such exclusion by the CSC was supplied.

415. "Glide Boycotts Firms That Won't Hire Homosexuals." THE ADVOCATE, 1, 3 (November, 1967), 2.

A news article reprinted from the Berkeley Barb on the activities of a task force on fair employment practices created at Glide Methodist Church. The church, together with its foundation and trustees, has adopted a policy of refusing "to buy goods and services from firms which discriminate against homosexuals." Studies are in progress to pinpoint firms which have carried out such policies. Contemporary efforts at aiding servicemen expelled on suspicion of homosexuality by attorneys volunteering as part of the War on Poverty are also outlined.

416. "Cross Currents." THE LADDER, 13, 1/2 (October-November, 1968), 37-42.

Among the news stories covered in this column is that of Benning Wentworth, who had filed suit against the U.S. Civil Service Commission to regain a lost security clearance, and news of a lesbian in Philadelphia who lost her position in the civil service for being homosexual.

417. "Cross Currents." THE LADDER, 13, 3/4 (December, 1968-January, 1969) 37-38.

This column contains note of a column written by Sydney J. Harris in the Chicago Daily News, dated September 11, 1968, advocating the removal of restrictions on homosexuals so that occasions for blackmail and security risks could not occur. The Jenkins case of 1964 is cited as an example.

418. "Teacher Appeals License Loss." THE ADVOCATE, 3, 5 (May, 1969), 2.

A reprint of a news item from the newsletter of the ACLU chapter of Southern California covering an appeal to that state's Supreme Court of an appellate decision. Said decision involved the revocation of the teaching credentials of an unnamed individual by the California Board of Education on grounds of having engaged in homosexual acts. Defense arguments are attacking the use of sexual conduct as a valid basis for credential suspension.

419. "S.F. Firm Fires Gay, Stirs Protest." THE ADVOCATE, 3, 5 (May, 1969), 3.

> A brief summary of the case of Gale Whittington, dismissed from his post at the State Line shipping firm in San Francisco following publication of a same-sex picture in the Berkeley Barb. The newly-created Committee for Homosexual Freedom organized a picket line in protest on April 9, 1969.

420. "Government Created Employment Disabilities of the Homosexual." HARVARD LAW REVIEW, 82 (June, 1969), 1738-1751.

> A note commenting upon the structure and regulations of both the Civil Service Commission and the Department of Defense which serve as legal bases for the exclusion of homosexual persons from these branches and from private employ requiring security clearances. Federal action is seen as setting the standards of leadership in liberal employment policies: hence, impact of decisions at this level is extensive. Following a review of the statutory bases for CSC actions, criticism focuses on defining the term "efficiency" as it relates to position responsibilities, a dispute resting on the usage of the work "character." Applications of this statute by the Commission indicate a broad interpretation of the concept. Stating that "it is difficult to justify the Commission's exclusion of homosexual workers if a narrow interpretation of "efficiency" is adopted" (p. 1742), the argument of disruptive effects by a homosexual on his co-workers is examined. Conjectured damage for the system through retention is viewed as possibly equal to the loss of trained personnel. Industrial clearances and what judicial review of policies had occurred as of mid-1969 are then explored. Specific cases mentioned here are those of *Dew vs. Halaby* and Benning Wentworth's suit against the Department of Defense. The note concludes that "it is unlikely that the courts will be afforded opportunity to review basic government policies. . . The inability of the courts to intervene in the lack of . . . spokesmen for homosexual workers, creates a situation where the governmental process does not offer adequate protection to a minority group which lacks the political resources to protect itself" (p. 1751). Class action suits are viewed as a possible means of permitting such review. "Moreover, the exclusion of a large group of workers from three million jobs based on

an educated guess may still be criticized as poor administrative policy" (p. 1744).

421. McIntire, Dal. "State Lines Picketing Spreads to Los Angeles." THE ADVOCATE, 3, 6 (June, 1969), 1, 11-12.

News coverage of three days of picketing at the Los Angeles, California offices of the State Lines shipping firm in protest over the dismissal of an openly homosexual employee in San Francisco. Detailed descriptions of company and public reactions are included. Demands being made of the company by the Committee on Homosexual Freedom are listed.

422. "Being Gay No Longer a Bar to NYC Civil Service." THE ADVOCATE, 3, 6 (June, 1969), 1.

In May, 1969, Judge William B. Herlands of New York affirmed a new employment policy of the city's Civil Service Commission eliminating homosexuality as grounds for discrimination in hiring. Brief background information on the inception of the policy is presented.

423. "Pickets Win: Tower Records Rehires Boy." THE ADVOCATE, 3, 7 (August, 1969), 6, 35.

Following two weeks of demonstration, an employee of a San Francisco record store dismissed on suspicion of homosexuality was rehired. Negotiations with the Committee for Homosexual Freedom are profiled.

424. Kepner, Jim. "Can't Fire Gay Just Because He's Gay, Court Tells CSC." THE ADVOCATE, 3, 8 (September, 1969), 4.

A review of the July, 1969 decision by the District of Columbia Court of Appeals prohibiting the dismissal of federal civil service employees on grounds of homosexuality without demonstration of a "reasonable connection" between the individuals' proclivities and their assigned jobs. Lengthy excerpts from the court's decision are included and arguments are summarized.

425. "Cross Currents." THE LADDER, 14, 1/2 (October-November, 1969), 29-41.

This column contains four news stories involving employment discrimination:

a) Civil rights for city employees in New York City were guaranteed on May 10, 1969, by an order of the City Civil Service Commission, which stated that homosexuality would no longer be accepted as grounds for refusing employment. This move was prompted by a lawsuit filed against the city by two welfare workers denied positions for this reason.

b) Gale Whittington, an accounting clerk with the State Lines Steamship Company in San Francisco, was fired in April, 1969 for being a homosexual. Massive demonstrations were organized by the Council for Homosexual Freedom and a picket line was set up at company offices in San Francisco and Los Angeles. Demands included full reinstatement with back pay and adoption of a fair employment pledge against further discrimination.

c) Following three weeks of negotiation, a San Francisco firm, Tower Records, agreed to rehire Frank Denaro, who had been fired for being homosexual. Further, the employees' union agreed to enforce a pledge of non-discrimination.

d) The U.S. Court of Appeals in San Francisco ruled on July 1, 1969 that federal civil service employees may no longer be fired simply because they are homosexual.

426. "Federal Employment of Homosexuals: Narrowing the Efficiency Standard." CATHOLIC UNIVERSITY LAW REVIEW, 19 (Winter, 1969), 267-275.

An analysis of the case of *Norton vs. Macy* and the legal arguments considered by the court in its resolution. Beginning with a background history of the Civil Service Commission's authorization to remove employees for "such cause as will promote the efficiency of the service," the particulars of the case are presented and the prior decisions of *Dew vs. Halaby* and *Anonymous vs. Macy* are examined. Attention of the chief justice of the U.S. District Court for the District of Columbia was "turned to the question which he had formulated, i.e., whether off-duty homosexual conduct is sufficient cause for dismissal on the grounds that termination will foster service efficiency" (p. 272). The CSC failed to provide proof of this claim, and a lower court decision removing Norton from his position with

NASA was reversed. This decision is seen as sharply limiting the ability of the Civil Service Commission in defining policy applicability and as "the first time that a circuit court has squarely faced a direct challenge to the Commission's policy of excluding homosexuals from federal employment" (p. 274). Application of qualified homosexual persons to government employment is also viewed as effected by this case.

427. "Cross Currents." THE LADDER, 14, 3/4 (December, 1969-January, 1970), 28-34.

A news item in this column follows the Benning Wentworth case. In 1966, Wentworth lost his security clearance on the grounds that, as a homosexual, he was vulnerable to blackmail. The counter argument introduced by the lawyers is that, since Wentworth admits his homosexuality, no possibility of blackmail exists, and hence no threat to the Department of Defense.

428. "State Can't Take Teacher's Credentials for Homosexual Act." THE ADVOCATE, 4, 1 (January, 1970), 3, 10.

A summary of the ruling by the California Supreme Court in the case of Marc Morrison, a teacher dismissed from his post following allegations of homosexuality. The court ruled that the Board of Education could not, in said case, revoke the defendant's teaching credentials, as it had not established that violation of California's education code statutes covering homosexual acts and "moral turpitude" had occurred.

429. "Dismissal of Homosexuals from Government Employment: The Developing Role of Due Process in Administrative Adjudications." GEORGETOWN LAW JOURNAL, 58 (February, 1970), 632-645.

A review article placing the case of *Norton vs. Macy* (1969) in a context of "judicial review of governmental dismissals that involve possible violations of constitutional rights" (p. 633). After summarizing the traditional approaches taken in such past cases as *Gadsden vs. United States* (which case requires an honest non-judgmental evaluation as the basis for dismissal), it is noted that agency discretion in defining the relationship between the grounds for dismissal and the "efficiency of the service" has been

ill-defined. A trend towards closer scrutiny of dismissals involving homosexuality is remarked, with *Dew
vs. Halaby* offered as example. The author notes that
constitutional theory has been applied little in such
cases because statutes which limit agency activities
usually offer sufficient employee protection in this
area. Due process as a factor has entered the picture
through court borrowing from decisions in licensing
cases involving the balancing of competing interests.
Norton vs. Macy is an example of court willingness to
look behind such terms as "immoral" when offered as
grounds by an agency, as "these terms are very broad
and encompass conduct having no appreciable effect upon
the efficiency of an agency" (p. 643). Its importance
also lies in the fact that it necessitates a re-examination of traditional attitudes towards homosexuality
in the sphere of federal employment.

430.   McIntire, Dal. "Kameny, Scourge of Federals, Continues
       Attack on Government, Military Bias." THE ADVOCATE, 4, 2
       (February, 1970), 3, 5.

       A lengthy exploration of the efforts being made by Dr.
       Franklin Kameny and Barbara Gittings of the Washington,
       D.C. Mattachine Society to assist four separate cases
       involving civilian employees of the federal government
       who have been dismissed on grounds of homosexuality.
       The cases of Benning Wentworth and Otto Ulrich are
       presented in detail, as are quotations outlining
       Kameny's opposition to the continued sanction of such
       discrimination.

431.   "Federal Court Rules Pentagon Can Bar Clearance for Gays."
       THE ADVOCATE, 4, 2 (February, 1970), 3.

       A note on the ruling by the U.S. Court of Appeals for
       the District of Columbia in the case of *Adams vs.
       Laird*. Said ruling held that the Pentagon regulations
       "include ample indication that a practicing homosexual
       may pose serious problems . . . emotional instability
       and possible subjection to sinister pressures." The
       plaintiff plans to appeal.

432.   "Cross-Currents." THE LADDER, 14, 5/6 (February-March,
       1970), 35-41.

On November 21, 1969, the Supreme Court of the State of California ruled that a teacher could not have their teaching credentials revoked on the grounds of having engaged in homosexual activity. Such revocation would be possible if adverse effects on the students could be detected as a result.

433. "Gays Picket ABC Station." THE ADVOCATE, 4, 3 (March, 1970), 9.

A report on protest demonstrations at the San Francisco and New York City affiliates of the American Broadcasting Company on January 16, 1970. At issue was the dismissal of news editor Leo Laurence from KGO-TV (San Francisco) for his public activities in the militant gay movement.

434. "Cross Currents." THE LADDER, 14, 7/8 (April-May, 1970), 31-38.

A demonstration was held at the offices of KGO-TV and radio in San Francisco on January 16, 1970, to protest the firing of Leo Laurence. Laurence, a news editor, had participated in another gay protest against the San Francisco Examiner. Union backing was obtained for the case.

435. "Ulrich, Gayer Cases Show Up Security Program As Vendetta Against Gays." THE ADVOCATE, 4, 4 (April, 1970), 7.

A review of recent developments in the legal cases of Otto Ulrich and Richard Gayer, both of whom have been discharged from security-clearance level positions within the federal system on grounds of homosexuality. Dr. Franklin Kameny, civilian counsel to both defendants, is interviewed, commenting upon the legality of the questions put to them and the reasons offered in support of the initial separations. Said questions do not address individual qualifications for the position or clearances.

436. "Minnesota Fires Gay Announcer for Blind Radio Network." THE ADVOCATE, 4, 4 (April, 1970), 9.

A summary of the case of Thom Higgins, an announcer for the Radio Talking Book Network of Minnesota, dismissed on grounds of being a homosexual. Network officials charged Higgins was incompetent. The Minnesota Department of Human Rights has agreed to handle the case.

437. "S.F. Commission Backs Gays on Job Rights." THE ADVOCATE, 4, 5 (29 April-12 May, 1970), 20.

In response to a petition from the Society for Individual Rights, the Human Rights Commission of San Francisco passed a resolution "supporting equal and fair employment rights for homosexuals." The city's Board of Supervisors was called upon to ascertain the existence of the practice in the city.

438. "High Court Turns Down Gays Fired for Off-Job Conduct." THE ADVOCATE, 4, 6 (12-26 May, 1970), 5.

On April, 20, 1970, the U.S. Supreme Court declined to review the cases of Richard Schlegel and Robert Adams, both involving dismissal from federal employment following identification as homosexuals. The positions of the court and the Justice Department are outlined.

439. Crumpler, William B. "Administrative Law--Constitutional Law--Is Governmental Policy Affecting the Employment of Homosexuals Rational?" NORTH CAROLINA LAW REVIEW, 48 (June, 1970), 912-924.

An overview examination of the grounds used to support federal employment policies towards homosexual persons as they existed in 1970. Citing the then-recent cases of *Schlegel vs. United States, Adams vs. Laird* and *Norton vs. Macy* (the last seen as threatening "an heretofore unquestioned federal policy of regarding homosexual acts as an ipso facto basis for dismissal from the Civil Service" [p. 914]), a rationale for this attitude is sought with a view toward preventing constitutional repercussions. Various causes of homosexual behavior (both psychological and physiological) are reviewed, with the conclusion that, whatever its nature, the source of homosexual behavior lies in individual personality development. Optimum adjustment of the homosexual to his society is seen as greatly hindered by "criminal and civil penalties" (p. 920). A lack of consideration of individual circumstances prior to penalization for homosexual conduct "may be deemed unreasonable and the policy adjudged as irrational.

That the policy is founded on public opinion makes it no less irrational" (p. 921). An accurate determination of fitness for employment, following the model offered in *Norton vs. Macy*, must therefore "turn on the whole of a person's personality and integrity rather than solely on his private . . . sexual conduct" (p. 923).

440. "Cross Currents." THE LADDER, 14, 9/10 (June-July, 1970), 33-40.

Two news stories involving discrimination in employment are among the items listed in this column:

a) Leo Laurence, the ABC news editor sacked by radio station KGO in San Francisco for admitting to homosexuality, was reinstated by his union on February 13, 1970. Immediately thereafter, the station once again initiated procedures to fire him.

b) The San Francisco Human Rights Commission has recommended that the city Board of Supervisors hold public hearings on city legislation prohibiting discrimination against homosexuals in public and private employment.

441. "Norton Awarded $80,000 for Dismissal from NASA." THE ADVOCATE, 4, 10 (8-21 July, 1970), 3.

A note on the cash awards made to Clifford L. Norton as back pay following his dismissal from the National Aeronautics and Space Administration in 1964 and subsequent reversal of the initial decision in 1969. Details of the case are briefly outlined.

442. "Survey Starts Drive on Job Discrimination." THE ADVOCATE, 4, 11 (22 July-4 August, 1970), 2, 4.

The homophile organization of the University of Minnesota has sponsored a survey of the employment practices of the twelve largest corporations in the Minneapolis-St. Paul region. The letter and survey questionnaire are presented with regard to homosexuals.

443. "Mattachine Raps CBS on Job Discrimination." THE ADVOCATE, 4, 11 (22 July-4 August, 1970), 4.

The Mattachine Society of New York has filed complaints against the Columbia Broadcasting System with the city Commission on Human Relations over the CBS policy of dismissal of job candidates if "homosexual tendencies" are discovered. Two recent cases are cited as evidence.

444. "Marriage Applicant's Job Up to Judge." THE ADVOCATE, 4, 14 (2-15 September, 1970), 23.

A partial transcript of the hearing held on August 5, 1970 in Minneapolis on the request from the Minnesota Civil Liberties Union that the university libraries of the University of Minnesota be compelled to honor the job offer made in April to J. Michael McConnell. McConnell was subsequently informed that a committee of the board of regents had recommended against his appointment. Details of the cross-examination of the chair of the committee are included. The objective of the MCLU case is "to establish that the State of Minnesota and its agencies . . . cannot legally discriminate against gays."

445. "Homosexuality Isn't Valid Reason to Deny Job, Court Tells University." THE ADVOCATE, 4, 16 (30 September-13 October, 1970), 1.

On September 9, 1970, federal district Judge Philip Neville of Minneapolis issued a permanent injunction forbidding the University of Minnesota to refuse to hire J. Michael McConnell "solely because he is a homosexual." The decision drew a distinction between homosexuality and sodomy. Legal precedents cited are summarized. McConnell's initial appointment as head of cataloging at the St. Paul campus will stand.

446. "Three Big Companies Say They Hire Gays." THE ADVOCATE, 4, 16 (30 September-13 October, 1970), 5.

A survey of hiring practices regarding homosexuals in force at the twelve largest companies in the Twin Cities area of Minnesota has produced four responses. Firms responding (in the affirmative) that homosexuals were not specially eliminated during employment screening were Pillsbury, General Mills, and the Dayton department store chain.

447. "Job Decision Appealed." THE ADVOCATE, 4, 17 (14-27 October, 1970), 1, 19.

> On September 11, 1970, the University of Minnesota Board of Regents executive committee determined to appeal the federal court ruling ordering the hiring of J. Michael McConnell, an admitted homosexual. Board members indicated that they felt "the university just couldn't afford to hire someone who made such a public display of being gay, at least not without doing everything possible to avoid it."

448. "GAA Attacks County Job Bias." THE ADVOCATE, 4, 17 (14-27 October, 1970), 7.

> The Gay Activists' Alliance of New York City has attacked the Suffolk County Civil Service Commission for what it terms an "extraordinary intrusion into the privacy of employees and prospective employees." In addition to being queried about "homosexual tendencies," the applicant is asked regarding epilepsy, venereal diseases and refusal of insurance.

449. "Librarians Ask McConnell Case Probe." THE ADVOCATE, 4, 19 (11-24 November, 1970), 3.

> The Minnesota Library Association, at its convention on October 16, 1970, adopted a resolution calling upon the Intellectual Freedom Committee of the American Library Association to investigate the recent employment discrimination case of J. M. McConnell and to censure the University of Minnesota regents if said investigation determined homosexuality was the basis for denial. Censure could extend to a warning to all librarians not to accept jobs at the university.

450. "Government Employment and the Homosexual." ST. JOHN'S LAW REVIEW, 5 (December, 1970), 303-323.

> A detailed examination of recent cases involving governmental employment policies towards homosexual persons indicates a degree of reversal of established and traditional stances. This article explores the scope of these changes. Decisions presented in detail are *Dew vs. Halaby* (1963), *Scott vs. Macy* (1965), *Norton vs. Macy* (1969), *Morrison vs. State Board of Education* (1969), *Schlegel vs. United States* (1969), *Adams vs. Laird* (1969) and *McConnell vs. Anderson*

(1970). The due process considerations raised in Norton, McConnell and Morrison are viewed as having impact upon then-current penal provisions outlawing or severely proscribing consensual homosexual activity. "Just as the impairment of agency efficiency must be evidenced in order to exclude homosexuals from government employment, some demonstrably inimical effect on society must be evidenced in order to outlaw nonconforming moral codes" (p. 320). Absence of a "legitimate public purpose in punishing private homosexual behavior" (p. 322) is seen as the paramount reason for liberalization of existing policies. Federal and state attitudes are seen to reinforce attitudes of private employers and "support the fallacious proposition that these individuals are incapable of leading socially productive lives" (p. 323).

451. "Cross Currents." THE LADDER, 15, 3/4 (December, 1970-January, 1971), 39-44.

On September 19, 1970, a decision was handed down in the case of *Michael McConnell vs. the University of Minnesota*. The federal district judge, Philip Neville, ruled that the university could not refuse employment to anyone simply for being an avowed homosexual. McConnell had been accepted for the position as head of the cataloging department in the university libraries and was being denied the position on these grounds. Mention is also made of his efforts to legally marry his lover, Jack Baker, and their application for a marriage license.

452. Harenstein, Neal G. "Homosexuals in the Teaching Profession." CLEVELAND STATE LAW REVIEW, 20 (January, 1971), 125-134.

A comment reviewing the status of homosexuals in the American educational system as it was in 1971. Noting that revocation of teaching credentials "is a matter of express statute" (p. 125) in all fifty states, a sample of article 291 of the California Penal Code is offered as example. Interview excerpts with Mr. Dorian Smith, assistant director of personnel for the Cleveland Board of Education and Mr. Bob Meloe, Vice-President of the Mattachine Society of New York present alternative opinions regarding the abilities of school systems to refuse employment to applicants known or suspected of being homosexual. Teachers requested to resign for reasons of homosexuality theoretically have the right to an administrative hearing, although Harenstein notes that this rule is not uniform, probationary teachers being a notable exception. "Dismissal for good cause" is raised as an issue, with *Morrison vs. State Board of Education* offered as example. Such decisions "by requiring the system to prove that an individual's sexual inclinations produced an adverse effect on his teaching service" (p. 133) are viewed as more professional grounds for evaluation.

453. "U. of Minnesota Moving Toward Anti-Bias Policy." THE ADVOCATE, 4, 23 (6-19 January, 1971), 2.

An outline of the proposed anti-bias policy presently moving through administrative channels at the University of Minnesota. If approved by the University Senate, said policy would bar firms using the campus placement office from discriminating against applicants except on the basis of academic records, work experience, personal references, physical abilities or relevant qualifications as established under federal law. Local activists anticipate using the policy to force changes at Honeywell, Inc.

454. "School Suspends Counselor After Appearance on TV." THE ADVOCATE, 4, 24 (20 January-2 February, 1971), 1, 11.

Kenneth Bland, a counselor at the American School for the Deaf in West Hartford, Connecticut was suspended from his position following an appearance on local television as a representative of the Kalos Society, Hartford's gay liberation group. The text of the letter of suspension is reprinted in full and parental reaction outlined.

455. "NY Councilmen Propose Gay Job Rights Laws." THE ADVOCATE, 52 (3-16 February, 1971), 1.

At a press conference on January 6, 1971, New York City councilmen Eldon Clingan and Carter Burden announced their introduction of a bill intended to expand existing discrimination legislation in housing, public accommodations and employment to cover sexual orientation. Support for the measure has been promised from prominent clergy and the Human Rights Commission.

456. "Boy's Counselor to Challenge Suspension in Court Action."
THE ADVOCATE, 52 (3-16 February, 1971), 5.

The Connecticut Civil Liberties Union has agreed to
represent Kenneth Bland in forthcoming legal action
against the American School for the Deaf. At issue is
Bland's dismissal over his homosexuality and subsequent
action taken by the school regarding said dismissal in
private hearings.

457. "L.A. Civil Service Puts Off More Liberal Hiring
Policies." THE ADVOCATE, 52 (3-16 February, 1971), 3,
12.

A detailed presentation of a hearing held on January 8,
1971 before the Los Angeles Civil Service Commission on
proposed revisions in those sections of city employment
policy barring hiring of persons "arrested on charges
involving sex, drugs or subversion, regardless of
whether they were convicted." A continuance of thirty
days was granted. Lengthy excerpts of the floor debate
on the proposals are included.

458. "Reforms on Housing Stall in L.A. City Council." THE
ADVOCATE, 53 (27 February-2 March, 1971), 10.

On January 20, 1971, the Personnel Committee of the Los
Angeles City Council deferred action on proposed revisions of city hiring policies regarding arrest records
on sex, narcotics or subversion. Lengthy quotes from
the testimony of councilman Arthur Snyder, author of
the initial suggestion for revision and Morris Kight of
the Gay Liberation Front are included.

459. "ACLU Sues on Security Clearances." THE ADVOCATE, 53 (27
February-2 March, 1971), 14.

On January 25, 1971, suit was filed in the U.S. District Court for the District of Columbia by the American Civil Liberties Union on behalf of Otto Ulrich.
The case seeks "to enjoin the Defense Department from
denying industrial security clearance to an individual
solely because he is a homosexual." Ulrich had previously been cleared of vulnerability to "blackmail or
coercion" in an internal Defense Department investigation prior to his suspension.

132

460. "Some Dayton Companies Throw Out Job Survey." THE ADVOCATE, 55 (17-30 March, 1971), 23.

A report on a survey of employment policies regarding homosexuals in the Dayton, Ohio business community was publicly rebuffed by two local firms. A third, National Cash Register, agreed to respond but declined comment.

461. "Minnesota U. Senate Backs Gay Librarian." THE ADVOCATE, 56 (31 March-13 April, 1971), 8.

On March 11, 1971, the University Senate of the University of Minnesota voted to adopt a recommendation of its library committee that the Board of Regents be urged to reverse themselves on the issue of hiring openly gay librarian J. M. McConnell. Proponents of the measure cited the Regent's objections to McConnell's public stance on homosexuality as a violation of freedom of expression.

462. "First Gay Complaint Filed in L.A. Job Equality Office." THE ADVOCATE, 60 (26 May-8 June, 1971), 4.

A review of the complaint filed on April 30, 1971 with the Los Angeles District Equal Employment Opportunities Commission office by Cheryl Thompson, fired for renting apartments to homosexuals. Note is also taken of an April 29 letter sent to President Nixon by the Los Angeles Gay Liberation Front requesting the appointment of a gay commissioner to the National Equal Employment Opportunities Commission.

463. "Commissioner Starts Library Hiring Row In Oklahoma." THE ADVOCATE, 60 (26 May-8 June, 1971), 4.

On April 15, 1971 at a meeting in Oklahoma City of the local county commissioners, the suggestion was made that all homosexuals currently employed in the metropolitan library system should be fired. The proposal met with severe criticism and possible legal action by persons separated for this reason was raised as a consequence.

464. "Teacher Appeals Firing." THE ADVOCATE, 60 (26 May-8 June, 1971), 4.

133

A summary of the case of Michael Roe, a high school human relations instructor in Iowa City fired for inviting a panel of local gay activists to address his eighth-grade class. The positions of Roe and the school board are outlined. A public hearing has been set for May 11.

465. "Gay Prof Out: College Denies Bias." THE ADVOCATE, 50 (26 May-8 June, 1971), 9.

A profile of the dismissal of sociology faculty member Michael Silverstein of California State College, Hayward for open involvement with campus gay activism. Silverstein's personal development of consciousness as a homosexual is illustrated in an interview.

466. "Catholic Group Favors End to Job Bias." THE ADVOCATE, 61 (9-22 June, 1971), 2

On May 4, 1971, the Commission on Social Justice of the Catholic archdiocese of San Francisco adopted a resolution supporting a proposed amendment to the city's ordinance on job discrimination. Said reform would extend the existing protections to include sexual orientation. The original request from the Society for Individual Rights had been referred to committee fourteen months previously.

467. "Job Hunter Need Not Hide Being Gay." THE ADVOCATE, 61 (9-22 June, 1971), 11.

A brief note on a ruling by the Los Angeles County Department of Public Welfare that a recipient of aid "cannot be forced to conceal his sexual identity" as a condition for continued assistance.

468. "Fired Sex-Ed Teacher Hired Back." THE ADVOCATE, 62 (23 June-6 July, 1971), 4.

A detailed news report on the May 11, 1971 hearing in Iowa City in the case of Michael Roe, a human relations instructor under dismissal for having brought local gay activists to address his class. Roe was rehired following evidence of massive popular support. The arguments used by the school board to fire Roe are presented.

469. "Federal Building 'Work-In' Protests U.S. Hiring Policy." THE ADVOCATE, 63 (7-20 July, 1971), 4.

An account of a protest against federal hiring policies towards homosexuals staged at the San Francisco federal building on June 7, 1971. Protestors attracted substantial media attention through operating elevators, posing as janitors and reporting to a public "unemployment office" following their ejection by security officers.

470. Stone, Jeannine. "American Library Assn. Adopts Anti-Bias Plank." THE ADVOCATE, 64 (21 July-3 August, 1971), 9.

A news report on the adoption of a broadly worded anti-discrimination resolution by the American Library Association at its 90th conference in Dallas. The full text of the resolution (drawn up by the Task Force on Gay Liberation) is included and other gay-related activities of the conference outlined.

471. "Gay Granted Reinstatement to Postal Job." THE ADVOCATE, 65 (4-17 August, 1971), 9.

At a press conference held at the University of Illinois, Chicago on June 23, 1971, the Chicago Committee for Gay People and the Law announced the decision of the civil service commission to reinstate Alvin Golden. Golden had earlier been dismissed on the grounds of a case of solicitation despite his acquittal.

472. "Gay, Straight Leader Push S.F. Hiring Law." THE ADVOCATE, 68 (15-28 September, 1971), 14.

A profile of the support within the city of San Francisco for a proposed amendment to the city charter extending protection in hiring to sexual orientation. A brief history of the proposal is included.

473. Aiken, David L. "Security Sex Snoops Lose: Judge Rules Out Prying to Bar Gay Clearances." THE ADVOCATE, 70 (13 October, 1971), 1, 26.

A report on the September 13, 1971 ruling of U.S. District Court Judge John H. Pratt in three cases involving use of personal information on federal job questionnaires and denial of employment or security clearances for refusal to answer such questions. Pratt held that the government may not ask applicants "probing personal questions" or use any personal sexual data it may obtain to deny employment without demonstrating a clear connection between the data and the job requirements.

474. "Ulrich Case Is Study of a Man Hell-Bent on Justice." THE ADVOCATE, 70 (13 October, 1971), 26-27.

An interview with Otto Ulrich, one of the three plaintiffs recently restored to federal security clearance status by Judge John H. Pratt in a decision prohibiting federal employers from barring homosexuals on grounds of sexual preference. The details of Ulrich's experiences with the federal bureaucracy are presented.

475. "Jack, Mike Lose on Job, Marriage." THE ADVOCATE, 72 (10 November, 1971), 1, 30.

A discussion of the October 19, 1971 decision by the Eighth Circuit Court of Appeals in St. Louis that the University of Minnesota had been justified in denying employment to activist Michael McConnell due to his desire to "pursue an activist role in implementing his unconventional ideas concerning the societal status to be accorded homosexuals . . . thereby to foist tacit approval of his socially repugnant concept upon his employer." McConnell's counsel termed the finding "outrageous" and plans to appeal.

476. "Won't Hire Gays, Says 'Ma Bell,' But . . ." THE ADVOCATE, 72 (10 November, 1971), 5.

A detailed report on demonstrations held against the Pacific Telephone company in San Francisco on October 13, 1971. At issue was the stated policy that the firm would "not knowingly hire a homosexual." Similar demonstrations have been held at the American Telephone and Telegraph company headquarters in New York City.

477. "McConnell Ruling Hit by Gene McCarthy." THE ADVOCATE, 73 (24 November, 1971), 1.

Quotations from presidential candidate Eugene McCarthy decrying the recent appeals court decision in the employment discrimination case of J. Michael McConnell, terming the issue one of "freedom of speech."

478.   "Hets, Gays Protest Job Ruling." THE ADVOCATE, 73 (24 November, 1971), 2.

A profile of the furor generated in Minneapolis by the recent appeals court decision in the case of J. Michael McConnell. The Minnesota Civil Liberties Union has requested that the court review its decision, and massive campus demonstrations have been held to show support.

479.   "L.A. Hiring Reform Rejected." THE ADVOCATE, 73 (24 November, 1971), 3.

On November 1, 1971, the Los Angeles City Council rejected by one vote proposed reforms in the city employment policy eliminating consideration of past arrest records on sex or narcotics charges without regard for conviction.

480.   "Extension of Illinois Job Law Sought." THE ADVOCATE, 73 (24 November, 1971), 14.

A report on a proposal filed on October 26, 1971 with the Illinois Fair Employment Practices Commission by the Chicago Gay Alliance. The state agency was asked "to prohibit discrimination by private employers against male and female homosexuals and against single persons." A history of the proposal and media debate on the question is also provided.

481.   "U. of Oregon Job Policy Facing Legal Challenge." THE ADVOCATE, 73 (24 November, 1971), 16.

A profile of the challenge mounted to the equal employment opportunity policy of the University of Oregon by local activists. The Seattle regional civil rights office of the Department of Health, Education and Welfare has been asked to reject the present policy because homosexuals are not covered.

482. "Minn. Court Rules Library May Deny Homosexual Post."
LIBRARY JOURNAL, 96 (December, 1971), 4046, 4048.

A detailed account of the reaction within the American
library community to the refusal of the University of
Minnesota to hire a qualified candidate because he was
homosexual. Protests took the form of requesting
censure of the university and charges that the Intel-
lectual Freedom Committee of the American Library
Association had deliberately delayed ruling on the
matter.

483. "Agencies at Odds Over Fired Clerk." THE ADVOCATE, 74 (8
December, 1971), 4.

The Civil Service Commission has requested the resignation of a staff member of the National Bureau of
Standards whose homosexuality is a matter of public
record. The Bureau, however, has stated its satisfac-
tion with the employee's work record and wishes to
retain him. A class-action suit is planned.

484. "Teachers Win Okay in Holland." THE ADVOCATE, 74 (8
December, 1971), 5.

Two leading Catholic education organizations of the
Netherlands have stated that "the rejection of a
teacher on grounds of homosexuality is not
permissible." The 1970 case which occasioned this
ruling is described and subsequent discussions
summarized.

485. "S.F. Job Law Prospects Brighten." THE ADVOCATE, 76 (5
January, 1972), 8.

A summary of the political conditions in the city of
San Francisco with regard to passage of a proposed
amendment to the city charter's anti-discrimination
clause extending protection to homosexuals. Details of
past debate on the issue are presented.

486. "Minnesota U. Senate Reviews McConnell Hearing Demand."
THE ADVOCATE, 76 (5 January, 1972), 14.

The University of Minnesota Senate has repeated a
demand that its Board of Regents reverse their decision

not to hire librarian Michael McConnell and have called for "an open hearing" with the Senate to settle questions relating to "personal characteristics irrelevant to the fundamental mission of the university."

487. "U.S. Bows, Restores Clearances." THE ADVOCATE, 78 (2 February, 1972), 1.

A description of the various legal efforts engaged in by the Defense Department in an effort to avoid restoring the security clearances of Otto Ulrich and Richard Gayer as mandated by court order. These included an attempted appeal to the Supreme Court. A September 13, 1971 decision by Judge John Pratt had indicated that a "nexus" had to be established between a person's private life and job performance before sexual preference could legitimately be used as grounds.

488. "ACLU Files Washington Job Suit." THE ADVOCATE, 78 (2 February, 1972), 2.

A brief overview of a case filed with U.S. District Court in Washington, D.C. by the American Civil Liberties Union. The class-action suit seeks a permanent injunction against the U.S. Civil Service Commission to halt "all investigation of the sexual activities of government employees or of those applying for government work." The background of the four plaintiffs is sketched.

489. "Lindsay Issues Anti-Bias Order." THE ADVOCATE, 80 (1 March, 1972), 1, 9.

News coverage of the executive order issued on February 8, 1972 by Mayor John Lindsay of New York City directing that "private sexual orientation" may not be considered in city employment procedures. The effect of this order on attempts to pass a pending gay civil rights bill for the city is explored.

490. "ACLU Takes McConnell Case to Top Court." THE ADVOCATE, 80 (1 March, 1972), 13.

A petition for a writ of certiorari has been filed with the U.S. Supreme Court by the Minnesota and American Civil Liberties Union in the case of Michael

McConnell's job discrimination suit against the University of Minnesota. An October 18, 1971 decision by a St. Louis appellate court is challenged as being at variance with prior federal decisions affecting employment of homosexuals.

491. "Mayors Reject Hiring Gays." THE ADVOCATE, 81 (15 March, 1972), 16.

The responses of the mayors of the Rhode Island cities of Providence, Cranson and Warwick to New York Mayor John Lindsay's executive order forbidding use of sexual orientation as a factor in city hiring is sketched. All three condemned the idea of having "diseased individuals" working for local government. Activist reaction is noted.

492. "Top Court Rejects McConnell Case." THE ADVOCATE, 84 (26 April, 1972), 1, 19.

On April 3, 1972, the U.S. Supreme Court refused to consider an appeal of a St. Louis court decision supporting the University of Minnesota refusal to hire gay librarian Michael McConnell. Details of the case are presented.

493. "Ooops, East Lansing First with Hiring Law." THE ADVOCATE, 85 (10 May, 1972), 1, 4.

On March 7, 1972, the city council of East Lansing, Michigan passed an amendment to the city's personnel rules banning "discrimination in hiring on account of homosexuality." The history of the amendment, the first by an American city in this area, is discussed in detail.

494. "The McConnell Decision." NEW REPUBLIC, 166 (13 May, 1972), 9-10.

A concise summary of the legal history of the employment discrimination suit filed by Michael McConnell against the University of Minnesota Board of Regents. Opinions given at various steps in the adjudication process are quoted.

495. "S.F. Hiring Law Goes Into Effect." THE ADVOCATE, 86 (24 May, 1972), 3.

A discussion of the April 27, 1972 amendment to the San Francisco civil rights ordinance barring firms doing business with the city or county from discriminating against homosexuals in hiring policies. The bill was signed by Mayor Joseph Alioto on April 21.

496. "Restore Wentworth Clearances, Says Judge." THE ADVOCATE, 88 (21 June, 1972), 1.

A summary of the May 26, 1972 decision of the Washington, D.C. District Court in the security clearance case of Benning Wentworth, a civilian employee of the Defense Department. Judge John Pratt ruled that being a "practicing homosexual" is not sufficient grounds for denial of clearance and that Defense Department policy in the area precluded plaintiffs from receiving "a fair and impartial hearing."

497. "Fired Because of Rumor, Rural Teacher Fights Back." THE ADVOCATE, 88 (21 June, 1972), 1.

A profile of the case of Peggy Burton, a schoolteacher in Salem, Oregon dismissed from her position due to a "rumor" that she was homosexual. Ms. Burton has retained counsel, as present Oregon consensual sex legislation has removed all criminal sanctions against homosexuality except in cases of rape.

498. "D.C. School Board Bans Gays, Bias." THE ADVOCATE, 88 (21 June, 1972), 3, 11.

Commentary upon the text of a resolution passed May 23, 1972 by the District of Columbia Board of Education banning "discrimination in employment on the grounds of sexual orientation." The full text of the resolution is included. Said measure is believed to be the first in the United States.

499. "PT & T Eyes Hiring Policy." THE ADVOCATE, 89 (5 July, 1972), 13.

Pacific Telephone Company, which supplies communications services to the city of San Francisco, is reviewing its legal position on hiring homosexuals. Prior policy of refusing to do so is discussed in light of recent changes in the city civil rights policy.

500. "Ma Bell Will Ignore S.F.'s Gay Ordinance." THE ADVOCATE, 90 (19 July, 1972), 4.

The text of a letter to The ADVOCATE from the vice president in charge of personnel of the Pacific Telephone and Telegraph Company indicating that the recent civil rights legislation adopted by the San Francisco government would not affect the firm's refusal to hire homosexual persons. The history of the dispute is briefly summarized.

501. "Teacher Sick? Or Board?" THE ADVOCATE, 92 (16 August, 1972), 15.

Excerpts from an editorial run by the Bergen Record newspaper of northern New Jersey attacking the Paramus school board over the case of John Gish. Gish had been ordered to submit to a psychiatric examination following public statements supporting the civil rights of homosexuals.

502. "'We Don't Ask,' Bell System Claims." THE ADVOCATE, 93 (30 August, 1972), 4.

An article discussing the hiring policies of the American Telephone and Telegraph Company and its constituent corporations with specific reference to the treatment of minorities. Recent queries on the employment of homosexuals are placed in context.

503. "Bay Area Firms Sign Hiring Pledges." THE ADVOCATE, 93 (30 August, 1972), 4.

Discussion of recent action by twenty-seven firms doing business with the combined city-county government of San Francisco on affirmative action agreements barring discrimination for "sexual orientation." The history of the agreements is outlined and participating firms listed.

504. "Teaching Ticket Held off for Penn State Gay Grad." THE ADVOCATE, 93 (30 August, 1972), 14.

> A summary of events in the case of Joseph Acanfora, a graduate of Pennsylvania State University whose state teaching certification is being delayed pending a decision on his gay activist involvement.

505. "Gay Wins Credentials to Teach." THE ADVOCATE, 96 (11 October, 1972), 1.

> Certification to teach earth and space science in the schools of Pennsylvania was awarded to Joseph Acanfora on September 15, 1972 by State Secretary of Education John Pettenger. At issue was Acanfora's involvement with a gay rights group at the Pennsylvania State University. Debate on the question is summarized in detail.

506. "Gay Teacher Wins Fight Against Mental Exam." THE ADVOCATE, 96 (11 October, 1972), 17.

> On September 8, 1972, the New Jersey Superior Court issued a temporary injunction against the Paramus school board's effort to force teacher John Gish to undergo psychiatric examination due to his homosexuality. Gish has been removed from classroom teaching and denied campus privileges.

507. "Damage Payment Offered Fired Teacher in Oregon." THE ADVOCATE, 96 (11 October, 1972), 18.

> Legal counsel for the Cascade Union High School has been authorized to offer dismissed lesbian teacher Peggy Burton a cash settlement. Said offer was suggested by Judge Robert Belloni who dismissed the grounds for Burton's initial firing but declined to order her reinstatement. Burton's lawyers have rejected the monetary settlement and continue to request "judicial determination" of the legality of her firing.

508. "Joe's War Starts Over." THE ADVOCATE, 97 (25 October, 1972), 2.

A news article on the transferral of earth science teacher Joseph Acanfora from classroom teaching to administrative work following publication of the story of his dispute with Pennsylvania State University over his certification in the New York Times. Local education groups in Montgomery County, Maryland have opposed the suspension and are exploring legal action.

509. "New Security Clearance Fight Erupts." THE ADVOCATE, 97 (24 October, 1972), 5.

A lengthy news article covering the case of Allan L. Rock, a civilian electronics engineer employed by the Department of Defense, presently facing revocation of his security clearances due to his homosexuality. Details of a September 21 hearing in San Francisco comprise the bulk of the article.

510. "U.S. Agency Backs Down on Firing." THE ADVOCATE, 98 (8 November, 1972), 3.

A profile of the dispute between the Civil Service Commission and the Government Printing Office over the attempted dismissal of computer programmer George Strasser. The latter agency appealed the CSC recommendation that Strasser be dismissed as his homosexual activities "would not promote the efficiency" of the agency. The request was withdrawn.

511. "Acanfora Files Suit Over Job." THE ADVOCATE, 99 (22 November, 1972), 2, 13.

Notice of the suit filed in federal district court in Baltimore by science teacher Joseph Acanfora over his suspension from his junior high classroom following publicity relating to his certification dispute with the state of Pennsylvania involving gay activism.

512. "I Loved You Then, I Love You Now." THE ADVOCATE, 99 (22 November, 1972), 13.

A summary of a television interview with Joseph Acanfora taped for distribution as part of a series on public television station WNET in New York. Entitled "How Do Your Children Grow?", the series segment pre-

sented familial reactions to Acanfora's employment
suits in Pennsylvania and Maryland.

513. "New Jersey Teacher Goes on Hunger Strike." THE ADVOCATE,
100 (6 December, 1972), 2.

On October 31, 1972, Paramus high school teacher John
Gish began a "modified" hunger strike in protest over
his exclusion from the school cafeteria under instructions barring him from access to the campus. Details
of the legal dispute over an ordered psychiatric examination are included.

514. "Illinois Gays Appeal to New Governor." THE ADVOCATE, 101
(20 December, 1972), 21.

In a meeting of nine gay organizations held at Northern
Illinois University in DeKalb on November 17-19, 1972,
a coalition for legislative action was formed. Its
first act was the drafting of a letter to Governor
Daniel Walker requesting an executive order barring
employment discrimination against homosexuals by state
agencies.

515. Chaitin, Ellen and V. Roy Lefcourt. "Is Gay Suspect?"
LINCOLN LAW REVIEW, 8 (1973), 24-54.

The authors of this analysis "show how the psychological approaches to homosexuality taken by the different
schools of psychology can be utilized for purposes of
legal argument . . . generalizations about the psychological make-up of homosexuals are as flimsy and inadequate as the generalizations about their physical
characteristics" (p. 33). Attention is then given to
the legal definition of a suspect class using the
example of race discrimination. Characteristics used
in this category are presented as preliminary argument
for similarly defining homosexuals as a suspect class
entitled to legal protections. Five characteristics
are noted: victims of historical discrimination,
victims of stereotyping, group internalization, group
culpability and exclusion from the political process.
Homosexuality as a mutable or immutable quality is
likewise examined and the various implications for
legal discrimination set forth. Chaitin and Lefcourt
conclude that homosexuals do indeed constitute "a
clearly defined politically important minority" (p. 54)

which is subject to laws rendering a moral judgment rather than a legal one. Extant laws are seen to be in need of re-examination.

516. Johanns, Michael. "Constitutional Law--Freedom of Speech --Maryland Federal District Court Upholds Transfer and Dismissal of Teacher Because of 'Repeated' and 'Unnecessary' Public Appearances Made to Explain His Plight As a Homosexual Teacher--Acanfora vs. Board of Education, 359 F Supp. 843 (D. Md. 1973).

An analysis of the case of *Joseph Acanfora vs. the Montgomery County (Maryland) Board of Education* with specific reference to the constitutional issues involved. While the district court decided that the plaintiff "had a constitutional right to be a homosexual" (p. 95) without declaring such right a suspect classification under the equal protection clause of the fourteenth amendment, its attention focused on Acanfora's four appearances in the media. These interviews were regarded as violating "a sense of discretion and self-restraint . . . to avoid speech or activity likely to spark added public controversy which detracts from the educational process" (p. 95). Johanns criticizes the approach taken by the district court to the question of Acanfora's first amendment rights and "whether likelihood of imminent turbulence" is sufficient to curb these rights. Under the precedent set forth in the 1966 case of *Burnside vs. Byars*, the Supreme Court held that school districts must demonstrate that conduct would materially disrupt institutional functioning. The school system avoided dealing with the issue of first amendment limitation by not examining the relationship between Acanfora's homosexuality and system function, and by limiting the plaintiff to appearances which filled its own nebulous idea of "reasonable self-defense." Such an approach prevented it from reaching the constitutional issues involved. Johanns notes that "the real impact of extending constitutional protection to sexual preference is that the state or school system may bear a substantially greater burden of proof" (p. 103).

517. "Ma Bell Clings to Anti-Gay Policy in Liberated S.F." THE ADVOCATE, 102 (3 January, 1973), 6.

A news article discussing the latest challenge to the anti-gay hiring policies of Pacific Telephone. The city attorney's office issued a ruling that "the telephone company can discriminate against homosexuals in employment because it is a monopoly and is a unique contractor within the city."

518. "ACLU Fights Firing." THE ADVOCATE, 104 (31 January, 1973), 16.

A summary of a brief filed by the Wisconsin Civil Liberties Union Foundation on behalf of a houseparent at Southern Wisconsin Colony and Training School. State officials had stated at a personnel hearing that "the fact that the man was a homosexual was grounds for dismissal." The position is being challenged as a violation of due process.

519. "Gay Lawyer's Disbarment Kept in Force." THE ADVOCATE, 104 (31 January, 1973), 17.

On January 9, 1973, the appellate division of the New York Supreme Court rejected an argument by lawyer Harris Kimball that his 1958 disbarment for homosexuality should be vitiated due to changed social conditions. Further challenge to the decision is planned.

520. Graham, Kathleen M. "Security Clearances for Homosexuals." STANFORD LAW REVIEW, 25 (February, 1973), 403-429.

A detailed description of the bureaucratic structure and procedures created by the federal government for the awarding of security clearances. Instructions for applicants who have been denied or have had their status revoked are also included. Sections of the directive issued by the Department of Defense listing five criteria commonly invoked in clearance cases involving homosexual individuals indicate that "while the sexual perversion criterion is always applied to homosexual conduct, it is generally not the only reason cited" (p. 409). Three principal justifications are advanced by administrators in such cases: blackmail, criminal conduct and psychopathic or unstable personalities. Each of these assumptions is examined on a factual basis and severely criticized as lacking. Changes in public attitudes and increasing openness on the part of homosexual individuals have vitiated the blackmail issue. As regards the second and third assumptions, Graham notes that "the government has not argued that conviction for these crimes is a bar to security clearance, but rather that the very existence of laws against homosexuality should preclude homosexuals from confidential jobs . . . In effect, spokesmen for the government appear to believe quite seriously that individuals who deviate from the norm in their sexual preferences are emotionally unstable and dangerously psychopathic" (pp. 413-414). Legal theories which had been applied to the problem up to 1973 are then evaluated, with the desired goal of utilizing available information on homosexuality to bring federal procedures into line. Issues raised in these theories are the right to privacy, compelling state interest, conditional privilege, equal protection, substantive and procedural due process. Summaries of individual cases which have raised these points indicate to Graham that "recalcitrance in complying with the present court orders demonstrates that greater judicial pressure on the Department of Defense is necessary to secure equitable treatment for homosexuals" (p. 429).

521. "Wall Street Journal Says Yea, Nay on Gay Lawyer." THE ADVOCATE, 105 (14 February, 1973), 15.

Commentary on an editorial on the disbarment case of Harris Kimball which appeared in the January 19, 1973 issue of *The Wall Street Journal* outlining the issues raised by the case.

522. "U.S. Judge Says Teacher's Firing Unconstitutional." THE ADVOCATE, 106 (28 February, 1973), 3.

A profile of the decision rendered January 18, 1973 in the case of *Burton vs. Cascade School District* which awarded the plaintiff all remaining salary plus costs but did not reinstate her as a teacher. The Oregon statute used in the case was condemned as "unconstitutionally vague."

523. "Library Group May Still Condemn Gay's Firing." THE ADVOCATE, 106 (28 February, 1973), 7.

A report on the challenge and rejection of a committee recommendation to the American Library Association that a request for censure of the University of Minnesota libraries for refusal to hire Michael McConnell be dismissed.

524. Bell, Arthur. "Despite Liberal Attitudes in Show Biz, Few Admit Being Gay." THE ADVOCATE, 106 (28 February, 1973), 32-34.

A reprint of an article originally published in *Playbill* magazine on the status of gay persons in the entertainment industry. Interviews with Joanna Merlin, Mary Crowley, Milton Berle, Lillian Roth, Lotte Lenya, Ben Vereen and Tennessee Williams comprise the text.

525. "Anti-Gay Teaching Law Upheld." THE ADVOCATE, 107 (14 March, 1973), 18.

A reprint of the decision by a California state appellate court that a law permitting suspension of teaching credentials following conviction for a sex offense is valid. Recent debate on the issues raised by the case of a San Francisco teacher is summarized.

526. "N.Y. Faculty Supports Gays." THE ADVOCATE, 108 (28 March, 1973), 7.

A note of two resolutions passed by the faculty senate of the State University of New York at Buffalo supporting civil rights for homosexuals in the hiring process and tenure considerations.

527. "Honeywell Faces Bias Charge at Minnesota U." THE ADVOCATE, 110 (25 April, 1973), 8.

A complaint filed by a graduate student at the University of Minnesota protesting the anti-gay employment policies of Honeywell, Inc. is profiled. Said complaint was framed under a 1971 university policy barring from placement facilities employers who discriminate among applicants on bases other than job aptitude, grades, experience or formal education.

528. "Lawmaker Rails at Gay Profs." THE ADVOCATE, 110 (25 April, 1973), 16.

A summary of the efforts of state representative James Lemon calling for an investigation of homosexual faculty at the University of Missouri-Columbia. Excerpts from a local editorial which began the controversy were termed "an insult to this institution" by university officials.

529. "Gay Teacher Called Good for Students." THE ADVOCATE, 111 (9 May, 1973), 5.

Detailed coverage of testimony offered during four days of hearings at U.S. District Court in Montgomery County, Maryland on the suit brought by gay teacher Joseph Acanfora for reinstatement as an earth science instructor. Background on the case is provided.

530. "Social Workers Face Issue of Whether Gay Is Okay." THE ADVOCATE, 111 (9 May, 1973), 10.

A note on a draft policy on homosexuality scheduled for debate at the May 9, 1973 convention of the National Association of Social Workers. The text calls upon delegates to support consensual sex legislation and oppose employment discrimination based on sexual orientation.

531. "Madison GLF Entering Wisconsin Employee's Case." THE ADVOCATE, 111 (9 May, 1973), 23.

The details of an amicus curiae brief filed by the Madison Gay Liberation Front in the case of a house-parent at a state training school dismissed on grounds of homosexuality are reviewed.

532. "Illinois Gays Press Governor." THE ADVOCATE, 112 (23 May, 1973), 12.

A profile of the efforts of the Illinois Gays for Legislative Action organization to force Governor Daniel Walker to make good on a campaign promise to issue an executive order barring discrimination against homosexuals. Walker has evaded the issue through repeated references to the state constitution which contains no sexual orientation provisions.

533. "Acanfora Loses: Judge Says He Talked Too Much." THE ADVOCATE, 115 (4 July, 1973), 5.

A report on the denial of the request for an injunction against the Montgomery County, Maryland school system by Joseph Acanfora. Judge Joseph Young indicated that publicity attending the case generated by the plaintiff via statements and a television appearance had exceeded "the bounds of reasonable self-defense." Acanfora's transfer out of the classroom was supported and possible "deleterious" impact upon students explored.

534. DuBay, William. "Seattle Mayor Admits Prejudice." THE ADVOCATE, 115 (4 July, 1973), 19.

In an interview with leaders of Seattle's gay and lesbian community, Mayor Wes Uhlman stated his support for a policy of discrimination against hiring homosexuals for the police force and fire department "because they would be subject to blackmail." Discussions with Rev. Robert Serico of the local M.C.C. congregation are summarized and demands for inclusion of "sexual orientation" in the Seattle executive order outlawing discrimination in city hiring are outlined.

535. "National Teacher's Group Kills Gay Rights Resolution." THE ADVOCATE, 117 (1 August, 1973), 14.

The annual convention of the National Education Association meeting in Portland voted down a gay civil rights resolution. If adopted, the measure would have placed the organization "on record as opposing discrimination against gay teachers." The history of the proposal and reception of gay issues at the conference are outlined.

536. "Court Says Gay Lawyer Can Be Fit." THE ADVOCATE, 118 (15 August, 1973), 2, 14.

A report on the decision of the New York State Court of Appeals in the disbarment case of Harris Kimball requiring a lower court to reconsider his application for readmission to the bar. Kimball had been disbarred in 1957 for having committed sodomy. The 1973 decision ruled that "a . . . lawyer cannot be barred from practice solely on the basis of being homosexual."

537. "Gish Still Fighting Psychiatric Test." THE ADVOCATE, 118 (15 August, 1973), 16.

A profile of the efforts made since June, 1972 by New Jersey English teacher John Gish to fight a psychiatric examination ordered by the Paramus school board on the basis of his homosexuality. Measures include a lengthy series of appeals and counsel from the ACLU.

538. "Canada Gays Protest Admitted Bias Policy." THE ADVOCATE, 119 (29 August, 1973), 9.

During a conference in the Canadian House of Commons on security on July 11, 1973, Prime Minister Pierre Trudeau admitted that "suspected homosexuality, emotional instability and sexual abnormality" are used by his government in granting individual security clearances. Reaction from the gay community to these statements is reviewed.

539. "Battle of Ma Bell Spreads to Minneapolis." THE ADVOCATE, 119 (29 August, 1973), 14.

A summary of the protests and debate occasioned in the Twin Cities area by the statement of Northwestern Bell Telephone Company that it will not hire "admitted homosexuals" out of concern for its public image and community standing. Local criticism is reviewed.

540. "New Seattle Law Protects Gay Jobs." THE ADVOCATE, 122 (10 October, 1973), 1, 17.

A news report on the signing by Seattle Mayor Wes Uhlman of an ordinance prohibiting employment discrimination on the basis of several factors, among them age, sex and sexual orientation. The measure was sponsored by the city Human Rights Commission, the Women's Commission and the Seattle Division on Aging.

541. "ACLU Suit Will Challenge Northwestern Bell Hiring Ban." THE ADVOCATE, 122 (10 October, 1973), 12.

The Minnesota local chapter of the American Civil Liberties Union announced a forthcoming suit against the American Telephone and Telegraph Company "to force it to end its policy of never hiring gay people." The

Minneapolis case of Byron Schmitz is reviewed and legal precedents examined.

542. "Big Jersey Daily Scores Firing of Gay Teacher." THE ADVOCATE, 123 (24 October, 1973), 12.

A review of a stinging editorial supporting suspended gay teacher John Gish published September 24, 1973 in the Hackensack, New Jersey *Record*. The actions of the Paramus school board towards Gish were severely condemned and the argument that "adolescents can be recruited to homosexuality" decried for lack of evidence. The state of the Gish case at that time is also reviewed.

543. "Toronto Bans Anti-Gay Bias in City Jobs." THE ADVOCATE, 125 (21 November, 1973), 3.

Following six months of lobbying by the Gay Alliance Toward Equality, the city council of Toronto adopted a resolution on October 19, 1973 directing that "city employees are to be in no way discriminated against with regards to hiring, assignments, promotions or dismissals because of sexual orientation." Background on the measure is provided.

544. "Portlanders Will Vote on Employment Rights." THE ADVOCATE, 125 (21 November, 1973), 13.

A statement barring discrimination on the basis of "sexual identity" has been included in a new city-county charter which will be presented to the electorate of Portland, Oregon and Multnomah County in the May, 1974 primary election. The history of local activist efforts to have the provision included are described.

545. "Federal Judge Orders U.S. to End Hiring Ban." THE ADVOCATE, 126 (5 December, 1973), 3, 7.

Ruling in the case of Donald Hickerson, a Department of Agriculture gay employee fired in 1971, Judge Alphonse Zerpali of San Francisco stated that no attempt had been made to satisfy the "nexus" requirement established in the 1969 decision of *Norton vs. Macy*. Possible impact of the reinstatement order on other pending cases is explored through interview with Washington activist Dr. Frank Kameny.

546. "Berkeley Votes Gay Job Rights." THE ADVOCATE, 126 (5 December, 1973), 15.

By unanimous vote, the Berkeley, California city council passed an expanded version of a 1972 ordinance barring consideration of sexual preference in hiring.

547. "Holding Court." THE ADVOCATE, 126 (5 December, 1973), 29.

An edition of a regular legal affairs review column discussing the case of Joseph Acanfora and its implications for the right of free speech and employment discrimination in the education professions.

548. Aiken, David L. "Limit Upheld on Pentagon Sex Quizzes." THE ADVOCATE, 127 (19 December, 1973), 1, 17.

On November 16, 1973, a three-judge panel of a federal appeals court ruled that the Defense Department had "improperly denied" security clearances to Benning Wentworth, Otto Ulrich and Richard Gayer. All plaintiffs had previously won reinstatement decisions from U.S. District Court in Washington, D.C. which were then appealed. The decision permitted further investigations but prohibited questions "intrusive of the applicant's privacy."

549. "U.S. Asks Job Rules Keyed to Performance." THE ADVOCATE, 128 (2 January, 1974), 1.

A lengthy analysis of nine proposed criteria published in the December 3, 1973 issue of the Federal Register by the U.S. Civil Service Commission. Said criteria delineate the factors to be considered in determining a connection between applicants' or employees' homosexuality and federal employment responsibilities. The move was taken following court decisions declaring the prior blanket ban on gay hiring as unconstitutional. Washington activist Dr. Franklin Kameny is interviewed for opinion on the guidelines. A bulletin to heads of federal agencies listing cases where the Civil Service

Commission sees gay persons as continuing liabilities is extensively quoted.

550. "Fired Gay Supervisor of Retarded Boys Appeals to Supreme Court in Wisconsin." THE ADVOCATE, 128 (2 January, 1974), 19.

A news article summarizing events in the case of Paul Safransky, dismissed from a counseling post at a Wisconsin state home for the mentally retarded near Milwaukee in June, 1972 for blatant homosexual discussions. The legal history of the matter is profiled.

551. "Librarians Abandon McConnell." THE ADVOCATE, 129 (16 January, 1974), 17.

A report on the decision by the executive board of the American Library Association to take no action in J. Michael McConnell's dispute with the University of Minnesota libraries. The history of the professional society's efforts to avoid becoming involved in the employment discrimination case are summarized.

552. "Feds Must Grant Hearings on Security." THE ADVOCATE, 132 (27 February, 1974), 5.

A summary of the case of Otis Tabler, a mathematician denied security clearance by the Defense Department's Industrial Security Clearance Review office "on grounds of . . . homosexuality." A subsequent lawsuit filed on Tabler's behalf cited *Fitzgerald vs. Schlesinger*, a case wherein an applicant for similar clearance was accorded the right to a public hearing. Regulations on the issue were changed, effective January, 1974, "allowing open hearings if the clearance-applicant specifically requests them." Counsel David Isbell of the Washington ACLU is interviewed on the benefits of the change.

553. "Columbus Job Rights Measure Dies." THE ADVOCATE, 132 (27 February, 1974), 12.

A proposed revision of the city code of Columbus, Ohio intended to align the document with state law on homosexuality through granting job rights to gay persons was vetoed by both Mayor Tom Moody and the city council. Separate clauses providing protection in housing and public accommodations were adopted.

554. "Gay Teacher Sues for Damages, Claims Bias in Contract." THE ADVOCATE, 132 (27 February, 1974), 16.

A psychology instructor at Ames College in Greeley, Colorado has filed suit against the institution seeking reinstatement, wages and punitive damages. At issue is her dismissal following an invitation to members of the Denver Lesbian Center to address her class and subsequent discussion with the students. The suit claims denial of due process and accusations against the plaintiff's moral character. The involved, Susan Brown, is heterosexual.

555. "Out of the Closet, Fighting for Rights." THE ADVOCATE, 133 (13 March, 1974), 21.

A discussion of the case of California deputy state attorney general Glenn Taylor, dismissed on August 2, 1973 following investigation of a 1972 arrest in a raid on a Los Angeles bar. Arguments planned for use in Taylor's planned legal action are reviewed.

556. "Berkeley Aids Gays." THE ADVOCATE, 133 (13 March, 1974), 25.

A note on the passage of an ordinance in Berkeley, California by the city council permitting the city to refuse business to firms which "practice anti-gay employment bias."

557. "Gay Job Rights Backing Prompts Recall Attempt." THE ADVOCATE, 134 (27 March, 1974), 3.

News coverage of the controversy in Boulder, Colorado over a proposed gay employment rights ordinance. Opponents have mounted petition drives calling for a special referendum on the bill and the recall of the mayor and four council members who approved the initial reading.

558. "Tell of Job Losses in Massachusetts." THE ADVOCATE, 134 (27 March, 1974), 9.

A lengthy review of testimony on anti-gay discrimination in employment in the state of Massachusetts by
both public corporations and state agencies presented
to the state house Committee on Commerce and Labor in
hearings on bills H-2524 and H-2525. These latter
would prohibit such discrimination and extend protection to public accommodations as well.

559. "A Quiet Win: Honeywell Yields." THE ADVOCATE, 135 (10
      April, 1974), 13.

      A report on the announcement by Honeywell, Inc. that it
      "will no longer refuse to employ people because they
      are gay." A prior controversy over public statements
      supporting discrimination by the corporate vice presi-
      dent for employee relations were altered upon his
      retirement.

560. "Licensing Board May Ban Bias." THE ADVOCATE, 135 (10
      April, 1974), 14.

      A review of testimony given to the New York City Board
      of Examiners on the situation of homosexual teachers in
      the public schools and the need for "a clear,
      publicized statement" prohibiting such discrimination.

561. "Reverse State Bias, But Locals Stubborn." THE ADVOCATE,
      135 (10 April, 1974), 26.

      A report on a questionnaire distributed to local school
      systems throughout Denmark requesting information on
      their position on hiring openly gay teachers. Only
      forty responses were received, most stating a position
      based on professional credentials. Prior warnings by
      education minister Helveg Petersen that homosexuals
      should not seek "employment as teachers in Denmark" are
      clarified and placed in context.

562. "Acanfora Case Prepared for Supreme Court Appeal." THE
      ADVOCATE, 136 (24 April, 1974), 8.

      The National Education Association announced that it
      will pay the appeal costs for the presentation of the
      case of Joseph Acanfora to the U.S. Supreme Court. The
      legal history of the employment discrimination dispute

is reviewed. A request for certiorari will address both the validity of prior Supreme Court decisions used as bases for appellate decisions and the accuracy of lower courts in the use of said decisions.

563. "New Push for Illinois Job Rights." THE ADVOCATE, 137 (8 May, 1974), 8.

A summary of depositions made to the Illinois Fair Employment Practices Commission by members of state gay organizations in support of "correcting and prohibiting all job discrimination based on sexual orientation." Unsuccessful efforts in this area since the 1972 election of Gov. Daniel Walker are discussed.

564. "Ma Bell Will Switch, Not Fight Law." THE ADVOCATE, 137 (8 May, 1974), 12.

A report on the decision by Northwestern Bell Telephone Company to discard its policy of discrimination against gay persons in hiring. Said decision followed by three days the enactment by the Minneapolis city council on March 29, 1974 of an amendment to the city civil rights ordinance protecting gay people in housing, public accommodations and union membership as well as jobs. Pending legal action by the local ACLU chapter will continue.

565. Sasha, Gregory-Lewis. "Fired Teacher Rejects Settlement." THE ADVOCATE, 138 (22 May, 1974), 13.

An interview with Peggy Burton, discussing her dismissal from Cascade High School in Oregon on the basis of lesbianism and ensuing legal action.

566. Mendenhall, George. "Gay Nurses Set Convention on Ear." THE ADVOCATE, 142 (17 July, 1974), 11.

A report on the response to workshop and teaching activities sponsored by the Gay Nurses Alliance at the American Nurses Association 1973 annual conference in San Francisco. While official recognition was withheld, informal sessions were overcrowded for discussions on both fears for employment and quality of patient care given to gay persons.

567. "Cincinnati U. President Declares Sex Bias Ban." THE
ADVOCATE, 142 (17 July, 1974), 16.

On June 3, 1974, President Warren Bennis of the University of Cincinnati issued an executive order barring
the use of sexual orientation as a basis for discrimination in any university activity "including employment." The action was taken consequent to letters
received by Bennis documenting past abuses in this area
at the university, such as a 1964 panel created for the
purpose of "ferreting out homosexual faculty and
students."

568. "Defense Engineer Gets Job, Top Secret Clearance Back."
THE ADVOCATE, 142 (17 July, 1974), 19.

A note on a June 27, 1974 ruling by a federal district
judge in San Francisco restoring the security clearance
of Allan Rock following some two years of litigation.
Case history details are summarized.

569. "Honored Director Imprisoned." THE ADVOCATE, 142 (17
July, 1974), 20.

Following a trial in the city of Kiev, Soviet film
director Sergei Paradjanov was sentenced to a prison
labor camp for six years on charges of homosexuality
and "incitement to suicide." Background on
Paradjanov's film career and the circumstances of his
December, 1973 arrest are included.

570. "Seek Job Rights in Supreme Court." THE ADVOCATE, 143 (31
July, 1974), 23.

A news report covering the details of the appeal filed
with the U.S. Supreme Court in the employment discrimination case of teacher Joseph Acanfora. The petition
argues that permitting lower court denials of the
plaintiff's rights "would serve as an inhibiting discriminatory precedent against all homosexuals, preventing them from living open, productive and healthy lives
without fear of economic reprisals or financial
insecurity."

571. "Amnesty Group Looks Into Filmmaker's Plight." THE
ADVOCATE, 144 (14 August, 1974), 13.

An account of the current investigation into the case of Sergei Paradjanov being conducted by Amnesty International. If sufficient evidence is found, the imprisoned director will be adopted by the agency. The absence of media coverage of Paradjanov's treatment on charges including homosexuality in America is noted and decried.

572. "Librarians Finally Vote Probe of Job Bias." THE ADVOCATE, 144 (14 August, 1974), 16.

At the 1974 American Library Association convention in New York, a resolution was passed by the body's governing council repudiating an earlier recommendation of the Staff Committee on Mediation that no mediation was possible to assist J. M. McConnell. Citing the association's policy on equal opportunity employment, the council ordered "an immediate formal inquiry" into the 1972 case.

573. "Defense of Clearance Bias Pales Under Public Scrutiny." THE ADVOCATE, 145 (28 August, 1974), 1, 6.

A report on the public hearing held in Los Angeles into the revocation security clearance to Otis Tabler, a computer scientist working as a consultant to the Air Force, on grounds of susceptibility to blackmail due to his homosexuality. Detailed statements from both prosecution and defense witnesses are included.

574. "Northwestern Settles Pay Bias." THE ADVOCATE, 145 (28 August, 1974), 2.

Details of the August 2, 1974 settlement made in the case of *Byron Schmitz vs. Northwestern Bell Telephone*. The recent reversal of the firm's employment policy as regarded homosexuals is placed in context within changes in the communications industry.

575. "As Ma Bell Decrees . . . No More." THE ADVOCATE, 145 (28 August, 1974), 2.

A report of a statement in a recent issue of the AT&T News that personal information on sexual preference should not be requested of job applicants, as "an individual's sexual preference isn't a criterion either for becoming . . . or remaining an employee of the Bell System." The significance of the action for other large industries is noted.

576. "News & Views." COMMONWEAL, 101 (11 October, 1974), 26.

A news article on the dismissal of columnist Brian McNaught from his post as writer and reporter for *The Michigan Catholic* newspaper. The relationship of McNaught's activist work for gay liberation to the reshuffling is explored in a commentary by editor Margaret Cronyn.

577. "Catholic Newspaper Fires Brian McNaught Two Days After His Protest Fast Is Ended." THE ADVOCATE, 150 (6 November, 1974), 15.

A review of the dismissal on October 4, 1974 of activist columnist Brian McNaught from his position at *The Michigan Catholic* diocesan newspaper. Several of his recent actions, including a sixteen-day fast and an address to the Catholic Press Association are profiled. The Detroit Newspaper Guild has filed a grievance action in the matter.

578. "Gay Cops?: Los Angeles Board Balks at Lie Detector Test Intended to Screen Out Homosexual Recruit." THE ADVOCATE, 150 (6 November, 1974), 20.

A summary of events and arguments presented at an October 11, 1974 hearing before the Los Angeles Civil Service Commission on proposed disqualification standards for police recruits. Among the fourteen areas marking a candidate as unsuitable was "homosexual tendencies." Debate was deferred to November 1, 1974 pending a ruling by the city attorney's office on the constitutionality of this and other provisions of the standards.

579. "N.Y. Lawyer Striking Back at Old Florida Disbarment." THE ADVOCATE, 151 (20 November, 1974), 6.

Notice of the suit filed by attorney Harris Kimball in Southern District Court in Ft. Lauderdale challenging codes governing admittance to the Florida bar. Said codes, involving the "good moral conduct" of applicants, were used in 1955 to deny Kimball a certification. The suit claims the codes and related statutes violate rights to privacy and due process and are "unconstitutionally vague."

580. "'Sex Preference' Bias Ends at Two Major Newspapers." THE ADVOCATE, 151 (20 November, 1974), 16.

A news note on the inclusion of an anti-bias clause forbidding discrimination on the basis of sexual preference in an agreement between the American Newspaper Guild and two major Philadelphia newspapers.

581. "Court Refusal to Hear Acanfora May Be Hidden Victory." THE ADVOCATE, 151 (20 November, 1974), 20.

An analysis of the refusal by the U.S. Supreme Court to consider the appeal of Joseph Acanfora in his employment discrimination suit. This action is viewed as beneficial in that it upholds the decision by the Fourth Circuit Court of Appeals in Richmond "that homosexuality . . . was not a sufficient reason" for denial of employment.

582. "Educator's Future Unclear, NEA Says." THE ADVOCATE, 151 (20 November, 1974), 20.

An interview with Joseph Gewirtz, staff counsel for the National Education Association on the effects of the Joseph Acanfora case on the rights of gay teachers. Membership in homosexual organizations was seen as a liability on application forms. The original ruling that "a homosexual has the right to teach as long as he does not attract widespread publicity to his homosexuality" was not challenged by the Supreme Court and therefore remains valid precedent.

583. "Peggy Burton Ruling Upheld." THE ADVOCATE, 152 (4 December, 1974), 15.

A profile of the decision by a federal appeals court in San Francisco reaffirming a 1973 ruling declaring "teacher dismissal on the grounds of immorality" as unconstitutional. The decision to award lesbian teacher Peggy Burton back wages and costs was also supported. No ruling has yet been made on the rights of a non-tenured teacher to job protection.

584. Castillo, Kathy. "No Job Protection for Fired Analyst." THE ADVOCATE, 153 (18 December, 1974), 17.

A profile of the case of Vic Galotti, a credit analyst fired from his position at Motorola following his appearance in five television ads for the Gay People's Union at Stanford University. An investigation is being conducted by the San Francisco Human Rights Commission into the case.

585. Mendenhall, George. "Two Bay Area Cities Extend Equal Employment Rights to Gays." THE ADVOCATE, 153 (18 December, 1974), 17.

A summary of the effort by activist Arthur Carbin to extend employment codes to include sexual preference in the fifteen cities of Santa Clara County, California. Ordinances to this effect have been passed in Palo Alto and San Jose.

586. Reese, Susan Elizabeth. "The Forgotten Sex: Lesbians, Liberation and the Law." WILLAMETTE LAW JOURNAL, 11 (1974/1975), 354-377.

Noting that "a discussion of the law in relation to the lesbian is more accurately placed in the context of the legal treatment of women than in the context of the legal rights of male homosexuals" (p. 354), Reese examines the definition of a lesbian, both self-defined and in law. Attitudes towards lesbians in family law and employment cases heard up to 1975 are then presented with citations to relevant decisions. Problems of harassment, judicial mistreatment and confusion, and invisibility are noted, with opinion polls from southern California and Portland recording employer's attitudes. Reese concludes that legislation such as the failed Oregon House Bill 2637 (outlawing sexual orientation in public accommodations, housing and employment), while useful and necessary, must be accompanied by "a re-evaluation of social attitudes towards sexuality in general and toward women in particular" (p. 377).

587. "Gish Reinstated But Told to Take Psychiatric Exam." THE ADVOCATE, 154 (1 January, 1975), 9.

New Jersey State Education Commissioner Fred Burke has issued two decisions in the case of Paramus teacher John Gish. While requiring the local school system to reinstate Gish in his administrative post and pay withheld wages, Burke ordered the plaintiff to take a psychiatric examination in dispute since 1972. Gish had not reached a decision on the matter.

588. "Victory in Portland: Employment Bill Survives Barrage of Angry Opposition." THE ADVOCATE, 155 (15 January, 1975), 1.

A profile of debate and testimony in the city council of Portland, Oregon on a resolution authorizing the city's personnel department to investigate "all complaints of alleged violations on the basis of sexual orientation in all city employment." The resolution was subsequently passed, becoming the first item of gay rights legislation in the state.

589. "Gish Fights Back." THE ADVOCATE, 156 (29 January, 1975), 7.

Paramus, New Jersey teacher John Gish has appealed a recent ruling by the state education commissioner requiring him to submit to a psychiatric examination to determine his teaching fitness. The request is based upon the removal of homosexuality as a mental illness by the American Psychiatric Association and violations of his right to freedom of speech.

590. Buttry, Robert. "Gay Cops, Firemen? Of Course There Are." THE ADVOCATE, 156 (29 January, 1975), 8-9.

An interview with gay members of the New York City police and fire departments. Recruiting approaches and job related stresses are discussed.

591. "Employment Rights Roundup--Where We Are, Where We're Going." THE ADVOCATE, 156 (29 January, 1975), 9, 14.

A special report summarizing the state of change in gay employment rights legislation in city and county jurisdictions as it was in early 1975. Communities cited as examples include San Francisco, Seattle, Minneapolis and New York City. Both public debate and calm negotiation are seen as necessary.

592. "L.A. Police Department's Position on Gay People." THE ADVOCATE, 158 (26 February, 1975), 8.

Excerpts from a memorandum circulated unofficially within the Los Angeles Police Department in December, 1974 addressing a proposed ordinance barring discrimination in employment against homosexuals. Homosexuality is cited as being a mental "disturbance" and gay persons are seen as unfit to be police officers, as they "may turn against friends, family and even country."

593. "A Beginning of the End of Discrimination." THE ADVOCATE, 158 (26 February, 1975), 10.

A report on a letter issued January 24, 1975 by the personnel division of the New York City Board of Education to the Gay Teachers Association stating that "homosexuality is not a bar to entrance into teaching in New York City nor to the continuation of teaching in the city."

594. "Lobbying Against Employment Rights." THE ADVOCATE, 158 (26 February, 1975), 15.

A news note on the involvement of the Knights of Columbus in the New York area in opposition to Intro 554, a proposed employment rights bill prohibiting firings on the basis of sexual orientation. The bill is seen to permit the practice of "deviate and unnatural behavior in . . . educational employment and municipal structures of our city."

595. "Defense Department Official Says Yes on Security Clearance." THE ADVOCATE, 159 (12 March, 1975), 4.

An analysis of the December, 1974 decision by the Industrial Security Clearance Review Office to restore the clearance of Otis Tabler, a computer scientist denied the privilege in 1972 on the basis of homosexuality. A 1962 document stating that clearances

should not be granted to persons with "recent homosexual activities" recently uncovered is explored by
Dr. Franklin Kameny in reference to the security
clearance case of Allan Rock.

596. "Task Force Begins Discrimination Project." THE ADVOCATE,
159 (12 March, 1975), 5.

An announcement of a project by the National Gay Task
Force to survey the hiring and employment practices of
large publicly owned corporations. Contact information
is included.

597. "Employment, Housing: Connecticut." .THE ADVOCATE, 159
(12 March, 1975), 12.

A news note on efforts underway in Connecticut to add
the phrase "sexual orientation, marital status or lack
thereof" to extant civil rights legislation covering
employment, housing and public accommodations. Background on the state's political scene is given.

598. "Employment, Housing: Chicago." THE ADVOCATE, 159 (12
March, 1975), 12.

A review of the situation facing a reintroduction of
the 1973 gay civil rights ordinance to the Chicago City
Council during the 1975 council sessions. Endorsements
for the measure, which bars discrimination in housing
and employment, have been received from liberal alder-
men and the Association of Chicago Priests.

599. "The Official Fire Fighters Union Policy." THE ADVOCATE,
159 (12 March, 1975), 13.

The text of a resolution on "Homosexuals in the Fire
Service" approved in the summer of 1974 by the International Association of Fire Fighters. The document
calls upon all local unions to be aware of possible
legislation to permit homosexuals to work in the fire
services, where they "are excluded . . . with just
cause."

600. Convissar, Shelley Taylor. "The Concept of Attorney--Fitness in New York: New Perspectives." BUFFALO LAW REVIEW, 24 (Spring, 1975), 553-566.

A discussion of the facts of the cases *Florida Bar vs. Kimball* (1957) and *In re Kimball* (1971) within the context of New York state standards for determining the fitness to practice of a member of the bar. In 1957, Harris Kimball was expelled from the Florida bar following an inquiry involving commission of sodomy. On November 30, 1971, he was certified as having passed the New York State bar examination. The chief issues involved with all arguments were "whether past or present conduct should be the focal point of the fitness inquiry and whether past or present legal and ethical standards should be used to judge it" (p. 559). Following an initial appeal (which agreed that, while qualified for admission, plaintiff would have to be readmitted to the Florida bar first), the court of appeals reversed on two grounds: first, that Kimball's past conduct, while relevant to the case, was not a controlling factor, and that the New York courts were "free to exercise their independent judgment of the applicant's fitness" (p. 558). Convissar concludes by discussing the nexus requirement as developed in *Norton vs. Macy* (1969) and posits a relationship with the court of appeals decision.

601. "Another Broadcasting Network Offers Rights." THE ADVOCATE, 160 (26 March, 1975), 4.

A news report on the announcement by the Columbia Broadcasting System that "sexual preference" would be added to its minority hiring practices policy.

602. Singer, Shelley. "Governor Bans Discrimination in State Employment." THE ADVOCATE, 160 (26 March, 1975), 4.

A general executive order banning discrimination against gay employees of state government drafted by Pennsylvania Gov. Milton J. Shapp will be distributed in March, 1975. Terry Dellsuch, assistant to the governor for human services, is interviewed.

603. "'No Discrimination Here,' Seven More Say." THE ADVOCATE, 163 (7 May, 1975), 5.

An announcement by the National Gay Task Force of the forty responding corporations to a recent survey inquiring about employment policies on homosexuality. Sample companies were drawn from the Fortune 500 list.

604. "Peggy Burton Files Appeal." THE ADVOCATE, 163 (7 May, 1975), 13.

A review of the request for a rehearing in the discrimination case of Oregon teacher Peggy Burton by the full judicial complement of the Ninth Circuit of Appeals in San Francisco. At issue is an earlier decision awarding Burton damages but refusing reinstatement.

605. "Shapp Commits State to Ending Discrimination." THE ADVOCATE, 164 (21 May, 1975), 4.

On April 23, 1975, Governor Milton J. Shapp of Pennsylvania issued the first executive order in the United States committing the state to ending anti-gay discrimination. Negotiations preceding the announcement are reviewed.

606. "L.A.--'Hire Gay Cops.'" THE ADVOCATE, 165 (4 June, 1975), 6.

A report on the legal opinion on employment and hiring practices in the City of Los Angeles issued on May 9, 1975 by city attorney Burt Pines in response to a series of questions referred by the Civil Service Commission. The specific section dealing with the recommendation of disqualification for homosexual activity is extensively quoted. Pines' opinion cites this standard as raising constitutional questions of equal protection, job relatedness and privacy.

607. "Race Steward Sues for Job." THE ADVOCATE, 165 (4 June, 1975), 13.

A report on the $1,350,000 suit filed against the Ontario Racing Commission by John Damien, steward of that body, over his dismissal on grounds of homosexuality. Said legal action charges violation of a provision of the Ontario Human Rights code and seeks damages and reinstatement.

608. Brill, David. "Massachusetts Senate Defeats Job Rights Bill." THE ADVOCATE, 166 (18 June, 1975), 4.

A summary of the events surrounding the defeat on May 19, 1975 of Massachusetts House Bill 5868, which would have banned discrimination on the basis of sexual preference in public employment. A broader measure, S 272 has not yet been placed on the agenda for debate.

609. La Morte, Michael W. "Legal Rights and Responsibilities of Homosexuals in Public Education." JOURNAL OF LAW AND EDUCATION, 4 (July, 1975), 449-467.

A survey article examining reported decisions in case-law up to mid-1975 dealing with questions of hiring, revocation of teaching certificates and contract non-renewal or dismissal for homosexuals employed in the public education system. Specific cases examined include *Acanfora vs. Board of Education of Montgomery County*, the Peggy Burton case in Oregon, the dispute between James McConnell and the Board of Regents of the University of Minnesota, Board of Education, *El Monte School District of Los Angeles County vs. Calderon* (1974) and the California landmark case of *Morrison vs. State Board of Education* (involving revocation of teaching credentials). The author notes that "the case law is not well established and at times inconsistent" (p. 459) and observes that, to date, no definitive decisions on homosexuals in public education have been handed down by the U.S. Supreme Court. The only point of consistency in all cases reviewed is that, if there is no criminal violation, dismissal or revocation of credentials must be related to unfitness to teach. Other features noted are the general absence of empirical evidence, language which reflects an anti-homosexual bias on the part of some judges and "folk wisdom steeped in antiquity" (p. 462). Social trends which appear to be liberalizing the general attitude towards homosexuals in general are seen as potentially influential in public education decisions. Among these are lifestyle changes, increased sympathetic attention to homosexuality from the media, the upholding of private actions by teachers in related education law, and "the increasing use of the judicial test of establishing a nexus between conduct and teaching performance" (p. 462). Researchers should be aware that this article is frequently cited in subsequent legal literature addressing the question of homosexual employment in education.

610. Zeh, John. "Anti-Gay Bill Sneaks Through Pa. House." THE
      ADVOCATE, 167 (2 July, 1975), 5.

      By a vote of 162 to 30, the Pennsylvania House of
      Representatives passed an amendment to a bill dealing
      with campus police at state colleges. Said amendment
      bans gays from working in state institutions and serv-
      ing as state police. The measure was placed in the
      context of political gay rights events in
      Pennsylvania.

611. "Writers Won't Discriminate." THE ADVOCATE, 167 (2 July,
      1975), 5.

      During the 1975 annual conference of the National Union
      of Journalists in Cardiff, Wales, two resolutions were
      passed prohibiting members from discriminating against
      women and gay people in both employment and in
      materials written by them.

612. Mendenhall, George. "Teacher Rights Approved." THE
      ADVOCATE, 168 (16 July, 1975), 4.

      A report on the June 17, 1975 decision by the San
      Francisco Board of Education to extend a recent affirm-
      ative action resolution to include gay persons. Poli-
      tical activity related to the debate is summarized.

613. Shivers, Rob. "EEOC Charges Filed Against Government
      Agency." THE ADVOCATE, 168 (16 July, 1975), 7.

      A profile of the charges filed against the Texas State
      Health Department by nine-year employee Rachel Montoya.
      The plaintiff claims she has been denied transfer and
      promotion opportunities "because she is a Mexican-
      American lesbian." The Equal Employment Opportunity
      Commission and the American Civil Liberties Union are
      reviewing the case.

614. Aiken, David L. "Gay Is Now OK in 2.6 Million Federal
      Jobs." THE ADVOCATE, 169 (30 July, 1975), 4-5.

      An in-depth news report on the decision by the U.S.
      Civil Service Commission revising its regulations and
      guidelines to remove the ban on employment of homo-
      sexuals in civilian federal jobs. Said decision was

made to bring the agency policy into conformity with a 1973 court case, Society for Individual Rights and *Heckerson vs. Hampton* which declared a connection must be established between an applicant's homosexuality and stated job duties.

615.   "S.F. Rights Commission Takes on Ma Bell." THE ADVOCATE, 169 (30 July, 1975), 4.

On June 28, 1975, the Human Rights Commission of San Francisco issued a finding in response to a complaint against Pacific Telephone and Telegraph Co. over its stated policy of refusing to hire "manifest homosexuals." Under an existing non-discrimination ordinance, the city must move to void contracts with firms found in violation. A history of the dispute on this issue is provided.

616.   Willmore, Judy. "Police Hiring Standards Studied." THE ADVOCATE, 170 (13 August, 1975), 7.

A profile of the work of a current committee of Los Angeles officials charged with the formulation of hiring standards for the police department. The question of altering existing regulations to prevent discrimination against gay persons is explored in detail.

617.   Aiken, David L. "Pentagon Retreats on Security Clearance Issue." THE ADVOCATE, 171 (27 August, 1975), 4.

A report on the abandonment of the appeal filed by the Defense Department in the security clearance case of Otis Tabler. The move is seen as tacit acknowledgment that denial of clearance on the basis of homosexual identity is no longer viable. Coverage of debate on the issue since the first challenge in 1958 is included as background.

618.   Parisi, Joe. "Working in the Closet." THE ADVOCATE, 172 (10 September, 1975), 20.

A listing of responses to an informal survey of professional people in the Midwest on the issue of coming out and relations with office mates. While greater freedom was desired, most individuals were reluctant to take public actions for fear of affecting both work and family situations.

619.   "Q: Has Being Gay Helped or Hindered in Your Work?" THE ADVOCATE, 172 (September 10, 1975), 31-32.

A series of interviews with ten gay and lesbian professional people in Chicago, Detroit, San Francisco and New York City exploring the impact of being known as gay in a work environment. Fields reported as problem areas were banking and the law.

620.   Mendenhall, George. "State Employment Rights Bill Scuttled." THE ADVOCATE, 174 (8 October, 1975), 12.

A report on the defeat in the California legislature of a bill introduced by Assemblyman John Faran to extend the concerns of the State Fair Employment Practices Commission to include "sexual orientation." Recent political events on related legislation are used to place the debate in perspective.

621.   "Ex-Race Commissioner Sues." THE ADVOCATE, 174 (8 October, 1975), 16-17.

A detailed interview with John Damien, a race steward for the Ontario Racing Commission suing for reinstatement following dismissal for being gay.

622.   "Class Action Suit Filed Against Ma Bell." THE ADVOCATE, 176 (5 November, 1975), 15.

A note on the filing of a class-action lawsuit against the Pacific Telephone and Telegraph Company and the California Fair Employment Practices Commission by San Francisco gay activists. The suit seeks "to persuade the courts to order what negotiations have failed to produce--a ruling that gay people's employment rights are protected under state law."

623.   "High Court Denies Appeal." THE ADVOCATE, 176 (5 November, 1975), 15.

On October 4, 1975, the U.S. Supreme Court unanimously refused to hear the appeal for reinstatement sought by lesbian teacher Peggy Burton in the school system of the state of Oregon. Details of the case are provided.

624. Clark, Keith. "Governor Shapp Vetoes Antigay Bill Passed in Unanimous Senate Vote." THE ADVOCATE, 177 (19 November, 1975), 1.

News coverage of the debate over Pennsylvania Senate Bill 196, a bill bearing an anti-gay amendment passed by both houses of the legislature in the autumn of 1975. Gov. Milton Shapp vetoed the measure on October 21, terming it "a setback for the cause of fair and equal opportunity." Said measure was one of five anti-gay measures introduced by Pennsylvania legislators following Shapp's April 23 executive order barring discrimination in state employment on the basis of sexual preference.

625. "Gay Cops: An Issue Getting Attention Nationwide." THE ADVOCATE, 17 (19 November, 1975), 14.

A commentary on the continuing debate in Los Angeles and San Francisco on the fitness of gay persons to serve as police officers. The positions of police officials in Austin, Detroit, New Orleans, Chicago, Boston and Berkeley are reviewed.

626. "Attorney Rules." THE ADVOCATE, 178 (3 December, 1975), 10.

A report on an opinion issued by the office of the Attorney General of Pennsylvania declaring recent anti-gay legislation vetoed by Governor Milton Shapp to be unconstitutional. Said ruling vitiates the measure and frees state agencies from the obligation to enforce it.

627. Shilts, Randy. "The Final Appeal and the Aftermath." THE ADVOCATE, 178 (3 December, 1975), 16-18.

An historical review of the employment discrimination case of lesbian teacher Peggy Burton including interviews with both Burton and her legal counsel, Charles Hinkle.

628. Freiman, Arlene. *"Acanfora vs. Board of Education*: New Interpretations on Standing 1983 and Judicial Review of an Administrative Determination." TEMPLE LAW QUARTERLY, 48 (Winter, 1975), 384-396.

> A critical analysis of the decision rendered by the Fourth Circuit Court of Appeals in the case of Joseph Acanfora, an openly homosexual teacher protesting transfer to a non-teaching position in the school system of Montgomery County, Maryland. Freiman's attention rests upon the application made by the doctrine of standing under 42 U.S.C. #1983. This doctrine (as articulated in *Dennis vs. United States* [1966] is presented and the court's action in Acanfora viewed as inappropriate, as a prior case (*Johnson vs. Branch* [1966]) wherein a teacher was dismissed from duty for involvement in the civil rights movement and sued claiming violation of her constitutional rights) was neither adhered to nor overruled. Acanfora "was never afforded the due process hearing the law requires, and Montgomery County School Board was never given an opportunity to defend against Acanfora's claim that it had violated his constitutional rights" (p. 392). Freiman presents extensive commentary on all legal decisions of recent date whose findings bear on Sec. 1983, and regards the logic utilized as evidence that "the court simply did not wish to deal with the controversial issue of whether or not an employment transfer based on sexual preferences is a violation of the employed constitutional rights" (p. 396).

629. Myers, John E. B. *"Singer vs. United States Civil Service Commission*--Dismissal of a Government Employee for Advocacy of Homosexuality." UTAH LAW REVIEW 1, (1976), 172-185.

> An analysis of the decision in Singer on the basis both of legal precedent and restriction of protected First Amendment rights. In the case, a clerical employee of the federal government was dismissed on the grounds that "his speech and associations relating to homosexuality were immoral and notoriously disgraceful conduct" (p. 172). Myers presents precedents in cases wherein the legal interests of government as employer and the individual's constitutionally protected rights have come into conflict. Emphasis is placed on the balancing principle created in *Pickering vs. Board of Education* (1968) and the findings in *Norton vs. Macy* relating to governmental right of dismissal for private

homosexual conduct. The Singer case is considered not to have demonstrated the requisite connection between plaintiff's speech and associations and the efficiency of government service, but only to have relied on "such factors as the potential disruption . . . because of the possible revulsion of other employees . . . possible use of government funds . . . and possible embarrassment to the Federal civil service" (p. 183). Singer's dismissal was upheld by the appellate court. Myers views the decision as placing "an unhealthy discretion over government employees" (p. 183) in official hands. Exercise of the protected rights of speech and association is seen as threatened for all federal employees, homosexual or not.

630.   "Gay Cop Reinstated." THE ADVOCATE, 185 (10 March, 1976), 10.

A brief summary of the case of Douglas Wyman, a communication technician with the Seattle police force dismissed in October, 1974 after acknowledging his homosexuality in a routine personnel investigation. Judge Edward Henry of Washington State Superior Court ruled in favor of reinstatement, citing the finding in the case of *Burton* vs. *Cascade School District* as precedent.

631.   "Job Corps Won't Discriminate." THE ADVOCATE, 186 (24 March, 1976), 7.

Following a February 20, 1976 meeting with Bruce Voeller, head of the National Gay Task Force, officials of the Department of Labor's Job Corps announced the discontinuance of a technical supplement on "sexual deviation."

632.   "Immoral Conduct." THE ADVOCATE, 186 (24 March, 1976), 7.

A news note on the defeat of California Assembly Bill 820. Introduced by Howard Berman of Los Angeles, the measure would restrict dismissals of teachers for "immoral conduct" to cases in which "the questionable activity relates to fitness to teach." Reintroduction is planned.

633. "Remedial Balancing Decisions and the Rights of Homosexual Teachers: A Pyrrhic Victory." IOWA LAW REVIEW, 61 (April, 1976), 1080-1098.

> An examination of the problems attendant upon the necessity of clearly defining pertinent legal issues relating to the constitutional status of homosexuality, using the case of *Burton vs. Cascade School District Union High School No. 5* as example. This case involved a lesbian teacher's request for reinstatement to her position following discharge under an Oregon statute addressing teacher "immorality." A detailed presentation of the case history is shown to reveal two rationales in the thinking of the Board, namely the challenge of the original statute on grounds of vagueness, and at the same time stressing that "Burton was asserting a constitutional right to be a homosexual" (p. 1083). While the wrongfulness of the original firing was stipulated, discussion appeared to be centered upon "alleged community hostility to the litigant" (p. 1084). In light of cases cited as precedent, the Burton case is viewed as seriously misunderstanding the contemporary remedial balancing principle set forth in them. A detailed exploration of the role community hostility can play is shown from *Cooper vs. Aaron* with the result that "the defendant must find other ways of preserving public order than by infringing the plaintiff's civil rights" (p. 1089). Burton is seen to be a very narrow application of the broader Cooper finding. The question essential to the disposition of the case, "whether a public school teacher could constitutionally be discharged from employment solely because of her homosexuality" (p. 1094) was never addressed by the court. This reluctance to deal with the issue is reflected in various features of the final opinion. Burton is then compared with the cases of Joseph Acanfora and Michael McConnell. Final legal resolution is seen as dependent on a Supreme Court decision, "a prerequisite to such a decision, however, is the forthright confrontation of the lower courts of important legal issues involving the rights of homosexuals" (p. 1098).

634. "Set Back for Employment Rights." THE ADVOCATE, 188 (21 April, 1976), 10.

> A report on the ruling issued by the Ninth Circuit Court of Appeals in San Francisco in the case of civil service clerk John Singer of Seattle. The court stated

that "advocacy of gay rights causes and public admission of homosexuality constitutes 'flaunting' and therefore can be just cause for dismissal from a civil service job."

635. "Anita's Circle." TIME, 109 (2 May, 1976), 76.

A capsule summary of the effort by Anita Bryant and the Save the Children campaign to repeal a Dade County, Florida ordinance guaranteeing protection for homosexuals in public accommodations, housing and employment. Bryant is quoted as fearing that under said law, "religious and private schools will be forced to hire homosexual teachers."

636. "Faculty Member Will Appeal." THE ADVOCATE, 190 (19 May, 1976), 8.

A discussion of the issues of sex and gender being raised in the employment discrimination suit of Douglas Wilson against the University of Saskatchewan. Debate centers on the interpretation of provincial civil rights laws. A ruling in late January by the Court of Queen's Bench Chambers stated that the term "sex" as used in said laws indicates only gender and thus the protections do not apply to homosexuals.

637. "Medical Standards Approved." THE ADVOCATE, 191 (2 June, 1976), 11.

A report on the alteration of medical grounds for exclusion from civil service employment with the City of Los Angeles. The former section of text covering "overt homosexuality" was replaced by one discussing "psychological functioning and psychic aberrations."

638. Siniscalco, Gary R. "Homosexual Discrimination in Employment." SANTA CLARA LAW REVIEW, 16 (Summer, 1976), 495-512.

Legal developments in both the public and private sector (chiefly from the early 1970s) regarding employment discrimination against homosexuals are analyzed in this article. Emphasis is placed upon changes affecting private sector employers "for it is here that homosexuals are afforded the least legal protection"

(p. 495). While federal-level decisions such as *Norton vs. Macy* have provided a measure of protection, state and local courts have not taken similar actions, preferring to avoid confronting the issue. Protections legislated under Title VII of the Civil Rights Act of 1964 were not invoked in relevant private sector cases until 1975, either by the judicial system or the Equal Employment Opportunity Commission. Cases cited are *Smith vs. Liberty Mutual Insurance Co., Voyles vs. Ralph K. Davies Medical Center* and two cases from the EEOC record wherein "the Commission found that it lacked jurisdiction to deal with either complaint" (p. 503). The usual basis offered for such actions is that, when Title VII was enacted, protection of homosexuals was not intended. EEOC decisions evince the opinion that "homosexuality is a mutable proclivity . . . and therefore not within the protection afforded by Title VII" (p. 505). Siniscalco notes that other "mutable" characteristics have been considered as protected under Title VII and offers the "adverse impact analysis" model as a possible method of challenging neutral employment policies which are in fact exercised against homosexuals.

639. "Ma Bell Must End Bias." THE ADVOCATE, 193 (30 June, 1976), 10.

On May 28, 1976, a hearing panel of the San Francisco Human Rights Commission denied an appeal of a prior "cease and desist" order to the Pacific Telephone and Telegraph Company. Said order required the firm to abandon its stated practice of refusing to hire "manifest homosexuals," a violation of a San Francisco ordinance affecting firms doing business with the city.

640. "Integrating Career and Lifestyle: A 1970's Image: The Upfront Gay Professional." THE ADVOCATE, 194 (14 July, 1976), 13-16.

A group of interviews with openly gay professionals in the fields of law, medicine, and psychology discussing their problems and career satisfactions. Individuals interviewed are Earl Rick Stokes, Dr. William Garrard and Dr. John De Cecco.

641. "Fly the Not-So-Friendly Skies." THE ADVOCATE, 195 (28 July, 1976), 21.

> A news note on a complaint filed against Northwest Orient Airlines on June 23 by the Gay Air Line Pilots Association charging discrimination on the basis of "affectional preference" in hiring. The case of Guy Hurt, founder of the lobbying group, is summarized.

642. "Lesbians Suing." THE ADVOCATE, 197 (25 August, 1976), 10.

> A brief summary of the suit brought by two lesbian former employees against the Alameda Regional Criminal Justice Planning Board. The plaintiffs claim anti-gay attitudes exhibited by their former supervisor created a "hostile environment" which drove them to quit and seek psychotherapeutic counsel.

643. "Big Brothers Found in Violation of Rights Law." THE ADVOCATE, 199 (22 September, 1976), 10-11.

> A note on the ruling by the Minneapolis Civil Rights Department that Big Brothers, Inc. was in violation of city statutes in refusing volunteer status to a gay man. The conciliation agreement requires the admission of the plaintiff to the program, damages, and active recruitment of gay persons.

644. "UCLA Adopts Equal Employment Policy." THE ADVOCATE, 201 (20 October, 1976), 9.

> The text of a non-discrimination policy covering "sexual preference or orientation" adopted on September 1, 1976 by the University of California-Los Angeles.

645. "Rights Commission Tells Ma Bell 'Don't Discriminate.'" THE ADVOCATE, 203 (17 November, 1976), 9.

> A report on the unanimous ruling issued on October 28, 1976 by the San Francisco Human Rights Commission against Pacific Telephone and Telegraph, declaring that the firm had thirty days in which to issue "a new employment statement explicitly banning discrimination against gay people." Failure to do so will result in the suspension of all contracts with the city.

646. "Canadians Protest Treatment by Mounties." THE ADVOCATE, 203 (17 November, 1976), 10.

> A profile of a complaint issued by the Canadian National Gay Rights Coalition against the Royal Canadian Mounted Police over recruiting statements referring to homosexuality as a "character weakness" used to screen out unsuitable applicants. Representation has also been made to the Ministry of Justice requesting the inclusion of sexual orientation under the prohibited categories of discrimination in the proposed Canadian Human Rights Act.

647. "Teacher Loses Another Round." THE ADVOCATE, 205 (15 December, 1976), 10.

> On November 4, 1976, a New Jersey state appeals court ruled unanimously that Paramus teacher John Gish should submit to a requested psychiatric examination. The court also noted that local school boards could impose restrictions on free speech and that Gish's gay activist involvement showed "evidence of deviation from normal mental health."

648. "Temple Bans Bias." THE ADVOCATE, 207 (12 January, 1977), 43.

> A note on the new affirmative action policy adopted in November, 1976 by Temple University. Among its provisions are clauses barring discrimination on the basis of sexual orientation and marital status.

649. "Score One for High Court: Supreme Court Reverses Rights Ruling." THE ADVOCATE, 209 (9 February, 1977), 8.

> A brief summary of the January 10, 1977 decision by the U.S. Supreme Court reversing a lower court ruling in the case of John Singer. The plaintiff was dismissed in 1973 from a civil service post in Seattle for his advocacy of gay causes.

650. "Court Waffles: California Court Rules Rights a Legislative Matter." THE ADVOCATE, 209 (9 February, 1977), 8.

In January, 1977, the California Court of Appeals stated that an earlier superior court decision holding that gay persons were not covered by the scope of the Fair Employment Practices Commission was a valid finding, as "sexual orientation" had not been included under the term "sex" in the original legislation. The history of attempts to persuade the California government to institute this change is profiled.

651.   "Crazy Activists: New Jersey Teacher Appeals Psychiatric Ruling." THE ADVOCATE, 209 (9 February, 1977), 9.

A note on the decision of John Gish to appeal a court of appeals ruling mandating his acceptance of a demand by the Paramus school board that he undergo a psychiatric exam to prove his fitness to teach. No date of presentation to the New Jersey Supreme Court has been set.

652.   "State Dept. Lifts Gay Ban." THE ADVOCATE, 211 (9 March, 1977), 17.

A report and summary of a statement issued by the U.S. Department of State on February 9, 1977 announcing that its previous automatic prohibition of gay persons for employment will be altered to the consideration of each case on the merits of the individual.

653.   "Aumiller Reinstated." THE ADVOCATE, 221 (10 August, 1977), 41.

In June, 1977, U.S. District Judge Murry Schwartz ruled that Professor Richard Aumiller should be restored to his position in the drama department of the University of Delaware and awarded the plaintiff back pay and damages. Aumiller had been fired following the publication of statements supportive of gay rights in 1976.

654.   Merrow, Ed.D., John. "Gay Sex in the Schools." PARENTS MAGAZINE, 52 (September, 1977), 66.

A commentary directed to concerned parents addressing the possible influences homosexual teachers may or can exert on their students. After reviewing research findings on the issue and citing specific coping strategies forced upon gay educators, the author concludes that "the real issue is sexuality." Morrow calls for a rethinking of the entire matter by both parents and the educational community in general.

655. "Fighting for Their Jobs." THE ADVOCATE, 223 (7 September, 1977), 10.

Summaries of the employment discrimination suits presently in progress involving naval commander Gary Hess, computer engineer Roy Fulton and Tacoma high school teacher James Gaylord.

656. "Koch Says 'No Quotas.'" THE ADVOCATE, 224 (21 September, 1977), 11.

Representative Edward Koch (New York) has amended his federal gay civil rights bill "to specify that employers would not have to hire quotas of gay men and women to make up for past discrimination." The claims of the opponents of a similar measure defeated in Dade County, Florida, that passage would institute quota hiring, are cited as prompting the textual change.

657. "Gay Police: Controversy Heats Up." THE ADVOCATE, 225 (4 October, 1977), 12.

A review article summarizing the positions of the police departments and city administrations of Cleveland, Atlanta, San Francisco and San Diego on the question of hiring openly gay officers.

658. "Lesbian Sues for Her Job." THE ADVOCATE, 225 (4 October, 1977), 12.

The American Civil Liberties Union has filed suit in Brooklyn Federal Court on behalf of Sallie Herson, a veteran teacher in the New York City schools recently dismissed following discussion of homosexuality with her students.

659. "Schools and School Districts--Admission of Status as a Homosexual by Teacher Held Sufficient Cause for Dismissal on the Basis of Immorality. *Gaylord vs. Tacoma School District No. 10*, Wash. 2d, 559 P 2d (340, cert. denied 46

U.S.L.W. 3220 [1977])." JOURNAL OF FAMILY LAW, 16 (November, 1977), 129-134.

A summation of the history and arguments presented by both plaintiff and defense in the trial involving the 1977 dismissal of James Gaylord by the Tacoma school system. Grounds used were Gaylord's admission of homosexual identity (and thus violation of then-current Washington State law) and consequent impairment of teaching effectiveness. Questions raised by the dissent involving the due process rights of the plaintiff are also examined.

660. "State Dept 'AID' Clears Gay Workers." THE ADVOCATE, 227 (2 November, 1977), 10.

The United States Agency for International Development has determined that "homosexuals are not unsuitable for employment . . . in the Foreign Service." This reversal of agency policy was made as part of the settlement of a discrimination case filled by a former employee.

661. "Education Now." SATURDAY REVIEW, 5 (12 November, 1977), 53-54.

An opinion column dealing with the possibly deleterious effect on children of being exposed to homosexual teachers. Topics addressed are child molesting, stereotypes and the right to privacy, with the author noting that "abuse is much more likely to be rooted in hostility or stupidity than in homosexuality."

662. "Efforts to Forge Coalition to Fight Briggs Initiative." THE ADVOCATE, 228 (16 November, 1977), 17-18.

A detailed analysis of political organizing efforts in California to create effective opposition to the initiative proposed by state Senator John Briggs. Current petitions circulated by Briggs would place a proposition allowing local school districts to dismiss instructors and other employees "who are known to be gay" on the ballot in June, 1978.

663. "Dallas, D.C. Vote on Gay Teachers." THE ADVOCATE, 229 (30 November, 1977), 13.

A news summary examining recent debate in the city council of the District of Columbia and the school system of Dallas, Texas on the hiring of gay teachers and employment protection for them. The Washington, D.C. body affirmed the 1973 Human Rights Act mandating protection, while the Dallas superintendent stated that "any school teacher identified as a homosexual will be asked to resign immediately."

664. Oddone, Maureen. "Of All, the Most Vulnerable: Homophobia Hits the Classroom." THE ADVOCATE, 230 (14 December, 1977), 15-17.

An interview with Jan Zobel and Marilyn Beckstrom, discussing the gay and heterosexual positions in the teaching profession in California in light of the proposed Briggs initiative Proposition 6.

665. Hansen, Kent A. "*Gaylord vs. Tacoma School District No. 10*: Homosexuality Held Immoral for Purposes of Teacher Discharge." WILLAMETTE LAW JOURNAL, 14 (Winter, 1977), 101-114.

This article presents and examines the facts and arguments utilized by the Supreme Court of the State of Washington in the case of James Gaylord. The plaintiff had served as a social studies teacher in the Tacoma schools for some twelve years, earning consistently favorable ratings. Through a set of circumstances, his homosexuality became known to the vice-principal and he was immediately discharged on grounds of "immorality." Hansen notes that most of the case law relating to homosexuals in public education "is the product of the federal courts and the California State courts" (p. 103). These decisions have all dealt with two common areas: the constitutional rights of the homosexual and proper application of the rational nexus test (a demonstrable link between undesirable conduct/qualities and job efficiency). In Gaylord, three issues were considered by the Supreme Court--vagueness of the local school board policy, whether Gaylord's homosexuality impaired his fitness as an instructor, and "whether homosexuality was 'immoral' within the meaning of the school policy" (p. 109). All three topics were decided against the plaintiff. Hansen draws particular attention to the fact that in Gaylord, the court assumed immoral conduct had occurred simply because the plaintiff had admitted being an overt homosexual. Legal decision and precedents are reviewed and "there is no recent support for the proposition that a person can be discharged from public employment solely on the basis of sexual orientation. . . The Gaylord decision stands virtually alone in its conclusion that mere homosexual status can impair job fitness" (p. 113).

666.   Levine, Ellen. "Legal Rights of Homosexuals in Public Employment." ANNUAL REVIEW OF AMERICAN LAW, 1978, 455-491.

A survey article presenting and analyzing "the leading cases in the fields of teaching and federal government service" (p. 455) involving job discrimination against homosexuals heard up to 1978. Cases examined are *Norton vs. Macy* (1969), *Morrison vs. State Board of Education* (1969), *McConnell vs. Anderson* (1971), *Burton vs. Cascade School District* (1973), *Gaylord vs. Tacoma School District No. 10* (1977), *Board of Education vs. Jack M* (1977), *Acanfora vs. Board of Education* (1973), *Aumiller vs. University of Delaware* (1977), *Gish vs. Board of Education* (1976-1977), and *Singer vs. United States Civil Service Commission* (1976). Stress is placed upon the establishment of a rational nexus between homosexuality and unfitness for continued employment (as articulated in Norton and evidenced in the prosecution of Singer) and the "varying degrees of rigor" (p. 490) with which the courts have responded to arguments based on First Amendment rights. The Acanfora and Aumiller cases are viewed as strong precedents for successful use of this argument in cases involving employment discrimination against homosexuals.

667.   Wood, Robin. "Responsibilities of a Gay Film Critic." FILM COMMENT, 14 (January, 1978), 12-17.

Based upon a lecture given at London's National Film Theatre, this article presents a personal account of the evolution of gay consciousness in a leading British critic and the manner in which this has affected his work.

668.   "Teacher Gets Raise." THE ADVOCATE, 234 (8 February, 1978), 11.

A note on the promotion of Paramus, New Jersey teacher John Gish to an administrative post following the refusal by the U.S. Supreme Court to hear his case. Said action removed Gish from the classroom and ended several years of litigation over a psychiatric exam requested by the school board.

669. "Bill Threatens Gay Activism." THE ADVOCATE, 235 (22 February, 1978), 6.

A review of the significance of S. 5274/HR 120, a bill under debate which prohibits members of the armed forces from joining organizations whose purpose includes negotiation with the government over working conditions. The definition of "labor organization" is viewed as broad enough to include "all outside assistance to service personnel" which would exclude counsel from assisting gay service people. The constitutionality of the measure is regarded as questionable.

670. Flygare, Thomas J. "Schools and the Law." PHI DELTA KAPPAN, 59 (March, 1978), 482-83.

A summary of the legal decisions in the case of *James Gaylord vs. Tacoma School District No. 10* written by the counsel for the university system of New Hampshire. Extensive quotation from selected rulings is provided.

671. Hechinger, Grace and Fred M. "Should Homosexuals Be Allowed to Teach?" McCALLS, 105 (March, 1978), 100.

A report on the findings of a survey commissioned by McCall's magazine on the question "Do homosexual teachers present a danger to the nation's young?" The researchers polled supporters, detractors and one thousand three hundred school officials for a range of opinions, concluding that "no rational obstacle should stand in the way of letting homosexuals remain and become teachers."

672. Dubay, William. "Alaska School Board Bans Gay Teachers." THE ADVOCATE, 236 (8 March, 1978), 12.

At its meeting in early January, 1978, the school board of Copper River District in Alaska passed a resolution barring "moral turpitude" among teachers. Homosexuality was classed with cohabitation as constituting grounds of unfitness to teach, as it was "inconsistent with decency, good order and propriety of personal conduct." Details of the debate between liberal and conservative factions are presented.

673. Dressler, Joshua. "Gay Teachers: A Disesteemed Minority in an Overly Esteemed Profession." RUTGERS-CAMDEN LAW JOURNAL, 9 (Spring, 1978), 399-445.

The author of this article focuses on homosexual teachers as living under two sets of social stereotypes and misperceptions, namely the behaviors expected of all homosexuals and the "puritanical lifestyle" (p. 399) expected of a teacher as the moral model and influence on children. Following a highly detailed review of legal history and causal theories relating to homosexuality, ten prevalent beliefs about homosexuals are presented. Similar treatment is then given to the social role of the teacher, followed immediately by summaries of the proceedings and decisions in light of court cases involving gay and lesbian teachers. Beginning with *Sarac vs. Board of Education* (1967), "the first appellate decision in the nation to deal with homosexuality" (p. 418), two major principles are discerned: First, that discharge from teaching positions commonly rests upon proof of unfitness to teach. This quality is proven if the teacher's status or conduct jeopardizes student physical well-being, vitiates him or her as an effective role model, is likely to become known with consequent public reaction adversely affecting the school system, or prevents instruction in a subject required as part of the curriculum. The second factor in all such cases is the nature of the charges. Dressler notes three criticisms of the existing case law: "courts have become . . . willing to find unfitness on the basis of 'expert' testimony that is devoid of substance . . . unfitness may be found even when harm has not occurred . . . and most significantly, courts have shown themselves willing to uphold discharge on the basis of disruption resulting from community hostility" (pp. 432-433). Five recommendations for the legal system, the educational community and the general public are set out "about homosexuality--its realities and not the stereotype" (p. 445).

674. Hoffman, Stephen Clare. "An Analysis of Rationales in Homosexual Public Employment Cases." SOUTH DAKOTA LAW REVIEW, 23 (Spring, 1978), 338-357.

This article discusses the liberalizing trend in case law regarding dismissal of homosexual employees, focusing in particular upon the rationales advanced in cases which have not followed the model established in *Norton vs. Macy*. Three basic premises are explored: "prevention of activity contrary to the public mores, the prevention of emotional instability in employees, and the prevention of the spread of homosexuality" (p. 356). Cases examined are *Schlegel vs. United States* (1970), *McConnell vs. Anderson* (1972), *Gaylord vs. Tacoma School District No. 10* (1977), *In re Labady* (1971) and *Acanfora vs. Board of Education of Montgomery County* (1973). Arguments based upon the concept of the "prevailing mores of society" are seen as continuing repressive attitudes which might otherwise vanish, as well as being at variance with the concept of an open democratic society. Regarding homosexuality as a sickness in a legal context--as evidenced in *Gish vs. Board of Education of Borough of Paramus*--is seen as lacking substantive empirical proof. The idea that "if homosexuals are allowed to have jobs near other people then homosexuality, like a contagious disease, will spread" (p. 350) is likewise considered unsupportable by available evidence.

675. Trent, Michael. "On Being a Gay Teacher: My Problems-- and Yours." PSYCHOLOGY TODAY, 11 (April, 1978), 136.

A pseudonymous account by an elementary school instructor in New York City providing an insider's view of the charges laid against homosexual teachers.

676. "Gay Cops an Issue." THE ADVOCATE, 238 (5 April, 1978), 7, 14.

The situation of gay police officers on the forces of New York City, Seattle and Chicago is illustrated using current controversies over morale, hiring practices and popular perceptions of police effectiveness. Data from Los Angeles and San Francisco involving organizing efforts among gay police officers is included.

677. "Teachers Face Job Struggles." THE ADVOCATE, 238 (5 April, 1978), 9-10.

Two court cases involving actual or perceived lesbian-ism of school teachers from Des Moines, Iowa and Anchorage, Alaska are summarized in this survey.

678. Lowe, James H. "Civil Rights--Homosexual Teacher Dismissal: A Deviant Decision--*Gaylord vs. Tacoma School District No. 10*, 33 Wn. 2d 286, 559P.2d 1340, cert. denied, 95 S. Ct 234 (1977)." WASHINGTON LAW REVIEW, 53 (May, 1978), 499-510.

The dismissal of James Gaylord from his teaching posi-tion in the Tacoma School district on grounds that "public knowledge of his homosexuality impaired his academic efficiency and thus constituted sufficient cause for discharge under state law" (p. 499) is analyzed. Review of extant cases involving similar dismissals exhibits a pattern, with "at least one of three possible aggravating circumstances" (p. 503) present: sexual conduct occurred in public; said behavior is criminal and has already been separately judicially recorded, or that the plaintiff has invited greater publicity than would be expected to attend such an occurrence. The Gaylord decision is evaluated on all three counts and found lacking on all three. While acknowledging the freedom of the Washington Supreme Court to reach such a verdict, Lowe notes that "the policy implications of institutionalizing homophobia in the public school system, at the expense of dedicated teaching, are tragically retrogressive" (p. 510).

679. "Corporate Policies on Gay Rights." THE ADVOCATE, 242 (31 May, 1978), 12.

A survey of corporate hiring policies regarding gay persons conducted by the Houston Human Rights Defense Foundation is reviewed. Specific firms profiled are IBM, Eastern Airlines, McDonald's, Adolph Coors Brewing Company and the Bell System.

680. "Friends Befriend Gay People." THE ADVOCATE, 243 (14 June, 1978), 9.

As a result of discussions in June, 1976, the board of directors of the American Friends Service Committee created an affirmative action planning committee "to consider oppression and discrimination on the basis of sexual orientation in addition to race and sex." The final report of this committee and its provisions is reviewed.

681. "Court Rulings." THE ADVOCATE, 249 (6 September, 1978), 8.

On July 21, 1978, the Federal Employee Appeals Authority of the U.S. Civil Service Commission issued a ruling in the case of John Singer stating that "homosexuality is not sufficient grounds for dismissal of an employee who is performing his job satisfactorily." A brief history of the case is included.

682. Gengle, Dean. "Ending the Doctor's Dilemma: Bay Area Physicians Come Out." THE ADVOCATE, 249 (6 September, 1978), 12.

An interview with the officers of Bay Area Physicians for Human Rights, an organization of doctors and medical specialists formed in 1978. The situation of openly gay persons in the field of medicine is discussed.

683. "Chemist Can't Get Clearance." THE ADVOCATE, 250 (20 September, 1978), 8.

A review of the case of Alvin Ray Crook, a radiochemist employed at Oak Ridge National Laboratories, involving the suspension of a security clearance pending a hearing on his "attitudes and convictions regarding drug use and homosexuality."

684. "The New Issues. Gay Teachers." NEWSWEEK, 92 (2 October, 1978), 56.

A survey of issues planned for consideration by the California electorate in the November, 1978 referendum. Proposition 6 is briefly summarized.

685. "AFT Hedges on Rights." THE ADVOCATE, 251 (4 October, 1978), 8-9.

190

The American Federation of Teachers convention in August, 1978 debated and passed a resolution opposing California's Proposition 6. Specific language supporting the rights of gay teachers was voted down.

686. "A California Travesty." NEW REPUBLIC, 179 (28 October, 1978), 8.

An editorial comment by the management of the New Republic journal opposing the passage of Proposition 6, an initiative which, if passed, would authorize the dismissal of teachers who engage in "homosexual conduct."

687. "Illinois Governor Balks on Gay Rights Issue." THE ADVOCATE, 254 (15 November, 1978), 17, 19.

A report on the refusal by Illinois Gov. James Thompson to issue an executive order prohibiting discrimination based on sexual preference. The comments were made as part of an address to a statewide coalition of women's organizations.

688. "Teachers Win New 'Lifestyle' Clause." THE ADVOCATE, 255 (29 November, 1978), 9.

A news note on the ratification of a new contract containing a clause "protecting teachers against sexual orientation discrimination" by the Jefferson High School District near San Francisco. The provision is seen as a response to possible passage of Proposition 6.

689. Gusfield, Joseph R. "Proposition 6: Political Ceremony in California." NATION, 227 (9 December, 1978), 633-35.

An analysis of the political factors involved in the defeat of Proposition 6 in the California elections of November, 1978. The initiative is described as "a way whereby the meaning and place of homosexuality in American society could be defined and evaluated." The episode is placed in a context of American populism.

690. "Canadian Firing Is Gay Cause Celebre." THE ADVOCATE, 256 (13 December, 1978), 12.

A 1976 libel suit filed against more than twenty Canadian papers by the Ontario Racing Commission for their coverage of the John Damien gay employment discrimination case has been dropped. Background information on the case is sketched.

691. "Court Upholds Firing of Gay 'Disrupter.'" THE ADVOCATE, 258 (11 January, 1979), 16.

The dismissal of Patrick Batt, openly gay personnel director of the Marion Heights Nursing Home in Milwaukee, has been upheld by the U.S. Seventh Circuit Court. Said ruling stated that "private institutions supported by government funds are not required to follow Federal employment practices." Charges of having a "disruptive" lifestyle brought against Batt were not substantiated.

692. "Judge Rules in Favor of Fired Lesbians." THE ADVOCATE, 258 (11 January, 1979), 16.

U.S. District Judge Ray McNichols has ruled that six lesbian employees fired from the Boise, Idaho police force were terminated illegally. Evidence used against the plaintiffs included illegally recorded conversations. Local officials charged the women with misconduct, malfeasance, moral turpitude, inefficiency, associating with known criminals and lowering department morale.

693. "Corporate Gay Attitudes Shifting, Study Shows." THE ADVOCATE, 259 (25 January, 1979), 12.

A review of the results of a survey of corporate hiring policies relating to gay persons conducted in 1978 by the National Gay Task Force. Five hundred firms were contacted, with 122 indicating the issue of such discrimination does not exist for them. This figure represents a notable increase over the 1975 survey where only twelve companies out of one hundred reported equality in hiring.

694. "UC Trustees to Act on Gay Hiring Clause." THE ADVOCATE, 259 (25 January, 1979), 13.

A proposal to add age, sexual orientation and marital status to employment discriminations prohibited within the system of the California State University Colleges is to be considered by the trustees at their meetings January 23-24, 1979 in Long Beach. Background history on the recommendation is outlined.

695. Friedman, Joel Wm. "Constitutional and Statutory Challenges to Discrimination in Employment Based on Sexual Orientation." IOWA LAW REVIEW, 64 (March, 1979), 527-572.

A broad survey article dealing with the expanding body of case law and decisions dealing with discrimination against gay persons in both private and public employment as it existed in mid-1979. Then current practices of a discriminatory nature are evaluated under the obligations created by the equal protection and due process clauses of the Constitution and the texts of the Civil Rights Acts of 1866 and 1964. Researchers should be aware that many of the points explored in this article, such as differential impact and right of privacy, are dealt with in greater detail elsewhere in the legal literature. Friedman concludes that "the gay community's best hope for relief is through legislation aimed specifically at dismantling . . . entrenched discriminatory policies" (p. 572), as the courts have evinced an unwillingness to deal with issues raised in cases filed to date.

696. Pearldaughter, Andra. "Employment Discrimination Against Lesbians: Municipal Ordinances and Other Remedies." GOLDEN GATE UNIVERSITY LAW PERIODICAL, 8 (Spring, 1979), 537-558.

Stating that "little effort has been focused on documenting discrimination against lesbians" (p. 519), the author proceeds to attempt exactly that. The analysis begins with an outline of the problems involved in defining the problem in both legal and psychological terms. In the absence of common law prohibition against employment discrimination, private employees usually have no recourse unless contractual provision has been made for status protection. While state employment statutes bar discrimination based on Title VII of the 1964 Civil Rights Act, "no state equal employment statute explicitly or by construction prohibits discrimination on the basis of sexual preference" (p. 541). Although an amendment to Title VII expanding coverage to include such preferences has been proposed but not passed by Congress, local city governments (whether charter or general law in nature) do possess the power to enact gay rights ordinances (usually under the police power). As of 1982, twenty-six communities had passed such ordinances protecting homosexuals in employment, although the wording in these ordinances varies as regards specific language, definition of the protected class, employers covered and liberality of the standing requirement. Variation in enforcement mechanisms (from nothing to administrative agencies with the authority to issue cease-and-desist orders) is then explored. When present, such agencies "are often reluctant to enforce contract compliance provisions against employers who are important to the city's economy" (p. 550). Local ordinances are seen to be an effective means of working for change at the federal level although they themselves "often fail to provide actual assistance to victims of discrimination" (p. 552). The 1977 and 1978 campaigns against repeal of the Dade County, Florida basic civil rights ordinance and California's Proposition 6 are offered as recent developments on this level. Local legislation is seen as more usually effective in that "there may be support for gay rights in a local community but not in the state" (p. 557), as well as retaining the initiative for dealing with such issues to the local government.

697. Sarver, Tony. "The Decline and Fall of Britain's Jeremy Thorpe, M.P." THE ADVOCATE, 263 (23 March, 1979), 12-14.

A detailed exploration of the news coverage and political scandal occasioned in England by charges against Jeremy Thorpe, leader of the Liberal Party, of homosexual activities.

698. "Penn Adopts New Anti-Bias Policy." THE ADVOCATE, 264 (5 April, 1979), 11.

On January 17, 1979, the university council of the University of Pennsylvania adopted a nondiscrimination policy relating to sexual minorities, including "sexual or affectional preference." It is believed to be the most comprehensive of any Ivy League institution.

699. "Cal. Gay Jobs Bill: No Support." THE ADVOCATE, 265 (19 April, 1979), 7.

    A summary of the debate in the California legislature over Assembly Bill 1 and Senate Bill 3 which prohibit job discrimination based on sexual orientation. Opposition has been mounted by a group of fundamentalist churches.

700. "Brown Vows Ban on Bias in Hiring." THE ADVOCATE, 266 (3 May, 1979), 5.

    Discussion of a statement by Gov. Jerry Brown of California that an executive order prohibiting discrimination in state hiring on the basis of sexual orientation will be signed soon. Reaction from the California Human Rights Advocates and members of the state legislature is profiled.

701. "Brown Signs Order Banning Bias in Hiring." THE ADVOCATE, 267 (17 May, 1979), 7.

    The complete text of executive order B-54-79, signed by Gov. Jerry Brown of California on April 4, 1979, stating that the "government must not single out sexual minorities for harassment or recognize sexual orientation as a basis for discrimination."

702. "Tell Us What You Think About Gay Parents and Teachers." GLAMOUR, 77 (September, 1979), 34.

    A copy of a questionnaire issued in a survey of readers of *Glamour* magazine on teaching and employment fitness of homosexuals. Popular stereotypes and prejudices of the late 1970s on this issue are evidenced in the questions.

703. "FBI Holds Out: Gays Face Bias in Hiring." THE ADVOCATE, 276 (20 September, 1979), 16-17.

    Speaking at a press conference in August, 1979, FBI Director William Webster reaffirmed the agency's policy of refusing employment to "known gays," citing homosexual conduct as a factor to be considered in judging applicants.

704. Giteck, Lenny. "May the Force Be with Us: Recruiting Gay Rookies." THE ADVOCATE, 276 (20 September, 1979), 20-23.

An interview with candidates for the San Francisco police force discussing the police recruitment program for gay persons and its political consequences and opposition.

705. Giteck, Lenny. "Our Urban Plight? A Lineup of Gay Employment Problems." THE ADVOCATE, 277 (4 October, 1979), 16-17.

A discussion of the employment situation for gay people in San Francisco in light of that city's employment discrimination protections and intense competition. Underemployment and continuing discrimination are highlighted.

706. Kantrowitz, Arnie. "Arnie Kantrowitz on Teachers: The Human Cost of Coming Out." THE ADVOCATE, 277 (4 October, 1979) 22-23.

A personal and professional account of the situation of gay and lesbian teachers at all levels of instruction during the 1970s. The foundation of the Gay Teachers Association and the Gay Academic Union are profiled.

707. Dagani, Ron. "There's More Energy Than E=MC^2 when TGS Gets Gay Scientists Together." THE ADVOCATE, 278 (18 October, 1979), 17.

An interview with Larry White and Mike Young, co-founders of the Triangle Area Gay Scientists organization in North Carolina. The problems facing members in the physical and biological sciences and engineering are explored.

708. "Oklahoma Teachers Sue for Rights." THE ADVOCATE, 282 (13 December, 1979), 8.

A report on a class-action suit filed by four pseudonymous plaintiffs in Oklahoma City challenging the constitutionality of a state law which permits dismissal of teachers because of homosexuality. Opponents of the statute, known as the Helms Bill, charge that its provisions violate four amendments.

709. La Barde Scholz, Jeanne. "A Comment: Out of the Closet, Out of a Job: Due Process in Teacher Disqualification." HASTINGS CONSTITUTIONAL LAW QUARTERLY, 6 (Winter, 1979), 663-717.

"Any morally-based disqualification of teachers for conduct which is private and consensual, or which is otherwise protectible under the First Amendment, offends due process because it is patently arbitrary" (p. 717). This conclusion results from a detailed presentation of due process standards as evidenced in decisions of the U.S. Supreme Court prior to 1979; substantive standards developed by state and federal courts and the Civil Service Commission (and the results of their application in specific cases) and efforts toward creating more objective consideration of due process in cases involving the disqualification of gay teachers. State constitutions are viewed as the proper basis for the protection of these individuals, as "the United States Supreme Court's avoidance of cases posing due process problems in disqualification of gay employees does not preclude state supreme court recognition of employment protection" (p. 717).

710. Wise, Donna L. "Challenging Sexual Preference Discrimination in Private Employment." OHIO STATE LAW JOURNAL, 41 (1980), 501-531.

This article surveys issues commonly encountered in efforts to secure legal protection of the rights of gay persons employed in the private sector. Responses to claims of discrimination in the record of extant case law are based upon federal statutes relating to civil rights, state statutes, and common law. Specific portions of law cited are Title VII of the Civil Rights Act of 1964, Section 42 of the United States Code, 1985(c), the National Labor Relations Act, canon law, tort and contracts doctrines, and state/local statutes and ordinances where applicable. Approaches of argument examined are "disparate impact," conspiracy, sexual stereotypes, protected class and protected rights. Of particular interest to researchers is the section dealing with dismissal of employees for political beliefs as tortuous and its possible relevancy to gay activism. Wise endorses the passage of statutes and executive orders specifically prohibiting sexual preference-based discrimination, noting the harmful effects on the labor market and the process of democracy in general.

711. "Feinstein in D.C., Asks to End Antigay Bias." THE ADVOCATE, 287 (6 March, 1980), 8.

In a meeting with Jack Watson, President Carter's assistant for intergovernmental relations, Mayor Dianne Feinstein of San Francisco called for an executive order banning anti-gay discrimination in the federal government and the military, as well as a review of current immigration policy on homosexuals. Feinstein stated that such actions would be congruent with Carter's public position on human rights.

712. "Carter, in Letter to NGTF, Points to Record and Makes No Promises to Issue Progay Order." THE ADVOCATE, 290 (17 April, 1980), 7.

On March 3, 1980, a formal position statement on gay issues was issued by President Jimmy Carter, stressing past actions in the gay rights area but declining to confirm rumors of an executive order eliminating prejudicial hiring in federal employment.

713. "Homophobia: Effects on Scientists." SCIENCE, 209 (18 July, 1980), 340.

A letter from four members of the National Association of Lesbian and Gay Scientists discussing the formation and objectives of the group. The inhibiting effects of homophobia on members of the pure and applied scientific professions is explored.

714. "Gay Guidelines Upheld in Oklahoma Action." THE ADVOCATE, 299 (21 August, 1980), 19.

A profile of the case of an assistant financial aid officer at a technical institute in Oklahoma City. An attempt at dismissal on grounds of homosexuality was denied on the basis of state affirmative action laws.

715. "Police Detective Fired for Being Openly Gay." THE ADVOCATE, 302 (2 October, 1980), 12.

Steve Horn, a four-year veteran of the Mesa, Arizona police force, was fired under Arizona statutes governing "lewd and lascivious behavior" after admitting to superiors that he was gay. Counsel has been retained from the American Civil Liberties Union.

716. "Lesbian Wins Court Fight to Become Deputy." THE ADVOCATE, 302 (2 October, 1980), 12.

A detailed news report on the ruling by California Superior Court Judge Richard Calhoun in the case of Denise Kreps of Contra Costa County. The plaintiff had brought suit claiming she had been denied a post as deputy sheriff (after qualifying by examination) due to her lesbian identity. The court decision stated that county representatives had not presented "any evidence other than speculative" that Kreps' homosexuality made her unfit for the post. An appeal is planned.

717. "California Agency Seeks Data on Bias." THE ADVOCATE, 303 (16 October, 1980), 14.

The California State Personnel Board has requested information from state employees who believe they have experienced discrimination on the basis of sexual orientation. The project is based upon an April, 1979 executive order by Gov. Jerry Brown banning such practices in state hiring.

718. Bernstein, Mal. "Gay Arizona Police Detective Fights to Stay on the Force." THE ADVOCATE, 304 (30 October, 1980), 7.

An interview with Mesa, Arizona police narcotics officer Steve Horn, currently engaged in legal action to regain his position following disclosure of his sexual identity. Issues in the case are discussed.

719. "'Sexual Orientation' Missing in Guidelines." THE ADVOCATE, 305 (13 November, 1980), 9.

The National Gay Task Force has requested an explanation from the U.S. Department of Justice over the omission of the phrase "sexual orientation" from new regulations for police forces covering summary punishment and physical abuse. Provisions included are race, sex, national origin, color and religion.

720. "Philadelphia Adopts Bias Ban in City Hiring." THE
ADVOCATE, 307 (11 December, 1980), 9.

A report on the directive issued by Philadelphia Mayor
Wilson Goode adding sexual orientation to the nondiscrimination provisions of the city's employment legislation. Applying to "all employees, union or non-
union, civil service or exempt," the measure was drawn
up following discussions with community leaders.

721. "Southern California Gay State Employees Organize." THE
ADVOCATE, 309 (8 January, 1981), 7-8.

A report on the November 19, 1980 meeting establishing
a southern California chapter of Advocates for Gay and
Lesbian State Employees. A brief history of the organization is included.

722. "Lesbian Deputy Wins." THE ADVOCATE, 311 (19 February,
1981), 11.

Under an agreement signed by Sheriff Richard Rainey of
Contra Costa County, California, deputy candidate
Denise Kreps will be permitted to enter training with
one year of seniority. Background on an earlier denial
of promotion on the basis of Kreps' lesbianism is
summarized.

723. "Christians Oppose California Jobs Bill." THE ADVOCATE,
311 (19 February, 1981), 11.

A profile of lobbying efforts by a group of fundamentalist ministers from Northern California against a
pending bill barring employment discrimination against
gay people. Among the arguments advanced were that
such legislation would "protect immorality" and that
homosexuals did not need protection due to their
already high levels of disposable income.

724. "Agnos Fund to Back California Jobs Bill." THE ADVOCATE,
311 (19 February, 1981), 11.

A news note on the establishment of the California
Legislative Human Rights Fund, an organization dedi-
cated to fund raising in support of Assembly Bill 1.
The latter would provide legal protection for gay

people from job discrimination in the state of California.

725. "Gay Jobs Bill Dies in California Legislature." THE ADVOCATE, 317 (14 May, 1981), 10.

On March 31, 1981, Assembly Bill 1, the California legislation banning job discrimination against homosexuals, died in committee. Details of testimony offered at hearings on the measure are reviewed.

726. "Michigan Civil Service Bans Antigay Bias." THE ADVOCATE, 317 (14 May, 1981), 12.

A report on a letter to Rep. David Evans of Michigan from Michael Shively, chair of the state Civil Service Commission, responding to an earlier inquiry regarding the scope of state employment guidelines. Factors unrelated to employment, including homosexuality, were stated to fall within established protections.

727. Giteck, Lenny. "On the Beat with Cops: Fighting Harassment in San Francisco." THE ADVOCATE, 317 (14 May, 1981), 15.

An update on an earlier profile of programs to recruit and retain gay and lesbian officers being conducted by the San Francisco Police Department. Interviews with members of the force who have completed training recount efforts at harassment.

728. "Man Files Suit Against Utah Univ. Hospital." THE ADVOCATE, 323 (6 August, 1981), 16.

A report on legal action filed in federal district court in Salt Lake City by the children's play director at the University of Utah Medical Center. The plaintiff was dismissed from his position in December, 1979 following an appearance in a television documentary on Mormon attitudes towards homosexuality. Grounds for the suit are abridgement of the freedom of speech by a government-supported institution.

729. "Who Are the Gay Scientists?" SCIENCE, 2, 3 (4 September, 1981), 1100-1101.

A profile of the gay and lesbian membership in the American scientific community based upon letters received by the Office of Opportunities in Science of the American Association for the Advancement of Science. AAAS debate on the matter from its initial resolution of January, 1975 is outlined.

730. "Gayness No Bar to Bar, Florida Court Rules." THE ADVOCATE, 326 (17 September, 1981), 9.

In a five-to-two decision, the Florida Supreme Court ruled that the Florida bar "may not probe the homosexual backgrounds of candidates applying to practice law in Florida." The decision is placed in context with regard to existing sex law and legislation in the state.

731. "Chicago Cable TV to Ban Gay Job Bias." THE ADVOCATE, 332 (10 December, 1981), 13.

Discussion of a proposed ordinance on cable television being considered for the city of Chicago recently amended to include "sexual orientation" under job discrimination provisions. Activist efforts by Network Lambda, a group focused on development of gay and lesbian programming, are explored.

732. Clark, Penny M. "Homosexual Public Employers: Utilizing Section 1983 to Remedy Discrimination." HASTINGS CONSTITUTIONAL LAW QUARTERLY, 8 (Winter, 1981), 255-311.

Section 1983 of the Civil Rights Act of 1871 "prohibits any person from the deprivation of any rights, privileges, or immunities secured by the Constitution and laws" (p. 257). Litigation involving the application of this section involves examination of the protectable interests asserted by each party. This analysis sets forth the interrelated interests which may be raised by a homosexual plaintiff and the standards used to measure the action of government agencies. Topics addressed include the rational nexus approach *(Norton vs. Macy* set forth in detail as background) and protected interests (property rights, stigmas and reputation, status/classification, freedoms of speech and association, and the right to privacy). Extensive citation to relevant cases heard prior to 1981 is provided. Clark notes that "the strongest case a homosexual litigant can assert is one with the dual prongs of a property interest and a 'pure' liberty interest." "Most importantly, the homosexual litigant should act with confidence" (pp. 310-311).

733. Roberts, Leslie J. "Private Homosexual Activity and Fitness to Practice Law: Florida Board of Bar Examiners, *In re N.R.S.*" NOVA LAW JOURNAL, 6 (Spring, 1982), 519-534.

Private noncommercial homosexual acts between consenting adults are the focus of this examination, with especial reference to the legitimacy of such inquiry as related to the fitness to practice law in the State of Florida. Full background on the decision *In re N.R.S.* is provided. The chief impact of this decision was its denial of authority to the board of bar examiners to "question an applicant regarding his proclivity towards private homosexual conduct" (p. 520). Constitutional issues (in particular, due process guarantees and privacy) and related cases are set forth in detail. The Board defended its inquiry by noting that a lawyer is sworn to uphold the laws of the state where he practices, which the prohibition of homosexuality on the Florida books would force the plaintiff in N.R.S. to violate. While the Florida supreme court did not specifically address the constitutional issues raised in the case, it did use constitutional due process language in framing its decision. No "rational relationship" was established between the Board's inquiry and the attorney's fitness. "Mere preference for homosexuality" did not constitute a threat to the Board's goal of keeping "those morally unfit" to practice law "from membership in the Florida bar. Researchers will find this comment of interest for its consideration of language relating to immorality.

734. "NY Jobs Head Bans Antigay Discrimination." THE ADVO-CATE, 339 (1 April, 1982), 15.

On February 17, 1982, a memorandum to New York state agency chiefs asking for the adoption of equal employ ment policies barring sexual preference discrimination was issued by Meyer Frucher, director of the Office of Employee Relations. The action fulfills a provision of contract negotiations with the Civil Service Employees Association.

735. "Chicago Bans Bias in Cable TV Jobs." THE ADVOCATE, 340 (15 April, 1982), 10-11.

A summary of arguments presented to the Chicago City Council prior to passage of February 10, 1982 of an "enabling" ordinance forbidding cable television firms from discriminating against gay persons. Discussions took place as part of more general debate on establishing a cable system for the city.

736. "Despite Setback, Gay Arizona Cop Fights On." THE ADVOCATE, 344 (10 June, 1982), 15.

Former Mesa, Arizona narcotics officer Steve Horn has filed a motion of appeal to overturn a March 9, 1982 ruling by a local court. Said ruling stated that, as homosexuality was illegal under existing state law, Horn could not be continued as a member of the police force.

737. "British Civil Servants Get New Guidelines." THE ADVOCATE, 347 (22 July, 1982), 9.

A review of new security clearance rules for gay civil servants recently announced by Prime Minister Margaret Thatcher. While acknowledging that "a stable relationship between two consenting adult males" poses no threat in domestic positions, homosexuals will still be barred from the diplomatic service.

738. "Chicago Mayor Signs Gay Antibias Order." THE ADVOCATE, 348 (5 August, 1982), 9.

A news report on the executive order prohibiting anti-gay discrimination in city jobs, credit and services signed by Mayor Jane Byrne of Chicago on June 18, 1982.

739. "NGTF Publishes Discrimination Survey." THE ADVOCATE, 348 (5 August, 1982), 10.

A publication entitled *Employment Discrimination in New York City: A Survey of Gay Men and Women* has been issued by the National Gay Task Force as part of its employment assistance program. The contents cover results of a recent poll, problems and possible legal solutions including a city ordinance.

740.   "Top Civil Servants Back Security Clearance for British Gays." THE ADVOCATE, 354 (28 October, 1982), 10.

In a report recently issued by the Association for First Division Civil Servants, an organization representing senior British government officials up to the rank of under-secretary, Prime Minister Thatcher's May, 1982 recommendations barring gays from the diplomatic service were criticized, while domestic protections were heartily endorsed.

741.   "Md. Defeats Bill to Halt Lie Detector Queries on Job Seekers Sex Lives." THE ADVOCATE, 363 (17 March, 1983), 58.

A report on the defeat in the Constitutional and Public Law Committee of the Maryland legislature of a bill which would have barred questions involving sexual orientation or sex acts from being used by employers in that state. The bill was sponsored by state senator Thomas Reilly after a complaint from a female constituent.

742.   Bush, Larry. "AP Turns Down Union Request for Gay Job Protections." THE ADVOCATE, 365 (14 April, 1983), 9.

The Wire Service Guild reports that Associated Press has refused to include sexual orientation protections in contract negotiations. The history of the adoption of such provisions by United Press International is outlined.

743.   "Monitor Charged with Discrimination." MS, 11, (May 1983), 29.

A brief summary of the facts behind a fourteen-point lawsuit filed by editor Christine Madsen against the *Christian Science Monitor* newspaper. Following admission of her status as lesbian, Madsen was informed that, as official church policy viewed homosexuality as a "call for healing," she presented a personnel problem and was fired.

744. "'Notorious' Gay Teachers May Be Fired--W. Va. Attorney General's Office." THE ADVOCATE, 367 (12 May, 1983), 10-11.

A probe of the debate occasioned in West Virginia by an advisory opinion of the relation of homosexuality to teaching fitness given in February, 1983 by attorney general Clark Woodroe. Sexual orientation was held to be covered by a state law banning "immorality" in the grounds for dismissal of teachers.

745. "Gay Cop Trainee Ordered Reinstated in San Francisco." THE ADVOCATE, 371 (7 July, 1983), 65.

In May, 1983, the San Francisco Civil Service Commission ordered the city police force to reinstate trainee Thomas Cady. The history of the dispute since the initial complaint of discrimination by Cady in 1981 is summarized.

746. Freiberg, Peter. "Gov. Cuomo's Delay on Executive Order Angers Gays." THE ADVOCATE, 382 (8 December, 1983), 11.

Detailed coverage of the political maneuvering and protest related to Gov. Mario Cuomo's persistent delay in implementing a campaign promise of an executive order barring anti-gay discrimination by New York state agencies.

747. "Ohio Gov. Celeste Closes Out '83 by Protecting Gays in State Jobs." THE ADVOCATE, 387 (7 February, 1984), 9.

A report on the history and provisions of the executive order signed on December 30, 1983 by Ohio Governor Richard Celeste prohibiting discrimination on the basis of sexual orientation in state government employment.

748. "California Gov. Deukmejian Nixes Statewide Gay Employment Bill." THE ADVOCATE, 392 (17 April, 1984), 10.

A political analysis of the factors contributing to Gov. George Deukmejian's March 10, 1984 veto of Assembly Bill 1, which would have provided job rights protection for homosexuals in California. The measure was termed "divisive" by the governor, using voting patterns in the legislature as evidence.

749. "San Diego, Calif. Grand Jury Supported Sheriff's Ban Against Gay Deputies." THE ADVOCATE, 397 (26 June, 1984), 28.

A summary presentation of conclusions contained in a four-page interim report by the San Diego County grand jury on exclusionary hiring practices in force at the county jails. Homosexuals and their capacity to conduct strip searches as professionals occasioned the debate.

750. "Lesbians and Unions." THE ADVOCATE, 402 (4 September, 1984), 24-25.

A series of interviews with lesbians active in local unions in the San Francisco Bay Area and elsewhere in the state of California. Issues of coming out, credibility and support from the hierarchy are discussed.

751. Freiberg, Peter. "State Judge Strikes Down Koch's Executive Order 50." THE ADVOCATE, 404 (2 October, 1984), 13.

A review of events surrounding the ruling by New York State Supreme Court justice Alvin Klein that an executive order barring anti-gay discrimination in firms doing business with New York City was void. Klein stated that Mayor Edward Koch lacked the power to make such a step "without legislative authority from the city council."

752. Freiberg, Peter. "Gay Teachers: Lesbians Battle Prejudice in the Blackboard Jungle." THE ADVOCATE, 404 (2 October, 1984), 21-23.

A general survey of the legal status and social problems faced by lesbian teachers as of 1984. Relevant court cases currently underway are profiled and the plaintiffs interviewed.

753. Cort, Joan. "Supreme Court Finally Accepts a Gay Case." THE ADVOCATE, 406 (30 October, 1984), 22.

   The U.S. Supreme Court has agreed to hear arguments in the appeal filed by the National Gay Task Force of a lower court ruling upholding the constitutionality of an Oklahoma law permitting teachers to be fired for "advocating, encouraging or promoting . . . homosexual activity." Opponents have challenged the law as too vague and a violation of freedom of speech.

754. "Attorney General Issues Anti-Bias Policy in R.I." THE ADVOCATE, 408 (27 November, 1984), 19.

   Rhode Island Attorney General Dennis Roberts issued an order that anti-discrimination provisions of his office's employment policies be expanded to cover sexual preference. This action is set in context of the lesbian and gay community in Rhode Island.

755. Freiberg, Peter and Dave Walter. "Supreme Court Lets Two Antigay Rulings Stand." THE ADVOCATE, 417 (2 April, 1985), 10.

   An analytical report on the denial of appeal by the U.S. Supreme Court of the employment discrimination case of Marjorie Rowland. Details of the case and an accompanying brief involving the Detroit Metropolitan Community Church are explored.

756. Lassell, Michael. "New Mexico Governor Issues Order Banning Job Discrimination." THE ADVOCATE, 420 (14 May, 1985), 19.

   A news profile of the provisions of Executive Order 85-15, signed on April 1, 1985 by New Mexico Governor Tony Anaya following eight months of negotiation with state activists. The history and political climate surrounding the order are discussed. The text prohibits sexual preference discrimination in state employment and covers thirteen thousand staff of the executive branch.

757. "Maine Survey Shows Antigay Discrimination Widespread." THE ADVOCATE, 421 (28 May, 1985), 11.

The results of a survey of the gay and lesbian population of the state of Maine conducted between January 1 and March 5, 1985 are reviewed. 4640 of the respondents reported some type of employment discrimination, while 6790 "concealed being gay at times to avoid job bias."

758. Freiberg, Peter. "Rhode Island Governor Orders End to Bias in State Jobs." THE ADVOCATE, 429 (17 September, 1985), 14.

Governor Edward D. Prete's Executive Order 85-11, amending an extant executive order on discrimination through the addition of sexual orientation to the portion covering Rhode Island state employees is reviewed. The action was taken in early August, 1985 as fulfillment of a campaign pledge to provide job protection.

759. "Court Upholds Firing of Lesbian: Christian Science Monitor Reporter Refused to Be 'Healed.'" THE ADVOCATE, 430 (1 October, 1985), 13.

A summary review of the August 21, 1985 ruling by the Massachusetts Supreme Court in the case of *Christine Madsen vs. The Christian Science Monitor*. Madsen's 1982 firing from the paper's staff due to lesbianism was upheld on religious grounds, as she had refused to be "healed" of her condition by the church.

760. Walter, Dave. "NSA/CIA/FBI: Gays Need Not Apply." THE ADVOCATE, 438 (21 January, 1986), 10-12.

An examination of the historically anti-gay hiring positions of the CIA, FBI and the National Security Agency. The current case of Terry Sakellos is used as illustration. All the agencies deny placement on grounds ranging from poor judgment as a characteristic of homosexuals to fear that such hiring would impair their ability to "work well with informants."

761. "Washington Governor Signs Antidiscrimination Order." THE ADVOCATE, 439 (4 February, 1986), 15.

On December 24, 1985, Gov. Booth Gardner of Washington fulfilled a campaign promise through an executive order barring discrimination against gay persons in state employment. General affirmative action provisions for all state employees were also set in place with this text.

762. Freiberg, Peter. "Calif. Atty. Gen. Rules Labor Code Protects Gays in Private Firms." THE ADVOCATE, 448 (10 June, 1986), 17.

A report on an opinion issued by California attorney general John Van de Kamp that homosexuals, whether overt or closeted, are protected as employees of private firms under the state's Labor Code. The opinion is based upon a 1979 ruling by the state supreme court in this area.

763. Walter, Dave. "Federal Court Upholds CIA Dismissal of Gay Employee." THE ADVOCATE, 455 (16 September, 1986), 14.

A detailed summary of arguments used in the August 1, 1988 decision of the federal Court of Appeals for the District of Columbia in the case of *John Doe vs. William Casey* in which a CIA employee was terminated in 1982 without explanation of the grounds upon which his homosexuality made him unsuitable. The case was remanded to district court to establish the C.I.A.'s intent.

Censorship

764. "Danish Nudie Mags Get the Nod: Physique Books Can Enter U.S., High Court Rules." THE ADVOCATE, 1, 4 (December, 1967), 1.

This article reports a reversal by the United States Supreme Court of obscenity rulings in two lower court cases involving pornographic magazines imported from Denmark. Judgement was based upon an inability to prove that such materials met standard criteria defining obscenity. These decisions are seen to have implications for cases involving homosexually-oriented publications. The case of *Vennen*, a magazine published in Copenhagen, is given as an example.

765. "Vice Cop Arrests Mattachine Midwest Editor for Article." THE ADVOCATE, 4, 4 (April, 1970), 2.

David Stienecker, editor of Chicago's *Mattachine Midwest Newsletter*, was arrested by Officer John Manley of the city police at his home on February 7, 1970. Grounds used lay in an article which appeared in the September, 1969 issue of the newsletter, documenting Manley's massive use of tactics of entrapment and false arrest against homosexuals in the Lincoln Park neighborhood. No warrant was presented at the time of Stienecker's arrest.

766. "Chicago Editor's Trial Set May 6." THE ADVOCATE, 4, 6 (13-26 May, 1970), 7.

    The trial of David Stienecker, editor of the newsletter of the Mattachine Midwest organization, was postponed to May 6 during preliminary hearings April 16. At issue in this case is an article detailing the activities of a city police officer, John Manley, involved in up to twelve arrests per day on grounds of "public indecency."

767. "Judge Throws Out Suit Against Editor." THE ADVOCATE, 4, 10 (8-21 July, 1970), 22.

    A complaint of "criminal defamation" brought against the editor of Mattachine Midwest's *Newsletter* by a city police officer was dismissed by a Chicago court as "insufficient." The newsletter had published an article in September, 1969, describing the activities of officer John Manley in the Lincoln Park area.

768. "Double Standard for the Press?" THE ADVOCATE, 61 (9-22 June, 1971), 7.

    This article comments upon the reversal by the U.S. Supreme Court of a lower court injunction against police harassment obtained by a Dallas underground newspaper which had been raided twice by police. Refusal of press passes to the L.A. *Free Press* and *The ADVOCATE* by the Los Angeles Police Department is also reported. The authors note that, while the underground press continues to expand, "gay news and advertising in such papers has been a substantial factor in their troubles with the authorities."

769. "Ban Stands on Book with Gay Angle." THE ADVOCATE, 61 (9-22 June, 1971), 20.

    On April 21, 1971, Community School Board No. 5 in Flushing, New York voted to ban *Down These Mean Streets* by Piri Thomas from school libraries. The work is an autobiography detailing the writer's childhood in the "El Barrio" section of East Harlem.

770. "Gay Paper Seized in Porn War." THE ADVOCATE, 86 (24 May, 1972), 4.

A copy of the San Francisco publication *Gay Sunshine* was seized at an adult bookstore on Hollywood Boulevard, during a raid by the vice squad of the Los Angeles Police Department. Lt. Robert Loomis refused to issue any information beyond a summary statement that the raid had in fact occurred and publications had been seized. An official of the public affairs office of the LAPD stated that further questions would have to be submitted in writing. Refusal by the department to grant *The ADVOCATE* press accreditation is also noted. Spokesmen for the collective which published *Gay Sunshine* stated that their paper "concentrated on political articles, poetry, and graphics. In no sense of the word can the paper be called pornographic." Freedom of the press was seen as a basic issue in this affair.

771. "A First for the Gay Press." THE ADVOCATE, 91 (2 August, 1972), 3.

Guy Charles and David L. Aiken, reporters for *The ADVOCATE*, attended the Democratic National Convention in Miami Beach, having received press credentials after routine clearance by the U.S. Secret Service. This was the first time gay and lesbian media were represented at such an event. The reporters' clearance and accreditation in their home areas of New York City and Washington, D.C. is contrasted with the denial of similar credentials to staff reporters in Los Angeles by the city police department.

772. "Gay Women's Ladder Folds." THE ADVOCATE, 96 (11 October, 1972), 14.

The Ladder, a lesbian-oriented publication issued by the Daughters of Bilitis since 1956, ceased publication in September, 1972. It was the oldest continuously published journal of its type. In her parting editorial, Gene Damon condemned the subculture as a whole for failing to support the women's point of view.

773. "TV Story on Lesbians Didn't Fare So Well." THE ADVOCATE, 101 (20 December, 1972), 10.

This article reviews an episode of NBC-TV's program *The Bold Ones*, aired on October 31, 1972, involving a lesbian character. Both plot and rationale were found wanting. No opinion was offered on the presentation of a lesbian in prime time television.

774.   "Out of the Closet: Depicting Homosexuality on Television." TIME, 101 (5 March, 1973), 80.

Various portrayals of homosexuals, both male and female, on network television are noted, with the observation that the topic is being approached rather timidly. Programs mentioned include *Marcus Welby, Room 222, All in the Family* and the drama *That Certain Summer*. Activist reactions to network plans are also discussed.

775.   "*Gay* Faces Swansong As Newspaper: Straight Owners Eye Sex Magazine Format." THE ADVOCATE, 115 (4 July, 1973), 1.

The second largest homosexually-oriented magazine in the United States, *Gay,* ceased publication in 1973 after a three-year existence. This article reviews fiscal and management reasons for its demise and interviews the editors, Lige Clarke and Jack Nichols.

776.   "ADVOCATE Removed in Wichita Falls." THE ADVOCATE, 118 (15 August, 1973), 11.

On July 24, 1973, a bookstore in Wichita Falls, Texas was ordered by the county attorney to remove all "adult books" from its public shelves. The defining criterion appears to have been sexual explicitness. Among the items removed were current issues of *The ADVOCATE.* When contacted by newspaper staff, Timothy Eyssen, the attorney in question, agreed to review *The ADVOCATE.*

777.   "Editor Says British to Burn His Book on Gay Liberation." THE ADVOCATE, 127 (7 November, 1973), 9.

Speaking on a radio program on station KSAN, San Francisco, Len Richmond, editor of *The Gay Liberation Book,* reported that four hundred fifty copies of the anthology had been seized by British customs officials. The copies in question were en route to several bookshops in London. Although the anthology contained little or no sexually explicit materials--being chiefly poetry, cartoon, plays and memoirs--customs officials stated all copies in their possession would be burned as obscene literature.

778. "Author Outlines Plan for Gay Writers Guild." THE ADVOCATE, 133 (13 March, 1974), 4.

Referring to an article in Issue 131 (February 13, 1974) of *The ADVOCATE* discussing the difficulties of finding publishing outlets for quality fiction with homosexual themes, Paul Damon proposes a professional organization to deal with the problem. Advantages of such a group are detailed.

779. "ADVOCATE Ads Are Refused." THE ADVOCATE, 139 (5 June, 1974), 3.

Small display advertisements for *The ADVOCATE,* highlighting news content to promote sales of individual copies, were refused publication by the Boston *Globe* and *Los Angeles Times* newspapers. Neither paper would give reasons for the denial, having run stories in the past using both "gay" and "homosexual" without comment.

780. "Derisive Curtain Call Marks *Gay*'s Farewell." THE ADVOCATE, 142 (17 July, 1974), 19.

The final issue of *Gay,* a New York based homosexual publication which folded in 1974 for financial reasons, appeared as a satire on gay publishing written by the owners of the company. No indication of the humorous intent of the paper was given anywhere in its text. Activists indicated their displeasure with such misrepresentation and former subscribers report failure in their attempts to recover monies paid.

781. "Gay Books Escape Library Cage." THE ADVOCATE, 146 (11 September, 1974), 5.

On July 23, 1974, the Hollywood Public Library removed the closed-shelf restriction policy from books dealing with homosexuality. This event followed two-and-one-half years of protest by various local community figures and organizations. Prior to this, anyone wishing to use such materials was obliged to explain their need to know to the reference staff.

782.   "Encyclopedia Barrier on Gay Info Is Broken." THE
       ADVOCATE, 146 (11 September, 1974), 9.

       Officials of the *Encyclopedia Britannica* indicated
       willingness to add positive materials on homosexuality
       to their publication's essays on the subject and to
       note changes in the annual supplemental yearbook. This
       action comes in response to letters sent to publishers
       of the eight leading encyclopedias in the United States
       by the Gay Activist Alliance of New York. A history of
       the encyclopedia and dictionary project, and related
       efforts by the Social Responsibilities Round Table of
       the American Library Association is also provided.

783.   "R.F.D. Protests Mother Earth." THE ADVOCATE, 156 (29
       January, 1975), 38.

       Mother Earth News, a leading publication on contempo-
       rary country life, refused to list *R.F.D.,* a rural-
       oriented quarterly on similar subjects for gay people,
       in a news column.   *R.F.D.* staff responded with a
       letter to *M.E.N.* which generated other protests. A
       statement was then issued by the editors of *Mother
       Earth* that their publication did not discriminate
       against gay women and men.

784.   "Theatre Censoring Gay Material." THE ADVOCATE, 159 (12
       March, 1975), 14.

       The artistic board of The Vanguard, an experimental
       theatre in Los Angeles, decided to withdraw an invita-
       tion to perform extended to John Jack Baylin, a gay
       media satirist. Judith Stark, president of the board,
       explained that, after a preliminary viewing, Baylin was
       asked to present an audition to the entire board. Upon
       his refusal to do so--on the grounds that this was
       censorship--the board decided to make the audition a
       condition of performance. Bill Maritz, a gay man who
       worked as administrator of The Vanguard, was subse-
       quently fired from his post for scheduling Baylin.

785.   "Prison for Books." THE ADVOCATE, 179 (17 December,
       1975), 10.

       This news note reports that books on gay history are
       currently being kept in special locked stacks at the
       Stanford University Library. The local organization,

the Gay People's Union, is attempting to have this restriction removed.

786. "ADVOCATE Banned." THE ADVOCATE, 190 (19 May, 1976), 8.

The Hayden Library of Arizona State University in Tempe removed issues of *The ADVOCATE*, a leading gay periodical, from its shelves shortly after the creation of a local campus organization. Opinions of faculty members teaching in areas related to the study of homosexuality were not solicited prior to the removal. Helen Gaten, assistant to the University Librarian, stated that *The ADVOCATE* was eliminated because "it had little relevance to the curriculum of the University." A review of the decision will be taken by the university library committee.

787. "Police Raid L.A. Gay Paper." THE ADVOCATE, 191 (2 June, 1976), 11.

Five Los Angeles vice squad officers, armed with a search warrant, visited the offices of *News West* on May 13. Their warrant permitted them to seize all of Cost Plus Printing's corporate records in relation to another case. During the police visit, officers were observed going through the desk of Jeanne Barney, editor of *News West*.

788. "FBI Keeping ADVOCATE File." THE ADVOCATE, 194 (14 July, 1976), 7.

On June 23, 1976, confirmation was received by the editors of *The ADVOCATE* that a domestic surveillance file on their publication existed in the records of the Federal Bureau of Investigation (FBI). Earlier letters requesting release of such information under the Freedom of Information--Privacy Act (FOIPA) are noted and the process of confirming the file's existence are detailed.

789. "ADVOCATE Returned to Shelves." THE ADVOCATE, 198 (8 September, 1976), 9.

Arizona State University has agreed to return its collection of *The ADVOCATE* to public shelves and to purchase a back set of the publication on microfilm. This action rescinds an earlier ruling by the university library that *The ADVOCATE* was not relevant to curriculum content.

790. "No Gay Publications in Prison." THE ADVOCATE, 207 (12 January, 1977), 9.

In December, 1976, Norman Carlson, director of the U.S. Bureau of Prisons, announced he would not permit any gay publications in federal correctional facilities. This statement came after Rep. Edward Koch (N.Y.) appealed a decision of the warden of Leavenworth banning *The ADVOCATE* and *It's Time,* newsletter of the National Gay Task Force (NGIF). Given as the basis for these actions were possible damages to inmates should they be identified as homosexual, and unwillingness to further exacerbate the level of such behavior already present. The NGTF indicated plans to appeal Carlson's ruling.

791. Hall, Richard. "Once a Fad, Not Always a Fad: The Perils of Publishing Gay Books." THE ADVOCATE, 209 (9 February, 1977), 24-25.

This article is a condensation of a presentation given at the panel "Publishing Gay Writing" organized by the Gay Caucus of the Modern Language Association at their meeting in New York on December 29, 1976. After analyzing the structure and psychology of the contemporary American publishing industry, Hall discusses the growth of gay-oriented works and the overall ignorance of the gay market shown by major houses. Small presses are seen as vital to the development of this genre, as "the gay book has not been recognized as a valid category in American letters" (p. 24).

792. "On Trial for Blasphemy: Gay News Trial in Great Britain." TIME, 110 (25 July, 1977), 54.

In Court No. 8 at London's Old Bailey, charges of blasphemy were brought against *Gay News,* England's foremost homosexual newspaper, and its editor, Denis Lemon. At issue was the publication of a poem by James Kirkup on the Crucifixion. By a vote of ten to two, both parties were found guilty and fined $2500. Reactions included a proposal to abolish Britain's 279-year-old law on blasphemy.

793. "Rome Muzzles McNeill." THE ADVOCATE, 226 (19 October, 1977), 14.

> The Sacred Congregation for the Doctrine of the Faith of the Roman Catholic Church issued an order barring Fr. John McNeill, S.J. from speaking publicly on homosexuality or sexual ethics and removing ecclesiastical approval from his controversial work *The Church and The Homosexual*. McNeill was charged with presenting "advocacy theology" and promoting his position actively, rather than simply presenting his views to the church community for study. The reaction of Dignity, whose third convention McNeill was scheduled to address, is shown in the text of a press release condemning the action.

794. "Quixote Center Calls for McNeill's Freedom." THE ADVOCATE, 230 (14 December, 1977), 23.

> The Quixote Center in Mt. Rainier, Maryland, a Catholic-based center concerned with issues of equality and justice, sent a letter to the bishops and Jesuit provincials of the United States urging them to protest the silencing of John McNeill, S.J. Fr. McNeill, author of *The Church and the Homosexual*, was ordered to refrain from writing or speaking further on the subject. The letter compared this action of the Congregation for the Doctrine of the Faith to totalitarian rule.

795. "Police Raid Body Politic." THE ADVOCATE, 234 (8 February, 1978), 10.

> On December 30, 1977, the offices of *The Body Politic*, Toronto's gay newspaper, were visited by five officers from both local and Ontario provincial forces armed with a search warrant. Said warrant authorized them to seize materials which might support charges of using the mails for the transmission of obscenity. Twelve cartons of *Body Politic* property were removed, among them manuscripts, mailing lists and financial records. Clayton Ruby, attorney for the paper, criticized the breadth of the warrant (illegal under Canadian law) in that it "allowed seizure of almost anything on the

premises." Two criminal charges were subsequently filed against staff members.

796. "Lemon Loses." THE ADVOCATE, 241 (17 May, 1978), 9.

A British Court of Appeals panel of judges ruled against London's *Gay News* and its editor, Denis Lemon, in their effort to reverse conviction for blasphemous libel. Fines of one thousand pounds for the paper and four hundred for Lemon were let stand, although a nine month jail term was abolished from the decision. *Gay News* is consulting its readership to determine support for possible further appeals. Grounds for this decision were the publication of a poem about Christ by Professor James Kirkup.

797. "Gay at Bay: British Backlash Is John Bull-Headed." THE ADVOCATE, 242 (31 May, 1978), 7-8.

A conservative political organization in Great Britain, the Festival of Light, threatened the publishing house of W. H. Allen with an obscenity lawsuit if it proceeded with the distribution of John Rechy's novel-*cum*-documentary *The Sexual Outlaw*. General anti-gay violence in Britain is reviewed, including the activities of the National Front. An interview with Rechy constitutes the second half of the article.

798. "Jailed Gay Soviet's Poem." THE ADVOCATE, 255 (29 November, 1978), 9.

The complete text of "Letter from Prison," by Gennady Trifonov, the noted Russian poet presently serving four years at a Soviet labor camp for providing circulation of his gay love poetry. A brief discussion of the Trifonov situation and a call for further publicity to assist his case is presented. The poem was also published simultaneously by *The Body Politic* and Swedish and British gay periodicals to maximize impact.

799. "Gay Mags on Secret British Customs List." THE ADVOCATE, 260 (8 February, 1979), 8.

Guidelines for Customs and Excise officials in Great Britain include a list of twenty-six firms whose mailings are to be seized *pro forma*. Three of these firms produce gay periodicals, including *Forum* and *Gay News.* Seizure is only possible when there is "portrayal of deviant practices . . . associated with sexual detail."

800.   *"Body Politic* Protests." THE ADVOCATE, 262 (8 March, 1979), 7.

A photographic feature showing protests in San Francisco and New York City associated with the Canadian government charges of obscenity against the Toronto newspaper *The Body Politic.*

801.   *"Body Politic* Verdict Expected on Feb. 14." THE ADVOCATE, 262 (8 March, 1979) 9-10.

A summary of the Canadian government charges against and trial of the Toronto gay newspaper *The Body Politic,* based upon materials confiscated in a police raid on December 30, 1977. The trial is viewed as beneficial for establishing freedom of the press as applied to gay publishing and for shattering stereotypes. Details of the charges are supplied.

802.   "The Perils and Power of Publishing Gay Books." THE ADVOCATE, 243 (14 June, 1978), 20-23.

This article is a transcription of a meeting of seven gay writers and editors held in New York in March, 1978. Social reaction to the increasing visibility of gay literature was the chief theme of discussion, including a review of publicity reactions to proposed-or-current works. Members of the panel included Patricia Nell Warren, Richard Hall and Jane Arnold.

803.   Young, Ian. "Gay Presses: Growing Gutenbergs." THE ADVOCATE, 243 (14 June, 1978), 28-29.

Written by a noted gay poet, this article is a history of gay and lesbian publishing in both the United States and Great Britain from the 1890s to the late twentieth century. Houses mentioned include Naiad Press and Guild Press of Washington, D.C., the latter involved in several early obscenity trials. Common themes for all periods have been disinterest by mainstream houses and outright censorship under various legal prosecutions.

Young calls for greater support of this publishing than has been shown by the gay community, noting that women's publication houses have done quite well.

804. Hall, Richard. "The ADVOCATE at the ABA: Books, Booths, Prayers and Promises." THE ADVOCATE, 245 (12 July, 1978), 23.

An account by the book review editor of *The ADVOCATE* of the reception accorded the publication's booth at the American Bookseller's Association convention in Atlanta in May, 1978. Despite the foundation of a gay caucus headed by Deacon Maccubin of Lambda Rising Bookshop in Washington, D.C. and a panel discussion on "Understanding and Reaching the Expanding Gay Media," Hall also notes that "a book can be de-published, robbed of the in-house support needed for success." Little, Brown & Company of Boston and their lack of publicity for two gay titles is cited as an example.

805. *"Gaysweek* Patent Denied." THE ADVOCATE, 248 (23 August, 1978), 8.

On June 14, 1978, the U.S. Patent and Trademark office in Washington, D.C. rejected an application to register the publication name *Gaysweek* "because the mark is considered to consist of or to comprise immoral or scandalous matter." Publisher Alan Bell plans to refile the application, and letters of support have been obtained from several politicians including Patrick Moynihan.

806. *"Body Politic* Acquitted of Obscenity." THE ADVOCATE, 263 (22 March, 1979), 7.

Judge Sydney Harris acquitted *The Body Politic* and its publisher, Pink Triangle Press, of government charges of "using the mails for the purposes of distributing immoral, indecent or scurrilous materials." A brief history of the case and associated publicity is supplied. *Body Politic* will republish the original article in its upcoming issue along with a commentary on the court case and its significance.

807. "Prosecutor to Appeal *Body Politic* Acquittal." THE ADVOCATE, 267 (17 May, 1979), 9.

The Attorney General of the province of Ontario announced on March 6, 1979 that an appeal had been authorized against the acquittal of *The Body Politic* on charges of obscenity. The appeal brief lists eight alleged legal errors made by presiding Judge Sydney Harris and seeks a guilty verdict or a retrial. Venue for the appeal will be at the county court level in the fall of 1979.

808. Hall, Richard. "An End to Gay Literature: Will Gay Books Muscle into the Mainstream?" THE ADVOCATE, 268 (31 May, 1979), 17, 21.

Written by the book review editor of *The ADVOCATE*, this essay considers the shift occurring in homosexual literature, with gay and lesbian characters being used more commonly and playing diverse roles. Excerpts are offered from the works of John Cheever, Richard Price and Elaine Markson. Hall notes that this is all the more remarkable as "for long ages . . . the merest hint of homosexuality was enough to send a manuscript back to the writer. . . Homosexuality might be dressed in polite evasions . . . but no more" (p. 17).

809. "ABA Gay Caucus Forms." THE ADVOCATE, 272 (26 July, 1979), 7-8.

At the May, 1979 convention of the American Booksellers Association, approximately one hundred gay publishers and businessmen formed a caucus. Its stated purpose was "to combat homophobia among ABA members and in the publishing industry." Publicity is intended to familiarize dealers with the potential of the gay market.

810. "Ashland Gay Exhibit Removed by Library." THE ADVOCATE, 274 (23 August, 1979), 12.

Following almost three weeks of controversy, a Gay Pride Week exhibit was personally removed from the Ashland, Oregon library display area by the head of the county library system. This action overruled both the library board and the local libraries.

811 "Gay Vancouver Paper Loses Lengthy Lawsuit." THE ADVOCATE, 274 (23 August, 1979), 12.

After five years of litigation reaching to the Canadian Supreme Court, the Vancouver newspaper *Gay Tide* lost its suit against the Vancouver *Sun*. At issue was the latter's refusal to accept a promotional ad for the *Tide*. Stating that "an honest bias honestly entertained is not unreasonable," the court ruled in favor of the *Sun*.

812. "Obscenity Case Is Not Atlanta Cause Celebre." THE ADVOCATE, 274 (23 August, 1979), 13.

A brief summary of the arrest of an Atlanta publisher and two other individuals following the presentation of a series on teen prostitution on local television. Charges were sale and distribution of obscene materials. A fund-raiser, including a cruise and a weekly entertainment magazine from the gay community, will be held to finance efforts to fight the charges.

813. "Clayton Ruby's People Power: Lawyer for Canadian Gay Publication, *The Body Politic*." MACLEANS, 92 (22 October, 1979), 14, 16, 18.

This interview profiles Clayton Ruby, one of the leading activist lawyers of Canada and attorney for the Toronto gay newspaper *The Body Politic* in the 1977-1979 obscenity controversy. A brief history of the case is provided.

814. "How Do You Get Gay Books into a Library?" THE ADVOCATE, 280 (15 November, 1979), 11.

A pamphlet prepared by the Gay Task Force of the American Library Association is available describing library selection policies and appropriate responses if the library refuses the requested items. The title is *Censored, Ignored, Overlooked, Too Expensive: How to Get Gay Books into A Library*.

815. "Gay Blazes But Lesbian Sells." THE ADVOCATE, 281 (29 November, 1979), 12.

The widely distributed American publication *The Joy of Gay Sex* has been seized and banned by British customs officials. *The Joy of Lesbian Sex* was released to its distributor. No reason was given in either case.

816.　Anderson, Scott. "The Gay Press Proliferates--And So Do Its Problems." THE ADVOCATE, 282 (13 December, 1979), 19-20.

An overview of the problems faced by an increasingly diverse and expanding group of gay publishers. Among those noted are reaching people, distribution, staffing, advertising and censorship. An interview with Don Michaels, editor of the *Washington Blade,* is included.

817.　"Perspectives on Gay Press Problems--Editorial Comments." THE ADVOCATE, 282 (13 December, 1979), 21-23.

A group interview with Jeanne Cordova, editor of Los Angeles' *Lesbian Tide,* Richard Burns of *Gay Community News* in Boston and Chuck Ortleb of *Christopher Street* magazine. Common problems include fear of advertisers to support such papers.

818.　"Is St. Denis a Gay Press Martyr?" THE ADVOCATE, 282 (13 December, 1979), 24-26.

An interview with Denis Lemon, editor of London's newspaper *Gay News.* Discussion centers upon the court case for blasphemy which Lemon had to endure. An appeal is planned to the European Commission of Human Rights in Strasburg. Details of British customs seizure of imported gay books and the harassment of *Gay News* by both government and private industry are explored in detail.

819.　"*Body Politic* Fights Appeal of Acquittal." THE ADVOCATE, 286 (21 February, 1980), 11-12.

Toronto's *Body Politic* newspaper is scheduled to be in court February 7, 1980 to counter government claims that its acquittal on charges of public obscenity should be overturned. The judge will have the option of passing sentence or declaring a new trial. Maximum penalty for the obscenity charges is six months in jail.

820.　"*Body Politic*--Back to Court Once More." THE ADVOCATE, 290 (17 April, 1980), 7-8.

On February 29, 1980, County Court Judge George Ferguson upheld the appeal request of the Crown that the ruling finding *The Body Politic* had not violated the obscenity laws of Canada should be reviewed. *The Body Politic* has decided to carry the case to the Ontario Court of Appeals. The latter body will have the options of permitting the acquittal to stand, ordering a retrial or a retrial under specific conditions.

821.   "Policy Change: Inmates to Get Gay Periodicals." THE ADVOCATE, 291 (1 May, 1980), 8.

Norman Carlson, Federal Director of Prisons, has announced that "publications which are nonpornographic and do not jeopardize the order of running of the institutions" will be permitted to federal inmates. This follows a two-year lawsuit by various publications, the National Gay Task Force and the Lambda Legal Defense and Education Fund. Prior ban of such periodicals was based on the claim that the recipient would then be exposed to homosexual rape. A related lawsuit barring members of the Metropolitan Community Church and other gay clergy is also reviewed.

822.   "Virginia Gay Paper Out, Then In Library." THE ADVOCATE, 293 (29 May, 1980), 10.

Following complaints from local fundamentalists and members of the Virginia Beach City Council, the Norfolk, Virginia paper *Our Own* was removed from circulation, but retained as a reference item. A protest by the Unitarian Universalist Gay Community of Tidewater is quoted.

823.   Kann, M. A. "Perils of Publishing *The Lesbian Path*." THE ADVOCATE, 313 (19 March, 1981), T.4-5.

An interview with Margaret Cruikshank, editor of the anthology *The Lesbian Path,* about "her struggle to stay afloat in the frustrating world of gay publishing" (T.4). Among her experiences was the difficulty of finding a publisher willing to issue the work and having twice to threaten legal action over contract violations.

824. "Can't Seize Gay Mags, Judge Tells Customs." THE ADVOCATE, 332 (10 December, 1981), 11.

In a lawsuit brought by the Chicago newspaper *Gaylife,* Judge Milton Shadur ruled on October 13 that U.S. Customs offices must translate a substantial portion of the text of a foreign publication prior to making a determination of obscenity. At issue was the U.S. Customs' impounding of issues of *Revolt,* a Swedish publication with which *Gaylife* maintains an exchange policy. Cited were previous rulings such as *Miller vs. California* (1973).

825. "Canadian Paper Faces New Obscenity Trial." THE ADVOCATE, 334 (7 January, 1982), 9.

A new trial has been ordered for Toronto's *Body Politic* newspaper on charges of "using the mails to transmit indecent, immoral or scurrilous matter" based upon an article on pedophilia printed in the December, 1977/January, 1978 issue. Appealing a 1979 acquittal, Judge George Ferguson of the county court ruled that the initial justice should have determined obscenity and not dismissed for absence of a common standard set by the Crown. Ontario Court of Appeals upheld Ferguson, and the Supreme Court of Canada has refused to hear the case. *Politic* staff fears a more detailed case based upon material confiscated during a police raid on newspaper offices.

826. "ACLU Fights Prison Censorship in Oregon." THE ADVOCATE, 341 (29 April, 1982), 13, 15.

The Oregon ACLU has filed a class-action suit charging that state censorship of mail to inmates violates constitutional rights. A social worker with the Town Council Foundation of Portland provided the data. A 1978 ruling of then-governor Bob Straub permitting inmates to receive such mail was reversed in 1980 by Gov. Vic Atiyeh.

827. "Canadian Gay Paper, Bookstore Raided." THE ADVOCATE, 345 (24 June, 1982), 12-13.

On May 7, plainclothes Toronto police raided the offices of *The Body Politic* collective and threatened to charge the entire group with obscenity, a threat carried out on May 12. At issue was the authorship of an article written by a pseudonymous author. Glad Day Books, a Toronto gay and lesbian bookstore, was also recently hit and charged with possession with intent to sell of obscene materials. Both actions are viewed as individual efforts of homophobic officials to sabotage Chief Jack Ackroyd's work at improving police-community relations.

828. "State Censorship Kills Gay Magazine in Brazil." THE ADVOCATE, 346 (8 July, 1982), 11.

Under the influence of an antipornography campaign begun by Brazil's President Figueireido, the latest issues of *Journal do Homo/Plequei*, Latin America's only gay periodical, were removed from newsstands by the police. Aguinaldo Silva, the editor, decided to burn all copies of the first four issues and destroy the subscription list. These events are a repeat of the fate of an earlier periodical, *Lampiao*, which Silva edited.

829. "No Hearing for Gay British Paper." THE ADVOCATE, 347 (22 July, 1982), 10.

On May 7, 1982, the European Human Rights Commission declined to hear the complaint brought by London's *Gay News* and its former editor, Denis Lemon, regarding their 1977 conviction on grounds of blasphemy. As specific grounds for rejection were not given, this prevents *Gay News* from pursuing other avenues of appeal.

830. "Lesbian Book Busted in Vienna." THE ADVOCATE, 347 (22 July, 1982), 10.

A Woman's Touch, a sexually explicit book produced by lesbians, was confiscated by Austrian police under Paragraphs 220 and 221 of the Austrian criminal code. These provisions cover the depiction of sexual activities. A demonstration was held May 13 in support of the book.

831. "*Body Politic* Wins But Faces More Charges." THE ADVOCATE, 348 (5 August, 1982), 13-14.

Provincial Court Judge Thomas Mercer ruled that the publisher and three officers of the *Body Politic* were innocent of the charge of distributing immoral and indecent matter through the mails. While agreeing that the article in question did advocate the practice of pedophilia, the judge ruled that mere advocacy was not sufficient grounds for a charge of immorality. Members of the collective will stand trial on a new charge in the fall of 1982, that of publishing obscene material based on an article which appeared in the April, 1982 issue.

832. *"The Body Politic* Faces a Third Trial for the Same Offense." THE ADVOCATE, 349 (19 August, 1982), 15.

The office of the Canadian attorney general has announced a second appeal of the acquittal of Toronto's newspaper *The Body Politic.* The announcement was made on July 13, less than one month after the recent court decision. This third trial will be limited to the Pink Triangle Press, publisher of the paper. As Canadian law has no protection against double jeopardy, "there is no legal limit to the number of times the Crown can appeal an acquittal." The news sparked a demonstration at the Canadian embassy in Washington, D.C.

833. Bate, Neel. "A Gay Magazine Ahead of Its Day." THE ADVOCATE, 349 (19 August, 1982), 41.

In March, 1937, the magazine *Bachelor* began a nine-month run of publication. This article examines its contents and format and presents speculation as to the reasons for its demise.

834. "P.W. Interviews." PUBLISHER'S WEEKLY, 222 (24 September, 1982), 6-8.

This article is an interview with openly gay novelist Edmund White. Among the topics discussed are his emergence and growth as a writer and the difficulties he experienced attempting to have his works published.

835. Dubow, David. "The People Who Brought England Its Gay News." THE ADVOCATE, 352 (30 September, 1982), 30-33.

An historical look at London's *Gay News,* its development and change. Substantial attention is paid to the famous blasphemy trial of 1977.

836. *"Body Politic* Wins Acquittal on New Case: Second Pending." THE ADVOCATE, 357 (9 December, 1982), 11-12.

On November 1, Judge Thomas Mercer ruled that the Pink Triangle Press, the legal corporation of *The Body Politic,* was not guilty of publishing obscene matter in connection with an article which appeared in April, 1982. Charges were dismissed against the collective's membership on grounds that mere appearance of a name in a masthead was insufficient proof of involvement. A second appeal of a case regarding use of mails to distribute immoral or indecent material will be heard on January 6, 1983, some five years after the original charges were filed.

837. "Censorship Charged in Virginia Seizure of 'Taxi zum Klo.'" THE ADVOCATE, 358 (23 December, 1982), 10.

On October 5, 1982, police in Norfolk, Virginia seized a print of the German award-winning film *Taxi zum Klo,* charging that the content violated the city's obscenity statute. The ACLU is representing the firm to retrieve the print, while the theater has agreed to pay $500 in fines. A counsel for the ACLU said charges will be filed if the police refuse to return the film, which has been widely shown elsewhere with little difficulty.

838. Steakley, Jim. "Anniversary of a Book Burning." THE ADVOCATE, 369 (9 June, 1983), 18-19, 57.

An historical piece covering the fiftieth anniversary of the sacking of the Institute fur Sexualwissenschaft in Berlin on May 6, 1933 by members of the fascist German Youth League as part of a move to "purge Berlin's libraries of un-German books" (p. 19). Virtually the entire contents of the institute research data and library collection, as well as many irreplaceable photographs, were confiscated and the building itself badly damaged. Materials were publicly burned in the opera square on May 10, 1933, along with confiscated materials from other libraries, following a speech by Joseph Goebbels denouncing Dr. Magnus Hirschfeld. Some twelve thousand volumes were destroyed.

839. *"Body Politic* Finally Wins Obscenity Case." THE ADVOCATE, 379 (27 October, 1983), 13.

Upholding two previous decisions of acquittal, Judge Patricia R. German ruled on September 14 that *The Body Politic* was not guilty of transmitting "scurrilous materials" through the mail. Roy McMurty, Ontario Attorney General and initiator of the six-year litigation, stated that he had no plans to pursue the matter further.

840. "Queen Drops Charges Against Body Politic." THE ADVOCATE, 381 (24 November, 1983), 13-14.

A review of the six-year court battle of Toronto's gay community paper, *The Body Politic.* The case is placed in the context of Ontario cultural background and regional attitudes. Of particular interest is the speculation that the real purpose of the initial 1977 raid was to silence a "lively critique of the brutally antigay Toronto police" (p. 13).

841. "Customs Officials Raid London Gay Bookstore." THE ADVOCATE, 395 (29 May, 1984), 10-11.

British customs officers raided London's *Gay's the Word,* the largest bookstore in England stocking homosexual literature, and confiscated some eight hundred books, approximately one-third of the total stock. All titles seized had been imported from the U.S. The store may now face possible charges of importing "indecent" literature. A partial list of materials seized is included and the community response reported.

842. "Yale Gays Win Furor Over Ad in Alumni Magazine." THE ADVOCATE, 399 (24 July, 1984), 18-19.

An article discussing the placement of an advertisement placed in the university's alumni magazine by the Yale Gay and Lesbian Alumni (GALA) and the resulting debate. A history of the group's creation and establishment of chapters is included.

843. "God Save the Queens: Homophobia on the Thames." THE ADVOCATE, 409/410 (11 December, 1984), 39-42.

An opinion piece describing the climate of public opinion and government action towards the gay community in Britain in 1984. Fully half the article is concerned with the wave of seizures of materials by customs and excise officers from *Gay's the Word* and other bookstores, as well as police raids on the newspaper *Gay Times*. Books intended for the International Feminist Book Fair and consignments to community organizations in Scotland have also been seized under the Obscene Publications Act.

844. "News Briefs." THE ADVOCATE, 425 (23 July, 1985), 28-29.

The May, 1985 issue of the Maine gay monthly *Our Paper* was banned from the Portland Public Library by a unanimous vote of the Board of Trustees due to a "safe sex" test printed in that issue. The library director was quoted as describing the chart on safe sex practices as "outright pornography." *Our Paper* has warned that if the ban was not lifted, legal action would be taken.

845. Cummings, Peter. "'Gay's the Word' Bookstore on Trial Over Banned 'Obscene' Literature." THE ADVOCATE, 427, (20 August, 1985), 16-17.

On June 24, 1985, hearings began in London on the suit brought by Her Majesty's government against *Gay's the Word* bookstore. Under an 1876 law, the store is being charged with one hundred charges of "conspiracy to import obscene or indecent literature." At evidence is a large group of books imported from the United States, some of which have been legally sold by mainstream shops for years. A full discussion on the powers of the Customs and Excise office, and the legal background for their action comprise the bulk of the article. The British literary community's outraged reaction and that of American creditors is also reviewed. The author notes that "American gay publications are virtually unobtainable. . . Most American gay magazines haven't been seen in London since mid-1984" (p. 16).

846. "Antigay Rabbi Loses Fight Over Booklist." THE ADVOCATE, 428 (3 September, 1985), 14.

On July 30, 1985, the Brooklyn Public Library announced the reinstatement of a gay reading list for all branches. Removal of the list was initially ordered by library director Kenneth Duchac following a meeting with the Family Defense Coalition and Rabbi Yehuda Levin. Rabbi Levin described the fifteen-item anno-tated list as "an affront to family values." The library received substantial pressure from sources within the profession as well as the National Coalition on Censorship and the NYCLU. Reference is made to the American Library Association's Bill of Rights under which library material evaluation "is not to be used as a convenient means to remove materials presumed to be controversial" (p. 14).

847. "Gentlemen's Agreement." ESQUIRE, 104 (November, 1985), 127-128.

Rumors that one of the potential candidates for the Presidency in the 1988 election has a homosexual past are discussed with staff members of the *Los Angeles Times, New York Times, Wall Street Journal* and the White House correspondent for National Public Radio. General agreement is exhibited that an "unacknowledged code of silence" (p. 127) on homosexuality exists among reporters and that such an issue varies in relevance to a political career.

848. Pally, Marcia. "William Burroughs: A Literary Treasure, Lost for Thirty Years, Is Finally Published." THE ADVOCATE, 427 (7 January, 1986), 68-70.

An interview with writer William Burroughs, discussing his views on the current problems (including possible censorship recommendations by the Meese Commission). Particular note is taken of the decision to finally issue his novel *Queer*, originally written in 1953. Recalling the initial reception, Burroughs notes that "my publisher said he'd go to jail . . . it was the homosexuality. Absolutely, it was completely taboo." A useful sum of several decades' activity in regard to U.S. attitudes on censorship.

849. Karlinsky, Simon. "The Case of Gennady Trifonov." NEW YORK REVIEW OF BOOKS, 10 April, 1986, 44.

This article summarizes the harassment endured by openly gay Russian poet Gennady Trifonov since the early 1970s, including four years at hard labor under article 121 of the Soviet criminal code, which prohibits homosexuality. The chief evidence used to convict him was his own writings. Unable to find employment except as a stevedore, Trifonov has been consistently refused an exit visa. At the time of writing, a new case was being constructed which threatened further imprisonment. Karlinsky's article is intended to publicize the situation of a "man being framed for being a homosexual." Letters of support are solicited.

850. Cummings, Peter. "British Customs Drops Obscenity Case: Gay's the Word Wins Without Court Battle." THE ADVOCATE, 452 (5 August, 1986), 17.

On June 27, the Customs and Excise Division of Great Britain returned all but nineteen of 142 titles seized in an April, 1984 massive raid on the largest gay and lesbian bookstore in London. One hundred pending charges were dropped on the order of Treasury Secretary Peter Brooke. Political considerations, both domestic and those of a recent decision by the European Supreme Court, are believed to have caused this action. In future, Customs will state in advance whether books are indecent rather than burning them at the ports of entry. MP Chris Smith has introduced a bill on July 2 recommending the scrapping of the provisions of the 1876 Customs Law used as a basis for the raids.

851. Karlinsky, Simon. "The Soviet Union Vs. Gennady Trifonov." THE ADVOCATE, 453, (19 August, 1986), 42-49.

A history of the life of the contemporary Russian poet Gennady Trifonov, including a detailed record of his trials and incarceration by the KGB. Grounds for these actions are stated to be Article 121 of the Soviet criminal code, which "forbids homosexuality--not the committing of any homosexual acts, but the mere fact of being a homosexual" (p. 46). Trifonov has circulated his poetry in samizdat format, given readings in private homes, and has sent copies abroad where critical reception has been favorable. Efforts in the West to aid Trifonov are called for.

852. "FCC Investigates Radio Broadcast of Gay Play." THE ADVOCATE, 460 (25 November, 1986), 17.

The Federal Communications Commission has received a complaint with regard to an August 31, 1986 late night broadcast of Robert Chesley's play *Jerker* over Los Angeles radio station KPFK-FM. The complaint was filed by Rev. Larry Poland, an evangelical pastor. At issue is the possible effect of what Poland refers to as "porno broadcasting." *Jerker* portrays a relationship between two men exchanging sexual fantasies by phone and culminates in the death of one of them from AIDS. An FCC official noted that this is the first such investigation for obscene broadcasting since 1978. If convicted, Pacifica Foundation, the owners of KPFK, could face up to a twenty thousand dollar fine and the loss of their license.

853. "The New York Times Vs. Gay America." THE ADVOCATE, 461 (9 December, 1986), 112-115.

A profile of the treatment and coverage accorded gay people and the subject of homosexuality by *The New York Times* newspaper. Topics addressed include representative coverage of community events, terminology, and editorial policies. While recent improvement is noted, severe criticisms are also leveled by community organizations. The *Times* editorial staff declined comment when solicited for this piece.

Religion

854. Ross, Kenneth N. LETTER TO A HOMOSEXUAL. London: The Talbot Press (S.P.C.K.), 1955.

   A pamphlet on homosexuality by a member of the Anglican clergy expressing concern for then-current British laws on the subject and advising a life of continence, chastity and avoiding temptation to the homosexual Christian.

855. "Church Rules on Homosexuality." THE LADDER, 2, 2 (November, 1957), 21.

   A 155 to 138 vote by the executive committee of the Church of England destigmatizing homosexual acts between consenting adults is reported. The Wolfenden Commission report is seen to have been influential in producing this ruling.

856. "Methodists Take Stand on Homosexuality." THE LADDER, 2, 11 (August, 1958), 13.

   A report on the recommendation by the Methodist Church of England that homosexual acts in private by consenting adults should be legalized forms this news item. This action was taken to support the conclusions of the Wolfenden Report.

857.   Wood, Robert W. CHRIST AND THE HOMOSEXUAL (SOME OBSERVATIONS). New York: Vantage Press, 1960.

Rev. Robert Wood's attack on the morality of the condemnation of homosexuals by the Christian church--and, to a lesser extent, the societal influence of religious pronouncements--is one of the most important early writings on this issue. The first section, entitled "Snapshots of the Landscape," begins with the statement that "the homosexual community is a vast complex segment of society," and presents seven vignettes which together graphically portray the situation of American homosexuals in the 1950s and early 1960s.

The homosexual community in the United States and its influence as part of social changes between 1942 and 1960 is next profiled, with the third section discussing "the homosexual's problems." The opening sentence states that "no one, knowing all the personal and social problems which the homosexual must face in contemporary America, would voluntarily choose to become a member of the homosexual community" (p. 63). Employment discrimination, blackmail, military discharges and social isolation are all examined.

Section IV, "Where Is the Church?," evaluates the historic role played by the church with regard to homosexuality, in areas as diverse as civil rights and scriptural prohibitions. Three chief reasons are cited as supporting a negative attitude: ignorance, refusal to examine the situation, and oppression. Reverend Wood then proposes that the Church "should immediately implement its message of love by positive acts of concern for the homosexual and his affliction" (p. 119). This can be done through various means, such as a reinterpretation of relevant Biblical passages and establishing an "Institute of Homosexual Studies."

While researchers will find prejudices of the time clearly visible, Christ and the Homosexual remains one of the first works to have raised the issue of organized religion and its attitudes towards gay people.

858.   "N.Y. Mattachine Convention." THE LADDER, 6, 4 (January, 1962), 19-22.

New York Mattachine's 1961 convention was addressed by two speakers whose topics were the attitudes of organized religion towards homosexuality and improved sex laws. Rev. William Zion detailed both the Catholic and Anglican official positions on this issue, as well as exploring the idea of celibacy. Sex law improvement was seen as a function of changing public opinion towards the subject, a matter in which religious attitudes are extremely influential.

859.   "Changing Religious Attitudes." THE LADDER, 7, 1 (October, 1962), 7-10.

Rev. Robert Wood, prominent author of the controversial *Christ and the Homosexual*, spoke on the attitudes of established religion towards homosexuality at the ninth annual conference of the Mattachine Society. Acknowledging a need for ministry to the homosexual community, his discussion moved to recent instances of debate and change. Specific topics mentioned were the problems of homosexual members of the clergy, civil liberties and the role of the Church, the need for constructive dialogue and whether homosexual marriage was permissible within a religious context.

860.   "Changing Religious Attitudes Toward Homosexuality." THE MATTACHINE REVIEW, 8, 11 (November, 1962), 4-12; and 8, 12 (December, 1962), 21-29.

Rev. Robert W. Wood, author of *Christ and the Homosexual*, delivered this address at the Ninth Annual Conference of the Mattachine Society in San Francisco on August 25, 1982. Beginning in 1955, he examines the trends in various religious denominations to acknowledge and address the need for ministry to homosexuals. The general issue of sexuality is also raised. Both positive and negative statements are included, creating a clear picture of a very tangled debate.

861.   "Towards a Quaker View of Sex: Introduction and Basic Assumptions." THE MATTACHINE REVIEW, 9, 4 (April, 1963), 26-34.

This article is an excerpt from the report on sexual matters issued by the Society of Friends in 1963, and covers the history of the project and the ethical views of the Society as a whole with regard to the morality of love.

862. "Towards a Quaker View of Sex, Part II: Normal Sexual Development." THE MATTACHINE REVIEW, 9, 5 (May, 1963), 4-10, 23-34.

Continuing the exposition of the Quaker attitude towards sex, this chapter from the "Quaker Report" provides a clear statement of their views on usual human sexual development and orientation.

863. "Towards a Quaker View of Sex, Part III: Homosexuality." THE MATTACHINE REVIEW, 9, 6 (June 1963), 4-20.

A considered view of the subject of homosexuality (as perceived by the study group of the Society of Friends which produced the "Quaker Report") is presented in this article. Beginning with the statement that "one should no more deplore homosexuality than left-handedness," attention is given to both male and female homosexuality, their origin and society's response. This latter begins with the persecution of Constantine's sons and Justinian and extends to an examination of then-current English law. Legal reform efforts in this matter prior to the Wolfenden Report are also reviewed.

864. "Biblical References to Female Homosexuality." THE LADDER, 7, 9 (June, 1963), 16-18.

A brief summary of a lecture given by the Rev. Robert Wood to the New York chapter of the Daughters of Bilitis on April 27, 1963. Homosexual references in the Bible are noted and placed in cultural context as Hebrew condemnation of practices associated with paganism.

865. "The Church and the Homosexual: A New Report." THE LADDER, 8, 12 (September, 1964), 9-13.

Representatives of five Protestant denominations and four major homophile organizations met in retreat near San Francisco from May 30 to June 2, 1964. Questions addressed centered about the attitudes of established doctrines (as distinct from basic theological dogma), the vagueness of sex law and legislation and proposed activism in religion and society. As a result of this meeting, the Council on Religion and the Homosexual was formed.

866. "Clergy Shatter Another Taboo." CHRISTIAN CENTURY, 81 (23 December, 1964), 1581.

> An editorial opinion on the purposes of the newly-created Council on Religion and the Homosexual. While the stated goal of dialogue between gay persons and organized religion is viewed as laudable, the writer sees it as insufficient. The Council is seen as a means of both reconciliation and "rehabilitation of those homosexuals who can be restored to a sexual life of the kind approved by the Christian church."

867. "National Church Group Discusses Homosexuality." THE LADDER, 10, 7 (April, 1966), 13.

> This article summarizes a meeting held on January 7, 1966 at the headquarters of the National Council of Churches. Participants included clergy, homosexuals and professional people. The object of the gathering was to develop working principles to guide active ministry to the gay community. As a recommendation issued afterwards states, "the basic problem for the churches is to find some means of understanding their own role with the homosexual: i.e., we ought to be more concerned with the churches' problem of ignorance, rejection and condemnation, than with problems of what homosexuality is."

868. "They're Still At It." THE MATTACHINE REVIEW, 11, 1 (July, 1966), 21-26.

> A conservative fundamentalist organization known as Teen Challenge was created in 1960 in an attempt to cope with juvenile delinquency on the streets of New York City. With its expansion to ten major United States cities, it began to shift focus to other groups, including homosexuals. This article consists of excerpts from two pamphlets distributed by the group to aid these efforts. The aim is to "cure" homosexuals through a program of absolute self-denial.

869. "Cross Currents." THE LADDER, 11, 1 (October, 1966), 24.

> Noteworthy in this column is the first recorded public execution of a homosexual in Yemen. Ahmed el-Osamy, sixty years of age, was shot in the central square of the city of Sana'a before six thousand witnesses.

Islamic law decrees that any man convicted of homosexuality should be thrown from the highest point in
the city.

870. "Friends in the Morning: The Church in Action." THE
LADDER, 11, 2 (November, 1966), 4-14.

This article summarizes presentations given at the
Daughters of Bilitis national convention, San
Francisco, August 20, 1966, on the topic "The Homophile
Community and Civic Organizations--How Well Do They
Relate?" Speakers represented included Methodist
clergy and activists from the Council on Religion and
the Homosexual. The role of organized religion for
gays and lesbians was a chief theme of the day's discussions.

871. "God and the Homosexual." NEWSWEEK, 69 (13 February,
1967), 63.

An interview article with clergymen in the San
Francisco Bay Area involved with the Council on Religion and the Homosexual. Both positive and negative
theological stances are profiled.

872. "Judaism and Homosexuality." THE LADDER, 11, 6 (April,
1967), 18-20.

Rabbi Elliot Grafman, speaking at the January, 1967
annual meeting of the Council on Religion and the
Homosexual, explored the position of Judaism relative
to gay activity. After citing the traditional texts
condemning such behavior (Leviticus 20, Verse 18), he
called for further education of the population in
general to reduce resistance to accepting gays and
lesbians, and pointed out that contemporary Judaism was
engaged in debate on this issue, among others.

873. "Homosexual Wedding." NEWSWEEK, 70 (17 July, 1967), 59.

A news report of a joining ceremony for a male couple
in Rotterdam, Holland involving a Catholic priest.
Local diocesan reaction evaded the issue of official
sanction of a same-sex union.

874. "The Bible and the Homosexual." CHRISTIANITY TODAY, 12 (19 January, 1968), 24-25. Reply, 12 (1 March, 1968), 23.

An unsigned opinion piece addressing proposed alterations in the manner of viewing homosexuals by professing Christians. "Compassion for the deviate" is stressed while traditional Biblical condemnations such as Paul and the Book of Leviticus are reaffirmed. A reply letter from a clergyman supports this view.

875. "Homosexual Acts Morally Neutral, Priests Say." THE ADVOCATE, 2, 2 (February, 1968), 4.

On November 28, 1967, Project H, a day-long conference of Episcopal clergy of the greater New York area on the church's approach to homosexuality, was held at the cathedral church of St. John the Divine. The featured speaker was Dr. Wardell Pomeroy, co-author of the Kinsey report on female sexuality. Opinion favored viewing homosexual acts per se as worthy of being judged by criteria other than automatic condemnation. Both majority and minority views are given. This piece originally appeared in the *New York Times* for November 28, 1967.

876. "Religious Group Urges Recognition of Homosexual's Rights." CHRISTIANITY CENTURY, 85 (5 June, 1968), 744-745.

A review article presenting the goals and objectives of the Council on Religion and the Homosexual in the areas of public education, sexual law reform and civil rights. The author notes that Christians can endorse these goals while not approving of homosexuality per se.

877. Wood, Robert. "Homosexuality and the Church." THE LADDER, 13, 3/4 (December 1968-January, 1969), 4-13.

Rev. Robert Wood begins by listing problems confronting American society with which the Church must deal. Including moral readjustment of individuals and institutions among these, he calls the Church to task for its attitudes and past behavior towards gay people. Stating that "the dialogue has never broken down for it has never been established," twelve moral areas affecting gay persons are noted as requiring effort on the part of the establishment. These are: law reform, increased activism by military chaplains on behalf of accused homosexuals, education of the clergy on the subject of homosexuality, civil rights, elimination of discrimination in admission to seminaries, fair employment practices, corporate attitudes, full church membership for homosexuals and admission of the existence and validity of homosexual marriage, childless couples, homosexuality on campus and Biblical texts as the basis for discriminatory practices.

878. "Homosexuality in the Bible and the Law." CHRISTIANITY TODAY, 13 (18 July, 1969), 7-10.

An essay by an Australian theologian exploring the relationship of Christian morality and civil legislation as regards homosexuality. The author notes that, as traditional legal restraints in this area have been demonstrably ineffective, the provisions of the Wolfenden Report offer a less draconian alternative to Scriptural treatment of homosexuality as a capital crime.

879. "Cross Currents." THE LADDER, 14, 1/2 (October-November, 1969), 29-41.

Among the news items in this column is a note on the meeting of the Council for Christian Social Action of the United Church of Christ on April 12, 1969. At this meeting, a document supportive of homosexuals was adopted. Entitled "Homosexuals and the Law," it was to be presented to the national conference of that denomination in August, 1969.

880. Davidson, Alex. THE RETURNS OF LOVE: LETTERS OF A CHRISTIAN HOMOSEXUAL. Downers Grove, IL: InterVarsity Press, 1970.

A collection of letters written by the author to a friend exploring the deeply-felt conflict between personal emotional needs for a satisfying same-sex relationship and Christian ethical strictures.

881. "Churches and the Homosexual." AMERICA, 124 (6 February, 1971), 113-117. Discussion, 124 (20 March, 1970), 273.

A news report examining and evaluating the efforts of four San Francisco Bay area religious organizations to open a dialogue with the homosexual community. Groups included are the Newman-Lutheran Campus Ministry at Berkeley, the Council on Religion and the Homosexual, the Pacific School of Religion and the Metropolitan Community Church. The accompanying letter of commentary refers to the attitude of the Roman Catholic church towards homosexuality as "retardation in full flower" (p. 273).

882.   "Priests Call for Homosexual Rights." THE ADVOCATE, 4, 4 (April, 1970), 3.

At a meeting in Berkeley, California, the Convention of the Episcopal Peace Fellowship passed a resolution calling upon their church to "stop sitting on her hands" and to act to remove the effects of oppression on both women and homosexuals.

883.   "Cross Currents." THE LADDER, 14, 7/8 (April-May, 1970), 31-38.

Daniel Gorham was dismissed from the Immaculate Conception Seminary in Conception, Missouri on January 15, 1970. Grounds for this action lay in a letter printed in *LOOK* magazine on January 13, 1970 wherein Gorham described himself as president of The Vineyard ("an organization founded in 1967 for both homosexuals and heterosexuals who wish to give themselves to the church"). In the letter Gorham stated his beliefs that the church had not turned its back on gays and that homosexual activity was no bar to membership. Humorously, Gorham also admitted to being a heterosexual.

884.   "Should Bless Union, Cleric Says." THE ADVOCATE, 4, 8 (10-23 June, 1970), 1.

Speaking at a meeting of the Homosexual Law Reform Society in Auckland, New Zealand, Anglican clergyman Rev. Morris Russell stated that the Christian church should find a way to welcome committed homosexual couples into membership and that homosexual acts "expressing love and tenderness" could not be considered sinful.

885.   "Cross Currents." THE LADDER, 14, 9/10 (June-July, 1970), 33-40.

 The Episcopal Diocese of Detroit deprived St. Joseph's Church and its rector, the Rev. Robert Norrison, of its allocated funds as punishment for allowing a homosexual group to use the church as a meeting place.

886.   "Presbyterian Report on Homosexuality: It's a Sin--Or Is It?" THE ADVOCATE, 4, 9 (24 June-7 July, 1970), 2.

 At its annual General Assembly in Chicago, The United Presbyterian Church approved for study a thirty-four-page report intended as a guide to the development of "Christian ethical sensibilities." While stating that they had found "no systematic ethical guidance from interpretation which relied solely on the laws or stories of the Bible" in the three years' research which preceded the conference, a final paragraph added at the assembly condemned homosexuality and premarital relations as sinful.

887.   "Homosexuality Not So Bad, Lutherans, Unitarians Decide." THE ADVOCATE, 4, 12 (5-18 August, 1970), 1.

 A report on the decisions of the Lutheran Church in America and the Unitarian Universalist Association to "accept homosexuals fully into the life of the church." Both resolutions were passed in the first week of July, 1970 and complete texts are included.

888.   "13th Century Theologian Knew Some Men Must Love Men." THE ADVOCATE, 4, 12 (5-18 August, 1970), 8.

 A comment upon a portion of the Summa Theologica of St. Thomas Aquinas which states that relations between men who are attracted to other men could not be considered as unnatural. The observation was part of a lecture given at the ONE Institute reception on July 8, 1970 by Dr. Hermann Van De Spyker, a Dutch sociologist who had written on homosexuality. The views of contemporary Dutch society and clergy on homosexuality are included.

889.   "Homosexual Church." CHRISTIANITY TODAY, 14 (11 September, 1970), 48-50.

An investigative report on the foundation, theology and activism of the Metropolitan Community Church as it existed in 1970.

890. "Catholic View: It's a No-No." THE ADVOCATE, 4, 14 (2-15 September, 1970), 22.

A news report on the publication in *L'Osservatore Romano* of an article by Franciscan theologian Fr. Gino Concetti warning against the legalization of same-sex marriages, terming them "moral aberrations that cannot be approved by the human conscience."

891. "Homosexual Church." NEWSWEEK, 76 (12 October, 1970), 107.

A brief interview with Rev. Troy Perry, founder of the Metropolitan Community Church, discussing the purposes of the denomination.

892. "Cross Currents." THE LADDER, 15, 1/2 (October-November, 1970), 24-31.

Two items in this edition of the popular news column relate to religion:

a) A decision in July, 1970, by the General Assembly of the Unitarian Universalist Church, calling for an end to discrimination against homosexuals. One resolution specifically admits the presence of homosexuals and bisexuals in both the clergy and the membership of the church in general.

b) An editorial in the *San Francisco Chronicle* of July 7, 1970, examining homosexual marriage. The Metropolitan Community Church services are mentioned and a call is issued for the right of gay people to have such sanctions for their relationships.

893. "Gays Tell It Like It Is at Catholic Seminar." THE ADVOCATE, 4, 21 (9-22 December, 1970), 7.

From November 9-13, 1970, a seminar on "Theology and Homosexuality" was held at the Catholic University of America in Washington, D.C. This article reviews the papers presented and highlights the conflicts between traditional psychiatric views of homosexuality and the call for theological reinterpretation. Speakers included Dr. Franklin Kameny and Fr. Charles Curran.

894. "The Roman Catholic Lesbian: The Old Order Changeth." THE LADDER, 15, 3/4 (December, 1970-January, 1971), 15-22.

This article discusses the changes occurring within the Catholic Church consequent to reforms enunciated by Vatican II and their relationship to the life of Catholic lesbians. Traditional arguments against homosexuality--based on "natural law"--are presented, and relevant points of dogma and theology concisely explained. Changes affecting lesbian Catholics cited are the Dutch Catechism and more individual interpretation of church teachings by local clergy. The author's own experiences are shared for the purposes of illustration.

895. "Rebel Catholic Priests Start Ministry for Gays." THE ADVOCATE, 4, 24 (20 January-2 February, 1971), 3.

An outline of the origin and purposes of the Community of St. John the Beloved, a new ministry for the gay community begun in San Francisco in 1971 by Rev. Robert J. Richards, S.H.J. and other dissident Catholic clergy. Background on the founders is provided.

896. "Church Should Bless Gay Marriages." THE ADVOCATE, 52 (3-16 February, 1971), 3.

Michael De-La-Noy, former press secretary to the Archbishop of Canterbury, in a sermon at St. Margaret's Anglican church in King's Lynn on January 3, 1971 called for the acceptance of gay unions by the church. He had been sacked following publication of articles condemning the hierarchy's attitude towards sexual problems.

897. "The Church and Gay Liberation." CHRISTIAN CENTURY, 88 (3 March, 1971), 281-285.

A thoughtful exploration of the challenges posed to organized Christian thought and practice by the nascent gay liberation movement. Topics addressed include stereotypes, the most effective use of gay clergy and the growth of homosexual religious bodies such as the Metropolitan Community Church.

898. "Oakland Catholics Deny Gays Banned at Mass." THE ADVOCATE, 57 (14-27 April, 1971), 4.

A news story on the truth behind an alleged ban on Masses or meetings for homosexuals by Bishop Floyd Begin of the Diocese of Oakland. Misunderstanding of an earlier order to a community center is seen as the cause of this rumor.

899. "Philadelphia Pickets Confront Rev. McIntire." THE ADVOCATE, 58 (28 April-11 May, 1971), 3.

On March 28, 1971, protestors from two Philadelphia area homosexual groups confronted the Rev. Carl McIntire at his church in suburban Collingwood. At issue were statements made by McIntire placing homosexuality "in the corrupt realm which God forbids and does not judge."

900. "Lutheran Seminary Bans 'Gay House' Co-Ordinator." THE ADVOCATE, 58 (28 April-11 May, 1971), 4.

A news report from Minneapolis on the barring of local activist and candidate for the Episcopal priesthood John Preston by the Northwestern Theological Seminary in St. Paul from taking one course. Details of the debate are included.

901. "Cross Currents." THE LADDER, 15, 7/8 (April-May, 1971), 38-42.

A news item in this column reports on a statement from King's Lynn, England dated January, 1971. In that month, Michael De-La-Noy, director of the Sexual Law Reform Society, appealed to officials of the Anglican Church to consider blessing permanent homosexual unions.

902. "'I Do' Rites Stir Hassle in New York." THE ADVOCATE, 59 (12-25 May, 1971), 2.

On April 21, 1971, Rev. Robert Clement, pastor of the Church of the Beloved Disciple in New York City, was informed that city clerk Herman Katz considered the "services of holy union" used to join same-sex couples as illegal and misdemeanors. Katz refused press comment and direct contact with Clement but plans legal action.

903.   "Gays Won't Wait, Churches Told." THE ADVOCATE, 59 (12-25 May, 1971), 2.

A profile of statements made at the First National Conference on Religion and the Homosexual held in New York City. Speakers included Rev. Robert Woods, author of *Christ and the Homosexual* and Rev. Robert Clement. Organizations from Lincoln, Nebraska and Methodist, Presbyterian, Lutheran and Episcopal clergy were represented.

904.   "Outspoken Anglican Ires Memphis Christians." THE ADVOCATE, 69 (12-25 May, 1971), 3.

During a speaking engagement at Memphis State University, Dr. Norman Pittenger, an Anglican theologian, called for churches to help homosexuals find fulfillment in their lives. Fundamentalist reaction from the community was severe.

905.   "Florida Fellowship Rejects Miami MCC." THE ADVOCATE, 60 (26 May-8 June, 1971), 8.

An application for membership in the Fellowship of Churches in Southern Florida by the Miami chapter of the Metropolitan Community Church was rejected "on the basis that MCC lacks the morals and faith of other member churches."

906.   "Evangelists Re-Damn Gays." THE ADVOCATE, 61 (9-22 June, 1971), 8.

Meeting in Westchester, California, a suburb of Los Angeles, the Twenty-Ninth Annual Convention of the National Association of Evangelists restated its belief that there is no Biblical basis for approval of homosexuality. Christian sociologists, psychologists and physicians are called on to find the cause and cure.

907. "Baptists Disapprove, Plan Study." THE ADVOCATE, 61 (9-22 June, 1971), 8.

A news story on the creation in Minneapolis by the Committee on Social Concerns of the American Baptist Convention of a task force on homosexuality. Said group is charged with the drafting of a major policy statement on the issue for presentation to the 1972 annual meeting. The confrontation between John Preston of the local Gay House community center and the committee is detailed. Preston criticized the committee for not including gays or persons who did not view homosexuality as a pathology on the committee.

908. "Homosexual Minister?" NEWSWEEK, 77 (14 June, 1971), 114.

A brief news article on the suspension of Rev. Gene Leggett of the Southwest Texas Conference of the United Methodist Church on grounds of homosexuality.

909. "Homosexuality, Aquinas and the Church." CATHOLIC WORLD, 213 (July, 1971), 183-186.

Written by a professor of philosophy, this article examines the traditional position of the Catholic church on homosexuality with special attention to the teachings of St. Thomas Aquinas. The logic of such positions is questioned.

910. "Texas Methodists Sack Admitted Gay Minister." THE ADVOCATE, 62 (23 June-6 July, 1971), 4.

A detailed summary of the events attending the dismissal of Rev. Gene Leggett of Dallas from the Southwest Conference of the United Methodist Church on grounds of homosexuality.

911. "Cross Currents." THE LADDER, 15, 9/10 (June-July, 1971), 40-46.

An article is noted in the periodical *The Christian Century* on the church and gay liberation, focusing particularly on the desire of gay men and lesbians for monogamous, legally sanctified marriages.

912. "Catholic Priests Listen to Gays." THE ADVOCATE, 63 (7-20 July, 1971), 8.

A report on the dialogue between Michael McConnell and some sixty Catholic clergy and lay persons at a retreat at St. John's University near Minneapolis on June 6, 1971. The speeches occurred as part of a discussion of pastoral concerns for the gay lifestyle.

913. "Unitarians Form Own Gay Group." THE ADVOCATE, 64 (21 July-3 August, 1971), 15.

A description of the formation of a gay and lesbian caucus within the Unitarian Universalist Association by Richard Nash and Elgin Blair at that denomination's general meeting June 6-12, 1971. The organizers cited instances of discrimination by church officers in Dallas, Los Angeles and Toronto despite a 1970 resolution condemning anti-gay prejudices.

914. "Father Clement Scheduled to Wed His Longtime Mate." THE ADVOCATE, 65 (4-17 August, 1971), 4.

The pastor of New York City's Church of the Beloved Disciple has scheduled a union ceremony for himself and his partner despite the contention by the city clerk that such joinings violate a provision of the state penal code covering unlawful solemnization of marriages. Father Clement has performed more than forty such unions for same-sex couples.

915. "Catholic Gay Ministry Planned." THE ADVOCATE, 66 (18-31 August, 1971), 15.

Discussions on the possibility of establishing a ministry to the gay community were held at the Community of St. John the Beloved, a non-affiliated Catholic commune in San Francisco. Discussants were seven members of the Catholic clergy and a specialist in canon law.

916. "Gay Church." TIME, 98 (23 August, 1971), 38-39.

A profile of developments in Christianity in the early 1970s relating to homosexuality. These include the establishment of the Metropolitan Community and American Orthodox Churches, the theologies of which are considered in detail.

917. "Cross Currents." THE LADDER, 15, 11/12 (August-September, 1971), 37-43.

Activities of the Church of the Beloved Disciple in New York City in the area of performing Holy Union ceremonies for lesbian and gay couples are noted.

918. "Bishop Reprimands Cleric, Protests Save His Job." THE ADVOCATE, 70 (13 October, 1971), 32.

A description of the controversy surrounding Rev. Roger Lynn of Minneapolis following his performance of a union ceremony for two men in a private residence. Reaction from the Methodist hierarchy and the popular press is presented.

919. Laurence, Leo. "Quakers Launch Major Gay Study." THE ADVOCATE, 71 (27 October, 1971), 10.

At the 1971 Pacific Yearly Meeting in Salem, Oregon of the Society of Friends, the Ministry and Oversight Committee decided to establish a research project on homosexuality which would "seek ways by which homosexuals can be assured that they need not hide their identity . . . within local churches." Documentation from local meetings which have dealt with the subject are requested.

920. "Toronto Priest Performs Double Gay Wedding." THE ADVOCATE, 72 (10 November, 1971), 15.

An interview with Father Boniface, a Toronto priest who recently performed a private double union ceremony. A description of the difficulties attending the event is provided.

921. "Mass for Gays Draws Criticism." THE ADVOCATE, 73 (24 November, 1971), 6.

On October 19, 1971, the Gay Christian Activists of Chicago leafleted a Legion of Mary Mass being held at St. Sebastian's Church. At issue was the refusal of

John Cardinal Cody to permit semi-monthly "masses for gays" to be publicly announced. Further protests are planned for the central cathedral.

922. "Priest Group, MSNF Talk." THE ADVOCATE, 73 (24 November, 1971), 9.

A report on the opening of dialogue in Buffalo, New York between the Mattachine Society of the Niagara Frontier and the local Catholic Priest's Association. The chair of the Society's legal committee urged the Association to "make a positive statement in support of state and local gay rights bills." Membership in the unofficial Association comprises approximately one-fifth of the clergy in the Buffalo diocese.

923. Dubay, William. "Gays Should Avoid Condemning All Religion." THE ADVOCATE, 75 (22 December, 1971), 27.

An article by a former Catholic priest on the role played by churches in fostering social change in the U.S. Criticism of all religion by gay activists is discouraged in favor of developing institutions to supplement the work being done by churches.

924. Perry, Rev. Troy D. THE LORD IS MY SHEPHERD AND HE KNOWS I'M GAY. THE AUTOBIOGRAPHY OF THE REV. TROY D. PERRY. Los Angeles: Nash Publishing, 1972.

One of the very few autobiographies available for a contemporary leader of the gay religious community, this thought-provoking volume details Reverend Perry's history from childhood to his present role as founder and leader of the Metropolitan Community Church. Its foundation on October 6, 1968 grew out of the alienation felt by many gay people due to the official position of many established faiths that "one couldn't be a homosexual and a Christian too" (p. 7). Accounts of harassment of both Reverend Perry and the MCC illustrate graphically several common attitudes of religious homophobia.

925. "S.F. Quakers Endorse Gay Rights." THE ADVOCATE, 76 (5 January, 1972), 31.

On November 14, 1971, the local meeting of the Society of Friends in San Francisco approved a broad statement supporting civil and religious rights for homosexuals. The full text is enclosed. Debate on homosexual issues in the Southern California meetings of the Friends is profiled.

926. "Church Hires Gay Activist." THE ADVOCATE, 76 (5 January, 1972), 31.

A report on the appointment of Minneapolis activist John Preston as director of minority outreach programs at the Universal Episcopal Center. Duties will include adult education programs and fund raising" to fulfill the social responsibilities which Episcopalians have traditionally considered important."

927. "Church Backs Rights Law." THE ADVOCATE, 79 (16 February, 1972), 9.

A report on the addition of the Episcopal Diocese of California to religious groups supporting efforts to include homosexuals under San Francisco's anti-discrimination law. Other groups involved are the United Church of Christ and the Methodist Church.

928. "Methodist Faction Set to Block Nod to Gays." THE ADVOCATE, 79 (16 February, 1972), 10.

A profile of the conservative position of members of the Methodist hierarchy regarding the ordination of homosexuals to the pastorate. Bishops Gerald Kennedy of Los Angeles and Thomas Pryor of Chicago are interviewed, and the recent cases of Rev. Gene Leggett and Rev. Charles Lamont summarized. As of February, 1972, no petition for recognition of gay clergy had been received by the church.

929. Bjornsen, Lars. "Presbyterian Head Would Welcome Gays." THE ADVOCATE, 81 (15 March, 1972), 17.

An interview with Lois Stair, moderator of the United Presbyterian Church U.S.A. She calls for the church to recognize its responsibility in the area of sexuality education "so we do not immediately denounce and condemn other persons . . . for behavior we really know

256

nothing about." Her experiences with gays in her home church in Waukesha, Wisconsin is related.

930. "Gay Rights Fight Looms at Methodist Conclave." THE ADVOCATE, 81 (15 March, 1972), 17.

A petition seeking "civil rights for homosexuals" has been submitted to the United Methodist National Board of Christian Social Concerns by Rev. Tom Maurer of the Glide Memorial Methodist Church in San Francisco. Debate is expected to center upon a statement from the church Family Life Committee which reportedly considers the homosexual lifestyle as a viable alternative. The group has no plans to address the qualifications of homosexuals to serve as Methodist clergy.

931. "Nearly 40 Ministers, Social Workers Rap with Gays at Seminar." THE ADVOCATE, 82 (29 March, 1972), 5.

A summary of the discussions held in a day-long seminar, The Church and the Gay Community in St. Paul, between forty Methodist, Lutheran, Presbyterian and Baptist clergy and social workers and representatives of the gay community. Opinions on gay issues were marked by a willingness to question traditionally held positions. The event was sponsored by the community center for gays.

932. "Chicago Minister Faces Suspension." THE ADVOCATE, 82 (29 March, 1972), 13.

A profile of the case of the Rev. Charles Lamont, dismissed from the Methodist Northern Illinois Conference on grounds of homosexuality. The procedural details of the dismissal under the Methodist Discipline are provided. The suspension took effect on February 14, 1972.

933. "Methodists Due Challenge." THE ADVOCATE, 82 (29 March, 1972), 13.

Debate on religious and civil rights for homosexuals will occur on four levels at the United Methodist Conference in Atlanta April 15-20, 1972: a new "social creed" stating the acceptability of homosexuality, two civil rights proposals and the plans of Rev. Charles

Lamont to push for protection of homosexual clergy. Conservative bishops plan opposition to any alterations in traditional positions on homosexuality.

934. "Catholic Outreach." THE ADVOCATE, 83 (12 April, 1972), 1.

The National Federation of Priest's Councils meeting in Denver on March 16, 1972 approved a resolution calling for the removal of "social and psychological stigma" from clergy who work with homosexuals and to develop a model for ministry to the gay community. A report on ways of implementing such a model is due to the federation by August 31, 1972.

935. "Open Up, Petitions Ask Methodists." THE ADVOCATE, 83 (12 April, 1972), 11.

A review of the contents of petitions filed with the secretary of the United Methodist Church for consideration at the April, 1972 general meeting in Atlanta. Those relating to homosexuality address questions of ordination and freedom from discrimination. The general reaction of Methodists to the question of homosexuals is presented.

936. "Methodists Give Gay Group $2000." THE ADVOCATE, 84 (26 April, 1972), 14.

A report on the gifts of $1000 to the Mattachine Society of the Niagara Frontier and the Rochester Gay Liberation Front by the United Methodists of Western New York. The general atmosphere within the church on the issue of homosexuality in 1972 is briefly outlined.

937. "Baptists Hit Proposed Ohio Consent Code." THE ADVOCATE, 85 (10 May, 1972), 4.

News coverage of the presentation made by four Baptist clergymen to hearings held in Columbus on April 4, 1972 before the Ohio Senate Judiciary Committee. At issue was a provision in the revised penal code covering consenting adults, which was condemned as "legalizing homosexuality and adultery."

938. Laurence, Leo and Richard Gayer. "Church of Christ to Ordain Gay: Decision Shatters Religious Tradition." THE ADVOCATE, 36 (24 May, 1972), 1, 12-13.

A detailed news report of the decision by the United Church of Christ to ordain William Johnson, a candidate for ministry who is open about his homosexuality. The full text of support and questions from the floor during the April 30, 1972 debate are included.

939. "Absolutely Not, Say Methodists." THE ADVOCATE, 86 (24 May, 1972), 1, 13.

A summary of actions taken on the question of homosexuality at the Atlanta general conference of the United Methodist Church, April 16-28, 1972. Proposals for the liberalization of church law on homosexuality were voted down, as was a provision of the Methodist Discipline permitting homosexuals to be ordained. While describing homosexuals as "persons of sacred worth," the statement finally approved by the delegates termed homosexuality "incompatible with Christian teaching."

940. "Clement Sees Turning Point." THE ADVOCATE, 86 (24 May, 1972), 9.

Excerpts from the text of a sermon delivered on April 23, 1972 in New York City's Church of the Beloved Disciple by Rev. Robert Clement, calling upon parishioners to follow their conscience in the expanding possibilities of the gay and lesbian movement, as "the church must not be remiss or slow to take its part if it is called upon to witness to moral or ethical truths."

941. "Church Backlash Against Gay Ordination Hinted." THE ADVOCATE, 87 (7 June, 1972), 2.

A profile of the reaction within the United Church of Christ to the decision by the Golden Gate Association of the North California Conference to permit the ordination of openly gay minister William Johnson. The possibility of censure at an upcoming annual meeting of the regional United Church of Christ is raised.

942. "Dear Church, Will You Miss Us When We're Gone?"
CHRISTIAN CENTURY, 89 (7 June, 1972), 660-661.

A pseudonymous personal account of one woman's evolving
lesbian consciousness and her views of organized
religion, wondering if all homosexuals who wished to
remain in churches were to leave, whether they would be
truly missed.

943. "Unitarian District Funds Bid for Gay Affairs Office."
THE ADVOCATE, 87 (7 June, 1972), 14.

A news brief on the provision of funds to the Unitarian
Gay Caucus by the parent church. Said monies will be
used to establish a full-time Office of Gay Concerns.
Efforts by Rev. Richard Nash of San Francisco in
successfully presenting a resolution on sexual minorities to the Pacific/Southwest District of the church
are summarized.

944. "Lamont Suspending Fight to Remain Methodist Cleric." THE
ADVOCATE, 88 (21 June, 1972), 8.

A report on the decision by Methodist clergyman Charles
Lamont of Chicago not to oppose current efforts to
defrock him. Church officials refused media comment
other than that Lamont was personally irresponsible.

945. "Fears for Children Figured Heavily in Methodist Debate."
THE ADVOCATE, 88 (21 June, 1972), 8.

An analytical article discussing the official transcript of testimony and discussion which occurred at the
1972 general conference of the Methodist Church about
homosexuality. A common theme was the fear of homosexuals preying upon and killing young boys. Detailed
coverage of the decisions taken on suggested textual
changes is provided.

946. Golder, W. Evan. "Ordaining a Homosexual Minister."
CHRISTIAN CENTURY, 89 (28 June, 1972), 713-716.

A detailed account of the debate over and ordination of
William Johnson to the ministry of the United Church of
Christ. At a ceremony in San Carlos, California in
late June, 1972, that denomination became the first

major religious body in the United States to "knowingly" ordain a homosexual to its clergy.

947. "Lamont Suggests Forcing Church Confrontations." THE ADVOCATE, 89 (5 July, 1972), 10.

Speaking in Miami, the Rev. Charles Lamont outlined possible strategies of protest for gay and lesbian members of the United Methodist Church. These include refusing communion, silent prayer as disobedience and otherwise denying participation in the liturgy.

948. Laurence, Leo. "Lutheran Head Against Ordination." THE ADVOCATE, 89 (5 July, 1972), 10.

Excerpts from remarks made to a San Francisco news conference by Rev. Robert J. Marshall, president of the Lutheran Church of America on June 5, 1972 indicating his opposition to homosexual clergy in that denomination. A follow-up interview with *The ADVOCATE* comprises the bulk of the article and is useful as a summary of views of the Lutheran community and hierarchy on homosexuality in 1972.

949. "Congregationalists Defeat Backlash." THE ADVOCATE, 89 (5 July, 1972), 11.

A news article covering the June 4 vote by members of San Francisco's First Congregational Church defeating a resolution which declared homosexuals "psychologically unfitted for ordination into the ministry of the United Church of Christ." A brief outline of the opposing position is given.

950. Gayer, Richard. "United Church of Christ Ordains a Homosexual." THE ADVOCATE, 90 (19 July, 1972), 10.

On June 25, 1972, in San Carlos, California, Rev. William Johnson became "the first declared homosexual to be ordained into the Christian ministry." Full details of the ceremony and Johnson's sermon are given in this news article.

951. "Not Because They Are Gay." CHRISTIANITY TODAY, 16 (28 July, 1972), 23.

An editorial on the idea of religious blessing of same-sex relationships. Such requests are viewed as impossible due to specific Biblical proscription of homosexuals as among those "who will not inherit the Kingdom of God."

952. Martin, Robert A. "Quakers 'Come Out' at Conference." THE ADVOCATE, 91 (2 August, 1972), 8.

A detailed news summary of the development in Ithaca, New York at the biennial convention of the Friends General Conference regarding homosexuality and bisexuality. The coming-out speech of Rev. Ronald Mattson of Minneapolis is noted.

953. "Chicago Pastor Gets Church Job." THE ADVOCATE, 93 (30 August, 1972), 16.

News coverage of the appointment of Rev. David Sindt of Chicago to a staff position at the Lincoln Park Presbyterian Church, where he plans "a program of outreach" into the area's "gay ghetto." Sindt was ordained in 1965 and is currently the secretary of the Chicago Gay Alliance.

954. "Cleric's Gay Ministry 'On The Line.'" THE ADVOCATE, 97 (25 October, 1972), 11.

A profile of the gay counseling ministry being conducted by Rev. Robert Hamilton of the Presbytery of Cleveland. That body will vote on October 17, 1973 whether to uphold Hamilton's status as an ordained minister and the validity of his work. Details of a September 26 hearing on the matter provide background.

955. "Priest Hits Catholic Oppression of Gays." THE ADVOCATE, 98 (8 November, 1972), 15.

Content summary of a pseudonymous article appearing in the September, 1972 issue of U.S. Catholic, a popular religious monthly magazine. The author (a middle-aged Minnesota priest) cites Catholic moral theological positions on sexuality and calls for change in this "narrow and repressive" approach to homosexuality.

956. "'Liberated' Church Calls Gay Catholics." THE ADVOCATE, 100 (6 December, 1972), 7.

> An interview with Fr. Laurence Gerard, pastor of Berkeley's St. Procopius Church, a "liberated" Orthodox Catholic congregation calling gay and lesbian Catholics to worship. Father Gerard notes the dissatisfaction some gay Catholics feel with the services of the Metropolitan Community Church.

957. "Ecumenical Bid in N.Y." THE ADVOCATE, 100 (6 December, 1972), 7.

> A joint program of worship services worked out by the MCC and the Episcopal Church of the Holy Apostles in New York City is reviewed. The church was formerly the site of the meetings of the Church of the Beloved Disciple.

958. McCaffrey, Joseph A., ed. THE HOMOSEXUAL DIALECTIC. Englewood Cliffs, NJ: Prentice-Hall, Inc., 1973.

> This anthology of fifteen articles was gathered "to indicate the depth and makeup of the dialectic as perceived by . . . different fields and . . . to portray homosexual reactions to a society where they are not only a minority, but a minority that is generally despised" (p. 2). The first section, "Straight Perspectives," contains excerpts from the Kinsey report (1948) and the National Institute of Mental Health Task Force on Homosexuality study (1967), as well as articles on female homosexuality, law and the homosexual, stereotypes and the changing self-image. In response, the second section is composed chiefly of articles written by gay and lesbian activists of the 1950s and 1960s, such as Paul Goodman and Franklin E. Kameny.

959. Dubay, William. "Gay 'Seekers' Are Free to Find Own Answers to Life." THE ADVOCATE, 102 (3 January, 1973), 37.

> A commentary by a former priest on the spiritual opportunities for growth open to gay people outside traditional religious institutions. Emphasis is placed on transcending "culturally conditioned ways of looking at things."

960. "Homosexuality in Biblical Perspective." CHRISTIANITY TODAY, 17 (16 February, 1973), 12-14.

An extended interview with Swiss theologian Dr. Klaus Bockmuhl discussing arguments based upon the idea that homosexuality is an inborn condition not subject to moralistic strictures. Bockmuhl opposes the position vehemently, citing the prescriptive nature of Christian ethics.

961. "Gays Test Liberality of Dallas Unitarians." THE ADVOCATE, 106 (28 February, 1973), 10.

A review of panel discussions on homosexuality held at the Dallas Unitarian Church in January, 1973. Dialogue was extensive and included debate centered upon removing reactions based upon stereotypes.

962. "Roman Catholic Priest Preaches at Gay Church." THE ADVOCATE, 106 (28 February, 1973), 18.

A news report from New York City on the sermon given to the Church of the Beloved Disciple by Fr. William Lewis as part of Unity for Prayer Week. This is believed to be the first such event on the East Coast.

963. "New Life for Gays in Judaism." THE ADVOCATE, 108 (28 March, 1973), 13.

A descriptive account of the dedication of the Torah at Beth Chayim Chadashim, the gay Jewish temple in Los Angeles. A brief history of the origin of the congregation is provided. The rare news report illustrates changes made towards equality such as deciding to include a woman cantor.

964. "The Homosexual and the Church." COMMONWEAL, 98 (6 April, 1973), 99-100.

An editorial comment calling upon members of the Christian church to support civil rights legislation for homosexuals in employment, housing and public accommodations and "cooperate with sex researchers . . . and homosexual Christians to reformulate guidelines for Christian sexual behavior."

965. "Contemporary and Christian Contexts." COMMONWEAL, 98 (6 April, 1973), 103-106. Discussion, 98 (1 June, 1973), 311-313.

A discussion of moral, religious, political and psychological aspects of the question "can the Christian church affirm homosexuality as a valid behavior and way of life?" The social context of religious debate on homosexuality in the early 1970s is clearly illustrated.

966. Fink, Peter E. "A Pastoral Hypothesis: It Was Gay Pride Week and the Church Stayed Home. . ." COMMONWEAL, 98 (6 April, 1973), 107, 110-112. Discussion, 98 (1 June, 1973), 311-313.

An essay discussing "what mission does the church have toward gay people, and what service can it render?" The author explores the forces within gay and straight society (as well as personal psychological dynamics) which stress gay persons and contrasts the passive attitude of organized religion in this area with its active involvement in the civil rights movement.

967. "Church Group Gives an Ear to Gay Lib." THE ADVOCATE, 109 (11 April, 1973), 15.

On February 28, 1973 at the National Council of Churches meeting in Pittsburgh, members of Gay Alternatives Pittsburgh petitioned for time to address the assembly. The statement on the church from the October, 1972 gay rights convention was then read and copies were distributed.

968. "Unitarians Appoint Nash Minister for Gay Concerns." THE ADVOCATE, 110 (25 April, 1973), 9.

A news release on the appointment of Rev. Richard Nash to a specialized ministry to the gay community by the Unitarian Universalist Association. The action was taken in recognition of "the need on the part of the denomination for greater sensitivity toward and affirmation of gay people." Nash's background and training are covered.

969.   "Church Funds Lesbian Center." THE ADVOCATE, 110 (25 April, 1973), 9.

A grant from the Women in Leadership project of the United Presbyterian Church has been awarded to Minneapolis' Lesbian Resource Center. Activities sponsored by the Center include counseling and consciousness-raising groups.

970.   Foust, Carl. "What Really Happened at Sodom?" THE ADVOCATE, 110 (25 April, 1973), 26, 35.

An analysis of the various problems of textual exegesis and interpretation surrounding the traditional study of the destruction of the cities of Sodom and Gomorrah.

971.   "Minister Defies Bishop, Marries Men in Historic Church." THE ADVOCATE, 111 (9 May, 1973), 3.

A detailed description of the wedding of two men cele-brated in Boston's Old West Church by Methodist clergy-man Rev. William Alberts. The text of a letter from the regional bishop forbidding said ceremony is included. Both partners are activists in the Boston community.

972.   "Methodists Give $1800 to Gay House." THE ADVOCATE, 111 (9 May, 1973), 3.

United Methodist Voluntary Services has awarded a grant for operating expenses to the Gay Community Services of Minneapolis. Recent history of involvement with similar groups in Minnesota is summarized.

973.   Wells, Charles W. "Is Catholic Church Moving Toward Change in Views on Love, Gays?" THE ADVOCATE, 111 (9 May, 1973), 37.

An opinion piece by the president of the Los Angeles chapter of Dignity commenting upon the April 6, 1973 issue of *Commonweal* magazine. That issue editorial-ized on the situation of gay Catholics and the church, calling strongly for reform. The contents of lengthy articles by a Jesuit priest and a professor of theology on the same topic are explored.

974. Jackson, Ed. "No Christian Gays, Says Plain Truth." THE ADVOCATE, 112 (23 May, 1973), 40.

A presentation of the views on homosexuality expressed through the popularly circulated religious tract *The Plain Truth*. Its claims are considered ill-informed and full of quasi-accurate information.

975. "Boston Minister Who Married Men May Lose Job." THE ADVOCATE, 113 (6 June, 1973), 8.

Methodist minister Rev. William Alberts of Boston, who officiated at a same-sex marriage on April 7, 1973 has been placed on disability leave and charged with mental illness by Bishop Edward G. Carroll. Background information on the situation is included.

976. "Office on Gay Affairs Created by Unitarians." THE ADVOCATE, 115 (4 July, 1973), 10.

On June 2, 1973, the Unitarian Universalist Association, at its annual meeting in Toronto, created an "office of gay affairs" by a two-thirds majority vote. The full text of the resolution is reprinted. This is the first such office in a major North American religious denomination.

977. "Ax Falls on Socially Conscious Boston Minister." THE ADVOCATE, 116 (18 July, 1973), 10.

A lengthy news article analyzing the forced retirement of Rev. William Alberts following refusal of a church trial by the Methodist Church. Local parish support for the clergyman is strong. Charges made against Alberts subsequent to his joining of two men in a ceremony on April 7, 1973 are reviewed.

978. "Gay Minister's Ordination Affirmed." THE ADVOCATE, 117 (1 August, 1973), 11.

A review of the case of the Rev. Tom Maurer, counselor and lecturer for the program in human sexuality at the University of Minnesota, whose credentials in ministry were recently reaffirmed by the United Church of Christ in the Minneapolis region.

979. "Lutherans Adopt Anti-Gay Position." THE ADVOCATE, 117 (1 August, 1973), 11.

A news article on the adoption of a resolution by the Lutheran Church-Missouri Synod terming homophile behavior "intrinsically sinful." Details of the heated debate are given in full. The action was taken at the denomination's annual convention in New Orleans.

980. "Johnson Says Church Still Major Oppressor." THE ADVOCATE, 117 (1 August, 1973), 11.

Quotations from a speech delivered by Rev. William Johnson at a Church of Christ meeting on human sexuality in Minneapolis on July 5, 1973. Johnson, the first openly gay person to be ordained to a major denominational ministry, criticized the Christian church's approach to homosexuality as "theological perversions to put down a whole group of human beings."

981. "Ousted Boston Pastor May Sue." THE ADVOCATE, 118 (15 August, 1973), 3.

Dr. William Alberts, former Methodist clergyman forcibly retired for performing a same-sex wedding, announced his intention to sue Bishop Edward Carroll at a Boston press conference on July 20, 1973.

982. Kepner, Jim. "Gays and Religion: The Stew Thickens." THE ADVOCATE, 118 (15 August, 1973), 37.

An essay touching upon the development of scriptural positions on homosexuality and, in part, feminism from the original Aramaic and the early Gnostic gospels to the later condemnations of St. Paul.

983. "Lutheran Youth Gathering Hears Talk by Gay Cleric." THE ADVOCATE, 120 (12 September, 1973), 6.

A report on the address given to a Lutheran Youth meeting discussion group in Houston during that denomination's annual meeting by Rev. Tom Maurer, an openly gay cleric of the United Church of Christ.

984. "Homosexuals and the Church." CHRISTIANITY TODAY, 17 (28 September, 1973), 8-10.

Written as a reply to an article in the July/August, 1973 issue of the Presbyterian magazine *Trends*, this essay restates Biblical strictures against homosexual conduct and harshly condemns the arguments and liberal attitude towards homosexuals presented in the *Trends* piece.

985. "Church Council Plea Backed." THE ADVOCATE, 122 (10 October, 1973), 10.

At a conference in Kansas City, Missouri on September 11-12, 1973, twenty-five delegates from the major Protestant denominations formed a National Task Force on Gay People in the Church. The group will "press the National Council of Churches to open its doors to gay Christians." Profiles of the six task force members are included. Plans are to approach the council at its upcoming meetings in New York City on October 12, 1973.

986. "Baptists Nix Dual Affiliation for MCC." THE ADVOCATE, 122 (10 October, 1973), 11.

A news report on the rejection of the application of the Orange County Metropolitan Community Church for alignment with the American Baptist Church. Positive and negative viewpoints are summarized.

987. Bjornson, Lars. "Catholic Order Plans National Ministry to Gays." THE ADVOCATE, 124 (7 November, 1973), 12-13.

A news report on the decision of the Society of the Divine Savior of Milwaukee, Wisconsin to create "a national ministry to the gay community." A lengthy history of the proposal and interview with Br. Brant-Michael Fitzgerald, chair of the planning task force, comprises the bulk of the article. Among the goals of the ministry will be an examination of admission and expulsion policies of religious orders.

988. "Episcopalians Duck Gay Justice Issue at Louisville Meet." THE ADVOCATE, 124 (7 November, 1973), 13.

A profile of events at the triennial convention of the Episcopal Church held in Louisville, Kentucky in October, 1973. A conservative atmosphere prevented effective creation of a gay caucus, and the ordination of women was defeated.

989. "Church Council Breakthrough." THE ADVOCATE, 125 (21 November, 1973), 10.

On October 15, 1973, the National Council of Churches voted to recognize the National Task Force on Gay People in the Church as a legitimate body. Excerpts from the statement presented to the Council and an outline of the proposed program of action envisaged by the group are included and biographical data on interested clergy is provided.

990. "Maryland Quaker Convention Passes Gay Lib Resolution." THE ADVOCATE, 127 (19 December, 1973), 10.

A report on the adoption by the Baltimore Yearly Meeting of the Society of Friends of a resolution urging that "myths that perpetuate deep-rooted discrimination about bisexuality and homosexuality" be dispelled. Members of the meeting were also called upon to support the removal of oppression of persons due to their sexual orientation.

991. "Boston Unitarians Approve Gay Office." THE ADVOCATE, 127 (19 December, 1973), 10.

The Unitarian Universalist Association Board of Trustees in Boston determined that an "Office of Gay Affairs" would be established, but that funding would have to be sought from sources outside the church budget.

992. Enroth, Ronald M. and Gerald E. Jamison. THE GAY CHURCH. Grand Rapids, MI: William B. Eerdmans Publishing Company, 1974.

This is a sociological study of the Metropolitan Community Church, its origin, theological positions and history from 1968 to 1974. The role of MCC in organized religion in America and its outreach efforts to various groups both within and outside the gay communi-

270

ty, and groups such as Dignity and Integrity working within established denominations are profiled in some detail. Differences among such mainstream religious bodies as the National Council of Churches provide useful background. Researchers should utilize Enroth and Jamison strictly as a basic outline for more detailed discussion.

993.   Gearhart, Sally and William R. Johnson. LOVING WOMEN/ LOVING MEN: GAY LIBERATION AND THE CHURCH. San Francisco: Glide Publications, 1974.

This volume is composed of five separate essays written in or before 1974. Each approaches the question of the relationship of gays and lesbians with organized religion from a different perspective.

Donald Kuhn, in the opening section "The Church and the Homosexual," recounts a consciousness-raising seminar near San Francisco in 1964 which resulted in the creation of the Council on Religion and the Homosexual. It provides an excellent picture of the attitudes held by both clergy and laity prior to the beginnings of political gay actions in 1969. A second article by Robert L. Treese discusses the biblical texts upon which condemnation of gays is based, together with the ethical contribution to homosexual relationships possible for the church.

Sally Gearhart and Bill Johnson present an overview of the gay movement in the church profiling efforts at change in established denominations as well as the birth and expansion of the Metropolitan Community Church. Historical material is included for the United Church of Christ, the Society of Friends (Quakers), the United Presbyterian Church and the Unitarian Universalist Association as well as Catholicism.

The fourth essay, entitled "The Good News of Gay Liberation," merits special attention. Its author, Rev. Bill Johnson, was himself the subject of a heated debate regarding his ordination as an openly gay minister in the United Church of Christ. In a spirited and lucid presentation, Rev. Johnson places gay liberation into a theological context and addresses the need for a reconsideration of both Scriptural texts and the philosophy they support.

"The Miracle of Lesbianism" sets forth the issue of lesbian/feminist women and their role in a church which has historically neglected them.

Researchers should bear in mind that many of the views expressed in these writings should be updated with later works on a particular denomination.

994. Swicegood, Tom. OUR GOD TOO. BIOGRAPHY OF A CHURCH AND A TEMPLE. New York: Pyramid Books, 1974.

The story of the founding and first five years of the Metropolitan Community Church (MCC) forms the focus of Swicegood's account. From an initial meeting in a suburban Los Angeles living room in 1968 to the destruction of the first church building by arson in 1973, many voices of MCC members illustrate the positions of established religions--Christianity and Judaism--on homosexuality which forced MCC into being. The work is also useful for historical information on the rise of the gay liberation movement in the city of Los Angeles.

995. "Church at Odds Over Magazine Treatment of Gays." THE ADVOCATE, 131 (13 February, 1974), 10.

A news report on the response of the Presbyterian Lay Committee, Inc. of Philadelphia to a 1973 issue of *Trends*, an official church periodical, which devoted an entire issue to the "views of gay people with respect to religion and organized churches." *Presbyterian Layman*, the Committee's journal, has called for censure and dismissal of those responsible and stated that "there should be total and absolute retraction of the concepts of the issue of *Trends*."

996. "Navy Agents Hunt Gays in Church." THE ADVOCATE, 131 (13 February, 1974), 13.

An interview with the Rev. John Hose of the San Diego Metropolitan Community Church on repeated visits by Naval security agents inquiring regarding a same-sex union ceremony performed by Reverend Hose in which one of the couple was a Navy man.

272

997. "Catholic Homosexuals: Views of Dignity." COMMONWEAL, 99 (15 February, 1974), 479-482. Discussion, 100 (23 March, 1974), 51 and (12 April, 1974), 141.

A theological evaluation of the doctrinal position taken by Dignity, an organization for gay members of the Roman Catholic Church. While the theology of acceptance is viewed as valid, the author sees the organization as most effective in espousing a minority opinion rather than seeking special status from the hierarchy.

998. "Christians Guilty of Bias: Council." THE ADVOCATE, 133 (13 March, 1974), 10.

A news report on the position statement on homosexuals issued by delegates to the Australian Council of Churches meeting in Melbourne. Homosexuality is to be accepted "as a part of creation." Australia's Parliament voted in 1973 to abolish homosexuality as a crime.

999. "Gay Catholics' Confession Guide: 'Change or Abstain--Sex Isn't All.'" THE ADVOCATE, 134 (27 March, 1974), 11.

A profile of a newly-released guide for priests being circulated by the National Council of Catholic Bishops. Homosexuals are called upon to either become heterosexual or be celibate. Discussion is planned for the meeting of the National Federation of Priests' Councils meeting, at which the Salvatorian order will present their proposal for a gay ministry for discussion.

1000. Young, Allan. "Church Sanctions Gay Ministry." THE ADVOCATE, 136 (24 April, 1974), 12, 18.

A news report and interview with Father Paul Shanley of Boston, designated "minister to gay and bisexual people" in that city's diocese. His views on sexuality and recent conservative measures within the Church are presented.

1001. "Priests Reject 'Gay Is Sin,' Call for Consenting Sex Laws." THE ADVOCATE, 136 (24 April, 1974), 13.

On March 21, 1974, the National Federation of Priests' Councils meeting in San Francisco called for the "repeal of laws proscribing consensual homosexual acts between adults" and an end to discrimination against gay persons in employment and government service. These resolutions are opposed to a guide issued by the National Council of Catholic Bishops which declared homosexuality to be a sin. Said resolutions were proposed by the delegates of Milwaukee's Society of the Divine Savior. Profiles of the conference's papers and discussion sections are given.

1002. "Anonymous Funds Provided to Support Gay Church Work." THE ADVOCATE, 136 (24 April, 1974), 16.

A profile of the program and funding status of the National Task Force of Gay People in the Church, as well as a listing of its members. While several Protestant denominations have contributed monies to the group, public recognition is to be avoided "for fear of repercussions."

1003. "Metropolitan Community Church: Deception Discovered." CHRISTIANITY TODAY, 18 (26 April, 1974), 13-14.

A description of "the heresy of the MCC" and denial of the validity of its interpretation of those portions of Scripture which relate to homosexuality.

1004. Zeh, John. "Bible-Beaters Replace the Firemen in Philly." THE ADVOCATE, 141 (3 July, 1974), A-3, A-15.

A report on the active and vocal opposition raised by religious fundamentalist groups at recent public hearings on Philadelphia City Council Bill 1275. Said bill would prohibit anti-gay bias in housing, jobs and public accommodations. Clergy testifying at the two-day hearings said passage of 1275 would condone "an immoral lifestyle that would corrupt youth and ruin the family."

1005. "Episcopal Diocese Authorizes Open Door for Gays in Church." THE ADVOCATE, 142 (17 July, 1974), 16.

Meeting in Detroit, the Episcopal Diocese of Michigan voted to adopt the essence of a special diocesan report on the position of gay persons with respect to the Church's ordination policies. The text calls for civil rights, urges clergy to speak out in support of law reform and repudiates police harassment tactics.

1006. "Lutherans Join Tide, Form Caucus." THE ADVOCATE, 142 (17 July, 1974), 17.

An announcement of the creation of a caucus of gay and lesbian people within the Lutheran denomination in the United States. The group, Lutherans Concerned for Gay People, is the tenth such organization and was formally constituted on June 17, 1974. Background and objectives are given by the director, Rev. Jim Siefkes of Minneapolis.

1007. "'No Special or Moral Reason Exists to Withhold Rights' Says Baptist." THE ADVOCATE, 142 (17 July, 1974), 17.

Note on a letter sent by James Christman, executive secretary of National Ministries of the American Baptist Church to the president of the Philadelphia city council in support of pending gay rights legislation.

1008. "LCA Praises Marriage Ban." THE ADVOCATE, 142 (17 July, 1974), 20.

A news item on the endorsement of the barring of same-sex marriages in the province of Manitoba by the Lutheran church, which cautioned against "offenses against public decency."

1009. "Bishop Balks on Rights Measure." THE ADVOCATE, 143 (31 July, 1974), 16.

On June 17, 1974, a statement was issued by Bishop Bernard Flanagan of Worcester, Massachusetts opposing proposed gay civil rights legislation pending in the city council. This action makes a break with a previously indicated stance of neutrality towards the bill.

1010. "Cardinal Is Against Bias Despite Church's View." THE ADVOCATE, 143 (31 July, 1974), 17.

A portion of the text of a statement released by the archdiocese of Boston opposing discrimination but remaining morally opposed to homosexual acts. The action by Humberto Cardinal Medeiros is seen in sharp contrast to recent speeches by New York's Cardinal Cooke.

1011. "Pro-Gay Presbyterian Wins Top Job." THE ADVOCATE, 144 (14 August, 1974), 17.

A report on the choice of Rev. Robert Lamar as moderation of the United Presbyterian Church in the U.S.A. and the role played by Presbyterians for Gay Concerns in evaluation. A brief precis of the caucus' activity is included.

1012. "Unitarian Gay Caucus Gets Regular Funding." THE ADVOCATE, 144 (14 August, 1974), 17.

Thirty eight thousand dollars has been designated by the Unitarian Universalist General Assembly as a budget for that denominations' gay caucus. This is the first such action in the United States.

1013. "Nation's Reform Jews Accepting Gay Temple." THE ADVOCATE, 146 (11 September, 1974), 24.

A news report on the acceptance by the Union of American Hebrew Congregations of Beth Chayim Chadashim, the first gay temple. Rabbi Erwin Herman, director of the Los Angeles synagogue, outlines its origin and general reception in Judaism since its formation in 1972.

1014. "Youth Group Urges: 'End Church Bias." THE ADVOCATE, 148 (9 October, 1974), 16.

The Council on Youth Ministry of the United Methodist Church has adopted a resolution stating that gay persons should be ordained and will ask that the 1976 convention to remove all anti-gay language from its practices and statements.

1015. "'Homosexuality Is Subversive.'" THE ADVOCATE, 148 (9 October, 1974), 17.

A brief note on the statement on homosexuality issued at the 29th annual convention of the Antiochian Orthodox Church, calling for "medical and psychological care leading to the full attainment of maturity by homosexuals."

1016. "The Fast Is Over." THE ADVOCATE, 149 (23 October, 1974), 16.

The fast by Brian McNaught, a Catholic journalist who began fasting on September 21, 1974 in atonement for Catholic actions and attitudes towards homosexuals, broke off on October 4 following pledges of support for change from three Episcopal and Catholic bishops in the Detroit area.

1017. Steakley, Jim. "Gay Bishop Consecrated in New York." THE ADVOCATE, 150 (6 November, 1974), 14.

A detailed and illustrated report on the consecration of Rev. Robert Clement of New York City to the episcopate of the Eucharistic Catholic Church. A brief history of the group is provided.

1018. "Catholic Newspaper Fires Brian McNaught Two Days After His Protest Fast Is Ended." THE ADVOCATE, 150 (6 November, 1974), 15.

A news report on the dismissal of openly gay journalist Brian McNaught from his post at the weekly paper of the archdiocese of Detroit. Background on the case is provided.

1019. "Mormon President Raps Homosexuals." THE ADVOCATE, 150 (6 November, 1974), 15.

Quotations condemning homosexuality from the speech delivered by President Spencer Kimball at the 144th conference of the Church of Jesus Christ of Latter-Day Saints.

1020. "Anglican Study May Determine Role of Gays." THE ADVOCATE, 150 (6 November, 1974), 15.

A twelve-member working party, chaired by Bishop John Yates of Whitby, has been appointed by the Anglican Church to carry out an eighteen-month analysis of gay persons and the homosexual lifestyle. Social, medical, pastoral and moral viewpoints will be examined. The envisioned report will be presented to the 1976 General Synod for discussion.

1021. "National Church Council Asks Step-Up in Dialog, Proposals." THE ADVOCATE, 152 (4 December, 1974), 14.

The National Council of Churches of Christ has requested the preparation of proposals for discussion and action by March, 1975. An interview with Rev. William Johnson of San Francisco, a member of the Task Force of Gay People in the Church, notes that Council membership for the Metropolitan Community Church is likely to be an issue.

1022. "Bible School Wants His Degree." THE ADVOCATE, 153 (18 December, 1974), 14.

A profile of the case of Jerry Sloan, coordinator of the Des Moines congregation of the Metropolitan Community Church. His alma mater, the Baptist Bible College in Springfield, Missouri, has demanded the return of his diploma "because we wanted the public to know that we abhor what he is doing."

1023. "Gay Rights Statement at World Church Meeting." THE ADVOCATE, 153 (18 December, 1974), 15.

A statement on human rights containing a gay rights statement drafted by Rev. William Johnson of San Francisco was presented to the World Council of Churches International Conference on Human Rights in Vienna by the delegate from the National Council of Churches (U.S.). It was the only one of the thirty-four statements entered into the record to discuss the topic.

1024. Ginder, Richard. BINDING WITH BRIARS: SEX AND SIN IN THE CATHOLIC CHURCH. Englewood Cliffs, NJ: Prentice-Hall, Inc., 1975.

A general exploration of the attitude of the Roman Catholic Church towards sexuality. Considering the impact of such modern Vatican documents as the 1968 Humanae Vitae, Father Ginder notes societal changes, doctrinal controversies within the church, and problems facing all Catholics. Homosexuality and gay liberation are reviewed as they existed in the mid-1970s, with chapter thirteen entitled "The Other Love." Church reform such as that urged by Fr. John McNeill is also considered. The author is a priest in the Diocese of Pittsburgh who "began the book as a conservative and ended a liberal" (p. viii).

1025.   Philpott, Kent. THE THIRD SEX? SIX HOMOSEXUALS TELL THEIR STORIES. Plainfield, NJ: Logos International, 1975.

The life histories of three gay men and three lesbians are presented in the form of lengthy interviews. Using these as illustrations, the author attempts "to bring together the salient features of homosexuality" (p. 159). Subjects addressed under this evaluation are the process of becoming homosexual, growth of self-awareness, prior religious experience and "deliverance and infilling of the spirit" (p. 168). Deliverance is defined as "demons were cast out of them" (p. 168). The general orientation of the volume is as a counselor's guide for pastors and others seeking to help homosexuals readjust to heterosexual behaviors. Advice on the fitness of several types of persons to work as counselors is also included. Philpott concludes with a warning that "without a firm conviction of the truth of God's Word concerning homosexuality, the homosexual will receive no help at all" (p. 187).

1026.   "Unitarians Open Gay Church Office." THE ADVOCATE, 154 (1 January, 1975), 15.

The Board of Trustees of the Unitarian Universalist Association has voted a budget of $38,000 to the new office of Gay Concerns. This action overrides vehement opposition by Dr. Robert Nelson West, president of the denomination. Actions taken by the office will be monitored by the church's gay caucus.

1027.   "Detroit Priests Support Gay Rights." THE ADVOCATE, 155 (15 January, 1975), 6.

On December 10, 1974, the priests' senate of the archdiocese of Detroit approved a resolution in support of
gay civil rights in housing, jobs and government
service, and called upon Cardinal Dearden to appoint a
formal liaison between the church and the local lesbian
and gay community. Said resolutions were occasioned by
debate over the case of journalist Brian McNaught. No
change in the moral view of homosexuality was discussed
by the senate.

1028. "Lutherans to Study Gay Bible References." THE ADVOCATE,
156 (29 January, 1975), 15.

In response to requests from the denomination's lesbian
and gay caucus, three theologians at a Lutheran seminary in St. Paul, Minnesota will conduct a study of the
texts in Leviticus, Romans and the Pauline letters
which touch upon homosexuality.

1029. "Presbyterians Want New Zealand Reform." THE ADVOCATE,
156 (29 January, 1975), 15.

A news report of statements made during the General
Assembly of the Presbyterian Church of New Zealand
concerning homosexuality. While calling for repeal of
laws prohibiting consensual sex between members of the
same gender, the Assembly also viewed the creation of
treatment agencies for homosexuals as a desirable
government project.

1030. "Unitarians Appoint Concerns Director." THE ADVOCATE, 156
(29 January, 1975), 15.

A news report on the appointment of Arlie Scott of New
York City as director of the Unitarian Office of Gay
Concerns. Her background is briefly summarized.

1031. "Priests Polled." THE ADVOCATE, 157 (12 February, 1975),
10.

A summary in brief of the results of an informal telephone and mail survey of Catholic priests in the Philadelphia area on homosexual issues done by Rev. Myron
Judy of Temple University. Topics addressed were legal
punishments for homosexual conduct and the social

contributions being made by the gay liberation movement.

1032.   "Methodist Group Asks Dialogue." THE ADVOCATE, 157 (12 February, 1975), 10.

A report on the semi-annual meeting in Nashville of the Council on Youth Ministry of the United Methodist Church. Support for gay presence in Church hiring and "an awesome task of constituency education" on homosexual matters were addressed.

1033.   Erickson, Howard. "Good News Isn't So Good After All." THE ADVOCATE, 158 (26 February, 1975), 15.

An interview with Rev. C. Philip Henerman of Minneapolis, a conservative Methodist fundamentalist cleric heading that church's Good News Movement. The group's opposition to the ordination of homosexual clergy is summarized.

1034.   "A Denunciation of Gay Ministry Status." THE ADVOCATE, 159 (12 March, 1975), 17.

An account of the opposition of the Pennsylvania Baptist Ministers Conference to a proposed gay civil rights bill for the city of Philadelphia.

1035.   "Support for Rights, But Not Funds." THE ADVOCATE, 159 (12 March, 1975), 17.

The Unitarian Universalist Association's formation and funding of an office for the concerns of gay people has been criticized on grounds of allocation of funds in violation of more urgent priorities. A brief summary of both positions in this debate is presented.

1036.   "Homosexual Demons: 'You Have No Right to Possess This Body.'" THE ADVOCATE, 159 (12 March, 1975), 17.

An account of the exorcism of the "demon" of homosexuality by a charismatic preacher in Oregon from one of his parishioners.

1037. "NCC Declares Discrimination Immoral." THE ADVOCATE, 160 (26 March, 1975), 5.

> On March 6, 1975, the National Council of Churches adopted "A Resolution on Civil Rights Without Discrimination As to Affectional Sexual Preference." A portion of the full text is reprinted.

1038. "Conform Or Quit." THE ADVOCATE, 161 (9 April, 1975), 17.

> An account of the support for reform of civil rights legislation in New Zealand by Father Felix Donnelly of Auckland. The local hierarchy has stated that priests "should conform with the church's teachings on homosexuality or resign."

1039. "Battle Heating Up." THE ADVOCATE, 161 (9 April, 1975), 17.

> A summary of the controversy within the United Methodist Church over the ordination of homosexuality as members of the clergy.

1040. "'At Least 338,900 Gay Lutherans." THE ADVOCATE, 163 (7 May, 1975), 19.

> An estimate of the number of gay members of their church has been drawn up by Lutherans Concerned for Gay People, based upon a 1972 sample of congregations regarding homosexual conduct.

1041. "Baptists Accept Gay Report." THE ADVOCATE, 164 (21 May, 1975), 16.

> A convention of state American Baptist Churches meeting in Providence, Rhode Island has accepted a task force report on homosexuality admitting "gay people often have been mistreated (and) denied equal protection under the law."

1042. "Presbyterian Plans for Assembly." THE ADVOCATE, 164 (21 May, 1975), 16.

The Presbyterian Gay Caucus plans to submit the reports required for recognition to the May 13-21 general assembly of the denomination in Cincinnati. Rev. David B. Sindt of Chicago will also coordinate several caucus meetings during the assembly.

1043.   "Gay People Protest at Cathedral." THE ADVOCATE, 164 (21 May, 1975), 16.

A news report of a confrontation at St. Andrew's Cathedral in Sydney, Australia between two dozen gay protesters and the Rt. Rev. Lance Shilton, the Anglican Dean of the city. At issue were statements made "equating gay people with adulterers and murderers and condemning the organization of the Metropolitan Community Church in Australia by Rev. Lee Carlton."

1044.   "Defrocked Minister Gets Another Chance." THE ADVOCATE, 165 (4 June, 1975), 17.

St. Stephen's Methodist Church of San Antonio, Texas voted to support the effort of former minister Gene Leggett for restoration of his credentials. Leggett was suspended in 1971 following announcement of his homosexuality. This action obliges the Southwest Texas Annual Conference of the Methodist Church to vote on the issue.

1045.   Kantrowitz, Arnie. "I Am Part of My People . . . I Am a Gay Jew." THE ADVOCATE, 165 (4 June, 1975), 17.

A personal account of reconciliation between the identities of being Jewish and being gay by a staff writer for *The ADVOCATE*. A profile of Beth Simchat Torah, New York City's gay synagogue, is included.

1046.   "Polling Methodists." THE ADVOCATE, 166 (18 June, 1975), 15.

A report of an opinion poll conducted by the *United Methodist Reporter* on the question of the church's position on homosexuality. Of the 8,610 respondents, the majority rejected ordination of gay clergy and favored a stance which "expresses the church's disapproval of a homosexual lifestyle in stronger terms."

1047.   "Ordination Plea Shelved." THE ADVOCATE, 167 (2 July, 1975), 15.

    The Council on Youth Ministry of the United Methodist Church has abandoned plans to request the denomination's 1976 annual meeting to endorse the ordination of gay clergy. This action is seen as a response to increasing polarization of the membership on the issue.

1048.   "'No' to UPC Caucus." THE ADVOCATE, 167 (2 July, 1975), 15.

    A report on the refusal of recognition to the gay caucus of the United Presbyterian Church by the 187th general assembly meeting in Cincinnati.

1049.   "Appeal for Baptist." THE ADVOCATE, 167 (2 July, 1975), 15.

    A profile of the case of Rick Mixon, a graduate of a Baptist seminary denied ordination in August, 1974. The Executive Committee of the American Baptist Church of the West has granted him an appeal of the original decision. Mixon's credentials are presented and plans for appeal to the national church discussed.

1050.   McNaught, Brian. "Church Study Debunks Roman Catholic Stand." THE ADVOCATE, 168 (16 July, 1975), 10-11.

    A discussion of the contents of a report recently completed by the American Theological Society's Committee on Sexuality. Traditional Catholic positions on homosexuality, Scriptural authority and liturgy are questioned, and the self-worth of gay persons as church members affirmed. Background to the research efforts of the committee is included.

1051.   "UCC Endorses Rights Laws." THE ADVOCATE, 169 (30 July, 1975), 6.

    On July 1, 1975, the 10th General Synod of the United Church of Christ, meeting in Minneapolis, adopted a resolution supporting "civil liberties without discrimination related to affectional or sexual preference." The resolution parallels a similar statement adopted by

the National Council of Churches. Local congregations
were urged to work for passage of civil rights laws and
a study of "human sexuality in a theological context"
commissioned for 1977.

1052. Stoneman, Donnell. "Episcopal Priest and Gay Activist."
THE ADVOCATE, 169 (30 July, 1975), 14.

An interview with Rev. Robert Herrick discussing both
his work for the National Gay Task Force and areas of
concern regarding ordination and general change on the
issue of homosexuality within the church.

1053. McQueen, Robert. "Outside the Temple Gates, the Gay
Mormon." THE ADVOCATE, 170 (13 August, 1975), 14.

A personal account by an editor of *The ADVOCATE* of
the disciplinary treatment meted out to discovered
homosexuals by the Mormon Brigham Young University and
five suicides consequent to said counseling which
occurred in 1965. The church's attitudes are described
and condemned.

1054. McQueen, Robert. "Dogma According to Kimball." THE
ADVOCATE, 170 (13 August, 1975), 14, 16.

A consideration of the official position of the Mormon
church on homosexuality as presented in the literature
authored by Spencer Kimball, president of the L.D.S.
faith. Three documents, *So Many Voices, Crime Against
Nature and The Mormon Homosexual* are cited and
analyzed. Contemporary anti-gay activity at Brigham
Young University is seen as encouraged by Kimball's
condemnatory tracts.

1055. McQueen, Robert. "BYU Inquisition." THE ADVOCATE, 170
(13 August, 1975), 14.

A reconstruction from private accounts by seven victims
of anti-gay "witch-hunt" tactics utilized by the campus
security officers at Brigham Young University in Provo,
Utah. Victims were subjected to intimidation to reveal
names of others who were homosexual, as "anyone
possessed with homosexuality needs all the help he can
get." Those who cooperated were eventually excommunicated. The events related occurred between 1973 and
1975.

1056. Brill, David. "A Call for 'Empathy.'" THE ADVOCATE, 171 (27 August, 1975), 20.

> A reprint of text from a pastoral letter sent by Humberto Cardinal Medeiros of Boston to all city parishes which was read at services on July 20, 1975. Clergy and congregation alike are called upon not "to give tacit or explicit support to any homosexual thought or deed."

1057. Shilts, Randy. "Gay, Jewish and Proud." THE ADVOCATE, 172 (10 September, 1975), 12-13.

> A survey article of the growth and development of gay Jewish congregations in the United States and elsewhere. Temples used as examples are New York's Beth Simchat Torah, Los Angeles' Beth Chayim Chadashim and B'nai Haskalah of Boston. Problems of adapting traditional liturgies to fit special needs are discussed.

1058. "Methodists." THE ADVOCATE, 172 (10 September, 1975), 13.

> A news note on the formal creation of the United Methodist Gay Caucus in Evanston, Illinois during a meeting July 25-27, 1975. Statements of purpose were drafted and task forces formed by the lay, clergy and seminarian delegates.

1059. Baker, Joe. "McNaught: Gay and Catholic." THE ADVOCATE, 173 (24 September, 1975), 17.

> An interview with Detroit journalist Brian McNaught on his struggle with the Catholic church as part of Dignity and personal odyssey of growth. Details of his suit against *The Michigan Catholic* are provided.

1060. Whitmore, George. "Theocracy Condemns New York Rights." THE ADVOCATE, 174 (8 October, 1975), 9.

> A news report on the defeat of Intro 554, the proposed gay civil rights bill for New York City. The role of religious bodies and groups in opposing the legislation is noted.

1061. "Minister Comes Out." THE ADVOCATE, 174 (8 October, 1975), 21.

> A report on the public "coming out" sermon delivered on September 14, 1975 by Rev. Edward Hougen of a congregational church near Boston. Reaction to the news was divided. Hougen is one of the candidates for the pastorate of the Metropolitan Community Church in Boston.

1062. "Gay Mormons Talking Back." THE ADVOCATE, 175 (22 October, 1975), 23.

> A collection of five letters taken as a sample of the massive response received by *The ADVOCATE* to the articles on Mormonism and homosexuality by Robert McQueen which appeared in mid-1975. Several were requesting excommunication.

1063. "Baptists Deny Appeal." THE ADVOCATE, 176 (5 November, 1975), 20.

> A detailed report of the affirmation by the American Baptist Church of a prior refusal of ordination to Randle R. Mixon. This case is the first in the history of this denomination "that an avowedly gay person had sought ordination." The decision leaves Mixon free to seek either legal redress or ordination by a local congregation, the Lakeshore Avenue Baptist Church of San Francisco.

1064. "Recognition." THE ADVOCATE, 176 (5 November, 1975), 20.

> A Committee on Homosexuality was recognized and budgeted by the Philadelphia Yearly Meeting of the Society of Friends. The body has been operating unofficially since 1973. A list of questions for discussion at the meeting will be prepared.

1065. "Resolution Passed." THE ADVOCATE, 178 (3 December, 1975), 19.

> The complete text of a resolution passed by the Episcopal House of Bishops meeting in Portland, Maine. Dialogue with "gay leaders and awareness of the needs of gay persons" are called for.

1066.   Gengle, Dean. "Ban on Theologian Lifted--Almost." THE
ADVOCATE, 180 (31 December, 1975), 8.

An interview with Catholic theologian John McNeill,
profiling his personal struggle to have his book, *The
Church and the Homosexual*, published and the evolution
of his challenge to traditional dogma and the hierarchy's response.

1067.   Orbach, William. "Homosexuality and Jewish Law." JOURNAL
OF FAMILY LAW, 14, 3 (1975-1976), 353-381.

Beginning with a definition of the sources of traditional law in Judaism--the Talmud and Midrash--as well
as the rabbinical commentaries of the Halacha and
Aggadah, this article examines chronologically the
attitudes evinced toward homosexuality. Extensive
quotes from the above-named sources are included and
evaluated. The legal position of the rabbinate with
regard to the definition of a homosexual act (as well
as variation involving age of the participants and use
or absence of force) is presented in detail. Modern
opinions on the issue are seen as unclear, although
traditional condemnations (short of capital punishment)
are retained. An interesting note is that "the recent
revival of homosexuality from its category as a mental
illness by psychologists strengthens condemnation of it
according to Jewish Law" (p. 371). Condemnation is
viewed as rooted in two sources--Biblical injunctions
relating to marriage and sexual practices (such as the
Levitical code) and the consideration of homosexual
practices as an "heathen abomination" which must not be
admitted into Israel. The history of the laws of the
State of Israel on the topic is also included. Orbach
notes the declining birth rate among American Jewry and
the struggle for survival of Israel and he concludes
that "there seems to be no viable gay alternative in
Judaism" (p. 381).

1068.   McNeill, John J. THE CHURCH AND THE HOMOSEXUAL.
Kansas City, Missouri: Sheed Andrews and McMeel, Inc.,
1976.

Father McNeill's exploration of the moral and pastoral
issues surrounding the responsibility of the Catholic
Church to its homosexual members excited great debate
and discussion upon its publication. Beginning with a
general consideration of theology in modern times, he

focuses quickly on the origins of anti-homosexual belief in traditional theology, covering textual exegesis and interpretation of the Sodom and Gomorrah story in some detail. The influence of the Stoic school of philosophy and the writings of St. Thomas Aquinas are included as well.

Having established the development of a theological stance on homosexuality--and a legal tradition of prohibition based upon a misinterpretation of the Sodom and Gomorrah story--Father McNeill turns to the condition of the modern homosexual community and how the Church could help to improve it. Topics discussed include anti-gay violence, reform of civil law, and the failure of pastoral ministry. As a clear and lucid summary of areas of concern and the historical roots of homophobia, this volume is invaluable. Researchers examining the changing position of the Church in the mid-1970s will find it particularly useful.

1069. Erickson, Howard. "Presbyterians Confront Ordination Issue." THE ADVOCATE, 181 (14 January, 1976), 18, 41.

A review of recent controversies over gay and lesbian clergy and seminarians within the United Presbyterian Church. Cases from Palo Alto, California, Chicago, New York City and West Hollywood are covered. Specific individuals involved are the Rev. David Sindt, Joan Abrams and Ken Forbes.

1070. "Congregationalists Oppose Discrimination." THE ADVOCATE, 181 (14 January, 1976), 40.

The Corporate Responsibility Committee of the Northern California Conference of the United Church of Christ has sent a mailing to all major corporations in which they hold stock requesting that they adopt a nondiscriminatory policy towards gay people.

1071. "Methodist Board Pro-Gay." THE ADVOCATE, 182 (28 January, 1976), 13.

A news report on a pro-gay statement issued by the United Methodist Church's Board of Church and Society intended as a replacement for a policy declaring homosexuality to be "incompatible with Christian teaching."

The proposal will be debated at the denomination's 1976 convention in Portland, Oregon.

1072. McNaught, Brian. "The Crowd Whispers, The Crowd Laughs." THE ADVOCATE, 185 (10 March, 1976), 16-17.

A critical commentary on the Vatican Declaration on Certain Questions Concerning Sexual Ethics. Its views are seen as inconsistent with reality. Popular reaction is indicated. In the document "the Vatican proclaims . . . that homosexuality is the result of 'rejecting God.'"

1073. "N.Y. Lesbian Ordained." THE ADVOCATE, 185 (10 March, 1976), 30.

A news report on the ordination of Ellen Marie Barrett to the deaconate of the Episcopal church on December 15, 1975 by Bishop Paul Moore. Her credentials are summarized and excerpts from Bishop Moore's remarks included. Researchers interested in a fuller exposition of this case should consult Moore's *Take A Bishop Like Me.*

1074. Aiken, David L. "Gay Ministers: One Accepted, One Removed." THE ADVOCATE, 185 (10 March, 1976), 30-31.

A discussion of the cases of Rev. Vic Brittain and Robert M. Moore of the Methodist church in the Washington, D.C. area. Brittain has been removed as pastor of three rural congregations following coming-out while Moore has been certified with a license to preach, the first step to full ordination. Detailed summaries of both cases are provided.

1075. "Open Doors to Gays: Grounds for Separation?" CHRISTIANITY TODAY, 20 (12 March, 1976), 53.

A description of the furor caused by the vote of the Santa Clara County Council of Churches in California to admit the Metropolitan Community Church congregation of San Jose to membership.

1076. "Bishop Supports Gay Rights." THE ADVOCATE, 186 (24 March, 1976), 28.

A report on the pastoral letter issued by Bishop
Francis Mugavero of Brooklyn in response to the recent
Vatican declaration on sexual ethics. Gay persons are
told not to limit their self-images to their sexuality.
Parishioners are called upon to "explore ways to secure
the legitimate rights of all citizens regardless of
sexual orientation."

1077. "Diocese Sends Representative." THE ADVOCATE, 189 (5 May,
1976), 7.

Gerald D'Avolio, legislative agent for the Massachusetts Catholic Conference, appeared at hearings on
H.2501, a proposed revision of the state criminal code
sections on private homosexual and heterosexual acts.
The bill was first filed in 1970. D'Avolio spoke
against passage.

1078. "Malcolm Boyd to Speak at Integrity Convention." THE
ADVOCATE, 189 (5 May, 1976), 15.

The national convention of Integrity, the organization
for gay Episcopalians, for 1976 will be held in San
Francisco August 6-8. The featured speakers will be
Rev. Malcolm Boyd, Rev. Laud Humphreys and Canon
Cleston Jones, author of a work on counseling.

1079. "Episcopalians Oust Founder." THE ADVOCATE, 190 (19 May,
1976), 14.

A news note on the expulsion of Dr. Louie Crew, founder
of Integrity, the Episcopal gay organization, from the
congregation of St. Luke's Church in Fort Valley,
Georgia. The move is regarded as a possible first step
towards excommunication.

1080. Judy, Myron. "The Last and Great Crisis Facing the
American Catholic Priesthood." THE ADVOCATE, 191 (2 June,
1976), 20-21, 54.

"By refusing to deal meaningfully with the entire
question of homosexuality in our society, Church leaders are setting the stage for a mass rejection of many
of their own." This article, reprinted from the
February, 1976 issue of *The Sword*, explores homo-

phobia in the Catholic priesthood and hierarchy and its costs in terms of credibility and human pain.

1081.   "Catholic Board Takes Forward Step." THE ADVOCATE, 196 (11 August, 1976), 19.

A report on a statement issued by the Young Adult Ministry Board of the United States Catholic Conference, a portion of whose text claims that gay persons are alienated from the Church due to discrimination "based on myth and questionable ' scriptural interpretation."

1082.   Gengle, Dean. "Beth Chayim Chadashim: Model for a Creative Community." THE ADVOCATE, 197 (25 August, 1976), 16-17.

An historical piece discussing the origin, growth and programs of the gay temple Beth Chayim Chadashim.

1083.   "Gay Episcopalians (and Friends) Get a New Constitution." THE ADVOCATE, 198 (8 September, 1976), 15.

A news article covering the 1976 convention of Integrity in San Francisco, August 6-8, 1976. This was the second conference of the Episcopalian gay organization, and meetings focused on discussion of a draft constitution for the group and provision of counseling services. Keynote speeches were given by Barbara Gittings and Fr. Malcolm Boyd.

1084.   Gengle, Dean. "ADVOCATE, Survey Part II: Religion." THE ADVOCATE, 200 (6 October, 1976), 18.

A report on a recent survey of gay organizations conducted by *The ADVOCATE*. Seventy-five religious groups were included. Their typical functions in both social and spiritual spheres are outlined, and political activity examined. Metropolitan Community Church and Dignity are profiled.

1085.   Gengle, Dean. "Moral Theology As a News Event: Fr. McNeill Speaks." THE ADVOCATE, 201 (20 October, 1976), 6-7.

An interview with Fr. John McNeill, S.J. author of *The Church and The Homosexual.* His personal views of sexuality and spirituality and the controversy surrounding his work are discussed.

1086. Shilts, Randy. "A Gay Back Seat on the Nirvana Express." THE ADVOCATE, 202 (3 November, 1976), 8.

An investigative report on the approach of six contemporary "cult" groups to the question of homosexuality. Groups reporting are the Divine Light Mission, Nichiren Shoshu Buddhism, Rev. Sun Myung Moon's Unification Church, Scientology, Buddhist Church of America and the Children of God. No pattern of approval, disapproval or neutrality is visible.

1087. Chalgren, Jim. "Small Gains for Gay People: Women Gain Ordination Rights from Episcopal Convention." THE ADVOCATE, 202 (3 November, 1976), 11-12.

A detailed news report on the chief events of the 65th General Convention of the U.S. Episcopal Church, September 11-23, 1976 in Minneapolis. In addition to revising the prayer book and approving the ordination of women, a resolution stating that "Homosexual persons are children of God who have full and equal claim with all other persons upon . . . the acceptance, pastoral care and concern of the church" was adopted. Support for civil rights for homosexuals was also voiced. Interviews with leading Integrity clergy are profiled.

1088. "Minister Fired, Then Rehired." THE ADVOCATE, 203 (17 November, 1976), 23.

A brief summary of the case of Disciples of Christ minister Richard McAfee and his appointment to a St. Louis congregation acknowledging his gay status.

1089. "Catholic Conference Affirms Justice." THE ADVOCATE, 203 (17 November, 1976), 23.

A report on the deliberations of the 1,340 delegates attending the American Catholic bishops bicentennial meeting in Detroit October 21-23, 1976. In keeping with the conference theme of justice in society and church, portions of the documents on work, family and "personhood" called for equal treatment for gay persons.

1090. "Catholics Say Give People Justice." THE ADVOCATE, 205 (15 December, 1976), 10.

On November 11, 1976, the National Conference of Catholic Bishops issued a pastoral letter on moral values. Homosexuals were seen as having "a right to respect, friendship and justice," although enjoined to chastity. Said letter is compared with other recent church documents on homosexuality.

1091. Quinn, Brian. "Christian Science: Homophobia Strikes the Hierarchy." THE ADVOCATE, 205 (15 December, 1976), 15-17.

A discussion of charges of homosexuality brought by Reginald Kerry against members of the Board of Directors of the Christian Science Church. The position of the denomination on homosexuality and other issues is presented. The author is a minister of an affiliated church in the New Thought movement.

1092. "What Is 'Pastoral Concern?'" THE ADVOCATE, 206 (29 December, 1976), 15.

An examination of controversy within the Episcopal church over the ordination of women and an attempted union of two Washington, D.C. gay men. Participants in the latter case are interviewed.

1093. Geyer, Marcia Lee. HUMAN RIGHTS OR HOMOPHOBIA? THE RISING TIDES. Los Angeles: University Fellowship Press, 1977.

Composed by an interim minister of the Metropolitan Community Church of New York in the context of pastoral counseling and parishioner education, this volume "attempts to clarify the homophobic perspective, how it works in several dimensions of experience and to present an alternative point of view" (p. viii). Reverend Geyer offers a framework for the consideration and understanding of homophobic behavior, beginning with George Weinberg's definition of the concept. Succeeding chapters relate this fear to sexism, lesbian and gay identity and self-image, the 1970s human rights struggle, specific charges advanced by Anita Bryant and the Save the Children crusade and Scriptural authority. Human rights efforts of all types are seen as rooted in the Christian social gospel of acceptance, although as Geyer regretfully notes, "it is not possible to answer questions motivated by fear from a human rights perspective." A selection of cartoons and photographs from both mainstream and gay presses is used to illustrate the text.

1094.   Macourt, Malcolm, ed. TOWARDS A THEOLOGY OF GAY LIBERATION. London: SCM Press Ltd., 1977

This collection of ten selected papers on theological discussions occasioned by the gay civil rights movement in Great Britain is drawn from two sources: a September, 1975 supplement to *Movement*, the journal of the Student Christian Movement, and a conference held April 3-May 2, 1976 at the SCM Conference House near Bristol. Both the supplement and the conference carried the same title as this present collection. Additional contributions have been made by respondents. Four topics are addressed: Christian perspectives on homosexuality (both historical and current), Biblical bases of homophobia, gay challenges to traditional ideas regarding human sexuality, and newer theological perspectives on such issues as Christian bases for gay relationships and the definition of liberation. The authors include members of the Anglican, Roman Catholic and Church of Scotland clergy, and the Society of Friends, a social statistician and the research editor of London's *Gay News*. Researchers should begin with the third entry by Malcolm Macourt which outlines the basic positions commonly held by both theologians and gay liberationists. Further background to the attitudes and positions discussed here will be found in John Boswell's *Christianity, Social Tolerance and Homosexuality*.

1095.   Oraison, Marc. THE HOMOSEXUAL QUESTION: AN ATTEMPT TO UNDERSTAND AN ISSUE OF INCREASING URGENCY WITHIN A CHRISTIAN PERSPECTIVE. New York: Harper & Row, 1977.

An exploration by a well-known French priest and psychoanalyst of the complex nature of homosexuality and the questions it poses for both personal development and pastoral concerns. Researchers should evaluate Dr. Oraison's conclusions in light of the relatively limited number and types of homosexuals encountered in his clerical experience. He considers that "the condition of a person with homosexual tendencies is rooted in the strange incompleteness of all human sexuality" (p. 131) and utilizes Freudian concepts extensively in his analysis.

1096. Philpott, Kent. THE GAY THEOLOGY. Plainfield, NJ: Logos International, 1977.

"The test, trials, and troubles a former homosexual faces and how such problems can be dealt with . . . this is the intent of this entire volume" (p. 76). Written as a sequel to the author's *The Third Sex* (1975), the first four chapters present interviews with men and women who claim to have overcome homosexual desires through conversion to Christianity. The remaining five sections address ministry to the gay community, evaluate pro-gay theological arguments, and reprint a series of newsletters issued from the Love in Action ministry in San Rafael, California. A repeated theme is that homosexuals can be redeemed from their lifestyle through religious experience.

1097. Boyd, Malcolm. "An Ambiguous Synthesis: Gay Religious Consciousness." THE ADVOCATE, 208 (26 January, 1977), 13-14.

A survey of a two-month trip across the United States by a leading gay Episcopal clergyman in September and October, 1976. Objectives were to assess U.S. religious consciousness as regarded social change in general and homosexuality in particular. Local religious and movement leaders in Harlem, Houston, San Francisco, Toronto, New York City, Chicago and Portland, Oregon are interviewed. Boyd sees vitality in religious groups in the churches among the women's movement and gay caucuses such as Dignity, Integrity and the Metropolitan Community Church.

1098. "Homosexuality and Christian Faith: A Theological Reflection." CHRISTIAN CENTURY, 94 (16 February, 1977), 137-142.

A theological article exploring "the vocational character of homosexual inclination" and the "temptations" of homosexual lifestyle.

1099. "New Caucus for Brethren." THE ADVOCATE, 210 (23 February, 1977), 23.

A brief news note announcing plans for the formation of a gay caucus within the Mennonite Church and the Church of the Brethren. Temporary headquarters for the group will be in Lancaster, Pennsylvania. Contact information is provided.

1100. "Gay Jews International." THE ADVOCATE, 210 (23 February, 1977), 23.

A profile of events scheduled for April 21-24, 1977 in New York City for an international gay Jewish conference for those "who seek to express and enhance their commitment to gay Jewish life." Delegates from thirteen American congregations and four foreign nations are expected. Sponsoring group for the meetings is Congregation Beth Simchat Torah.

1101. "Norfolk Unitarians Host Gay Conference." THE ADVOCATE, 213 (6 April, 1977), 36.

From June 10-12, 1977, the first Unitarian gay conference in the Tidewater region will be held in Norfolk, Virginia. A brief summary of the program is given.

1102. "UFMCC Passes Anita Resolution." THE ADVOCATE, 214 (20 April, 1977), 13.

A report on a press release distributed nationally by the Board of Elders of the Universal Fellowship of Metropolitan Community Churches condemning the anti-gay campaign in Dade County, Florida being led by Anita Bryant. The text cites Ms. Bryant for "selected use of scriptures taken out of context, unlearned interpretations of such scriptures, and faulty theological concepts."

1103.   Gengle, Dean. "Talking with One of God's Question Marks:
        Rev. Ellen Barrett." THE ADVOCATE, 214 (20 April, 1977),
        31-33.

        A lengthy interview with Rev. Ellen Barrett, the first
        open lesbian to be ordained a priest in the Episcopal
        Church. The discussion covers her evolving sense of
        vocation and place within both church and community.

1104.   Beck, Jern. "Christian Heritage Or Jesuit Pottage?" THE
        ADVOCATE, 215 (4 May, 1977), 36.

        A reprint of an essay originally published in the
        newsletter of the Los Angeles chapter of Dignity. The
        refusal of the Jesuit order to ordain Thomas Sweetin is
        seen as an example of hierarchical rigidity, and the
        author calls upon gay Christians not to "waste the
        pentecostal   opportunities"   by   supporting   such
        attitudes.

1105.   "Gay Get-Together." CHRISTIANITY TODAY, 21 (3 June,
        1977), 33-35.

        A report on a retreat on the theme "Gay and Christian"
        held at the Kirkridge Center near Bangor, Pennsylvania
        in May, 1977. Participants included Fr. John McNeill
        and Malcolm Boyd. The goal of the eighty-five dele-
        gates was to focus on ways in which homosexual Chris-
        tians could be true to both their faith and their
        sexual orientation.

1106.   "Confronting the Homosexual Issue." CHRISTIANITY TODAY,
        21 (8 July, 1977), 36.

        A brief survey article noting the deep involvement of
        religious organizations in the recent repeal of the
        Dade County homosexual rights ordinance.

1107.   "Sexual   Differences: A   Cultural   Convention?"
        CHRISTIANITY TODAY, 21 (8 July, 1977), 8-10. Reply, 22 (7
        October, 1977), 11.

        Stating that "our society is going through a period of
        profound cultural unrest and open moral degeneration"
        this article by a theologian reasserts the Biblical
        position on homosexuality and calls upon Christians to
        minister to people "trapped by their own sins."

1108. "Rome Muzzles McNeill." THE ADVOCATE, 226 (19 October, 1977), 14.

> Fr. John McNeill, S.J., author of *The Church and the Homosexual*, has been informed by superiors in Rome that his 1973 order of silence is once more in effect. He is forbidden "to speak publicly on homosexuality or sexual ethics" and Vatican approval is to be withdrawn from all future editions of his work. The Dignity convention, which McNeill was to have addressed in San Francisco, issued a news release repudiating charges of "advocacy theology" as stated by the hierarchy. Full details of the official church position on McNeill are provided.

1109. "Set the Captives Free." NEW CATHOLIC WORLD, 220 (November, 1977), 292-295.

> A lengthy interview with Episcopal priest Paul Shanley of the Boston diocese, discussing his historical involvement with ministry to the gay community and his situation in the archdiocese.

1110. "Disciples Decide: Homosexuality Issue and the Christian Church, Disciple of Christ." CHRISTIANITY TODAY, 22 (18 November, 1977), 56-57.

> A news report on the actions taken by the biennial 1977 General Assembly of the Disciples of Christ. Details of the debate on homosexuality and the adoption of an eight-thousand-word document on the subject for official study are noted.

1111. "Leveling of John McNeill." COMMONWEAL, 104 (9 December, 1977), 778-783.

> A lengthy critical philosophical exploration of the treatment and censorship of Fr. John McNeill by the Roman Catholic Church, written by a leading activist clergyman.

1112. "Gay Rights + Women Priests = Episcopal Schisms." THE ADVOCATE, 231 (28 December, 1977), 45.

> A report on the conference of the House of Bishops of the Episcopal Church held in October, 1977 at Port St.

Lucie, Florida. Dissent within the denomination over the ordination of women and acceptance of homosexual clergy are profiled. A statement by Bishop C. Kilmer Myers of San Francisco supporting the licensure of Rev. Ellen Barrett is quoted in part.

1113. "American Lutheran Church." THE ADVOCATE, 231 (28 December, 1977), 45.

A report of a planned "consultation on human sexuality" currently being organized for April 6-7, 1978 by the American Lutheran Church. Local congregations are being asked to respond to a draft of an official statement on homosexuality prepared in March, 1977 by Dr. Carl Reuss which condemns homosexuality but supports gay civil rights.

1114. Boyd, Malcolm. TAKE OFF THE MASKS. Garden City, NY: Doubleday & Company, Inc., 1978.

Malcolm Boyd, one of the leading gay religious philosophers of the twentieth century, shares his life in this autobiography. Along with stories of his work in the civil rights movement of the 1960s and his own growing awareness of his gay nature, he provides the reader with a scathing indictment of homophobic attitudes in society in general and Christianity in specific. The cry of pain from one who has been, and remains, both cleric and gay man is eloquently expressed in these pages.

1115. Evans, Arthur. WITCHCRAFT AND THE GAY COUNTER-CULTURE: A RADICAL VIEW OF WESTERN CIVILIZATION AND SOME OF THE PEOPLE IT HAS TRIED TO DESTROY. Boston: FAG RAG Books, 1978.

This volume presents a view of the persecution of homosexual men and women in the context of survivals of pagan practices and Church teachings on witchcraft, along with the renascence of feminist interest in reinterpretating traditional versions of historical events. Researchers should note the chronology of events and the extensive bibliography.

1116. Horner, Tom. JONATHAN LOVED DAVID: HOMO-
SEXUALITY IN BIBLICAL TIMES. Philadelphia: The
Westminster Press, 1978.

Perhaps no one work has been so consistently adduced as
justification for various anti-gay and anti-lesbian
laws and practices as the Bible. Accordingly, it is
vital that the passages used as evidence of divine
condemnation of homosexuality be understood in their
cultural and temporal context. Horner's readable and
cogent presentation begins with a general description
of the Middle Eastern cultural background out of which
the Bible came. Special attention is paid to the Epic
of Gilgamesh and its prototypical couple of male
heroes/lovers. Moving to the Biblical texts themselves, its stories of David and Jonathan, Ruth and
Naomi, and the men of Sodom and Gibeah are next
explored. The final chapters deal with topics as
varied as male cult prostitution in Canaan, the letters
of St. Paul and the teachings of Jesus on sexual
matters. A brief annotated bibliography and index
complete the work. Horner's book should be used as a
general introduction to the scriptural basis of ecclesiastical homophobia and recent debates as to its
validity.

1117. Kirk, Jerry R. THE HOMOSEXUAL CRISIS IN THE
MAINLINE CHURCH: A PRESBYTERIAN MINISTER
SPEAKS OUT. Nashville: Thomas Nelson Inc.,
Publishers, 1978.

In November, 1975, the New York Presbytery of the
United Presbyterian Church requested the General
Assembly of that denomination to appoint a special
committee to provide "definitive guidance" on the
question of ordaining avowed homosexuals to the
ministry. The committee issued its report to the
assembly in 1978, recommending that such individuals
could be ordained if otherwise qualified. This book
was written by a conservative member of the Presbyterian clergy opposing any alteration of traditional
positions on homosexuality. His attitude is best
summarized as "the issue before us is not gay rights,
but God's rights" (p. 37). Thirteen chapters examine
responses made to the gay rights movement by other
American denominations, positions on sexuality drawn
from patristic literature, and sharply question the
organization of a church which has permitted such
debate. A call is issued to all Presbyterian members

to oppose the recommendation in the next session of the General Assembly.

1118. Lovelace, Richard F. HOMOSEXUALITY AND THE CHURCH. Old Tappan, NJ: Fleming H. Revell Company, 1978.

A text addressing the 1978 recommendations of the United Presbyterian Task Force on homosexuality by the leader of the conservative minority bloc of that body. Positions taken in the final minority report of the task force have been expanded and clarified to form the present. Liberalization is condemned and homosexual Presbyterians are called upon to "repent from sin," with Rev. Lovelace urging the church to "discipline those who publicly announce their own practice" (p. 121). Extensive Scriptural quotations are included.

1119. Scanzoni, Letha and Virginia Ramey Mollenkott. IS THE HOMOSEXUAL MY NEIGHBOR? ANOTHER CHRISTIAN VIEW. San Francisco: Harper & Row Publishers, 1978.

This exploration of the moral challenge facing Christians in a re-examination of religious and social attitudes on the topic of homosexuality was published shortly after the Anita Bryant campaigns of 1977-1978. In it, two theologians address the issue through literature, sociology, human sexuality and religious studies. Of particular interest is the ninth chapter, entitled "Proposing a Homosexual Christian Ethic," which offers an alternative theological model for human sexuality embracing committed homosexual relationships. A brief annotated list of reading materials is appended.

1120. Woods, Richard. ANOTHER KIND OF LOVE: HOMOSEXUALITY AND SPIRITUALITY. Garden City, NY: Image Books, 1978.

Written by a Dominican clergyman with six years experience of ministry to "gay Catholics and other Christians" in the Chicago metropolitan area and as counselor to that city's chapter of Dignity, this text is oriented to both pastoral and lay audiences. Its theme is "an essay in spirituality," exploring homosexuality "as a fact, rather than as an undesirable or desirable situation" (p. 16). Topics addressed include acceptance, American cultural willingness to discuss homosexuality as it existed in the late 1970s, the place of religion in gay life and social dimensions of spirituality. Woods calls for the development of a uniquely gay spirituality through the sharing of experiences and reflection. A brief bibliography of references completes the work.

1121. Gengle, Dean. "Hate in the Jesus Tunnel." THE ADVOCATE, 232 (11 January, 1978), 17-19.

An opinion piece on the "belief chauvinism" of fundamentalist Christianity, with extensive quotations of anti-homosexual rhetoric drawn from several periodicals.

1122. "Reform Judaism Passes Gay Resolution." THE ADVOCATE, 233 (25 January, 1978), 17.

The full text of a resolution on the rights of homosexuals passed by the Union of American Hebrew Congregations at its biennial meeting in San Francisco. The UAHC stated that discrimination in housing, employment and opportunity should be opposed.

1123. "Sex and Homosexuality, Protestant Episcopal Church Statement." CHRISTIANITY TODAY, 22 (14 February, 1978), 23-30.

The full text of a pastoral statement on homosexuality written by the Episcopal bishop of Atlanta.

1124. Gengle, Dean. "A New Logic in Judaic Thinking." THE ADVOCATE, 235 (22 February, 1978), 25-26.

A review of an article by Rabbi Hershel J. Matt which appeared in the Winter, 1978 issue of *Judaism*. Entitled "A Jewish Approach to Homosexuality," its logic and conclusions offer possibilities for dialogue on the issue within the rabbinate.

1125. "Concerned Lutherans Convene." THE ADVOCATE, 235 (22 February, 1978), 26.

A news report on the first national convening of Lutherans Concerned in Milwaukee, Wisconsin, July 7-9, 1978. The organization was founded in 1974 for "gay and non-gay people, pastors and lay people from the Lutheran Church."

1126. Shilts, Randy M. "The Polyester Plot: A Conspiracy of Belief." THE ADVOCATE, 236 (8 March, 1978), 7-9.

A detailed news story analyzing the background to and current controversies over city gay rights laws in St. Paul and Wichita. Fundamentalist clergy are interviewed, and their subcultural mores presented.

1127. "Presbyterian Study Presses for Gay Rights." THE ADVOCATE, 236 (8 March, 1978), 31, 37.

The report of the United Presbyterian Church Task Force to Study Homosexuality has been completed and will be presented to that denomination's general assembly during the May 16-24, 1978 meetings in San Diego. Majority and minority opinions are presented through extensive textual quotation. The group supported decriminalization of homosexuality per se and an end to harassment by police, while recommending that the church leave the question or ordination of gays to individual congregations.

1128. Gregory-Lewis, Sasha. "God Vs. the Good Guys in Rockford." THE ADVOCATE, 237 (22 March, 1978), 16.

An examination of the Congressional race in the 16th District of Illinois as a test case of neo-right involvement in efforts to "purge the Republican party of any progressive elements." Incumbent John B. Anderson, Chair of the House Republican Committee, has a record of supporting equal rights legislation. He is challenged by fundamentalist minister Donald Lyon.

1129. "Friends Befriend Gay People." THE ADVOCATE, 243 (14 June, 1978), 9.

The American Friends Service Committee has issued an affirmative action employment plan "aimed at gay people, women and Third World persons." Goals of the plan and history of the dialogue initiated on gay employment in 1975 are summarized.

1130. Gengle, Dean. "Chris Glaser: Minister As Activist." THE ADVOCATE, 243 (14 June, 1978), 33.

An interview with Presbyterian activist Chris Glaser, current director of a counseling ministry to the gay community of West Hollywood. His evolution and views on "process theology" are explored.

1131. Glaser, Chris. "Presbyterian Family Ousts Gay Ministerial Candidates." THE ADVOCATE, 245 (12 July, 1978), 13.

A news analysis and commentary upon the 190th General Assembly of the Presbyterian Church meetings in San Diego in May, 1978 and the significance of homosexuality in its debates. Actions taken by the Task Force on Homosexuality and Presbyterians for Gay Concerns did not prevent passage of a modified version of the study report on homosexuality. The accepted text evaded the issue of ordaining known gays.

1132. Saslow, James M. "Robert Wheatley: A Concerned Unitarian Heads OGC." THE ADVOCATE, 253 (1 November, 1978), 25.

An interview with Robert Wheatley, director of the Office of Gay Concerns in the Unitarian Universalist Association. A history of the agency since its creation in 1975 and contemporary programs of education and dialogue are outlined.

1133. "Archbishop Knocks 6." THE ADVOCATE, 254 (15 November, 1978), 15.

California Archbishop John Quinn, chair of the National Conference of Catholic Bishops, has condemned the controversial Proposition 6 legislation as "perilously vague" and stated that such employment prohibitions violated the civil rights to which all homosexual persons were entitled as citizens.

1134. "Gay Priests Ordained." THE ADVOCATE, 256 (13 December, 1978), 11-12.

A report on the ordination of four openly gay men to the priesthood of the Eucharistic Catholic Church by Bishop Robert Clement of New York. The sect does not follow Rome nor require celibacy of its clergy.

1135. Goodich, Michael. THE UNMENTIONABLE VICE: HOMO-SEXUALITY IN THE LATER MEDIEVAL PERIOD. Santa Barbara, CA: ABC-Clio, 1979.

European homosexuality from the eleventh to the early fourteenth century is the subject of this contribution to the emerging field of gay history. Five chapters cover general background information on medieval homosexuality, agrarian reform, scholasticism, the Fourth Lateran Council and secular law, and legislation of the church councils. These latter provide an excellent background to such works as Peter Damian's treatise *The Book of Gomorrah* (1049). A detailed discussion of the often tangled historical evolution of attitudes, moral precepts and laws dealing with homosexuality centers on the role played by the religious establishments of the day. An appendix gives a translation of a trial for sodomy which occurred in southern France in 1323/1324.

1136. Moore, Jr., Paul. TAKE A BISHOP LIKE ME. New York: Harper & Row, Publishers, 1979.

In 1977, Paul Moore, bishop of the Episcopal Diocese of New York, made church history by ordaining Ellen Marie Barrett to the priesthood of that denomination. Prior to this time, Moore had been enmeshed in the ongoing debate within the Episcopal Church regarding the fitness of women to serve in the diaconate and as priests. Ellen Barrett complicated matters by admitting to being a practicing lesbian. *Take A Bishop Like Me* recounts the history of that debate as well as the storm of criticism and praise which followed the ordination of Reverend Barrett. A unique feature of this volume is its inclusion of the full texts of church resolutions, speeches and documents relating to this case.

1137. "Openly Gay Rabbi in San Francisco." THE ADVOCATE, 265 (19 April, 1979), 8.

Congregation Sha'ar Zahav of San Francisco on March 2, 1979 announced the appointment of Allen B. Bennett as their rabbi. Bennett is the first rabbi to openly acknowledge his homosexuality and has served as chaplain in Rochester, Minnesota.

1138. "Methodist Women Vote to Retain Lesbian." THE ADVOCATE, 269 (14 June, 1979), 8.

A report on the refusal of the Women's Division of the United Methodist Board of Global Ministries to accept the resignation of Joan Clark, a field staff member who revealed her lesbian status in a research report prepared for that body. The report was the result of four months' investigation into homosexuality and homophobia.

1139. "National Church Council Offers Gay Guidelines." THE ADVOCATE, 269 (14 June, 1979), 9.

Summaries of recent ecumenical guidelines on abortion and homosexuality issued by the National Council of Churches.

1140. "Methodist Board Keeps Lesbian, Then Axes Her." THE ADVOCATE, 270 (28 June, 1979), 14.

In response to "vicious attacks and publicity," the Women's Division of the Methodist Board of Global Ministries has dismissed Joan Clark, a staffer who admitted being a lesbian. An April 23 decision to retain Clark as an employee sparked the controversy.

1141. "Tennessee Baptists Enter Sex Law Fray." THE ADVOCATE, 270 (28 June, 1979), 14-15.

A news note on the efforts of Bradley County, Tennessee Baptist ministers to repeal current sex offense legislation which is unclear on the status of homosexual acts. The group described such acts as "contrary to the laws of God, man and nature" and stated that they "cannot be tolerated in a civilized society."

1142. "Methodist Seminarians Are Put on Probation." THE ADVOCATE, 271 (12 July, 1979), 9.

Five students at the St. Paul School of Theology in St. Louis have been placed on probation for distributing a pamphlet prepared by a committee set up to "explore the relation between homosexuality and the church." Background to the incident is briefly sketched.

1143. "Christian Lobby Hits 'Immorality' of Gays." THE ADVOCATE, 271 (12 July, 1979), 9-10.

The Washington, D.C. lobbying organization Christian Voice has planned a direct-mail campaign to press members of Congress for passage of anti-gay legislation. Steve Endean of the Gay Rights National Lobby is interviewed for comment.

1144. "Gay Relationships Get Good Press." THE ADVOCATE, 271 (12 July, 1979), 10.

A news note on an article in the May, 1979 issue of *The Lutheran* by Dr. Leroy Aden of Philadelphia which was supportive of same-sex relationships. The publication is the largest circulation church magazine in the United States.

1145. "Court Says It's OK to Deny Gay's Degree." THE ADVOCATE, 271 (12 July, 1979), 10-11.

A profile of the case of Ottie David Vance, who is currently suing the Lexington, Kentucky Theological Seminary to obtain his degree of Masters of Divinity. Upon admitting his homosexuality in 1975, the executive committee and the board of trustees disapproved the awarding of the degree, although Vance had completed all requirements. The institution's denial has been based upon a phrase in the school's catalog requiring applicants to possess "character and personality which indicate probable effectiveness of the Christian ministry." A recent ruling by the Kentucky Court of Appeals indicating that the school is "under no obligation to grant a degree to an openly gay student" is noted.

1146. "Two Church Reports Address Gay Issues." THE ADVOCATE, 272 (26 July, 1979), 8.

The positions taken by study group reports on homosexuality recently issued by the American Lutheran Church and the Episcopal Church are summarized. The Lutheran report saw "no theological rationale" for revision of traditional opposition to homoerotic practices, while the Episcopalian committee suggested that gay persons could be ordained if their behavior was "wholesome." Both reports will be submitted to the next general conventions of the respective denominations.

1147.   "Fundamentalists Blast Carter for Gay Support." THE ADVOCATE, 272 (26 July, 1979), 9.

A brief summary of charges leveled at President Jimmy Carter by an alliance of clergymen opposed to homosexuality in light of a meeting at the White House with a delegation representing Third World homosexuals.

1148.   Giteck, Lenny. "Gay Rabbi Allen Bennett: The First in 5,000 Years." THE ADVOCATE, 272 (26 July, 1979), 19.

An interview with Allen Bennett, an openly gay rabbi of Congregation Sha'ar Zahav in San Francisco. His views on the debate on homosexuality within Reform Judaism are explored.

1149.   "Mormons Excommunicate Editor of ADVOCATE." THE ADVOCATE, 273 (9 August, 1979), 10-11.

On June 20, 1979, Robert McQueen, former member of the Mormon Church and editor of the gay newspaper *The ADVOCATE* since 1975, was formally excommunicated from the church. McQueen had written and published a harsh attack on the attitude of the Latter Day Saints church towards homosexuals. Previously, excommunication had been used to purge members critical of official church policy on blacks. A brief interview with McQueen is included.

1150.   "Methodists Are Asking--To Ordain Or Not To?" THE ADVOCATE, 273 (9 August, 1979), 11.

A news report of the decision by the New York Annual Conference of the Methodist Church to present a petition on homosexuality to the Judicial Council. At issue is "whether a 'self-avowed, practicing homosexual clergyperson' can be appointed under the language of Paragraph 71D of the Methodist Social Principles."

1151. "Boston Cardinal Knocks Gay 'Lifestyle,' Priests." THE ADVOCATE, 274 (23 August, 1979), 13.

A brief summary of the contents of a sixteen-page pastoral letter issued by Cardinal Humberto Medeiros of Boston, rebuking clergy who regard homosexuality as acceptable or who would approve same-sex unions.

1152. Glaser, Chris. "Presbyterian Gays Opening New Doors." THE ADVOCATE, 275 (6 September, 1979), 7.

At concurrent General Assembly meetings in Kansas City, Missouri, the United Presbyterian Church in the U.S.A. and the Presbyterian Church in the U.S. voted to adopt the former faction's policy statement of 1978 opposing ordination for gay persons. A short history of the debate on this issue in both churches is included. A progressive note was the acceptance of the annual report of the gay caucus, Presbyterians for Gay Concerns, which had been regularly refused since 1975.

1153. Burke, Pat. "Dignity, Now 10 Years Old, Faces the Catholic Future." THE ADVOCATE, 278 (18 October, 1979), 9, 13.

A summary of the events and speakers at the 1974 convention of Dignity International in San Diego, California on the tenth anniversary of the organization's founding. Newly-elected president Frank Scheuren and delegates Fr. Robert Nugent (New Ways Ministry), historian John Boswell and Fr. John McNeill are interviewed.

1154. Clem, Lance. "Episcopals: No Ordination Officially, But Door Is Ajar." THE ADVOCATE, 279 (1 November, 1979), 11-12.

On September 18, 1979, the national convention of the Episcopal Church meeting in Denver passed a non-binding resolution opposing the ordination of gay priests. Said resolution was answered by an opposing "statement of conscience" by eighty-one delegates. Donn Mitchell, convention spokesman for Integrity, the Episcopal gay organization, is interviewed for comment.

1155. "Methodists to Tackle Gays at Fall Meeting." THE ADVOCATE, 279 (1 November, 1979), 13.

The United Methodist Church Judicial Council's agenda for the October 24-27, 1979 meetings will include the question of the ordination of gay persons to the clergy. This decision is in response to a query from the annual conference of New York State, which recently upheld such an ordination and approved the individual's placement. At issue will be the legal effect of the denomination's social principles.

1156. "Gays OK for United Church of Christ." THE ADVOCATE, 279 (1 November, 1979), 14.

The 1979 biennial convention of the United Church of Christ has reaffirmed the policy of accepting qualified homosexuals into the clergy and leaving the question of the disposition of cases to local authorities.

1157. "Christian Cause Has New Antigay Militancy." THE ADVOCATE, 280 (15 November, 1979), 7.

The fundamentalist organization American Christian Cause is distributing a fund raising mailing "because militant homosexuals are being recruited as law enforcement officers."

1158. "Pope Toes Hard Line on Homosexual Acts." THE ADVOCATE, 280 (15 November, 1979), 7.

Speaking in Chicago during his American visit, Pope John Paul II reaffirmed "that the Catholic Church was right in regarding homosexual actions as sinful." Other positions taken by the pontiff on such issues as abortion and contraception are outlined.

1159. "Theology Students Ask Clark's Reinstatement." THE ADVOCATE, 280 (15 November, 1979), 11.

Fifty-three students at New York City's Union Theological Seminary have presented the Women's Division of the United Methodist Church a petition calling for the reinstatement of Joan Clark, a lesbian staff worker, and adoption of a policy of non-discrimination and education within the entire church.

1160. "Church of England Report Stirs Gay Controversy." THE ADVOCATE, 281 (29 November, 1979), 12.

The Board for Social Responsibility of the Church of England has released the results of a five-year study on the ordination of gay clergy and homosexuality in general. It recommends that "bishops not refuse to ordain a candidate for the clergy on the basis of homosexuality," as well as civil law reform. The recommendations will be considered by the general synod in February, 1987.

1161. "Church Opens Door to Gay Ministers." THE ADVOCATE, 282 (13 December, 1979), 8.

A report on the decision of the St. Louis General Assembly of the Christian Church (Disciples of Christ) "to allow regional bodies of the national congregation the right to ordain openly homosexual ministers."

1162. "Rev. Recommends Mass Death." THE ADVOCATE, 282 (13 December, 1979), 11.

A news note on the statement by Baptist pastor Rev. Daniel Lovely of Watertown, New York, that "homosexuals should be killed by government means."

1163. "Gay Minister Gets Nod." THE ADVOCATE, 283 (27 December, 1979), 7.

The controversy surrounding the appointment of Rev. Paul Abels as pastor of New York's Washington Square Church is reviewed. The Judicial Council of the United Methodist Church has declared him to be "in good standing" with the regional authorities. The larger question of general ordainment of gays was not addressed in the decision.

1164. Boswell, John. CHRISTIANITY, SOCIAL TOLERANCE, AND HOMOSEXUALITY. GAY PEOPLE IN WESTERN

EUROPE FROM THE BEGINNING OF THE CHRISTIAN ERA TO THE FOURTEENTH CENTURY. Chicago: The University of Chicago Press, 1980.

The interplay of the forces of religion and civil authority and their effect on homosexuals is chronicled in detail by John Boswell for fourteen centuries. Beginning with the laws and customs of imperial Rome, discussion shifts to the Christian traditions of scripture and theology. Tracing attitudes towards homosexuality, Boswell presents a deeply scholarly account of the changing patterns of homophobia through the Middle Ages to the beginning of the Renaissance. The text abounds with specific legal citations to both lay and canon law, illustrating the sharp increase in intolerant attitudes between the twelfth and thirteenth centuries. For anyone interested in the evolution of anti-homosexual beliefs and practices on the European continent, this volume provides essential introduction and background. A selected bibliography is included.

1165.   Willenbecher, Thom. "A G.A.L.A. Goodbye to God: Gay Atheists Come Out." THE ADVOCATE, 284 (10 January, 1980), 19-21.

A profile of the Gay Atheists League of America including interviews with founders Daniel Curzon and Tom Rolfsen. The organization's history since its formation in 1978 is outlined, with the purpose of seeking "to make gay people realize that their worst enemy is organized religion." GALA opposition both within and outside the gay community is examined.

1166.   "Gay Mormons Hold First Conference." THE ADVOCATE, 285 (7 February, 1980), 8.

A brief news item on the first national conference of Affirmation, the organization for gay and lesbian Mormons, in Los Angeles, California, December 7-8, 1979. The status of the group at that time is outlined and contact information provided.

1167.   "Lesbian Presbyterian Pressured to Resign." THE ADVOCATE, 285 (7 February, 1980), 9.

Jane A. Spaht, executive director of the Council of Oakland (California) Presbyterian Churches, submitted her resignation on December 12, 1979. Grounds for the action were the discovery of her homosexuality through personnel procedures. This event is in direct opposition to the denomination's official stance that sexual orientation is not a valid basis for discrimination.

1168. "Church: Always Resistant to Change." CHRISTIAN CENTURY, 97 (27 February, 1980), 237-238.

A personal thoughtful account of the reception of lesbian Episcopal priest and theologian Carter Heyward (in her first sermon since publicly acknowledging her sexual preference) written by a deacon of the Charlotte, North Carolina church which hosted her. The occasion's controversies are seen as opportunities for growth within the community.

1169. "Fundamentalist Rev Up Lobbies." THE ADVOCATE, 287 (6 March, 1980), 7.

A summary of efforts at generating a write-in campaign to kill proposed gay rights legislation pending in the House of Representatives by the fundamentalist religious organizations Moral Majority and Christian Voice. Quotations from their flyers on the issue are included.

1170. Boyd, Malcolm. "'I Accuse'--Episcopal Priest and Author Malcolm Boyd Points a Finger at the Hypocrisy of 'Churchianity.'" THE ADVOCATE, 288 (20 March, 1980), 19-22.

"This is the sin of the church concerning gays . . . a public lie and wheeling and dealing with the truth" (p. 19). An opinion commentary by leading gay clergyman Malcolm Boyd on the treatment of gay persons by organized religion. Emphasis is placed upon both the author's own experiences and official dogma.

1171. Anderson, Scott. "Working Within: Gay Religious Groups Call for Acceptance." THE ADVOCATE, 288 (20 March, 1980), 22-23, 47.

A brief survey of the efforts of religious gay caucuses and organizations to stimulate change in organized religion in the United States and the varying degrees of success obtained. Cases offered as evidence are Presbyterians for Gay Concerns, Dignity, Integrity and the gay synagogues.

1172. "No Gay Priest Here, Say Alaska Episcopals." THE ADVOCATE, 289 (3 April, 1980), 9.

A profile of the case of Tom Wilkenson of Anchorage, Alaska, who was recently denied ordination after five years' study for the Episcopal priesthood. Local conditions are outlined.

1173. "Reagan Won't 'Condone' Gays, Will Take Funds from Fundamentalists." THE ADVOCATE, 290 (17 April, 1980), 7.

In an interview given March 6, 1980 to a staff member of *Los Angeles Times*, presidential candidate Ronald Reagan stated his opposition to civil rights for gay persons. He characterized the gay liberation groups as "asking for a recognition and acceptance of an alternative lifestyle which I do not believe society can condone," citing Biblical authority. Christian Voice, a fundamentalist group, has stated it will undertake a massive mail campaign in support of Mr. Reagan.

1174. "Methodist Magazine Highlights Homosexuality." THE ADVOCATE, 291 (1 May, 1980), 10.

A report on a special issue of *Engage/Social Action*, the periodical of the United Methodist Board of Church and Society for March, 1980, dealing with homosexuality in a positive manner. Articles are included by the leaders of the denomination's gay and lesbian caucus as well as from non-gay clergy.

1175. "Methodists Grope for a Common Center." CHRISTIANITY TODAY, 24 (23 May, 1980), 40-42.

An omnibus article examining the decisions made at the April, 1980 quadrennial meetings of the United Methodist Church. A 1972 statement in the denomination's Social Principles terming homosexuality "incompatible with Christian teaching" and a ban on fiscal contributions to gay organizations were reaffirmed.

1176. "Methodists Vote Down Progay Resolution." THE ADVOCATE, 293 (29 May, 1980), 8-9.

> A report on the defeat at the general conference of the United Methodist Church of a proposal to delete the section of that denomination's Statement of Social Principles which condemns homosexuality. The vote was 779 to 225.

1177. "Is Our Church Big Enough for Gay Catholics?" U.S. CATHOLIC, 45 (June, 1980), 6-13.

> A lengthy detailed interview with Catholic journalist and activist Brian McNaught. His own experiences with religious discrimination and stereotypes are related and the conflict between the gay pride movement and societal conditioning explored.

1178. Kavanaugh, Julia. "My Son Is Gay." U.S. CATHOLIC, 45 (June, 1980), 14-15.

> An article written by the Catholic mother of a gay son, speaking of both her own evolution and growth and calling for change within the Church.

1179. "Jewish Group Adopts Antibias Resolution." THE ADVOCATE, 294 (12 June, 1980), 10.

> On May 4, 1980, the American Jewish Congress' biennial convention meeting in Washington, D.C. adopted a resolution opposing "all discrimination against homosexuals in employment, housing, military service and other areas." A similar motion introduced in 1978 was defeated.

1180. "Missouri Methodist Is First Open Gay." THE ADVOCATE, 296 (10 July, 1980), 8.

> On May 19, 1980, Keith E. Spare was graduated from the Saint Paul School of Theology to become the first openly gay United Methodist minister. Background on the case and church reaction is included.

1181. "SF Archbishop Rips Gays in Open Letter." THE ADVOCATE, 296 (10 July, 1980), 9-10.

Highlights of a recent pastoral letter issued by Archbishop John R. Quinn of San Francisco restating traditional Catholic positions on homosexual acts. Among them was the statement that "opposition to homosexuality . . . by the church or by society cannot be regarded as a prejudice."

1182. "Gay Adventists Win Official Recognition." THE ADVOCATE, 297 (24 July, 1980), 10-11.

A profile of a planned conference of the Seventh Day Adventist Church scheduled for Arizona, August 5-11, 1980. Dialogue between officials and members of Kinship, the sect's gay and lesbian caucus is expected.

1183. Saslow, James A. "Methodist Paul Abels Raises Quiet Cain for Gay Religion." THE ADVOCATE, 297 (24 July, 1980), 14-15.

An interview with Rev. Paul Abels of Washington Square Church in New York City, recently sustained in his pastorate by a vote of the United Methodist Judicial Council. He outlines the details of his case and cautions against reading too much into the decision in terms of liberalization and ordination.

1184. "Methodists: No Action Against Gay Cleric." THE ADVOCATE, 298 (7 August, 1980), 9-10.

On June 16, 1980, an investigative committee of the New York Conference of the United Methodist Church refused to level charges of "immorality and unchristian conduct" against Rev. Paul Abels of New York City. Said charges were demanded by another Methodist cleric due to Abel's open homosexuality.

1185. "Defrocked Priest Ruled 'Immoral' by His Church." THE ADVOCATE, 300 (4 September, 1980), 10.

On July 17, 1980, Rev. Johannes Kuiper of the Dutch Reformed Church was found guilty of the charge of "the offensive lifestyle of homosexuality" by the New York state ruling council and defrocked. Researchers seeking further data on this case should consult Kuiper's own account, *Hot Under The Collar*.

1186. "N.Y. Church Project Takes Aim Against Gay Rights." THE
       ADVOCATE, 308 (25 December, 1980), 7-8.

       A news report on the foundation of Americans Against
       H.R.2074 by the Gates Community Chapel of Rochester,
       New York. The group plans a direct-mail campaign to
       defeat the bill, which it claims, gives special rights
       to homosexuals and "is evidence of our country's moral
       decay."

1187. Malloy, Edward A. HOMOSEXUALITY AND THE CHRIS-
       TIAN WAY OF LIFE. Washington, D.C.: University
       Press of America, 1981.

       Admitting in his conclusion to this analysis that he
       has "been unable to reconcile the homosexual way of
       life with the Christian way of life," the author none-
       theless presents a detailed exploration of both homo-
       sexuality and organized religion's response to it. The
       volume opens with an overview of the language (both
       clinical and colloquial) used to describe all types of
       homosexual activities. Chapters two through seven
       touch upon the subjects of cultural context, statisti-
       cal prevalence, theories of causation, homosexual
       social institutions, and the civil rights struggle.
       The second section covers Christian ethics and their
       relationship to the issues raised by homosexuality, the
       acceptability of scriptural evidence and ethical argu-
       ments (both contemporary and traditional) as to the
       moral acceptability of the gay lifestyle are treated in
       some detail. Having closely compared this latter with
       a distinctly Christian lifestyle based upon a set of
       teachings drawn from Scripturally-sanctioned texts, the
       gay lifestyle is found wanting. Although somewhat
       heavily in debt to orthodox Christianity, researchers
       interested in the positions of both the gay community
       and organized religion in the early 1980s will find the
       work instructive.

1188. McNaught, Brian. A DISTURBED PEACE: SELECTED
       WRITINGS OF AN IRISH CATHOLIC HOMOSEXUAL.
       Washington, D.C.: Dignity, Inc., 1981.

       In 1974, Brian McNaught, a columnist for the Detroit
       newspaper *The Michigan Catholic*, came out as homo-
       sexual and was promptly sacked. This volume is a
       selection from his published column, "A Disturbed
       Peace," which has appeared in both gay and straight

newspapers and magazines in virtually every region of the United States. Ranging in time from May, 1975 to March, 1981, the dominant themes in these essays are the civil rights of gays and lesbians, creating social bonds and a new subculture, and the role of the Catholic Church in homosexual liberation. Of the twenty-six columns presented here, seven deal with this latter topic. A thoroughly readable volume which speaks about gay rights and spirituality with a very human voice.

1189. NOW THE SILENCE BREAKS: TOWARD A PASTORAL UNDERSTANDING OF HOMOSEXUALITY. Chicago: National Lutheran Campus Ministry, 1981.

A study guide for Lutheran congregations begun following a 1977 survey in the San Francisco Bay region of ten member churches. Chapters are structured to promote group discussions on attitudes, causes of homosexuality, scriptural teachings and pastoral concerns and the role of the Lutheran church in community. In January, 1978, after some eight months' study, a group of twenty-one San Francisco Lutheran pastors issued a statement stressing the need for greater pastoral outreach in the gay community and greater acceptance for homosexuals: a selection of textual study is provided in an appendix, together with a summary of the original 1977 survey findings. A short bibliography is also included.

1190. "Christian Leaders Launch 'Moral War' On Homosexuals." THE ADVOCATE, 313 (19 March, 1981), 9.

A news report on a planned anti-gay campaign slated for San Francisco by three religious fundamentalist groups. Specific groups involved are Moral Majority, Californians for a Biblical Morality and In God We Trust, Inc. Political leaders of the city have decried the proposed campaign, as well as statements that homosexuals be executed by capital punishment or publicly stoned.

1191. "SF Ecumenical Group Opposes Gay Baiting." THE ADVOCATE, 316 (30 April, 1981), 12-13.

The San Francisco Council of Churches, the San Francisco Conference on Religion, Race and Social

Concerns, and the Society of Friends have all issued statements opposing a fundamentalist media campaign aimed at repeal of the city's civil rights law, which advocates have termed a "moral war."

1192. "Episcopal Support for NYC Gay Bill." THE ADVOCATE, 318 (28 May, 1981), 10.

The partial text of a statement issued by Episcopal Bishop Paul Moore of New York City in support of a bill pending in the city council to ban discrimination based on sexual orientation.

1193. Hall, Richard. "Historian John Boswell on Gay, Tolerance and the Religious Tradition." THE ADVOCATE, 318 (28 May, 1981), 20-23, 26-27.

The complete transcript of an interview with Dr. John Boswell of Yale, author of *Christianity, Social Tolerance and Homosexuality*. The chief thesis of the work, "that Christianity and the Church were not a consistent foe of gay people until the 14th century" (p. 22) is explored in detail.

1194. "Pentecostal Journal Rebukes Its Own Gays." THE ADVOCATE, 320 (25 June, 1981), 10.

A news article reviewing an editorial published in *Logos Journal*, the leading journal of the American Pentecostal movement, calling for the expulsion of Dr. James Tenney for founding the Pentecostal Coalition for Human Rights. The organization has supported civil rights for gays as well as Hispanics and African Americans.

1195. "Mainstream Churches Support Gays." THE ADVOCATE, 321 (9 July, 1981), 10.

A review of letters of support for H.R. 1454, the proposed national gay rights legislation, received from religious organizations by the Gay Rights National Lobby. Groups on record as supportive include the Union of American Hebrew Congregations, the National Council of Churches of Christ and the Lutheran Council.

1196. "Methodists Endorse Gay Legislation." THE ADVOCATE, 323 (6 August, 1981), 16.

At its annual meeting in DeKalb on June 7-10, 1981, the Northern Illinois Conference of the United Methodist Church approved a resolution calling upon members to lobby for passage of gay rights legislation, enjoined its boards and agencies from anti-gay discrimination and planned a three-year study on homophobia.

1197. Regelson, Rosalyn. "Worldwide Conference Draws 250 Gay Jews." THE ADVOCATE, 325 (3 September, 1981), 10.

A summary of the events and speeches given at the Sixth Annual Conference of Gay and Lesbian Jews, held in Philadelphia over the Fourth of July weekend and hosted by Congregation Beth Aharah. Two workshops and the keynote speech by author Seymour Kleinberg are noted.

1198. "Chicago Church Groups Respond to New Right." THE ADVOCATE, 331 (26 November, 1981), 16.

A formal response to proposals advanced by the New Right has been issued by a group of Chicago theologians representing Roman Catholic, Evangelical, Anabaptist and Protestant denominations. "The Chicago Statement" includes "a compassion for homosexuals" among its Christian concerns.

1199. Boggs, Mark. "Censured and Censored: A Gay Priest Speaks Out." THE ADVOCATE, 332 (10 December, 1981), 17-18.

An interview with Fr. Richard Wagner, author of a study questioning the value of enforced celibacy. Based upon his dissertation research while a member of the Oblates of Mary Immaculate, the study led to Wagner's official censure and dismissal from the order. He discusses both the methodology and contents of the research and the need for church reform.

1200. Damian, Peter. BOOK OF GOMORRAH: AN ELEVENTH-CENTURY TREATISE AGAINST CLERICAL HOMO-SEXUAL PRACTICES. Waterloo, Ontario: Wilfrid Laurier University Press, 1982.

Writing to Pope Leo IX in approximately 1049 AD from the monastery of Fonte Avellana in central Italy, the monastic reformer Peter Damian called attention to homosexual abuses among the Catholic clergy of the time. Such reform activity was widely underway throughout the eleventh century in an effort to purify and reclaim Europe as a Christian society. The Book of Gomorrah marks the beginning of Damian's long fight against clerical laxity in many areas. While sent to the Pope, its text is addressed primarily to those persons guilty of a variety of male homosexual activities, in hopes of dissuading them from further action and toward repentance. The introduction added by the translator provides an excellent summary of previous ecclesiastical legislation on the topic. Damian's work is invaluable to anyone wishing a clear view of the historical roots of anti-gay discrimination by organized religion.

1201.   Fortunato, John E. EMBRACING THE EXILE: HEALING JOURNEYS OF GAY CHRISTIANS. New York: The Seabury Press, 1982.

While not recounting specific instances of ecclesiastical homophobia, John Fortunato's account deals with the effects of that homophobia on the psyches of gays and lesbians. As a practicing psychotherapist and gay man, he explores the path of individual emotional and spiritual regeneration necessary for recovery from clerically inflicted damage of many types. Its thoughtful and frank presentation makes excellent reading.

1202.   Nugent, SDS, Robert, Jeannine Gramick, SSND and Thomas Oddo, CSC. HOMOSEXUAL CATHOLICS: A NEW PRIMER FOR DISCUSSION. Washington, D.C.: Dignity, Inc., 1982.

Compiled by Dignity, an organization of gay Catholics, this short publication contains thirty-seven questions and answers on homosexuality and the church. Beginning with the official position and the rationale for it, discussion covers pastoral responsibility, scriptural teachings and gay rights activities as related to changes in established attitudes.

1203. Rueda, Enrique. THE HOMOSEXUAL NETWORK: PRIVATE LIVES AND PUBLIC POLICY. Old Greenwich, Connecticut: The Devin Adair Company, 1982.

> Fr. Enrique Rueda states in his preface that "the conclusion that the homosexual movement is a subset of the spectrum of American liberal movements is inescapable" (p. xix). Drawing chiefly on sources of information within the homosexual movement, Rueda opens his argument by examining the degree of acceptance homosexuality has achieved in contemporary American society and describing the gay subculture. Through an examination of the writings of leading gay and lesbian activists, the proposition is advanced that gay liberation is in fact a political movement. In the fourth and fifth chapters, components such as the National Gay Task Force are discussed and the general objectives of the gay movement presented. Organized religion and its relationship with an aware homosexual community are examined via three denominations: Metropolitan Community Church, Judaism and Catholicism. American liberalism, its links to gay and lesbian liberation organizations and the various sources from which such groups obtain financial support close the discussion. Twelve appendices cover alleged supporters of the homosexual movement: ideology, human rights, the Gay Pride March, *Communication* (an underground publication for certain homosexual clergy in Catholic Church), the texts of homosexual marriage rituals and rules of gay religious orders, Dignity and Integrity chapter listings, gay synagogues, student groups, political organizations, and special interest groups. Researchers should be aware that Father Rueda is a research fellow at the Free Congress Research and Education Foundation, which focuses on "trends affecting the stability and well being of American family life . . . by presenting traditional alternatives" (p. vii).

1204. "Miami Archdiocese Boots Gay Priest." THE ADVOCATE, 334 (7 January, 1982), 12.

> A news report on the suspension of the Rev. Philip Scheeding by the Miami archdiocese following his admission of homosexual identity. Scheeding told the media that he came out in an effort to show homosexuals "that they belong in the church."

1205. Nugent, Fr. Robert. "Catholic Symposium Draws 180 Leaders." THE ADVOCATE, 335 (21 January, 1982), 11.

A report on the "First National Symposium on Homosexuality and the Catholic Church" held in Washington, D.C. and sponsored by New Ways Ministry. Although officially endorsed by more than forty Catholic organizations, local diocesan officials would not approve the gathering, citing New Ways' counseling that "homosexual expression in the context of stable, faithful relationships is a moral good." Guest speakers and workshop topics are profiled.

1206. "Boulder Minister Out, Sent to Denver Church." THE ADVOCATE, 335 (21 January, 1982), 17, 70.

A news note on the transfer of Rev. Julian Rush to the position of outreach and community affairs minister at St. Paul's United Methodist Church in Denver. Rush's host congregation in Boulder became deeply divided following his admission of homosexuality while serving as minister of education there.

1207. "Episcopal Outreach Opens in the Castro." THE ADVOCATE, 335 (21 January, 1982), 70-71.

A review of the events surrounding the opening of The Parsonage, an outreach facility of the Episcopal Church in San Francisco's Castro district. Rev. William Swing commissioned more than twenty gay and lesbian lay ministers to staff the facility, which was suggested by Rev. Bernard Mayes.

1208. "U.S. Journal: Boulder, 10." THE NEW YORKER, 57 (25 January, 1982), 80-88.

Detailed coverage of the controversy surrounding gay Methodist clergyman Rev. Julian Rush within the Rocky Mountain Conference of that denomination.

1209. "Chicago Church Affirms Rights of Gays." THE ADVOCATE, 336 (18 February, 1982), 13.

The Lincoln Park Presbyterian Church of Chicago "has adopted a policy to prohibit discrimination against gay people as members and lay officers of its congregation." The move was part of the "More Light" movement within local Presbyterian congregations, which began in 1979 in response to official prohibition of ordination of gays as lay leaders.

1210. McNaught, Brian R. "Bigotry, Not Religion, Is the Real Enemy." THE ADVOCATE, 343 (27 May, 1982), 20-22.

A commentary by a leading gay Catholic author on the place of religious homosexuals in both the Church and the gay liberation movement. McNaught notes improvements in ecumenical relations but warns against the danger of elitism.

1211. Saslow, James M. "Speaking Out on Gay Rights: The Activist Rev. William Sloane Coffin, Jr." THE ADVOCATE, 343 (27 May, 1982), 25-27.

An interview with activist minister Rev. William Coffin of New York City's Riverside Church. The discussion explores a recent sermon in which traditional punitive stances towards homosexuals were decried, and the evolution of Coffin's views on contemporary moral leadership in the United States within organized religion.

1212. Nugent, Bob. "Gay Christians Meet in Washington, D.C." THE ADVOCATE, 345 (24 June, 1982), 16.

A news article summarizing the proceedings of the Third American Conference of Lesbian and Gay Christians held in Washington, D.C. Discussion centered upon common grounds for the building of a coalition, planning for a follow-up conference in November, 1982, and organizational structure, worship, ministry, political action and education.

1213. "National Council of Churches Puts Off MCC Application." THE ADVOCATE, 346 (8 July, 1982), 9.

The application of the Metropolitan Community Church for membership in the National Council of Churches has been deferred pending the findings of that body's Faith and Order Commission on "the fundamental issues about the nature of the church and human sexuality" contained in the MCC doctrine on homosexuality. Some council members have questioned this approach.

1214. "Methodists Will Not Try Pro-Gay Bishop." THE ADVOCATE, 346 (8 July, 1982), 9.

The Western Jurisdiction Committee on Investigation of the United Methodist Church has declined to place Bishop Melvin Wheatley of Denver on trial for his support of homosexuals. Charges of "disseminating false doctrine" and "undermining the authority of the Holy Scripture" were dismissed for lack of "reasonable grounds." Denominational attitude towards homosexual rights, as stated in the 1972 Social Principles amendment, are noted.

1215. "Texas Methodists Elect Gay Board Member." THE ADVOCATE, 347 (22 July, 1982), 14.

A note on the election of Troy Stokes Austin to the Church and Society Board of the Southwest Texas conference of the United Methodist Church. Stokes is the first open gay to be elected to a position in the history of the denomination in Texas. Local hierarchical officials endorsed the election as an opportunity for dialogue.

1216. "Why Gay Catholics Won't Be Locked Out of the Church." U.S. CATHOLIC, 17 (August, 1982), 6-12.

A group interview with seven ex-Catholics who are now members of the Metropolitan Community Church. Official Catholic positions on homosexuality and personal coping strategies such as repression and self-abnegation are criticized.

1217. "International Gay Group Sues Bishop." THE ADVOCATE, 349 (19 August, 1982), 16.

A lawsuit has been filed by the International Gay Association against Bishop Leon Elchinger of Strasbourg, France over his denial of space in a Roman Catholic hostel and references to lesbians and gay men as "cripples and morally handicapped" and "contaminating" the hostel. The planned Easter conference of the IGA was held in tents provided by civil defense agencies.

1218. "Methodists Condemn Homosexual Ministers." THE ADVO-CATE, 349 (19 August, 1982), 18.

The ordination of homosexuals as ministers was condemned in a resolution passed by the Northwest Texas Conference of the United Methodist Church as "contrary to the will of God." A portion of the resolution is appended.

1219. "Presbyterians Reaffirm Gay Ordination Ban." THE ADVOCATE, 352 (30 September, 1982), 9-10.

The 194th General Assembly of the United Presbyterian Church in the U.S. voted by a five-to-one margin to reaffirm official policy barring lesbians and gay men from ordination as elders or ministers. Other actions in support of civil rights for homosexuals are noted.

1220. "Homosexuals in the Churches." NEWSWEEK, 100 (11 October, 1982), 113-114.

A general news article on the changes in organized American religions being occasioned by homosexuals. The formation of minority gay caucuses and separate congregations such as the American Orthodox and Metropolitan Community Churches are emphasized.

1221. "At Bay in San Francisco." TIME, 120 (11 October, 1982), 67.

A brief review of the findings of a task force on gay and lesbian issues appointed by the Committee on Social Justice of the archdiocese of San Francisco. Its report, entitled *Homosexuality and Social Justice*, offered fifty-four proposals for church action, "including the end of sexual preference screening for parochial school jobs" and "admission of 'self-accepting' homosexuals as candidates to be priests and nuns." Popular reaction was mixed.

1222. "Landmark S.F. Report Urges Full Minority to Catholic Gays." THE ADVOCATE, 354 (29 October, 1982), 9.

The Task Force on Lesbian and Gay Issues of the Archdiocese of San Francisco released its report on July
13, 1982. Entitled *Homosexuality and Social Justice*,
the document is intended as a working paper, presenting
fifty-four recommendations, including one calling upon
the Church to dissociate itself from the "religious
demagoguery" of fundamentalist theology. Kevin Gordon,
the chair of the committee, is interviewed.

1223. "Episcopalians Back Gay Immigration, ERA." THE ADVO-
CATE, 354 (28 October, 1982), 10.

Support was expressed by the Episcopal Church's House
of Bishops and House of Delegates for H.R. 3524 during
the national triennial conference in New Orleans. The
bill would remove all existing barriers to immigration
of homosexuals to the United States. Events at the
immediately preceding conference of Integrity are also
summarized.

1224. "D.C. Pentecostal Church for Expulsion of Gay Leader."
THE ADVOCATE, 356 (25 November, 1982), 12.

Members of the Pentecostal Coalition for Human Rights
picketed Washington, D.C. over the expulsion of Dr.
James S. Tenney, founder of the gay caucus. Tenney was
expelled because he "could not be both homosexual and
Christian." Local media coverage of the protest is
outlined.

1225. "Over 300 Attend Dignity Mass Led by Baltimore
Archbishop." THE ADVOCATE, 357 (9 December, 1982), 12-
13.

On October 23, 1982, Archbishop William Borders of
Baltimore officiated at a service for the city's chapter of Dignity, and indicated that he was open to
dialogue on the issue of a civil rights bill previously
defeated in the city council.

1226. DiMaria-Kuiper, Johannes W. HOT UNDER THE COLLAR:
SELF-PORTRAIT OF A GAY PASTOR. Columbia, Missouri:
Mercury Press, 1983.

Johannes Kuiper, pastor in the Metropolitan Community
Church, shares his life in this smoothly written auto-

biography. Aside from the personal information, it presents a clear account of the attitudes encountered in the Dutch Reformed Church towards homosexuals in general and gay clergy in specific. Researchers should also consult Troy Perry's *The Lord Is My Shepherd and He Knows I'm Gay.*

1227. Ferm, Deane William. ALTERNATIVE LIFE-STYLES CONFRONT THE CHURCH. New York: The Seabury Press, 1983.

Written by a Protestant theologian concerned with the role of religion in coping with American social change, this volume presents the views of sixteen major churches. These range from the National Council of Churches and the United Church of Canada through most of the major American denominations. Two chapters are applicable to the question of homosexuality and religion, Chapter 2, "The Churches Respond" and Chapter 3, "Pilot Projects: Significant Local Ministries." Each group was queried as to its official position on service to different social groups, one of which was gay people. Responses range from denial of ordination to avowed homosexuals (United Presbyterian Church) to the complete acceptance of the Unitarian Universalist Association. Chapter 3 includes several examples of outreach ministry for the gay and lesbian community. It must be noted, however, that not all groups surveyed mention their attitudes towards homosexuals. A very useful summary of official positions ca. 1983, but should be supplemented with more detailed information on a particular sect.

1228. Nugent, Robert, ed. A CHALLENGE TO LOVE: GAY AND LESBIAN CATHOLICS IN THE CHURCH. New York: Crossroad Publishing Co., 1983.

In this collection of eighteen essays, leading liberal Catholic theologians re-examine and criticize the responsibilities (political and social) and problems of ministry facing the Church with regard to its gay members. Among the specific issues addressed are homosexual marriage, gay clergy, the role of the Christian gay or lesbian in creating a more humane society, and social justice for homosexuals and reform theology. Taken together, these articles create a forum where the positions and issues of debate and confrontation, both within and outside the Catholic church, on homosexuality in the 1980s are cogently summarized. A brief subject index is also provided.

1229. Scroggs, Robin. THE NEW TESTAMENT AND HOMO-SEXUALITY: CONTEXTUAL BACKGROUND FOR CONTEMPORARY DEBATE. Philadelphia: Fortress Press, 1983.

Homosexual activity in the Greco-Roman world, the practices and attitudes of that world towards it, and the New Testament passages adduced in discussing and condemning it are explored lucidly and in detail here. While designed as a guide to clergy involved in debate over homosexuals in the church, it provides useful analysis of the religious basis of many later homophobic edicts and laws. The author concludes that the cited passages of scripture are open to variant interpretations and that they must be considered in the cultural context of the times in which they were written. Hence, they are of no help in the current debate over gays in the church.

1230. "Minn. Church Council Calls for Protective Laws, Full Ministry to Gays." THE ADVOCATE, 359 (6 January, 1983), 14.

A news report on a statement endorsed in October, 1982 by the Minnesota Council of Churches supporting the presence of gay and lesbian members in local congregations. Four resolutions addressing bills planned for introduction in the 1983 session of the state legislature were also adopted. Topics covered by the latter were a repeal of state sodomy legislation, a call for a human rights law, police violence and harassment and child custody.

1231. Nash, Phil. "Speaking Out for Gay Humanity: Bishop Melvin E. Wheatley, Jr." THE ADVOCATE, 362 (3 March, 1983), 17-19.

A news report and interview with Bishop Melvin Wheatley of the United Methodist Church, covering his support for openly gay clergyman Julian Rush. The controversy over Rush's appointment to the parish of St. Paul in Denver by Wheatley is presented in detail.

1232. "Attempt to Disband Catholic Gay Task Force Falls Short in S.F." THE ADVOCATE, 363 (17 March, 1983), 15, 58.

On January 19, 1983, the San Francisco Catholic Commission on Social Justice defeated a proposal by chairman Monsignor Peter Armstrong that the body's task force on homosexuality be disbanded. Armstrong had criticized the group for its recent report recommending reforms within the church, terming it as "holding the church in contempt." The chief recommendations of the report are noted.

1233. "New Ways Ministry--A Bridge Between Catholic Gays and Nongays." THE ADVOCATE, 367 (12 May, 1983), 12-14.

In March, 1983, a series of workshops on homosexuality were conducted in the Midwest by Fr. Robert Nugent and Sr. Jeannine Grammick, the founders of New Ways Ministry, whose purpose is "to promote understanding and dialogue between gays and nongays in the church." The opening session in Chicago is offered as an example of the typical format used and a brief history of the ministry since its founding in 1971 is included.

1234. "Calif. Episcopal Bishop Intervenes, Gay Couple's 'Union' Ceremony Axed." THE ADVOCATE, 368 (26 May, 1983), 15, 56.

A scheduled "union" ceremony for a male couple set for April 2, 1983 at Trinity Church in San Francisco was cancelled by order of Bishop William Swing. A study of church recognition of gay relationships is planned.

1235. "Gay Catholics, Other Reject S.F. Archdiocese's Call for Gay 'Chastity.'" THE ADVOCATE, 373 (4 August, 1983), 13.

On June 28, 1983, a press conference was called by representatives of the Coalition for Human Rights, Dignity/San Francisco, Catholics for Human Dignity and the Task Force on Gay and Lesbian Issues. The purpose was to reply to a report completed by the Priests' Senate of the Archdiocese calling upon gay Catholics to be celibate, recently adopted by Archbishop John Quinn as official policy. All involved organizations rejected the policy as "a dreary repetition of church teaching."

1236. "United Church of Christ: Homosexuality No Bar to Ordination." THE ADVOCATE, 375 (1 September, 1983), 8-9.

A report on the approval by the General Synod of the United Church of Christ of a task force document calling for the elimination of sexual orientation as a ground for barring ordination of qualified candidates. Support for the proposal among delegates was widespread. Related developments in the United Methodist Church are profiled.

1237. "Gays and Religion: A Spiritual Survey." THE ADVOCATE, 375 (1 September, 1983), 24-26.

A survey article examining the involvement of gay people in religion across the United States and their view of the benefits and effectiveness such internal lobbying can produce. Groups reporting are Affirmation (Mormon), Lutherans Concerned, Affirmation (Methodist), Congregation Sha'ar Zahav of San Francisco, Dignity/ Cleveland and Integrity. Responses to the AIDS crisis and the role of women are also addressed.

1238. Anderson, Scott P. "Metropolitan Community Church: Into the Religious Mainstream." THE ADVOCATE, 375 (1 September, 1983), 27-29.

An analytical report on the efforts of the Universal Fellowship of Metropolitan Community Churches to gain membership in the National Council of Churches.

1239. Lusardo, Lonnie. "Protest, Progress Mark Meeting of 650 Gay Catholics in Seattle." THE ADVOCATE, 379 (27 October, 1983), 15.

A profile of the events at the Sixth biennial international convention of Dignity held in Seattle, Washington with the countenance of Archbishop Raymond Hunthausen. Delegates created a task force whose purpose will be to prepare a document on "theological and pastoral issues of sexual activity by gay people" for the next convention. Contemporary Catholic positions on homosexuality were decried.

1240. "National Council of Churches Refuses to Decide on Admitting a Homosexual Denomination." CHRISTIANITY TODAY, 27 (16 December, 1983), 42.

A news article reporting on the decision by the National Council of Churches to indefinitely postpone a decision on the eligibility of the Metropolitan Community Church for membership in that body. The original application for MCC membership was filed in 1981.

1241. Freiberg, Peter. "Church Council to MCC--A 'Polite No.'" THE ADVOCATE, 383/384 (22 December, 1983), 10-11.

On November 9, 1983, the National Council of Churches of Christ meeting in Hartford, Connecticut passed a resolution to "postpone indefinitely" the application of the Metropolitan Community Church for council membership. Reaction from the MCC itself is provided through an interview with founder Rev. Troy Perry.

1242. Edwards, George R. GAY/LESBIAN LIBERATION: A BIBLICAL PERSPECTIVE. New York: The Pilgrim Press, 1984.

A consideration of gay and lesbian liberation efforts within the dual framework of contemporary "theologies of liberation and Christian conceptions of love." Emphasis is placed upon biblical interpretation and the sociocultural factors which may significantly affect it. Edwards views the oppression of homosexuals "no less real because official church councils have not yet incorporated their outcry in the urgent agenda of social ministry" (p. 23). The author is a faculty member at Louisville Presbyterian Theological Seminary and served on that denomination's task force on the ordination of homosexuals.

1243. Uhrig, Larry J. THE TWO OF US: AFFIRMING, CELE-BRATING AND SYMBOLIZING GAY AND LESBIAN RELATIONSHIPS. Boston: Alyson Publications, 1984.

As pastor of the Metropolitan Community Church congregation in Washington, D.C., Larry Uhrig is uniquely qualified to describe the difficulties and joys of gay relationships. Presenting the problem from the spiritual needs of each couple, this is an excellent account of the situation in which gay and lesbian couples find themselves with respect to organized religion. Stories of several couples and their rites of "Holy Union" are included.

1244. Fraser, Thomas. "United Methodist Church Delegates Vote Ban on Gay Ministers at Historic Conference." THE ADVOCATE, 396 (12 June, 1984), 9.

A detailed analysis of the events leading to the decision by the general conference of the United Methodist Church in Baltimore in May, 1984 to reject the ordination of gay persons as ministers. Delegates also voted to deny proposals offering the civil rights of gay people, ministry to them or use of church facilities by gay groups.

1245. Warwick, Dixie. "The Reverend June Norris Ministers to Gays." THE ADVOCATE, 396 (12 June, 1984), 29-31.

A profile of Rev. June Norris of the Metropolitan Community Church written by her daughter. The evolution of her involvement with the denomination is explored.

1246. Nash, Phil. "Methodist Faction Aims to Defrock Gay Minister." THE ADVOCATE, 400 (7 August, 1984), 13.

Under revised church legislation adopted at the general conference in May, 1984, openly gay and lesbian individuals may no longer be appointed to ministerial positions in the United Methodist Church. The case of Rev. Julian Rush is expected to be challenged on this basis. Rush is presently serving as music and outreach minister at St. Paul's in Denver. Support within the Rocky Mountain Conference has been strong for the validity of his ministry.

1247. Marks, Jim. "Holy Union: A Celebration of Gay Love." THE ADVOCATE, 407 (13 November, 1984), 24.

A discussion of the practice of same-sex unions as presently conceived and the inadequacies of traditional definitions. Rev. Larry Uhrig of Washington is interviewed regarding his forthcoming book on such issues, *The Two of Us.*

1248. Walter, Dave. "Baptists Revoke Gay Minister's Ordination." THE ADVOCATE, 412 (22 January, 1985), 12.

A summary of the case of Rev. Brian Scott of the Southern Baptist Church whose ordination was revoked by congregational vote on December 16, 1984. Opponents termed his admission of homosexuality "heretical." The vote concluded proceedings begun in May, 1982 when Scott came out in a letter to the deacons of the local church in Bel Air, Maryland. Scott will continue to work at the Gay and Lesbian Christian Fellowship.

1249. Giteck, Lenny and Mark Thompson. "Troy Perry and Malcolm Boyd: Two Gay Clergymen Speak About Ecstasy, Sex and Spirituality." THE ADVOCATE, 417 (2 April, 1985), 32-36.

A joint interview with Rev. Troy Perry, founder of the Metropolitan Community Church and Episcopal priest Malcolm Boyd, author of *Take Off the Masks*, exploring the relationship of religious experience to the experience of being homosexual. The growing fundamentalist movement in the United States is also discussed.

1250. Lassell, Michael. "S.F. Episcopal Dispute: Blessing Same-Sex Couples." THE ADVOCATE, 421 (28 May, 1985), 16.

An analysis of the dispute within the Episcopal church in San Francisco between Bishop William Swing and Rev. Robert Cramey of Trinity Church over the latter's blessing of union rites for same-sex couples. A history of the confrontation is provided.

1251. Freiberg, Peter. "Cardinal Gives Qualified Support to Gay Rights." THE ADVOCATE, 421 (28 May, 1985), 17.

Extensive quotations from a three-page letter sent by Joseph Cardinal Bernardin of Chicago to the Illinois Gay and Lesbian Task Force. Said letter was a reply to inquiries as to his position on proposed gay civil rights legislation for the city. While supportive of civil rights, Bernardin stressed that he considered "homosexual activity" to be morally wrong.

1252. Freiberg, Peter. "Prominent Church Votes to Recognize Gay Relationships." THE ADVOCATE, 424 (9 July, 1985), 18.

On June 2, 1985, a statement was adopted at the annual
meeting of the congregation of Riverside Church in
Manhattan "upholding the validity of gay relationships," decrying anti-gay violence and pledging to work
against homophobia within and outside the church. Rev.
William Sloane Coffin and local gay leader John Elliott
are interviewed.

1253. Sanders, Don. "Christianity and Sex: Holy Water and Baby
Oil Don't Mix." THE ADVOCATE, 425 (23 July, 1985), 8-9.

An essay by the national director of American Gay
Atheists on "Christianity's erotophobic preoccupation."
The history of official Christian attitudes towards
sex, marriage and homosexuality are briefly summarized.
Sanders calls upon gay people to become proactive for
social change.

1254. Walter, Dave. "N.C. Priest Comes Out, Resigns Under
Pressure." THE ADVOCATE, 433 (12 November, 1985), 18.

A brief summary of the events surrounding the expulsion
of Episcopal priest Fr. Zalmon Sherwood from the church
following coming out in an essay for the national
church magazine *The Witness*. Researchers interested
in further details of this case should consult
Sherwood's account, *Kairos: Confessions of a Gay
Priest*.

1255. "Homosexual 'Marriage.'" CHRISTIANITY TODAY, 29 (22
November, 1985), 21-28.

Stating that the "love quality" of same-sex relationships "is not sufficient to justify them," this article
calls for reinterpretations of Biblical passages supportive of such relationships and homosexuality in
general. Discipline for church members "who refuse to
repent and willfully persist in homosexual relationships" is called for.

1256. "Norway Fines Preacher for Antigay Remarks on Radio." THE
ADVOCATE, 434 (26 November, 1985), 15.

On September 23, 1985, the supreme court of Norway
convicted fundamentalist preacher Hans Bratterud of
violation of a 1981 law prohibiting discrimination and

persecution of gay people and imposed a moderate fine. The basis for the case was remarks made by Bratterud that "it would be a good thing for the country if my prayer that open gay and lesbian people lose their jobs be fulfilled."

1257. Brown, Judith C. IMMODEST ACTS: THE LIFE OF A LESBIAN NUN IN RENAISSANCE ITALY. New York: Oxford University Press, 1986.

In the year 1619, Benedetta Carlini, abbess of a convent in Pescia, was investigated upon charges of being a mystic. In the course of this inquiry, it came to light that she was having a lesbian relationship with another nun. Judith Brown's account of her life presents us with one of the few historical instances of lesbianism so far documented. It is extremely useful as an indicator of ecclesiastical attitudes toward homosexual activity--among both clergy and laity--in seventeenth century Italy.

1258. Gallagher, John, ed. HOMOSEXUALITY AND THE MAGISTERIUM: DOCUMENTS FROM THE VATICAN AND THE U.S. BISHOPS, 1975-1985. Mt. Ranier, MD: New Ways Ministry, 1986.

This volume is composed of the collected texts of twenty documents on homosexuality issued by the Vatican and the Catholic bishops of the United States for the period 1975-1985. While oriented towards pastoral care, a wide range of opinion is represented. Clergy from Milwaukee, Baltimore, Seattle, Richmond, Boston, Washington, D.C., San Francisco, Brooklyn, St. Paul and Chicago are included.

1259. Uhrig, Larry J. SEX POSITIVE: A GAY CONTRIBUTION TO SEXUAL AND SPIRITUAL UNION. Boston: Alyson Publications, Inc., 1986.

Reverend Uhrig presents an analysis of the relationship between homosexuality and spirituality, terming traditional Judeo-Christian views a "sex-negative" system and calling for the development of a new theology of sexuality. Contemporary fundamentalist arguments with regard to the Bible and homosexuals are presented and evaluated.

1260. "Rev. Julian Rush: A Maverick Minister Puts the Methodists to the Test." THE ADVOCATE, 439 (4 February, 1986), 31.

An interview with and summary of the case of Rev. Julian Rush, openly gay Methodist minister and director of the Colorado AIDS Project.

1261. Di Stefano, George. "Gay Under the Collar: The Hypocrisy of the Catholic Church." THE ADVOCATE, 439 (4 February, 1986), 43-48.

An analytical commentary on the contemporary status of homosexual clergy within the Roman Catholic church. Both liberal and conservative members are interviewed, with change seen as vital through working from within. Personal accounts of experiences with the attitudes of the hierarchy are presented. Textual inserts review the case of Fr. Richard Ginder and outline the position of San Francisco Archbishop John Quinn.

1262. Cummings, Peter. "Gay Priests Struggle for Discreet Acceptance in Church of England." THE ADVOCATE, 442 (18 March, 1986), 40-41, 128.

The Church of England and its attitudes towards homo-sexuality in both the general public and its clergy are explored in this article. An interview with former vicar Richard Kerker, chair of the Gay Christian Movement, is included.

1263. Walter, Dave. "Openly Gay Minister Wins Round Against Methodists." THE ADVOCATE, 443 (1 April, 1986), 15.

The United Methodist Church's Board of Ordained Ministry has dismissed complaints brought against Rev. Julian Rush. At issue was a UMC law barring "self-avowed practicing homosexuals" from serving as ministers.

1264. Frieberg, Peter. "Openly Gay Minnesota Man Ordained As Episcopal Priest." THE ADVOCATE, 447 (27 May, 1986), 14.

A news article on the ordination April 12, 1986 of Rod Reinhart as an Episcopal priest by Bishop H. Coleman

McGehee of Detroit. Reinhart's personal history within the church is profiled.

1265. "New Briefs." THE ADVOCATE, 449 (24 June, 1986), 26.

At a retreat for members of the Episcopal clergy of Colorado on May 16, 1986, two resolutions were passed opposing the stance of Rev. Edward Osterlag (St. Barnabas, Denver) that he would be willing to bless committed gay couples. Both resolutions acknowledged the validity of Osterlag's ministry but termed marriage "a sacrament . . . reserved for heterosexuals."

1266. "News Briefs." THE ADVOCATE, 449 (24 June, 1986), 27.

A news note on the experience of Fr. Ottaviano Pizzamiglio of Turin, Italy, who was physically dragged from his office and forced to perform a blessing over the coffin of Bruno Delana. The priest had earlier refused to do so because Delana was a professed homosexual.

1267. Freiberg, Peter. "Quakers Establish Gay Outreach Program in Northwest." THE ADVOCATE, 457 (14 October, 1986), 14.

The American Friends Service Committee, a Quaker-based peace and justice organization has established an outreach program to the gay community within the Pacific Northwest region. Its goals are to work with designated community projects and to educate adherents of other religious groups on gay issues. Jim Holm, president of the Dorian Group, the Washington State gay organization, is interviewed for comment.

1268. "News Briefs--Minnesota." THE ADVOCATE, 459 (11 November, 1986), 26.

Following two years of counseling work with gay persons and their families, Rev. William Dorn of St. Cloud, Minnesota was dismissed from his position. At issue was an article published on September 18, 1986 in a diocesan newspaper calling upon Catholics to "regard homosexuality as part of the 'gift' of sexuality."

1269.   Freiberg, Peter. "Gay Catholic Controversy." THE ADVOCATE, 462 (23 December, 1986), 10-11, 24-25.

> A survey article on the unrest within the Roman Catholic Church over the issue of homosexuality profiling various actions taken by the Holy See with regard to it. These include a papal letter condemning Episcopal support for gay rights legislation, the silencing of critical theologians, and forbidding the use of church facilities by Dignity, the Catholic gay caucus. The cases of Fr. John McNeill, William Dorn and Jim Bussen of Dignity are explored.

1270.   McNaught, Brian. ON BEING GAY: THOUGHTS ON FAMILY, FAITH, AND LOVE. New York: St. Martin's Press, 1987.

> A collection of essays by a noted Catholic journalist deeply involved with homosexual rights and sexual education. Many of these pieces were contained in the earlier volume *A Disturbed Peace* published in 1981. Topics addressed include the AIDS epidemic, the Vatican's decree on homosexuality in 1987, dynamics of gay relationships, and sexism.

1271.   Sherwood, Zalmon O. KAIROS: CONFESSIONS OF A GAY PRIEST. Boston: Altson Publications, 1987.

> The frank account of a candidate for the Episcopal priesthood determined to proceed with ordination. His assignment to a parish in North Carolina and subsequent expulsion from it are openly chronicled in these letters to friends. An excellent, if disturbing, example of contemporary attitudes toward homosexuality in the clergy.

1272.   Feliz, Antonio A. OUT OF THE BISHOP'S CLOSET. A CALL TO HEAL OURSELVES, EACH OTHER, AND OUR WORLD. San Francisco: Aurora Press, 1988.

> A personal account of the evolution of gay consciousness in a ward bishop of the Church of Jesus Christ of Latter-Day Saints. Researchers will find his description of the history of the Mormon attitude towards homosexuality of particular value, as the author had access to primary documents at church headquarters in Salt Lake City.

1273.   Glaser, Chris. UNCOMMON CALLING: A GAY MAN'S STRUGGLE TO SERVE THE CHURCH. San Francisco: Harper & Row, 1988.

A personal account by a candidate for ordination in the Presbyterian church, both of his evolution as a self-aware gay man and the roles sexuality and spirituality can and should play in the life of self-aware gay Christians. Glaser was involved in the foundation of the gay and lesbian caucus within his church and held membership on the Task Force on Homosexuality which presented its report to the General Assembly in 1978. His activities within these policy-affecting bodies provide a rare glimpse into factors influencing ecclesiastical positions on homosexuality. The church subsequently refused to sponsor him as a candidate for full ministry.

1274.   Grammick, Jeannine and Pat Furey, eds. THE VATICAN AND HOMOSEXUALITY: REACTION TO THE "LETTER TO THE BISHOPS OF THE CATHOLIC CHURCH ON THE PASTORAL CARE OF HOMOSEXUAL PERSONS." New York: Crossroad Publishing Co., 1988.

On October 31, 1986, the Vatican published a "Letter to the Bishops of the Catholic Church on the Pastoral Care of Homosexual Persons." Intended in part as an update to the text of Persona Humana (a previous declaration of sexual ethics given in 1975), it provides counsel to local bishops on dealing with both doctrinal positions on homosexuality and organizations such as Dignity working for change within the church.

The present volume consists of the full text of the letter and twenty-five essays commenting upon it. The authors of those essays explore the ramifications of the basic theological and social positions against homosexuality and challenge the hierarchy to a continuing dialogue. They include the co-founders of New Ways Ministry, the Archbishop of San Francisco, theologians at seminaries of several degrees of liberalism and commentators from the Catholic press. Researchers should be aware that it was this document which inveighed against "organizations which seek to undermine the teaching of the Church, which are ambiguous about it, or which neglect it entirely" (p. 9), a position used to expel groups for homosexual Catholics from church property and facilities. Homosexuality is regarded in this document as immoral, with members of the clergy called upon to promote "a chaste life" for the homosexual and to "keep as their uppermost concern the responsibility to defend and promote family life" (p. 10). While the degree of criticism leveled at the document ranges from mild reproof to outright rejection, the general feeling is that continuing dialogue on the question is necessary between the Vatican and gay and lesbian Catholics. "Until the Congregation substantially modifies its anthropological and ethical model . . its chances of having any kind of import on the Christian community's sexual discernments will continue to decrease" (p. 214).

Police Attitudes
and Actions

1275. Satterfield, Val B. "The Education of a Metropolitan Police Department Respecting Sex Molestation." JOURNAL OF CRIMINAL LAW, CRIMINOLOGY AND POLICE SCIENCE, 42 (September/October, 1951), 403-406.

>   This is a brief summary of an educational course created by the St. Louis police department in 1948 and administered in the summer of 1949. Officers and recruits alike were involved in this series of two-hour lectures. Details of the curriculum are provided as a model for other agencies. The series was opened with "a reading from the Book of Leviticus of the Holy Bible, beginning at verse ten of chapter twenty" (p. 404) and progressed to considerations of social morality and its fluctuation. "Sex offenders" were discussed and "there was willingness to accept the sexual criminal as part of the general criminal population" (p. 405). Discussion sessions explored a wide variety of subjects relating to sexual crimes in general, including the influences of family training, bad associates, possible dangers to police officers, effects upon intelligence and character of sex perversion, and "the necessity of suppressing homosexuality." A statistical study of the St. Louis area was initiated by the department to clarify local patterns with a view towards assisting officers. This course is an example of the approach to education on the subject of homosexuality prevalent among U.S. law enforcement agencies during the twentieth century.

1276. "Alleged Homosexuals Victim of Lawless Mass Arrests." THE MATTACHINE REVIEW, 2, 3 (March, 1956), 5-7.

> This is a reprint from the March, 1956 issue of *ACLU News*, and relates a police raid on a bar in San Mateo County, California. As a result, some ninety individuals were detained. Those persons "recognized" by undercover agents as having shown homosexual behavior were ordered to step to one side . . . and were loaded into a van parked outside." All other patrons were released. The raid was justified by the police on the grounds that the bar was becoming known as a gathering place for homosexuals.

1277. "San Francisco Police Raid Reveals Lack of Knowledge of Citizens Rights." THE LADDER, 1, 2 (November, 1956), 5.

> This article reports on a raid on a San Francisco gay bar where thirth-six women were arrested, of whom thirty-two pled guilty. The case is cited as an example of ignorance vs. civil rights. A meeting of the Daughters of Bilitis is scheduled where attorney Benjamin Davis will speak on lesbians and the law.

1278. "Police May Not Incite Crime, Rule Washington Appeals Court Judge." THE MATTACHINE REVIEW, 2, 6 (December, 1956), 10-11.

> A case involving police entrapment of a homosexual male in a theater in the District of Columbia is presented along with subsequent legislative history. Initial conviction was eventually overturned by the U.S. Court of Appeals. The ruling cited a 1921 decision stressing that it was the duty of police to prevent crime, not create it for the purposes of prosecution. Thus, such police tactics as entrapment could not be considered legal.

1279. "Calling Shots." THE MATTACHINE REVIEW, 5, 4 (April, 1959), 14-18.

> Items cited in this review of news include increased police activity against homosexuals in Sausalito, California and Detroit, Michigan. The California police chief was quoted as saying "if they do anything out of line or break the law, they've had it."

1280. "Calling Shots." THE MATTACHINE REVIEW, 6, 2 (February, 1960), 4-6, 28-30.

> The case of the entrapment of twenty-five gay men over a period of three weeks at the University of Michigan in Ann Arbor is reported.

1281. "Calling Shots." THE MATTACHINE, 6, 3 (March, 1960), 18-20.

> This news report centers upon the recent anti-homosexual purges at the University of Florida and the University of Michigan. In both instances, plain-clothes policemen were used to entrap homosexual individuals, thirty-four in the case of Ann Arbor.

1282. "Calling Shots." THE MATTACHINE REVIEW, 6, 5 (May, 1960), 9-10.

> Further information on the police entrapment cases at the University of Michigan is given here. Of the thirty-four persons arrested, nine chose to plead guilty. Judge James Breakey is reported to have told the victims that if they had the temerity to ask for trial by jury and "waste his valuable time," that if convicted their fines and sentences would be greatly increased. One individual, whose case was scheduled to be heard on appeal at the Michigan Supreme Court (after being convicted) committed suicide.

1283. "Calling Shots." THE MATTACHINE REVIEW, 6, 10 (October, 1960), 21-23.

> The arrest of nine men, including a priest and a college official, during a police raid on Frame Park in Milwaukee is reported. Local newspapers carried ages, names and background of all arrested persons.

1284. "Calling Shots." THE MATTACHINE REVIEW, 7, 7 (June, 1961), 4-5.

> "Witch hunts" against gay people are reported from Ann Arbor, Michigan, the University of Florida at Gainesville and Delaware. In the last case, police pressure was being applied to arrested homosexuals to reveal

names of other individuals and obtaining firings of individuals based on hearsay evidence.

1285. "Fire Hoses Next?" THE LADDER, 5, 2 (September, 1961), 14-15.

An editorial dealing with the August 13, 1961 raid on the Tay-Bush Cafe, a gay establishment in San Francisco, at which 103 persons were arrested on vaguely worded charges. Police sources are quoted as stating that same-sex dancing was one of the causes of the raid.

1286. "Flash!" THE LADDER, 5, 2 (September, 1961), 25.

A report that the San Francisco Mattachine Society is supporting the ninety-eight persons still charged in the Tay-Bush raid. Legal counsel has been retained and briefs are being printed, with the Society bearing the expense.

1287. "65 Freed in 'Gay Bar' Case." THE LADDER, 6, 1 (October, 1961), 18.

Dismissal of charges against all but six of the remaining seventy-one persons arrested in the police raid on the Tay-Bush Cafe is reported.

1288. "For Want of a Chance." THE LADDER, 6, 1 (October, 1961), 10-13.

At the eighth annual conference of the Mattachine Society in San Francisco, the rehabilitation and reintegration of sex offenders, veterans with less than honorable discharges, and released prisoners was discussed. Of special interest was the report by the Society on the increasing trend towards arrests and convictions in homosexual-related cases by the San Francisco police.

1289. "Special Cops for Gay Bars." THE MATTACHINE REVIEW, 7, 11 (November, 1961), 4-8.

An article quoted from the *San Francisco Examiner* of October 12, 1961, discusses a newly-revealed entrapment practice of the city police. Plain-clothesmen were being sent into gay bars with the intent of verifying prohibited behaviors. Said evidence would then be used to revoke the bars' licenses. Coming at a time when attacks on riders on the city's transit system were increasing, the practice is sharply criticized as wasteful, expensive and unnecessary.

1290. "Cop Spying Illegal." THE MATTACHINE REVIEW, 8, 6 (June, 1962), 4-8.

On May 10, 1962, hidden police surveillance of public toilet facilities for the purpose of entrapment of homosexual individuals was ruled illegal by the California Supreme Court. The decision is presented here in full from the court records.

1291. "Court Rules for Restroom Privacy." THE LADDER, 6, 9 (June, 1962), 24.

In a case against three men using evidence obtained through police surveillance in a Long Beach, California rest room, the California State Supreme Court issued writs prohibiting trial. Grounds were that such actions violated the rights of individuals.

1292. "Crackdown on Homosexual Activity at University of Michigan." THE MATTACHINE REVIEW, 8, 9 (September, 1962), 11-17.

A two-part article from the student newspaper *The Michigan Daily* discusses police arrests of individuals on the university campus, as well as providing detailed position statements by administrators and law officers. Between 1958 and 1962, campus police conducted three campaigns of surveillance to rid the area of homosexuals. Penalties imposed differed: expulsion for the students, forced resignation for the faculty members.

1293. Jacobs, Harold. "Decoy Enforcement of Homosexual Laws." UNIVERSITY OF PENNSYLVANIA LAW REVIEW, 112 (1963-1964), 259-284.

"Since status of being a homosexual is not itself criminal, prosecution for homosexual acts must be conducted with due caution" (p. 260). This article then proceeds to explore in detail the uses of police officers as decoys in order to elicit conduct overt enough to permit arrest and possible prosecution. Topics addressed include the conduct necessary to establish a criminal homosexual overture (including both verbal and nonverbal communication and a legal definition of importuning), defenses used in decoy situations, the decoy as "victim," entrapment, problems of proof and credibility. Jacobs concludes his examination by observing that "in all homosexual overture offenses involving decoys the court must determine criminality on the basis of the conduct of both the defendant and the decoy. Decoys are the only practicable means of enforcing homosexual statutes" (p. 284). Full legal citation to referenced cases such as *McDermett vs. United States* and *Kelly vs. United States* are provided.

1294.   "Cross Currents." THE LADDER, 8, 4 (January, 1964), 7-8.

The edition of a regular news column reports publication of an article in the December 17, 1963 *New York Times* on police harassment of gay clubs. One club is noted as having been "visited" nineteen times. While the item also considers homosexuality as a treatable condition, its primary value lies in portraying police attitudes and actions.

1295.   "Cross Currents." THE LADDER, 8, 6 (March, 1964), 19.

This column contains a report on police raids on gay clubs in Dallas in which forty-seven people were arrested. May or Earle Cabell is cited as having instigated the anti-homosexual campaign.

1296.   "After the Ball." THE LADDER, 9, 4-5 (February/March, 1965), 4-5.

Massive police harassment as surveillance of a benefit costume ball in San Francisco for the Council on Religion and the Homosexual is reported in detail. Six persons were arrested. A subsequent press conference called by the clergymen involved attacked police actions and stated that "court action would be forthcoming."

1297. "Cross Currents." THE LADDER, 9, 9 (June, 1965), 14-16.

Of note in this column is the resolution of the court case resulting from police harassment of a benefit dance for the Council on Religion and the Homosexual. Instead of a decision safeguarding the rights of assembly and privacy, the case was thrown out of court on a technicality.

1298. "A Brief of Injustices." THE LADDER, 10, 2 (November, 1965), 4-7.

A Brief of Injustices is the title of a document prepared by San Francisco's Council on Religion and the Homosexual in September, 1965. The text details ten major injustices originating in harassment and oppression of homosexuals. The clergy and laymen who created this work sent it to all political candidates, prominent civic leaders and the city administration. The San Francisco police in particular were subjected to severe criticism.

1299. "Homosexual Voting Block Puts Pizzaz in Politics." THE LADDER, 10, 2 (November, 1965), 13-14.

Police brutality/harassment and the need for citizen supervision of police activity were a major topic of discussion at an open political meeting called by the Council on Religion and the Homosexual in San Francisco on September 21, 1965. Five municipal candidates appeared and participated. Note is also taken of a September 15 meeting on police abuse held in New York City.

1300. "Sex Spies: UCLA Study of Law Enforcement Policies and Practices." NATION, 202 (16 May, 1966), 572-573.

A report on a recent study published in the *UCLA Law Review* evaluating anti-homosexual law enforcement policies and practices with specific reference to Los Angeles County, California. While enforcement is limited to controlling public displays and harassment, the study noted widespread use of police decoys and clandestine observation. Although the laws in question are seen to have completely negative consequences, the author notes that "few readers of this report will fail to be disturbed by the implication that we are permitting in this area an active program of public spying" (p. 573).

1301. "Entrapment Attacked." THE LADDER, 10, 9 (June, 1966), 12-13.

Police entrapment of homosexual men in New York City and the controversy surrounding it are profiled in this piece. Police officials decried the practice while taking virtually no steps to halt it. Examples of entrapment occurring between February and April of 1966 are cited. An April 30 meeting called by Mayor John Lindsay to review grievances between police and residents of Greenwich Village resulted in open condemnation of the practice by both the mayor and the police commissioner. The latter further stated that orders to halt the practice had already been issued.

1302. "Action in the Courts." THE LADDER, 10, 9 (June, 1966), 13-14.

An update on the lawsuit filed against the City of San Francisco by the Council on Religion and the Homosexual is given. Damages asked totalled $1,050,000.

1303. "An Empirical Study: The Law Versus Private Morality." THE LADDER, 10, 11, (August, 1966), 10-12.

Written by a practicing attorney familiar with California sex law and legislation, this article evaluates a 1966 research project conducted by the University of California at Los Angeles Law School. It contains an overview of homosexual offenses, the kind of people who commit them, the representation the accused receives, the penalties and some statistical data on acquittals and convictions. The objective of the study was to examine the criminal law as a regulator of private morality. Detailed information on law enforcement techniques, routine patrol and harassment, California sex law and legislation (including broad categories such as vagrancy) and court procedure are also included. One interesting finding is that, for the most part, California courts treated public homosexual offenses as public nuisances.

1304.   "Acquaintances in the Afternoon: The Homophile Community and Governmental Agencies--Can They Relate?" THE LADDER, 11, 3 (December, 1966), 18-22.

> Continuing a two-part series of news articles from the Daughters of Bilitis 1966 convention, summaries are given of two presentations. The first was by Ms. Janet Aitken, assistant district attorney for Los Angeles. A member of Bishop Pike's Joint Committee on Homosexuality, she profiled the current attitudes of local government in San Francisco with regard to enticement/ entrapment by police officers, and California sex laws. Self-policing measures from within the gay community were, in her view, the most effective means of curtailing legal problems.

> Officer Elliott Blackstone, Community Relations Unit, San Francisco Police Department, gave the final lecture. While stressing that police-gay communication was desirable, he denied that his department had a specific attitude toward gay bars or that entrapment (in the legal sense) was being practiced, or that San Francisco police were informing employers of homosexual charges pending against a member of their staff. A brief profile of the Community Relations Unit closed the presentation.

1305.   "Vice Raid Silverlake Bar." THE ADVOCATE, 1, 1 (September, 1967), 3.

> A report on a raid conducted on a popular bar in the Silverlake area of Los Angeles by the Rampart division of the Los Angeles Police Department. Plainclothesmen arrested ten patrons, who were charged with violating California's lewd conduct law. A beating of a bar employee by vice squad officers during an earlier incident is noted.

1306.   "Court Affirms Black Cat Convictions: Higher Appeal Set." THE ADVOCATE, 1, 1 (September, 1967), 2.

> The convictions of six persons arrested in a New Year's Eve raid on the Black Cat Bar in Los Angeles have been affirmed by an appellate court. A lengthy interview with counsel Herbert Selwyn is included, addressing the validity of California's lewd conduct law.

1307. "L.A. Cops, Gay Groups Seek Peace." THE ADVOCATE, 1, 2 (October, 1967), 1, 2, 5.

>A report and partial transcript of a four-hour meeting between representatives of the Los Angeles Police Department and nine homophile organizations held in a private home on August 30, 1967. Topics addressed included police entrapment, bar arrests, dances and antihomosexual crimes such as assault.

1308. "Harassment? Hell, No!" THE ADVOCATE, 1, 2 (October, 1967), 6.

>An editorial on the need for dialogue between the homosexual community of Los Angeles and that city's vice squad. While recent meetings are seen as a useful beginning, the term "harassment" is challenged as being too weak for the type of treatment currently in practice.

1309. "Arrest Ends in Suicide for Pasadena Man." THE ADVOCATE, 2, 4 (April, 1968), 2.

>A review of an incident in Pasadena where the victim committed suicide following arrest, rather than face a court hearing on lewd conduct charges. Background on the case is provided.

1310. "The Fine Art of Entrapment: Victim Tells How Hollywood Vice Fracture the Law." THE ADVOCATE, 2, 5 (May, 1968), 1.

>A personal account of an arrest by Hollywood vice squad officers from the perspective of the victim.

1311. "Editorial from Our Philadelphia Chapter Newsletter." THE LADDER, 12, 7 (May/June, 1968), 22-23.

>This editorial from the Philadelphia chapter of the Daughters of Bilitis reports a police raid on March 8, 1968 of Rusty's, a popular lesbian bar. Twelve persons were arrested and charged with disorderly conduct. No illegal actions were taking place on the premises as defined by law.

1312. "Fuzz Fabricate, Arrange Facts, Lawyer Tells NLSU." THE ADVOCATE, 2, 5 (June, 1968), 2.

> In an address to the May, 1968 meeting of the National League for Social Understanding, attorney Joan Martin related her experiences with police testimony in homosexual cases. Her approaches include consolidation of cases and scattering defendants among spectators to test the validity of officer identification.

1313. "Editorial: You're an Accomplice." THE ADVOCATE, 2, 5 (May, 1968), 8.

> An editorial discussing tactics in use by the Los Angeles police to close down bars frequented by homosexuals. Readers are urged to continue patronizing these establishments to ensure their survival.

1314. "No Public Complaints Reported Since N.Y. Gay Harassment Ended." THE ADVOCATE, 2, 7 (July, 1968), 2.

> A report on the status of homosexual arrests in New York City in the past year following issuance of an executive order banning such arrests without a signed complaint from a private citizen. The total number of arrests has fallen from over one thousand a week to almost none and officers formerly on vice duty have been reassigned.

1315. "Anatomy of a Raid, Part I." THE ADVOCATE, 2, 7 (July, 1968), 6, 7. "Anatomy of a Raid, Part II." THE ADVOCATE, 2, 8 (August, 1968), 6, 8.

> This two-part article is a detailed account of a 1966 raid on a Los Angeles bar, beginning with the initial appearance of vice officers and continuing through booking, release and eventual court appearances. The author calls for opposition to such tactics.

1316. "'Patch' Raids Police Station: Cops Join Hoods in Harassing Bar." THE ADVOCATE, 2, 9 (September, 1968), 5.

> A review of a protest conducted at the Harbor Division station of the Los Angeles Police Department following two arrests at a popular city bar.

1317. "Cross Currents." THE LADDER, 12, 11/12 (September, 1968), 29-30.

> Dr. Charles Socarides, in an address to the American Medical Association on June 18, 1968, described gays and lesbians as suffering from a pathological condition. In response, a news conference was called on June 20 by the Daughters of Bilitis and the Council on Religion and the Homosexual, with six demands being clearly stated. Among them was a demand criticizing police harassment, entrapment, blackmail, enticement and witchhunts.

1318. "If You Witness a Raid. . . " THE ADVOCATE, 2, 10 (October, 1968), 10.

> Legal advice to persons who may witness police harassment of gays intended to increase their effectiveness as defense witnesses in possible court proceedings. Areas explored center on the types of observations useful and the need to make a written record as soon as possible after the event while memories are still fresh and detailed.

1319. "Cross Currents." THE LADDER, 13, 1/2 (October/November, 1968), 37-42.

> Improved relations between the San Francisco gay community and the police force of that city are noted in this edition of the popular *Ladder* news review.

1320. "Police, Court Should Not Regulate Morals--Hanson." THE ADVOCATE, 2, 11 (November, 1968), 2.

> A news report on an address given to the October, 1968 meeting of ONE, Inc. in Los Angeles by attorney Michael Hanson on police conduct and attitudes. Topics discussed included police training and existing legal controls over private consenting behavior.

1321. "Supreme Court Turns Down Black Cat Case." THE ADVOCATE, 2, 11 (November, 1968), 3.

> The legal case filed by attorney Herbert Selwyn against the Los Angeles police for the brutal activities occurring in a raid on a New Year's party in January, 1967

has been refused a hearing by the U.S. Supreme Court. With assistance from the American Civil Liberties Union, Selwyn had filed a brief arguing that the application of Californian "lewd conduct" law in this case deprived homosexuals of their constitutional right to equal protection under the law.

1322. "S.D. Drive Nets 75 at Parks, Beaches." THE ADVOCATE, 2, 12 (December, 1968), 3.

Undercover members of the police force of San Diego posted to two city parks and a popular beach area have arrested seventy-five persons on homosexual charges since September, 1968. The occupations of those arrested are included.

1323. "Mattachine Hits Chicago Raids." THE ADVOCATE, 3, 1 (January, 1969), 4.

The Midwest Mattachine Society has sent a letter of protest to the Chicago Police Department regarding raids on two bars in August, 1968. The text calls for equal treatment and elimination of "minority" status.

1324. "Torrance Cops Use Muscle to 'Straighten' Bar." THE ADVOCATE, 3, 2 (February, 1969), 3.

A news item on the alleged intimidation of a businessman in Torrance, California against his plans for converting his club into a gay bar to increase custom.

1325. "Rampart Heats Up: Vice Cops Hit Two Bars, Arrest Ten." THE ADVOCATE, 3, 3 (March, 1969), 1.

A detailed news story on a raid conducted by the Rampart division vice squad on a bar in the Silverlake area of Los Angeles. Possible political connections to candidates for city council are theorized.

1326. "Is the LAPD Working for Lamport?" THE ADVOCATE, 3, 3 (March, 1969), 1.

An editorial charging the Rampart Division of the Los Angeles police with carrying out raids against supporters of the opposition candidate, Jack Norman, who is

presently attempting to supplant Paul Lamport on city
council. Lamport has been an outspoken foe of homosexuals.

1327. "Death at the Dover: Witnesses Say Vice Cops Beat Man to
Death." THE ADVOCATE, 3, 4 (April, 1969), 1.

A summary of an incident which occurred at the Dover
Hotel in Los Angeles in which three members of the vice
squad physically abused an arrest victim. The man died
an hour later in a hospital emergency facility.

1328. "Beating Death of Handcuffed Man Ruled 'Excusable
Homicide.'" THE ADVOCATE, 3, 5 (May, 1969), 1, 3, 10.

A review of the testimony presented in the three-hour
hearing before a coroner's jury in the death of J.
McCann at the Dover Hotel, Los Angeles on April 4,
1969. Details of the police account were contradicted
as regards use of excessive force.

1329. "Report Scores Police Practices: One of 10 in County
Misbehaves." THE ADVOCATE, 3, 6 (May, 1969), 2.

A summary of findings contained in an investigative
report on the first three years of operation of the
police malpractice offices in Los Angeles. Released on
April 19, 1969 by the American Civil Liberties Union,
its conclusions indicate a pattern of innocent persons
being booked for "crimes against the police."
Statistics for the period 1966 to 1969 are provided.

1330. "L.A. Vice Silly Season Is On." THE ADVOCATE, 3, 5 (May,
1969), 9, 10.

A news report on renewed entrapment activity in Hollywood by vice squad officers. The author acknowledges
that while "the way to stop police enticement practices
is to make them more expensive for the city than they
are for the gay community, most victims are not in a
position to challenge their arrests successfully.

1331. "Lawyer Seeks 'Cave' Witnesses." THE ADVOCATE, 3, 6
(June, 1969), 1.

A request by an attorney defending seven men arrested in a police raid at a Los Angeles bar for witnesses to the event. All arrested were charged with violating "lewd conduct" laws and one with possession of marijuana.

1332. "Berkeley Vice Cops Shoot Man to Death in Park." THE ADVOCATE, 3, 6 (June, 1969), 2.

A report on the shooting death of Frank Bartley of Berkeley, California involving two members of that city's vice squad. Murder charges are pending against the two officers and attorney for the family, Mary Montgomery, is quoted on the location of the head wound.

1333. "Terror in the Tubs: The Raid That Wasn't." THE ADVOCATE, 3, 6 (June, 1969), 3.

A pseudonymous detailed account of a police raid on a private bath house in Los Angeles. Behavior of both plainclothesmen and regular officers is described.

1334. "Atlanta Police Launch Drive in Parks, Use Cameras." THE ADVOCATE, 3, 7 (July, 1969), 12.

A report on a drive to clean homosexuals out of the parks of Atlanta through the equipping of vice squad officers with flash cameras.

1335. "Gays Attack Law, Police in Three Separate Court Actions." THE ADVOCATE, 3, 8 (September, 1969), 1, 6.

Three separate lawsuits have been filed against the cities of Oakland and Berkeley in relation to the death of Frank Bartley at the hands of two vice squad officers. The case brought by the Society for Individual Rights is covered in detail. President Larry Littlejohn of SIR and attorney B. J. Beckwith are quoted.

1336. "Professor Dies After Vice Arrest in Oakland." THE ADVOCATE, 3, 8 (September, 1969), 5.

A report on the damage suit brought against the city of
Oakland by Mrs. Frances Kaplan on behalf of her late
husband. Dr. Phillip Kaplan died of a massive heart
attack following his arraignment on vice charges on
June 19, 1969. Excessive violence by the arresting
officers is alleged.

1337. "State Investigates Bartley Death." THE ADVOCATE, 3, 8
(September, 1969), 5.

The office of the California Attorney General is con-
ducting a separate investigation into the death of
Frank Bartley in Oakland. The relationship of this
study to a petition presented to that office by the
Society for Individual Rights of San Francisco is not
clarified. Said petition claimed the use of deadly
force in misdemeanor arrests is not justifiable.

1338. "LAPD Does No Wrong: 'Gays Should Obey Laws.'" THE
ADVOCATE, 3, 9 (October, 1969), 1, 25-26.

A summary of a group interview with Captain Donald
Wesley, newly-appointed head of the Hollywood division
of the Los Angeles police, and Lt. White, community
relations officer and the head of the Hollywood vice
squad. Police policy on entrapment, harassment, use of
plainclothes operatives and other tactics is stated.

1339. "SIR Seeks Info on Enticement." THE ADVOCATE, 3, 9
(October, 1969), 33.

San Francisco's Society for Individual Rights has
requested affidavits from "persons who have been
solicited, harassed or arrested by plainclothes-
policemen" as an adjunct to cases pending against the
Berkeley and Oakland police departments.

1340. "Policing the Third Sex." NEWSWEEK, 74 (27 October,
1969), 76.

A survey article presenting the charged climate of
relations between local police forces and the homosexual community following the Stonewall Riots in New
York City and the rise of the "gay power" movement.
Examples are given from Detroit, Atlanta, San Francisco
and New York City itself.

1341. "Cross Currents." THE LADDER, 14, 1/2 (October/November, 1969), 29-41.

> Three police-related items are contained in this edition of the news column:
>
> a) On March 9, 1969, Howard Effland was badly beaten by four members of the Los Angeles vice squad. Subsequent to this beating, he died of massive hemorrhaging from a ruptured pancreas. An inquest on April 4, 1969 ruled the death to be "excusable homicide."
>
> b) On April 17, 1969, in a local park in Berkeley, California, Frank Bartley was entrapped by police officers and shot to death while "resisting arrest." This outraged the local gay community, which picketed the police department and held a press conference to publicize their demands for fair treatment.
>
> c) On the night of June 29, 1969, New York City police attempted to close the Stonewall Inn, a gay bar on Christopher Street in Greenwich Village. This resulted in a riot with over 400 gay men and women participating. Rioters threw garbage, pennies and even uprooted parking meters at the police. Rioting spread quickly throughout Greenwich Village and was followed on July 2 by leafletting protesting conditions which had provoked the disturbances.

1342. "Cops Cleared in Kaplan Death." THE ADVOCATE, 3, 10 (November, 1969), 1.

> The Alameda County Grand Jury cleared the Oakland police department of any responsibility in the $1.3 million wrongful death suit in the matter of Dr. Phillip Kaplan. Background on the case is provided.

1343. "Mattachine Threatens Action in New Wave of Chicago Bar Raids." THE ADVOCATE, 3, 11 (December, 1969), 2.

> A total of twenty-three persons were arrested in separate raids on bars in Chicago by members of that city's police force in September and October, 1969. Mattachine Midwest has sent a strongly worded letter of protest to Captain Raymond Clark, newly-appointed head of the vice squad, calling for an end to harassment. Extensive quotes from the document are presented.

1344. "Sheriff, ABC Fuzz Invade, Search Anubis Clubhouse Without Warrants." THE ADVOCATE, 4, 2 (February, 1970), 1.

> On December 19, 1969, the clubhouse of the Society of Anubis, a social organization of male and female homosexuals situated near Azusa, California, was raided by police. When the president demanded to see their search warrant, the officers told her "she would be arrested if she didn't shut up." The Society was cited violations of the entertainment and liquor laws.

1345. "Sears Mum About John-Peepers in Stores." THE ADVOCATE, 4, 3 (March, 1970), 9.

> Officials of the Sears & Roebuck company have refused to answer inquiries regarding possible covert surveillance by police in store rest rooms and company policy in this area. Based upon testimony in the 1969 Alvin Buchanan case, a list of questions was presented to store management in Los Angeles by The ADVOCATE. The list is reproduced in full.

1346. "Atlanta Scene: Drive on Gays Eases, Tubs Reopen, Scene Brightens." THE ADVOCATE, 4, 3 (March, 1970), 11, 12.

> A profile of the situation of the homosexual community of Atlanta as it was in early 1970. Promises by an alderman to rid the city of "queers, hippies and other perverts" have spawned increased entrapment activity by local police. Resistance to the practice is mounting.

1347. "The Halo Slips." THE ADVOCATE, 4, 4 (April, 1970), 1, 28.

> An editorial reviewing extant practices of the Los Angeles Police Department, the Board of Police Commissioners and the District Attorney. Both the city and district attorneys have been charged by the American Civil Liberties Union with failure to prosecute policemen who had engaged in "criminal offenses committed against citizens." The department is called upon to remove the "exponents of 'instant' justice."

1348. "Atlanta Cops Shoot Audience." THE ADVOCATE, 4, 4 (April, 1970), 9.

A Unitarian minister, among those members of an audience at a screening of the Andy Warhol film *Lonesome Cowboys* photographed by Fulton County police, is suing to have the pictures destroyed. During the raid, officers announced that the photos would be matched against their files of "known homosexuals" and later told the media that audiences at such films were usually composed of "sex criminals."

1349.   "Cross Currents." THE LADDER, 14, 7/8 (April/May, 1970), 31-38.

Two items relating to police-community relations in California are cited in this column:

a) Anubis, a private club for gay men and women in Azusa, California, was raided by police on December 19, 1969. Harassment of patrons occurred and citations on the establishment's liquor license and entertainment registry were reported.

b) On January 18, 1970, six policemen (two military, four civilian) invaded the home of Arthur Ornales in San Francisco, searching for an AWOL soldier. When it became clear that Ornales could not help them, he was beaten up repeatedly. A complaint to the San Francisco Police Department elicited no reply.

1350.   "L.A. Vice Cops Kill Another Gay." THE ADVOCATE, 4, 5 (29 April-12 May, 1970), 1.

A report on the death of Larry Turner in an incident with members of the Los Angeles police. Background and subsequent legal actions are covered.

1351.   "Youth Falls from N.Y.C. Jail." THE ADVOCATE, 4, 5 (29 April-12 May, 1970), 1, 6.

A news report of continuing protests in New York City by the Gay Activists Alliance against discrimination and harassment of homosexuals by officers of that city's police force. Following a raid on a local bar which resulted in 167 arrests, one patron, Diego Vinales, attempted to escape from the police station's upper floor and was impaled upon the guard fence below. Details of GAA discussions with city officials are provided.

1352. "Gays Remember Dover Death With Rally, March." THE ADVOCATE, 4, 5 (29 April-12 May, 1970), 1, 3.

A memorial and protest was held on March 8, 1970 to mark the first anniversary of the death of Howard Effland (also known as J. McCann) at the Dover Hotel. Speakers, including Morris Kight of the Gay Liberation Front and Rev. Troy Perry, called for an end to sex-related arrests. Excerpts from a letter sent to Los Angeles police chief Ed Davis are included.

1353. "Cops Hit Aquarius: Nab 4 on 288a, 647a." THE ADVOCATE, 4, 5 (29 April-12 May, 1970), 2.

An account of police harassment and a later raid conducted on a bath in the northeastern portion of Los Angeles. Police attention had been focused on the establishment for several weeks prior to the raid on March 20, 1970. Four patrons were charged with lewd conduct and violation of a felony regulation.

1354. "New York Controversy Continues Over Snake Pit Mass Arrest." THE ADVOCATE, 4, 6 (13-26 May, 1970), 2.

The March 8, 1970 mass arrest of 167 persons at the Snakepit, an after-hours club on Manhattan, and its subsequent political fallout is summarized. The Mattachine Society of New York has offered legal assistance to arrested parties desirous of suing the city for false arrest, while Rep. Edward Koch has charged the police with resuming a policy of harassment and illegal arrests of homosexuals.

1355. "M M Protest Stops Illegal Tactics by 2 Chicago Cops." THE ADVOCATE, 4, 6 (13-26 May, 1970), 10.

A formal protest to the 18th District Police Commander Clarence Braasch by Jim Bradford, president of Mattachine Midwest, has resulted in a cessation of complaints against two members of the city of Chicago vice squad. Details of the entrapment tactics used by these two individuals are provided.

1356. "Police Stupidity in L.A. . . . And Other Places." THE ADVOCATE, 4, 6 (13-26 May, 1970), 22.

A profile of efforts by chapters of the Mattachine Society in Chicago, Buffalo and New York to address police actions and attitudes towards the gay community.

1357. "Anubis Case Dropped--Cops Entered Illegally." THE ADVOCATE, 4, 7 (26 May-9 June, 1970), 2.

On April 29, 1970, Judge Morrie Matcha dismissed charges against the Society of Anubis, ruling that a December 19, 1969 raid by police and officers of the alcohol control board had been conducted illegally. Background on the incident is provided.

1358. "Leave Baths Alone, Denver Police Told." THE ADVOCATE, 4, 8 (10-23 June, 1970), 2.

A temporary restraining order against the Denver police department was issued to prevent harassment of steam baths in that city. Attorneys for the establishment charged that a city ordinance allowing inspectors virtually unlimited entry was unconstitutional.

1359. "L.A. College Police Explain 30 Arrests As Result of a Homosexual Infestation." THE ADVOCATE, 4, 8 (10-23 June, 1970), 3, 21.

A lengthy interview with Harold Cole, chief of campus security at Los Angeles Community College on the recent wave of arrests of homosexuals there. Two pseudonymous personal accounts are included.

1360. "Cross Currents." THE LADDER, 14, 9/10 (June/July, 1970), 33-40.

A police raid on The Snake Pit, an after-hours bar in New York City, on March 8, 1970 resulted in 167 individuals being taken into custody. One man, Diego Vinales, fearing deportation for being a homosexual, broke free, ran to the second floor of the police station and hurled himself from a window. Impaled on an iron picket fence, he was cut free, taken to the hospital and charged with "resisting arrest." Rep. Edward Koch subsequently wrote a letter to the commissioner of police demanding an explanation for the raid.

1361. "Cops Raid Regency, Harass Corral Club." THE ADVOCATE, 4, 9 (24 June-7 July, 1970), 1, 4.

Two related news stories of raids by members of the Los Angeles vice squad on bath houses. Some twenty persons were arrested. Details of each inspection strategy and the behavior of the officers involved are provided.

1362. "L.A. Getting Hotter? Statistics Don't Show It." THE ADVOCATE, 4, 10 (8-21 July, 1970), 2.

An article comparing arrest statistics for adults and juveniles entered under the category of "sex offenses" in the *Monthly Crime and Arrest Digest* of the Los Angeles Police Department for 1969 and 1970. Available figures do not indicate a significant increase in homosexual arrests for the period. Researchers will find the definition of the categories useful for comparative purposes.

1363. "Little Leniency in LACC Cases." THE ADVOCATE, 4, 10 (8-21 July, 1970), 2.

The cases of some thirty individuals arrested by campus security personnel at the Los Angeles Community College under section 288a of the California Penal Code have been dispersed to municipal court for preliminary hearings on this felony charge. Several have already reached the Superior Court for trial.

1364. "Minnesota Court Says No Tearoom Spying." THE ADVOCATE, 4, 10 (8-21 July, 1970), 3.

A summary review of a decision by the Minnesota Supreme Court voiding a sodomy conviction on grounds that police surveillance tactics used to obtain said conviction violated the Fourth Amendment rights of the plaintiff. Judgment was based upon the 1967 decision of the U.S. Supreme Court in *Katz vs. United States*. A brief history of the case is provided.

1365. "ADVOCATE Writer Arrested in Bar, Says Cops Beat Him." THE ADVOCATE, 4, 11 (22 July-4 August, 1970), 1.

A personal account of police brutality and harassment
by the Los Angeles police of a staff writer at *The
ADVOCATE* in a bar raid.

1366. "Christopher West Pin Brings Lewdness Bust." THE
ADVOCATE, 4, 11 (22 July-4 August, 1970), 2.

A member of the Metropolitan Community Church of Los
Angeles en route to services wearing a button advocating equal rights for homosexuals was arrested and
intimidated into signing a statement confessing to lewd
conduct with a police officer. Legal action is planned
against the officers involved in the incident.

1367. "S.F. Busts Fall: Macy's Called Liar." THE ADVOCATE, 4,
11 (22 July-4 August, 1970), 7.

A wave of arrests in mid-1970 in several city parks of
San Francisco and a local department store is profiled.
Entrapment tactics used in the latter are criticized.

1368. "Police Active in San Antonio." THE ADVOCATE, 4, 13 (19
August-1 September, 1970), 7.

Following an hiatus of some two years, San Antonio
police resumed their activity against gays with a raid
on a bar in the central district of the city. Both
civilian and military police participated in the
action.

1369. "Scrap 'Victimless Crime' Laws, Police Official Urges."
THE ADVOCATE, 4, 12 (5-18 August, 1970), 1.

Robert K. Ruskin, commissioner of the New York City
police department of investigation, has called for the
repeal of "victimless crime" laws, those laws covering
actions "where society is not a victim of the particular act." Ruskin made the statement following the
arrest of two New York police officers who had
attempted to use the laws for purposes of extortion.

1370. "Gays Picket Macy's Over Busts." THE ADVOCATE, 4, 13 (19
August-1 September, 1970), 1.

A description of protest demonstrations held at the downtown store of Macy's in San Francisco on July 25, 1970. Organized by an ad hoc committee of the local community, the protests hit forty arrests made in the public restrooms at the store and the company's failure to work with local gay organizations to lower the charges facing those detained from felonies to misdemeanors.

1371. "L.A. Arrests: No Big Jump." THE ADVOCATE, 4, 13 (19 August-1 September, 1970), 3.

A tabulation of statistics drawn from the *Monthly Crime and Arrest Digest* published by the Los Angeles Police Department covering sex offense arrests for the period January through June, 1970.

1372. Lee, Charles. "Who's Lying? Battle of the Busts in S.F." THE ADVOCATE, 4, 14 (2-15 September, 1970), 1, 6.

A news report on the continuing legal controversy occasioned by recent arrests at the Macy's department store in central San Francisco. Profiles of the mutual charges exchanged between the firm and the district attorney's office are presented.

1373. "Police Group Plans to 'Expose' Liberal Lawmakers." THE ADVOCATE, 4, 14 (2-15 September, 1970), 3.

Meeting in Detroit, the International Conference of Police Associations announced a plan to "get rid of lawmakers who support liberal legislation, such as making it legal for members of the same sex to have sexual relations." Local efforts in San Diego and Dallas are cited as case studies.

1374. "Bar Police Harassment of Gay-In, Court Asked." THE ADVOCATE, 4, 14 (2-15 September, 1970), 3.

A federal court in Los Angeles has been requested to issue a prohibitory judgment against excessive policing and harassment at that city's third "Gay-In," scheduled for Griffith Park on September 5, 1970. Much of the article describes the massive police presence at a previous event and planned legal protections.

1375. "Buffalo Gays, Police Meet, Fail to Agree." THE ADVOCATE, 4, 15 (16-29 September, 1970), 1, 10.

> On August 18, 1970, a meeting was held in Buffalo, New York between Richard Dyer, president of the Mattachine Society of the Niagara Frontier and Captain Kenneth Kennedy, head of the city vice squad. The ninety-minute discussion produced denial of entrapment practices by the police force and plans for future talks. A lengthy description of the current situation between the police department and the gay community of Buffalo completes the article.

1376. "San Antonio Bars Deny Police Harassment." THE ADVOCATE, 4, 15 (16-29 September, 1970), 7.

> An interview with the owners of two San Antonio, Texas gay bars regarding their relations with the police, which are reported to be "very, very decent." An earlier report of a raid by both civilian and military police is explained as an exaggeration of a minor incident.

1377. "Court Rejects GLF Plea to Bar Gay-In Harassment." THE ADVOCATE, 4, 16 (30 September-13 October, 1970), 3.

> In a hearing in a Los Angeles district court, Judge Andrew Hauk ruled that the evidence presented in support of a prohibitory judgment against the Los Angeles Police Department did not substantiate special discrimination. Community leader Morris Kight stated that the affidavits would be retained for use in a possible class-action suit against the police force. Details of prior police actions regarding public celebrations in Griffith Park are included.

1378. "L.A. Arrests Still Off." THE ADVOCATE, 4, 17 (14-27 October, 1970), 5.

> A comparative note on the statistics of sex offenses recorded by the *Monthly Crime and Arrests Digest* of the Los Angeles Police Department. Totals of the first seven months for 1969 and 1970 indicate a decrease in the overall rate. Estimates of specifically homosexual-related offenses are also provided.

1379. "My Wife Woke Up Screaming 'Don't Kick Him Again'." THE ADVOCATE, 4, 18 (28 October-10 November, 1970), 1.

A report of an observed instance of police brutality against a homosexual man by two members of the Los Angeles police force vice squad.

1380. "S.F. Official, Gays Meet Police Chief." THE ADVOCATE, 4, 18 (28 October-10 November, 1970), 3.

A news report on a meeting held on September 25, 1970 between San Francisco Police Chief Alfred Nelder, representatives of the city's gay community and Dianne Feinstein, president of the Board of Supervisors. Topics addressed were the use of plainclothesmen, training films used in police academies which depicted homosexuals as violence-prone and police support of pending legislation to remove sexual conduct in private from California's felony statutes.

1381. "ADVOCATE Writer Cleared, Plans $600,000 Suit." THE ADVOCATE, 4, 18 (28 October-10 November, 1970), 6.

The charges against Darby Summers, a staff writer for *The ADVOCATE*, resulting from his arrest on June 25, 1970 were dropped at a hearing on October 1. Summers, who had charged police brutality, immediately filed a suit against the city of Los Angeles for unlawful arrest and grievous bodily harm. Background on the case is provided.

1382. "Took Payoffs, Cops Admit." THE ADVOCATE, 4, 18 (28 October-10 November, 1970), 25.

Four former members of the Seattle police force pleaded guilty to accepting payoffs from the owners of a local homosexual bar, with the understanding that such payments would help avert harassment of the businesses. Details of the case are briefly sketched.

1383. "KNBC Hit for Shelving Death Probe." THE ADVOCATE, 4, 19 (11-24 November, 1970), 5.

The United States Mission of Los Angeles has called for a public protest against station KNBC, charging that, during the filming of a documentary on the Los Angeles gay community, a reporter stated his intent "to secure an indictment for murder" against the policemen involved in the death of Howard Effland in March, 1969. This was because Mission officials had witnessed Effland's arrest and maltreatment.

1384.   "Police 'Visits' to Clubs Shake Up Houston Gays." THE ADVOCATE, 4, 20 (25 November-8 December, 1970), 6.

A news report covering a series of bar raids by Houston police officers resulting in charges of liquor violations and several arrests. This was seen by the police force as part of a general increase in liquor law violations throughout the city.

1385.   "Lindsay Says He'll Investigate." THE ADVOCATE, 4, 20 (25 November-8 December, 1970), 8.

New York City Deputy Mayor Richard R. Aurelio, in response to an inquiry from *The ADVOCATE*, indicated that complaints that police harassment was increasing again would be looked into. Aurelio made it clear that this was also the view of Mayor Lindsay. The recent resignation of police commissioner Howard Leary is noted.

1386.   "Stop Criminal Cops!" THE ADVOCATE, 4, 21 (9-22 December, 1970), 22.

An editorial condemning beatings of civilians by certain police officers of the Los Angeles force and calling for an investigation to remove the personnel responsible for these acts. The Rampart Division is cited as a particularly notorious example.

1387.   "Gavin Says KNBC Hasn't Copped Out on Slaying Probe." THE ADVOCATE, 4, 22 (23 December-5 January, 1971), 1, 10.

Replying to criticism from officials of the United States Mission, KNBC newsman Mike Gavin denied that his investigation into the 1969 death of Howard Effland had been terminated due to official pressure. A history of the investigation and a related documentary film *Out of the Shadows* is presented.

1388. "LAPD Entrapment Victim Fighting Back." THE ADVOCATE, 4, 22 (23 December, 1970-5 January, 1971), 11.

> John V. Platania, a member of the Los Angeles Gay Liberation Front who was arrested on October 29, 1970 by plainclothes officers, has opted for a jury trial and plans a public confrontation on the issue of entrapment tactics. The five bases of his defense and a brief summary of the incident are provided.

1389. "S.F. Gays Protest Shooting by Cops." THE ADVOCATE, 4, 23 (6-19 January, 1971), 1.

> A new report on an incident following the closing of a San Francisco bar which resulted in the shooting of a patron in the ankle and elbow by police. A detailed description of the incident is included. A letter of protest was sent to Mayor Joseph Alioto and the San Francisco Police Commission by three major homophile groups in the city.

1390. "S.F. Groups Calling for Macy's Boycott." THE ADVOCATE, 4, 24 (20 January-2 February, 1971), 2.

> The Society for Individual Rights and the Council on Religion and the Homosexual have called for a boycott of Macy's department store in central San Francisco in protest against some forty felony sex offense arrests carried out in June and July of 1970 in the store's rest rooms. All requests to have charges diminished have been rebuffed by the district attorney.

1391. "Cops Harass Bar, Beat Patron: Police Probe Hassle at Tradesman." THE ADVOCATE, 52 (3-16 February, 1971), 1.

> A report of a series of incidents of harassment of a gay bar in Los Angeles which resulted in the arrest of the owner's son for obstructing an officer. The pattern of regular harassment by the district officers is covered in full.

1392. "Rampart Fuzz Invade Home, Arrest Two in House for Lowd Conduct." THE ADVOCATE, 52 (3-16 February, 1971), 1.

> An account of a case of home invasion by eighteen members of the Rampart division of the Los Angeles

police following a call from a vice squad officer. The two occupants were charged with the commission of an indecent act. Details of the matter are given in full.

1393. "N.Y. Leaders Testify at Assembly Hearing on Gay Problems." THE ADVOCATE, 52 (3-16 February, 1971), 4.

On January 7, 1971, New York State Assemblymen Stephen Solarz and Antonio Olivieri held a public hearing at the State Office Building in Manhattan on the problems of the homosexual in New York. Organizations from Rochester, Albany and the city were represented. Police abuse was a common theme. Statements from Reps. Bella Abzug and Edward Koch on the subject were read into the record.

1394. "It's Not Illegal, But 'Contempt of Cop' Gets Instant Punishment Without Trial." THE ADVOCATE, 52 (3-16 February, 1971), 10.

An analysis of a review of Paul Chevigny's 1968 study *Police Power, Police Abuses* written by Michael Hannon, a former officer and practicing attorney. Emphasis is placed upon the need for reform and accountability of the force to the public.

1395. "We Are Bleeding." THE ADVOCATE, 52 (3-16 February, 1971), 22.

An editorial attacking recent instances of escalating disregard for the constitutional rights of the public and home invasion by members of the Los Angeles police force and calling for all gay community organizations "to unite in a legal attack on police practices."

1396. "Hollywood Police Station Target of L.A. March." THE ADVOCATE, 53 (17 February-2 March, 1971), 1, 3, 12.

A detailed news report on a demonstration against police brutality held in Hollywood, California on January 23, 1971. Speakers at the rally included Rev. Troy Perry and Morris Kight. Extensive quotations from the speeches are included.

1397. "Jury Acquits L.A. Gay in Park Entrapment Case." THE
       ADVOCATE, 53 (17 February-2 March, 1971), 2.

       A review of the court proceedings in the police entrap-
       ment case of John Platania, a Los Angeles activist.
       Details of police and defense testimony are supplied.

1398. "Christman Trial Slated: Funds Raised." THE ADVOCATE, 53
       (27 February-2 March, 1971), 2.

       A summary of legal preparations in the case of a gay
       man shot by police during an attack on a crowd leaving
       a bar in San Francisco. Several bullets remain in the
       plaintiff's body. Details of fund raising by various
       organizations are included.

1399. "S.F. Gays Launch Big Macy's Boycott." THE ADVOCATE, 53
       (17 February-2 March, 1971), 8.

       The Society for Individual Rights and the Council on
       Religion and the Homosexual have initiated a campaign
       requesting holders of charge plates from the Macy's
       department store chain to turn them in as protest over
       the firm's unwillingness to cooperate in recent police
       entrapment cases. A statement issued by the S.I.R.
       notes that "the issue is . . . whether any business
       establishment can direct a systematic program of
       entrapment against the homosexual community using
       illegal procedures."

1400. "New Orleans Chief Denies Entrapment." THE ADVOCATE, 54
       (3-16 March, 1971), 2.

       In a meeting with members of the Gay Liberation Front
       on February 10, 1971, police superintendent Clarence
       Giarruso denied that entrapment and harassment were
       being practiced by his department. A brief review of
       relations between the police and the New Orleans homo-
       sexual community is included.

1401. "Police Board Can't Avoid Class Suit, Court Decides." THE
       ADVOCATE, 54 (3-16 March, 1971), 5.

       A review of a ruling by the Ninth Circuit Court of
       Appeals that the Los Angeles Police Commission must be
       a defendant in a class action suit pending against the

city's police department by the black community. Plans for a similar effort by the gay community are summarized.

1402.   Charbonnet, Claude. "Cops in New Orleans Have Taking Ways." THE ADVOCATE, 54 (3-16 March, 1971), 9.

A news report on the tactics of entrapment and bribery being used by certain members of the New Orleans police force in pursuing sexual crimes. Media indifference to the problem is noted and reform called for.

1403.   "F.B.I. to Probe Death of Gay in N.Y. City Jail." THE ADVOCATE, 55 (17-30 March, 1971), 2.

U.S. Attorney Whitney North Seymour of New York City has requested the assistance of the F.B.I. in a case involving the death of a gay inmate in the Men's House of Detention in November, 1970. Brutal treatment by the guards is alleged. Formation of the Gay Community Prisoner Defense Committee "which will assist gay men and women in penal or mental institutions" is noted.

1404.   Collins, Don. "Christman Assault Trial Winds Up With Hung Jury." THE ADVOCATE, 56 (31 March-13 April, 1971), 2, 13.

A detailed report on the trial of Charles Christman for allegedly assaulting five members of the Los Angeles police force during a raid on a gay bar on December 12, 1970. Emphasis is placed on the use of excessive force by the officers. Christman attended the trial in a wheelchair.

1405.   "Hollywood Vice Chief, Gay to Debate at Meeting." THE ADVOCATE, 57 (14-27 April, 1971), 6.

The transcription of a dialogue between gay members of the audience and Lt. John McGilivray, head of the Hollywood vice squad, at a public meeting on March 24, 1971. Although entrapment was denied, activists repeatedly cited the case of John Platania as evidence that the tactic was being used in the city.

374

1406. "Baskett Grabbed in Long Beach Vice Raid." THE ADVOCATE, 59 (12-25 May, 1971), 9.

A description of the entrapment arrest of financial consultant Edward Baskett in Long Beach, California. He declined a proposal by ACLU counsel to plead guilty and plans to fight the charges in a jury trial.

1407. "16 Nabbed in Raid at Regency Baths." THE ADVOCATE, 60 (26 May-8 June, 1971), 2, 24.

A news report of a raid by vice squad officers on a bath house in Hollywood. Background on the history of mass arrest raids in the Los Angeles area is provided. Views of the police and district attorney's office are also included.

1408. "Christman Accepts Less Assault-On-Officer Charge." THE ADVOCATE, 60 (26 May-8 June, 1971), 2.

The case of Charles Christman, charged with five counts of assaulting police officers, was settled with the acceptance of a deal dropping said charges in return for a guilty plea to two misdemeanors. A fine was imposed.

1409. "Commission Ponders Role of S.F. Cops." THE ADVOCATE, 61 (9-22 June, 1971), 3.

In a forty-seven-page report to Mayor Joseph Alioto and the Board of Supervisors, the San Francisco Crime Commission reviewed the question of legal action against "crimes without victims" but reached no resolution of the issue. Statistics indicating the prevalence of such incidents in the San Francisco area are included.

1410. Bear, Dave. "Probe Promised in 2 N.Y. Incidents." THE ADVOCATE, 61 (9-22 June, 1971), 3, 8.

Representatives of the Gay Activists Alliance and the Daughters of Bilitis met with senior aides to Mayor John Lindsay in New York City regarding recent instances of police harassment of social events and Greenwich Village bars. An investigation has been promised.

1411. "Story on Gays Puts Heat on Bars." THE ADVOCATE, 61 (9-22 June, 1971), 6.

> A wave of harassment of homosexual bars in Long Beach, California is traced to a reaction by a vice squad officer enrolled in a criminology class at Long Beach State University which included a section on homosexuality. An article on changing attitudes towards homosexuals in *The Lantern,* the campus newspaper, is believed to have triggered the incident.

1412. "Jury Finds Baskett Guilty in Long Beach Lewd Trial." THE ADVOCATE, 61 (9-22 June, 1971), 11.

> Following three days of legal debate in Long Beach Municipal Court, a jury found Edward Baskett guilty of lewd conduct. A fine of $150 was imposed. Plans for appeal are discussed and the case history briefly summarized.

1413. Code, Rob. "Ex-Vice Cop Talks: 'Homosexuals Prefer Young Boys to Older Queers.'" THE ADVOCATE, 63 (7-20 July, 1971), 1-2, 17, 26.

> A transcription of an interview with Dr. John B. Williams, author of the 1964 study *Vice Control in California* which has been attacked for perpetuating inaccurate stereotypes of gay persons. Williams worked for the Los Angeles police force for eighteen years and is currently working on a new book with Dr. Edward Bloomquist. He expresses the view that homosexuality "tends to contaminate society."

1414. "Hamburger Stop Brings Nightmare Encounter with LAPD 8 Elite." THE ADVOCATE, 63 (7-20 July, 1971), 3, 15.

> An account of an incident of police brutality by members of a Los Angeles police department unit detailed to eliminate "undesirables" involving two gay men. Interviews with personnel from HELP, a local legal aid society, provide perspective on the affair.

1415. "Old Guard Holds Fast, Says Bloomquist." THE ADVOCATE, 63 (7-20 July, 1971), 26, 29.

An interview with Dr. Edward Bloomquist, a psychologist presently co-authoring a book on vice squad activity with a former member of the Los Angeles police force. Emphasis is placed on the attitudes towards homosexuality held by senior members of the police "that this is an immoral and illegal situation that must be prosecuted to the fullest extent of the law."

1416. "Stevenson: Vice Squad Entraps." THE ADVOCATE, 66 (18-31 August, 1971), 1-2.

Los Angeles city councilman Robert J. Stevenson has charged that the city's vice squad is practicing "illegal entrapment" and announced plans to present the police commission with evidence substantiating these charges. Reform of punitive morals legislation is seen as the best way to eliminate such practices.

1417. Beardslee, Doug. "S.F. Police Hassle Dance Bars." THE ADVOCATE, 66 (18-31 August, 1971), 1.

A news article exploring the increase in police activity in the Mission Park and Castro Street districts of San Francisco.

1418. "GCA to Sift Complaints Against Cops." THE ADVOCATE, 66 (18-31 August, 1971), 2.

The Gay Community Alliance of Los Angeles has established a hotline accepting "reports of harassment, intimidation, or entrapment . . . by members of the Los Angeles police." All reports will be verified and validated cases will be forwarded to Councilman Robert J. Stevenson for use in his efforts at police reform.

1419. "Buffalo Show Airs Charges Against Cops." THE ADVOCATE, 66 (18-31 August, 1971), 10.

A report on charges of entrapment leveled against the Buffalo, New York police force during broadcast of an eight-part television series on the local gay community. Capt. Kenneth Kennedy stated that enforcement was intended to protect "children and the heterosexual community." Grounds for this position were rebutted by a psychologist also appearing on the program.

1420. "Criminologist Eyes Attitude of Policemen." THE ADVOCATE, 66 (18-31 August, 1971), 24.

A review of an interview with Dr. Donald J. McNamara published in the July, 1971 issue of the journal *Sexual Behavior*. McNamara views police officers as becoming inured to human misconduct with the exception of child molestation and similar events to explain the lack of involvement with their victims in entrapment cases.

1421. "Pershing Square Bust Leading to 'Show Trial.'" THE ADVOCATE, 67 (1-14 September, 1971), 1.

The arrest of Rev. Richard Nash on charges of soliciting to commit an act of prostitution by Los Angeles vice officers is reviewed and planned legal action surveyed. Of particular interest is the reaction of the heterosexual clergy belonging to the Southern California Council on Religion and the Homophile. The full text of the resolution on the Nash arrest passed by that body is included in the article.

1422. "Appeal Hope on Lewd Conviction Tied to Semantics." THE ADVOCATE, 67 (1-14 September, 1971), 4.

A brief summary of the argument that section 647(a) of the California Penal Code is unconstitutional due to the vagueness of its language, resulting in violation of "the first essential due process of law." Said argument is being advanced by defense counsel in the case of Edward Baskett of Long Beach.

1423. "Long Island Brutality Stirs Huge GAA Zap." THE ADVOCATE, 68 (15-28 September, 1971), 1.

A report on a series of police beatings of gay persons on Long Island, New York and the massive demonstrations held demanding redress from the Suffolk County district attorney.

1424. "Kalos Offers Its Evidence in Bridgeport." THE ADVOCATE, 68 (15-28 September, 1971), 2.

Members of the Kalos Society of Bridgeport, Connecticut have presented documentation to that city's mayor substantiating their claims of police indifference to attacks upon gays and harassment. A brief history of the protests held prior to this meeting is appended.

1425. "Gays Decline to Show at Fuzz Abuse Hearings." THE ADVOCATE, 68 (15-28 September, 1971), 12.

Speaking at an August 24, 1971 meeting of the police, fire and civil defense committee of the Los Angeles city council, activist Jim Kepner reported on current efforts to document instances of "harassment, intimidation, entrapment, beatings and killings of homosexuals by police."

1426. McCabe, Charles. "Whose Law? What Order?" THE ADVOCATE, 69 (29 September-12 October, 1971), 3.

A reprint of a column originally appearing in the *San Francisco Chronicle* dealing with the use of plain-clothes police officers in entrapment. The attitude of police chief Al Nelder is seen to be that "the problem was a moral, not a tactical one." The author calls for the use of uniformed officers in their place.

1427. "Vice Cops Spin Fairy Tales to Convict, Lawyer Relates." THE ADVOCATE, 70 (13 October, 1971), 9.

Commentary upon testimony presented to a hearing of the police, fire and civil defense committee of the Los Angeles city council by attorney Cletus Hanifin. Topics included were police graft, brutality and the unwillingness of vice squad officers to submit to lie detector tests. Hanifin was appearing as a representative for the Gay Community Association.

1428. "Floridians Picket Police: Charge Gays Harassed." THE ADVOCATE, 71 (27 October, 1971), 1.

A report on a demonstration held at the city police department of Gainesville, Florida protesting police brutality against gays and general harassment. Personal testimony by one victim is included.

1429. "Court Slaps Down John-Peepers in May Co." THE ADVOCATE, 72 (11 November, 1971), 17.

A report on the court decision in the Superior Court of Los Angeles declaring police surveillance in restrooms to be the result of unlawful search and seizure and an invasion of privacy. Legal precedents and arguments are extensively quoted.

1430. "LAPD Target of Rights Complaint." THE ADVOCATE, 73 (24 November, 1971), 3.

The Gay Community Association of Los Angeles presented a formal complaint to the city attorney's office, charging that city's police force with "direct civil rights violations." Specific charges leveled were blackmail, entrapment by non-uniformed officers and random arrests by vice squad patrolmen. Plans include an appeal to the Justice Department for a federal investigation of police actions.

1431. "Complainant Names Cops: L.A. Hearing Closed." THE ADVOCATE, 74 (8 December, 1971), 2, 17.

A lengthy news report covering public hearings held by the police, fire and civil defense committee of the Los Angeles City Council on police actions. Issues raised include the rights of privacy as extended to officers, a report by the Board of Police Commissioners supporting current practices, harassment of gays and an eight-point complaint specifically aimed at the Harbor Division precinct office.

1432. "Won't Work with Gays, Says L.A. Police Chief." THE ADVOCATE, 74 (8 December, 1971), 3.

In a response to a requested letter setting forth the suggestion that a liaison be established between the Los Angeles police force and the city's gay community, Chief Ed Davis stated that "it is the policy of the chief of police not to conduct liaison with any group which deliberately engages in criminal actions." A similar system is already in place in San Francisco.

1433. Charles, Guy. "Long Island Arrests Touch Off Protests, New Probe Promises." THE ADVOCATE, 75 (22 December, 1971), 2.

A summary article on continuing demonstrations against police brutality and excessive force in Suffolk County, New York directed against gays. Police actions at a November 23, 1971 raid are discussed in detail.

1434. "LAPD New Target of Drive for Gay Rights." THE ADVO-CATE, 75 (22 December, 1971), 3, 14.

A week of demonstrations against the policies of the Los Angeles police force is planned for December, 1971 by that city's Gay Community Alliance. The bulk of the article covers a protest on November 23, 1971 and discussions between its leaders and police representatives.

1435. "LAPD Chief Compares Gays, Lepers." THE ADVOCATE, 76 (5 January, 1972), 1.

A news report on a letter sent to 14th Councilman Arthur Snyder by the Los Angeles Police Department Chief Davis explaining his refusal to establish a liaison with that city's gay and lesbian community. The full text of the letter is included, which compares homosexuals to lepers. Comment from various community and civic figures is appended.

1436. Charles, Guy. "Long Island Police Beat Gay Delegation." THE ADVOCATE, 76 (5 January, 1972), 1.

On December 14, 1971, a delegation of twenty-six gays and lesbians visited the Suffolk County, New York D.A. office to deliver evidence documenting police brutality. Upon requesting a receipt for the materials, the group was assaulted by plainclothes officers, resulting in split lips, broken noses and legs and a punctured lung. County officials promised an investigation.

1437. "Bribe Attempt Claimed in Effort to Purge Gays on D.C. Police Force." THE ADVOCATE, 76 (5 January, 1972), 2.

A news report of harassment and beatings of gay persons in the District of Columbia, along with an internal investigation of the city police force to eliminate suspected gay officers.

1438. "Raid, 30 Arrests Stun Louisville GLF." THE ADVOCATE, 76 (5 January, 1972), 13.

A news report of a police raid on the gay community center of Louisville, resulting in its closure. Police involved were members of the narcotics squad.

1439. "San Diego Harassment on Increase?" THE ADVOCATE, 76 (5 January, 1972), 27.

A report of a demonstration on November 21, 1971 at the San Diego police headquarters, protesting increased harassment. Examples of tactics used are given. The forthcoming Republican National Convention is seen as possible motivation.

1440. "Rochester Raids First in 30 Years." THE ADVOCATE, 76 (5 January, 1972), 30.

On December 2 and 3, 1971, two gay bars in Rochester, New York were closed by police and their owners arrested. Parties were charged with loitering. The ACLU has entered the case and local community leaders indicated mass demonstrations during the arraignments are planned.

1441. "Davis Explains Why He Can't Talk to Gays." THE ADVOCATE, 77 (19 January, 1972), 2, 7.

A transcription of a taped interview given by LAPD Chief Ed Davis to stations KPPC and KNBC on December 17, 1971 at the start of a week-long demonstration demanding his removal.

1442. "Hidden Police Spying in Restrooms Outlawed." THE ADVOCATE, 77 (19 January, 1972), 9.

A report on the ruling by the Southern California Court of Appeals in *People vs. Metcalf* overturning a series of appellate decisions upholding police covert surveillance in public facilities at Los Angeles' May Company department store.

1443. "L.A. Police Board Says Gays Imagining Things." THE ADVOCATE, 77 (19 January, 1972), 11.

The Los Angeles Board of Police Commissioners has stated that allegations of entrapment, harassment, false testimony and similar tactics by Los Angeles police officers lodged by the GCA in hearings in November, 1971 are groundless. The board has assumed responsibility for hearings on police misconduct.

1444. "Victimless Crime? No Such Thing, Says Chief Davis." THE ADVOCATE, 78 (2 February, 1972), 4.

Quotations from a speech delivered by LAPD chief Ed Davis to the Beverly Hills Bar Association on January 13, 1972, denying the existence of the concept of "victimless crime" and illustrating popular conceptions of the homosexual subculture.

1445. "San Francisco Rites Honor Gays Killed by Vice Cops." THE ADVOCATE, 82 (29 March, 1972), 3.

A news report on a demonstration held on March 8, 1972 in San Francisco to memorialize three victims of vice officers in Los Angeles and Berkeley and to demand abolition of the unit. Speakers included Morris Kight, Rev. Ray Broshears and activist Karen Wells.

1446. "S.F. Mental Health Board to Probe Gay Entrapment." THE ADVOCATE, 84 (26 April, 1972), 17.

Following presentation of sex complaints at its public hearing on April 4, 1972, the San Francisco Mental Health Advisory Board announced the formation of a committee to inquire into police entrapment. The relationship of punishment of sex offenders to mental health is rationalized. Information on the witnesses from SIR and the Daughters of Bilitis is provided.

1447. Gregory, Sasha. "S.F. Harassment Data Gathered." THE ADVOCATE, 86 (24 May, 1972), 16.

An announcement of the collection of "depositions of alleged police harassment" by the Neighborhood Legal Assistance Foundation of San Francisco pursuant to a possible class action suit against the city police. The NLAF is being sponsored by GAA, which hopes to file the court action in May, 1972. Background and details of the plans are provided.

1448. "L.A. Police Board Rejects Complaints." THE ADVOCATE, 87 (6 June, 1972), 9.

> The full text of a letter dated May 3, 1972 from the Los Angeles Board of Police Commissioners to HELP President Larry Townsend, and Townsend's response. At issue are charges of police harassment, which the board states "could not be true because the practices complained of are illegal." The LA city council has been requested to investigate "police malpractice in this city."

1449. "Supreme Court Refuses to Hear Baskett Appeal." THE ADVOCATE, 88 (21 June, 1972), 12.

> A request by Edward E. Baskett of Long Beach that a case involving police entrapment be heard by the U.S. Supreme Court was rejected on May 27, 1972. No reasons were given. The suit challenged the lewd conduct laws of California.

1450. Rusinow, Richard. "Philadelphia Panel Urges Control of Police." THE ADVOCATE, 92 (16 August, 1972), 10.

> A report by the Pennsylvania State Advisory Committee of the U.S. Commission on Civil Rights has urged the creation of a citizens board to monitor the actions of the Philadelphia police force, which it terms "a paramilitary organization." Other recommendations are procedures for the expunging of arrest records. Groups ordered as especial victims of police harassment were homosexuals, the young and blacks. The report is the first government-level agency documentation of specific charges against the Philadelphia police. Political conditions are not seen as favoring implementation.

1451. "Court OK's T-Room Vice Voyeurs." THE ADVOCATE, 93 (30 August, 1972), 7.

> A news report on the decision by the California Second Court of Appeals in the case of Leroy Trigg and the departure this decision indicates from the value of *People* vs. *Metcalf* as legal precedent vitiating covert surveillance as a legal police tactic against homosexuals.

1452. "4 Year Sex Arrest Climb Traceable to S.F. Mayor?" THE ADVOCATE, 93 (30 August, 1972), 11.

> Statistics for sex arrests in San Francisco for the period 1967-1971 are presented. A sharp increase in "miscellaneous sex violations" is believed to be attributed to the election of Mayor Joseph Alioto and his policies.

1453. Jackson, Ed. "Massive Bar Raid: Police Hit Legal Aid Society's Sunday Fund-Raising Party." THE ADVOCATE, 94 (13 September, 1972), 18.

> A news report on a police raid on the Black Pipe bar in Los Angeles where a local organization, the Homophile Effort for Legal Protection (HELP) was engaged in fund raising. Community response was explored. Opposition to the organization is believed to have been grounds.

1454. "Police Captain Explains Raid." THE ADVOCATE, 94 (13 September, 1972), 8.

> The Black Pipe raid is discussed by Los Angeles Police Captain Robert S. Tucker. Gambling is set up as the pretext.

1455. "Police Motives Sick, Says HELP." THE ADVOCATE, 95 (27 September, 1972), 6.

> A report on comment made by Larry Townsend, president of the HELP organization of Los Angeles, at the L.A. Press Club on August 30, 1972 regarding police motivation in a raid on the fund-raising drive. Legal action is outlined. Representatives of other community organizations were in attendance.

1456. "ACLU Gets Police Chief to Break Silence on Gays." THE ADVOCATE, 96 (11 October, 1972), 14.

> Reports of the rationale utilized by Chief Walter McQueeney of the Providence, Rhode Island police department in designing his officers' approach to homosexuals. The information was obtained by the executive director of the Rhode Island ACLU in a private conference. Meetings with officers of the

Rhode Island Gay Alliance have been repeatedly refused.

1457. "Beaten by Cops, L.A. Lesbians Say." THE ADVOCATE, 98 (8 November, 1972), 6.

An account of police violence directed against two lesbians in two separate incidents in the Los Angeles area.

1458. Vicker, Randy. "Police Target of Protesters on Two Coasts." THE ADVOCATE, 100 (6 December, 1972), 1.

A combined news article covering two demonstrations on November 4 and 11, 1972 against the Los Angeles police department and New York police respectively. Extensive background information on recent incidents of violence and indifference is provided.

1459. "Arrests Climbing in 'Gay' San Francisco--Why?" THE ADVOCATE, 100 (6 December, 1972), 4.

An in-depth treatment of the recorded rate of sex offense arrests in San Francisco for the period 1970-1972 made by George Brown, a local attorney. Full details on the legal background and specific portions of California law is included. No one factor is seen as contributing to the increase.

1460. "Teacher Claims Beating by N.Y. Police." THE ADVOCATE, 102 (3 January, 1973), 10.

A case incident of police use of excessive force against a teacher in New York City where the victim was beaten severely enough to require medical attention. A complaint has been filed with the New York City police complaint review board.

1461. "ACLU to Help Seattle Gays Counter Arrests." THE ADVOCATE, 103 (17 January, 1973), 16.

The Seattle chapter of the ACLU has agreed to provide counsel for individuals in court actions against the city police. A profile of recent harassment actions

386

and the political climate of Seattle at this time is provided.

1462. "Denver Daily Takes Hard Look at Cop's Treatment of Gays." THE ADVOCATE, 112 (23 May, 1973), 16.

A report on a news story on police relations with Denver's gay community which appeared in the April 23, 1973 edition of the *Rocky Mountain News*. Summaries of arrests and entrapment tactics are presented in detail.

1463. "Gay Payoffs: Evidence Furnished in Indictments of Chicago Cops." THE ADVOCATE, 104 (31 January, 1973), 1.

A profile of the federal indictment of twenty-four Chicago police officers for tavern shakedowns and the role played by the Mattachine Midwest organization in furnishing evidence.

1464. "Report and Investigation of Enforcement of Section 647(a) of the California Penal Code by the Los Angeles Police Department." THE ADVOCATE, 105 (14 February, 1973), 2-3, 24.

A reprint of the major portion of a study of LAPD policy and practice funded by two gay organizations and carried out by two law students. Testimony of officers at various levels of the force is solicited. Available evidence is seen to substantiate homosexual complaints that they are the victims of standards "that . . . allow for discrimination at every level of law enforcement."

1465. "About This Report." THE ADVOCATE, 105 (14 February, 1973), 2.

A preface to a following report on the LAPD providing historical background to similar studies in legal research.

1466. Evans, Arthur. "How to Get the Cops Off Our Backs." THE ADVOCATE, 105 (14 February, 1973), 105.

A commentary on methods of eliminating police harassment. While the merits of the educational approach are acknowledged, political action is seen to be more effective.

1467. "Won't You Step Into My Bus? Said the Cop to the Gay." THE ADVOCATE, 107 (14 March, 1973), 1, 21.

A report on a bizarre entrapment tactic used for a brief time by the Denver police department.

1468. "Augusta Vice Squad Halts 'Coming Out' Dinner." THE ADVOCATE, 107 (14 March, 1973), 12.

An account of the cancellation of a fund-raising dance planned by an Augusta, Georgia gay and lesbian group due to vice squad police pressure on the restaurant. Background on local history of the community is provided.

1469. "Tearoom Spying Banned." THE ADVOCATE, 108 (28 March, 1973), 2, 23.

A report on a unanimous ruling by the California Supreme Court that "police officers may not observe activity in public restrooms from clandestine areas." The decision supports a 1971 appellate court ruling and 1962 rulings in the same area. Background on relevant cases is briefly summarized.

1470. "These Cops Are Gay and Proud." THE ADVOCATE, 111 (9 May, 1973), 1, 22.

An interview with two openly gay New York City auxiliary policemen serving in Brooklyn Heights. Departmental duties and lack of negative reaction by professional officers are noted.

1471. "Must Consider Entrapment, Judges Told." THE ADVOCATE, 111 (9 May, 1973), 2.

On April 11, 1973, a three-judge panel of the Los Angeles Superior Court ruled that, in each case where a defendant is charged with violation of the California "lewd conduct" statute "that the judge must instruct the jury to consider a defense of entrapment . . . that charges of homosexual conduct are easy to charge and hard to disprove and that the jury is to examine the testimony of the police officer with caution." Failure to so instruct would be held as grounds for the reversal of a conviction.

1472. "Bar Owners Tell of Paying Chicago Cops." THE ADVOCATE, 120 (12 September, 1973), 2.

A report on the trial of twenty-three Chicago police officers who face charges of extortion and perjury for demanding payments from owners of some fifty-five bars. Owners cooperating were promised freedom from raids by the vice squad.

1473. "Gotham Cops To Be Nicer." THE ADVOCATE, 120 (12 September, 1973), 3.

A report on an order issued by New York City Police Commissioner Donald F. Cauley on August 19, 1973 forbidding usage of derogatory terms for gays or other members of minority groups. Recent instances of police-gay community relations are included as perspective.

1474. "Village Crackdown Whiplashes Gays." THE ADVOCATE, 121 (26 September, 1973), 3.

Coverage of actions taken by the Tactical Police Force of the New York police department in the Greenwich Village and Sheridan Square areas. The action is seen as a response to the complaints of residents about gay bars bringing "undesirables" into the neighborhood. Victims are either harassed or arrested.

1475. "Lavender Panthers, Preventing Muggings of Homosexuals in San Francisco." TIME, 102 (8 October, 1973), 73.

A profile of the Lavender Panthers, a gay self-defense patrol established in San Francisco by Rev. Ray Broshears to counter anti-gay violence. Relations with the city police department are described. Broshear's statistics indicate a larger number of incidents than police records, attributed to the reluctance of homosexuals to report assaults to the police for fear of being charged with soliciting.

1476. Jackson, Ed. "The Wages of Hate." THE ADVOCATE, 122 (10 October, 1973), 1-2, 20.

An editorial commenting on recent beatings of gay persons by plainclothes police officers in Los Angeles. Details of two incidents are discussed. The attitude of Police Chief Ed Davis towards homosexuals are blamed for creating the atmosphere where such events can occur.

1477. "L.A. Police Chief Davis Lashes Out at Gays: Oppose Sex Law Reforms." THE ADVOCATE, 122 (10 October, 1973), 3, 21.

A partial transcription and analysis of a statement made by LAPD Chief Ed Davis on a television conference show on September 16, 1973. The topic of discussion was the proposed repeal of California adultery and sodomy laws. Contradictions in logic were noted at several points. Public responses surveyed were negative but unsurprised.

1478. "Miami Beach Police Target of Gay Suit." THE ADVOCATE, 122 (10 October, 1973), 22.

A report on the initiation of a class-action lawsuit against the Miami, Florida police department by a member of the city's gay community. The brief charges verbal abuse, deprivation of the rights to assemble peaceably and be free of unreasonable search, and seeks both injunctive and declaratory relief.

1479. "L.A. Gays Gain Police Board Ear." THE ADVOCATE, 123 (24 October, 1973), 1.

Report on a ruling by the Los Angeles police commission that persons who believe they have "fallen prey to police excesses" may be represented at hearings by a spokesperson. On October 3, 1973, such representation was made by David Glascock of the Gay Political Action Council, presenting three complaints.

1480. "Indianapolis Police Hit MCC Meet." THE ADVOCATE, 123 (24 October, 1973), 1.

On October 2, 1973, the nascent congregation of the Indianapolis chapter of the Metropolitan Community Church was raided during a meeting in a private home. Legal action has been undertaken with the assistance of the Indiana Civil Liberties Union and a news conference held to publicize the church and the police action. No charges have been preferred.

1481. "Denver Group Prepares for Battle Over Vice Laws." THE ADVOCATE, 123 (24 October, 1973), 8.

A news report on preparations for a hearing on four proposals to revise Section 8 of Denver's criminal code. The provisions deal with the areas of "disorderly conduct," public indecency, female impersonation and baths. Local political conditions attending the debate are profiled.

1482. "Denver Survey Shows Vice Cops Trap with Words." THE ADVOCATE, 123 (24 October, 1973), 8.

Results of a survey of vice arrests in the city of Denver occurring during January and March, 1973 indicating that, out of some 171 persons arrested under a city ordinance covering solicitation for lewd acts, "almost half were arrested on the basis of 'conversation only.'"

1483. "MCC Pastor is Arrested in Seattle." THE ADVOCATE, 124 (7 November, 1973), 3.

A personal account by Rev. Robert Sirico, pastor of the Seattle chapter of MCC, of his arrest and detention by city police. He was charged with jaywalking.

1484. "Police Official, 18 Other Cops Convicted in Chicago." THE ADVOCATE, 124 (7 November, 1973), 5.

On October 5, 1973, nineteen members of the Chicago police department were convicted in federal court of extortion. Some fifty-three bars were involved, fifteen of them gay. Full background on the FBI investigation is given.

1485. "S.F. Stifles Cops Who Insult Gays." THE ADVOCATE, 124 (7 November, 1973), 8.

San Francisco Chief Don Scott has issued a general order prohibiting officers from using derogatory slang against homosexuals. Originally proposed by the Pride Foundation, the text was written by Elliot Blackstone, department liaison to the gay community.

1486. "Infiltrated D.C. GAA, Says Police, FBI Spy." THE ADVOCATE, 124 (7 November, 1973), 9.

A news summary on the case of Robert E. Merritt, a self-confessed police informant assigned to report on the activities of the Washington, D.C. Gay Activists Alliance. Motivations were the monitoring of anti-war activities.

1487. "A Ride with a Patrol Cop." THE ADVOCATE, 125 (21 November, 1973), 1, 22.

A personal description by David Glascock of the Los Angeles Gay Political Action Council of his evening spent riding as observer with a member of the Hollywood vice squad.

1488. "Raids Jar Hollywood Gays." THE ADVOCATE, 130 (30 January, 1974), 1.

News coverage of raids carried out at four locations in Hollywood on January 14, 1974 by police. The objective was to establish the existence of a conspiracy to produce hardcore pornographic films. Both private residences and businesses were affected.

1489. "Hollywood Businessmen to Monitor Vice Arrests." THE ADVOCATE, 131 (13 February, 1974), 2.

On January 23, 1974, the Hollywood Businessman's Association indicated its willingness to monitor district arrests by vice squad officers. The full text of a statement sent to area news media is included. Associate officials said that popular reaction to a clean-up campaign had been seen as specifically targeted to gay businesses.

1490. "Cops Fired for Sadistic Motel Raid." THE ADVOCATE, 132 (2 February, 1974), 1.

An account of the dismissal of three members of the Albuquerque, New Mexico police force for physically abusing and threatening two homosexual men while intoxicated.

1491. "Austrian Police Bust Gay Bars, Park-Goers." THE ADVOCATE, 134 (27 March, 1974), 18.

A report of recent police actions against homosexuals in the city of Innsbruck, Austria. The change in attitude, as well as the abandonment of hope for reform in those portions of the Austrian penal code covering homosexuality is viewed as a reaction to the publicity on the Houston mass murders in 1973.

1492. "Hollywood Accord Near--Police Reveal Vice Policy." THE ADVOCATE, 136 (24 April, 1974), 2.

Following cancellation of a planned boycott of Hollywood businesses by homosexuals, Los Angeles City Attorney Burt Pines agreed to work out a policy with the city police to curb vice squad harassment actions. The full text of the order is included.

1493. "Mayor Shackles Million Dollar Vice Squad." THE ADVOCATE, 136 (24 April, 1974), 3.

A news report on massive changes within the Seattle, Washington police department occasioned by the dismissal of an officer charged with assaulting a gay man while the man was a prisoner. The position of the new chief of police is seen to be more flexible with regard to enforcement by the vice squad of consensual sex laws.

1494. "Sheriff: Thumbs Down on SB 39." THE ADVOCATE, 136 (24 April, 1974), 20.

A summary statement of the views of San Francisco Sheriff Richard Hongisto regarding California Senate Bill 39, a proposed revision of that state's criminal code. Hongisto opposes the bill due to its outdated priorities and philosophy, which he sees as repressive.

1495. "ACLU Condemns Practices, Priorities of L.A. Vice Cops." THE ADVOCATE, 137 (8 May, 1974), 2.

The full text of a resolution passed on April 16, 1974 by the Hollywood chapter of the American Civil Liberties Union "condemning police oppression of gay citizens."

1496. "Everything in Plain Sight When ACLU Watches Cops." THE ADVOCATE, 140 (19 June, 1974), 9.

Quotations from a statement by Ramona Ripton, executive director of the ACLU of Southern California, on the style of monitoring to be used in the current gay rights project which began in April, 1974. Members of the Los Angeles police force had been informed that observers would attempt to use secret tape recorders, a charge Ripton denied as being against California law.

1497. "Collecting Evidence of Police Malpractice." THE ADVOCATE, 141 (3 July, 1974), 17.

A commentary article on the California ACLU project to investigate alleged police malpractice in the Selma Avenue district of Hollywood. Two incidents are discussed in detail and police reactions to the observers are noted.

1498. "Those Police Field Reports Look Like Secret Dossiers." THE ADVOCATE, 145 (28 August, 1974), 10.

A report on the increased use of field interrogation-observation reports by members of the Boston police department. The Massachusetts Civil Liberties Union and local gay organizations charge that the mere presence of such a report in a file marks the person, should later police attention be desired. Police officials state that the reports are not meant to be used as punitive devices and promised an investigation of abuses.

1499. "Activist Coalition Formed to Fight Philly Police Abuse." THE ADVOCATE, 145 (28 August, 1974), 21.

A report on the emergence of the Coalition Against Police Abuse in Philadelphia through an agreement among twenty-four gay organizations. Its objectives are both to watchdog the police and to compile statistics and documentation on police brutality and harassment, as well as offering legal counsel to victims.

1500. "San Francisco Police Tarnish Liberal Image." THE ADVOCATE, 147 (25 September, 1974).

A report on increased police harassment of gay people in the Castro Village section of San Francisco. Efforts at correcting the situation currently being made by community leaders Rev. Ray Broshears and Harvey Milk are explored in detail.

1501. "Book Trains Cops for Bigotry." THE ADVOCATE, 16 (25 September, 1974), 16.

A commentary on the volume *Vice Control in California* used as a textbook "for students and teachers of police science and personnel of police service." The inaccurate and clearly prejudiced position of the author on many issues and homosexuality in specific is explored.

1502. "Hollywood Lewd Busts Off 48%." THE ADVOCATE, 148 (9 October, 1974), 5.

A review of statistics on lewd conduct arrests in Hollywood, California for the period June-August, 1974, which show a sharp decline. The reduction is attributed to both the monitoring policy of the ACLU and a more relaxed attitude by city attorney Burt Pines.

1503. Bjornson, Lars. "Minneapolis Gays Cite 'Queer-Bashing', Ask Protection." THE ADVOCATE, 149 (23 October, 1974), 15.

A review of the relationship between police and the gay community of Minneapolis in late 1974. Police investigation of gay complaints of violent attacks by teenage gangs is seen as half-hearted, with prosecution on minor charges increasing.

1504. Anderson, Lee. "Denver Free: Months of Legal and Political Maneuvering Pay Off as Police Chief Signs Accord to Halt Harassment." THE ADVOCATE, 150 (6 November, 1974), 3.

A report on the signing on September 19, 1974 of a written agreement between the Denver police force and the gay community formally halting harassment. Said document was the outgrowth of a sixteenth-month formal complaint on the basis of past actions filed by the Gay Coalition of Denver. Legal details are given in full.

1505. "The Killing of Emma Jones 1: Gay Pensacola Becomes a Nightmare of Corruption and Bigotry." THE ADVOCATE, 153 (18 December, 1974), 8.

The first of a series of three articles covering recent anti-homosexual activity, including harassment and arson in Pensacola, Florida. A brief summary of the history of local gay-community relations is included.

1506. "The Killing of Emma Jones 2: Who is Responsible?" THE ADVOCATE, 154 (1 January, 1975), 4, 36.

The second in a series of articles on recent anti-gay violence in Pensacola, Florida, focusing on background to the local business establishment as a framework for the events of the summer of 1974. Police action is covered.

1507. "Police Are Sued." THE ADVOCATE, 161 (9 April, 1975), 11.

A new report covering the filing of a class-action lawsuit against the Fort Worth police by Ken Cyr, director of AURA, a local gay-rights group. The suit stems from police actions at the Texas Gay Conference, held June 22, which included registration of license plate numbers of attendees and subsequent publication of same. Charges included invasion of privacy, deprivation of civil rights and continued harassment. Cyr has since been fired from his position at Texas Christian University.

1508. "Bar Shakedown Investigated." THE ADVOCATE, 162 (23 April, 1975), 12.

> A federal grand jury in Chicago is presently investigating two police lieutenants for allegedly extorting payoffs from two bar owners in return for keeping their businesses free of harassment and arrest raids.

1509. "Vice Harassment Investigated." THE ADVOCATE, 163 (7 May, 1975), 14.

> Report from Ottawa on an investigation conducted by a local organization, Gay People of Ottawa, into the recent arrest of fourteen persons charged with operating a "homosexual vice ring." One committed suicide by leaping to his death from the roof of his apartment building.

1510. Aiken, David L. "D.C. Council Vote: 'Abolish Special Department.'" THE ADVOCATE, 165 (4 June, 1975), 6.

> The District of Columbia City Council has voted to abolish the city police forces "prostitution, perversion and obscenity" division as a part of budget recommendations. The action is viewed as likely to cause controversy before the appropriate committees of the House and Senate which pass on the District's budget.

1511. Rothenburg, David. "Gay Cops." THE ADVOCATE, 172 (10 September, 1975), 23.

> A brief survey article delineating the situation of gay and lesbian members of police forces who must remain invisible to retain their professional status.

1512. Willmore, Judy. "Is It Entrapment?" THE ADVOCATE, 178 (3 December, 1975), 11.

> An essay exploring various viewpoints on the subject of entrapment. Testimony is provided by a vice squad officer and an attorney. Confusion of case law on the issue is noted.

1513. "St. Louis Police Scandal." THE ADVOCATE, 188 (21 April, 1976), 12.

> A detailed news report covering an arrangement involving payoffs from bail bond firms to members of the St. Louis police force. Increased arrests of eight persons in the city of Forest Park provided victims for the shakedown. Local political background to the events is covered.

1514. Willmore, Judy. "The Great Slave-Market Bust: A Story Only Los Angeles Could Produce." THE ADVOCATE, 189 (5 May, 1976), 13-14.

> A detailed news article covering police arrest of some forty participants in a charity "slave auction" held to raise funds for a community center. Local political repercussions are discussed as well as police actions at the event.

1515. "Homophobic Police Studies Exposed." THE ADVOCATE, 195 (28 July, 1976), 34.

> Training materials used at the Alameda County Sheriff's Academy which described homosexuals in derogatory terms and perpetuated inaccurate information and stereotypes are discussed. Examples of the curriculum are given as illustration.

1516. "Minneapolis Police Harassment Escalates." THE ADVOCATE, 200, (6 October, 1976), 13.

> Increased police harassment in Minneapolis in mid-1976 is seen as a consequence of local political conditions in the sheriff's office. Community reaction has taken the form of increased organization and legal action.

1517. "A Philadelphia Story: Police Terrorize Gay Men." THE ADVOCATE, 203 (17 November, 1976), 11-12.

> A case history of police abuse and brutality dating from 1974, originally reported as a front-page feature in the *Philadelphia Inquirer*. The officers involved were convicted of assault but harassment has continued. No disciplinary action was taken by the department.

1518. "Canadians Take to the Streets." THE ADVOCATE, 231 (28 December, 1977), 10.

> A report on a massive demonstration against police harassment of gay people which occurred in Montreal on October 22, 1977. One hundred and forty-five people were arrested by officers in attendance, some of whom were armed with submachine guns. The political effects of the event are outlined.

1519. "Police Raid *BODY POLITIC.*" THE ADVOCATE, 234 (8 February, 1978), 10.

> A description of the police raid on the Toronto gay newspaper *The BODY POLITIC* which occurred on December 30, 1977. Twelve cartons of materials were seized pursuant to their search warrant involving use of the mails for transmission of "anything obscene, indecent, immoral or scurrilous." Background on the case and subsequent legal action is provided.

1520. "Boston Cops Censored." THE ADVOCATE, 256 (13 December, 1978), 12.

> A news summary of the suspension of two members of the Boston, Massachusetts police force for verbal and physical abuse of three gay men and for filing false arrest statements. Police commissioner Jordan is on record as opposing such tactics within the city of Boston.

1521. "Houston Study Seeks Data on Antigay Bias." THE ADVOCATE, 265 (19 April, 1979), 8.

> Operation Documentation, a project of the Houston Gay Political Caucus, has requested testimony to be used before the U.S. Department of Justice Civil Rights Commission. At issue are "alleged activities of the Houston Police Department, including harassment, entrapment, raids or illegal surveillance." Contact information is provided.

1522. "Laguna Beach Police Act to Protect Gays." THE ADVOCATE, 267 (17 May, 1979), 11-12.

Foot patrols have been stepped up in predominantly gay areas of Laguna Beach, California in response to an increase in attacks on residents. Background on this problem is included.

1523. "Cops Hit Denver Bars." THE ADVOCATE, 267 (17 May, 1979), 12.

A summary news report of increased police harassment of gay establishments in Denver since March 23, 1979. These actions are believed to be linked to the upcoming municipal elections. Information on the relationship of Mayor William McNichols to the city's gay community is provided.

1524. "Gay Houstonians Rally Against Police Violence." THE ADVOCATE, 268 (31 May, 1979), 7.

On April 10, 1979, a peaceful demonstration was held at Houston City Hall to coincide with the beginning of a federal investigation into the city's police department for alleged civil rights violations. Speeches and local media coverage are noted.

1525. Linger, David William. "Dozens Are Arrested in Chicago Bar Raids." THE ADVOCATE, 270 (28 June, 1979), 10-11.

A news report on three raids on Chicago bars and clubs by plainclothes uniformed police officers. Community reaction, including that of Mayor Jane Byrne, is profiled and police conduct deplored.

1526. "Police-Gay Dialogue Initiated in Chicago." THE ADVOCATE, 272 (26 July, 1979), 7.

The Office of Professional Standards, an internal investigative arm of the Chicago Police Department, has requested witnesses to corroborate reported police violence in three recent bar raids. Mayor Jane Byrne has evinced her support of a gay rights bill presently stalled in the city council and has ordered police to give "equal treatment" to gay citizens of Chicago.

1527. Cohen, Sheri. "Houstonians Testify on Antigay Violence." THE ADVOCATE, 273 (9 August, 1979), 9-10.

On June 12, 1979, representatives of the Houston Gay Political Caucus appeared at a hearing of the U.S. Commission on Civil Rights to present documentation of over one hundred cases of abuse, unproductive correspondence between the caucus and the police department and selective enforcement of crime law. The hearings were part of a nationwide effort to ascertain the impact of police forces on civil rights. Reaction of both committee members and local politicians is explored.

1528. "Cop Paper Suggests Eugenics for Gays." THE ADVOCATE, 275 (6 September, 1979), 12.

A report on an article in *The Policeman*, the newspaper of the San Francisco Police Officers Association, suggesting genetic engineering as the solution to having openly gay officers on the force. The author states that "insisting on recruiting a certain percentage of homosexuals into the field of law enforcement is as reasonable as insisting on the same representation of diabetics, epileptics, child molesters and rapists."

1529. "Portland Police Chief Says He'll Hire Gays." THE ADVOCATE, 277 (4 October, 1979), 9.

A report on the announcement that the Portland, Oregon Police Bureau "does not discriminate on the basis of sexual orientation" and invites applications from qualified lesbian and gay candidates.

1530. "No Charges Filed Against Houston Police." THE ADVOCATE, 279 (1 November, 1979), 11.

Following hearings held in Houston by the Commission on Civil Rights, the Justice Department has announced that no charges of civil liberties violations will be filed against the city's police force. Local gay and lesbian leaders termed the announcement "premature". Details of the testimony given before the commission is briefly outlined.

1531. "Man Socks Boston with Suit for Half Million." THE ADVOCATE, 283 (27 December, 1979), 11.

One of the "library defendants" arrested as part of a plain-clothes operation at the Boston Public Library in 1978 has filed suit against the city charging entrapment. Nearly half of the one hundred persons involved have been acquitted and media attention has made the affair an embarrassment to the administration.

1532. Willenbecher, Thom. "What's Behind the Badge? Force of Bigotry or Rule of Law?" THE ADVOCATE, 291 (1 May, 1980), 13-14.

A review article on the state of police relations with the gay community with specific advice for victims of anti-gay crime as regards police procedures and methods of furthering cooperation. Cities cited as examples are San Francisco, Boston, New York and Philadelphia.

1533. "Seattle Police Create Panel on Antigay Crime." THE ADVOCATE, 307 (11 December, 1980), 12.

The problem of increasing numbers of attacks on gay persons in the Seattle area will be addressed by a task force composed of representatives of community groups and the police. Its charge will be to design a crime prevention program to eliminate the current situation.

1534. Rosen, Steven A. "Police Harassment of Homosexual Women and Men in New York City, 1960-1980." COLUMBIA HUMAN RIGHTS LAW REVIEW, 12, 2 (Fall/Winter, 1980-81), 159-190.

A detailed historical and political analysis (based on both written documentation and the oral histories of the New York City gay and lesbian community) of the events and atmosphere between that city's police force and said community for the indicated period. Harassment is defined as "active police conduct for reasons unrelated to individual or public safety, directed at persons believed by the police to be homosexual, which has the effect of annoying, impeding, embarrassing, injuring, threatening or intimidating such persons" (p. 161). Specific topics addressed include the preconditions which sparked the Stonewall Riots of 1969, the decision of the New York Court of Appeals in *People vs. Onofre* (which held the New York statute used during the 1960s as the legal basis for police harassment to be unconstitutional) and attempts by gay activists to introduce a balanced curriculum on the topic to the New York Police Academy. Fifteen cases of harassment, ranging from verbal abuse and threats to physical brutality occurring in the period 1961-1980 are offered as evidence. Rosen notes that "it is not yet clear whether the physical and political resistance to harassment by the homosexual community will prove sufficient to bring about major attitudinal changes among police officers" (p. 189).

1535. "Straight Talk in Gay Town." MACLEANS, 94 (February 23, 1981), 27-8.

A recent raid on four bathhouses by the Toronto police force which resulted in 286 arrests and substantial property damage is examined. Consequences for the city's gay community and political scene are explored.

1536. "Growing Terror of Gay Bashing." NEWSWEEK, 97 (23 March, 1981), 30.

A news article on the increase in hate crimes against homosexuals and the various strategies attempted to cope with the problem.

1537. Holley, Steve. "New Police 'Liaison' Meets With Gay Community." THE ADVOCATE, 315 (16 April, 1981), 30.

In December, 1980, Police Commander Ken Hickman was appointed liaison to the Los Angeles gay and lesbian community. This article is an interview with Hickman prior to the March 6, 1981 meeting which produced a community agenda to be presented to the police. Topics addressed included the concept of gays as a minority, police policy on lewd conduct arrests and city hiring practices.

1538. "Chicago Cadets Get Training on Gays." THE ADVOCATE, 318 (28 May, 1981), 13.

Through a joint program of the Gay Horizons Community Center and the Illinois Gay Rights Task Force, educational classes on gay and lesbian issues are being given as part of training for recruits at the Chicago Police Department Academy. Since its inception in January, 1981, more than 170 cadets have participated.

An interview with Bobbie Russell, one of the instructors, is included.

1539. "Chicago Police Say 30 Arrests Not Crackdown." THE ADVOCATE, 324 (20 August, 1981), 10-11.

Details of incidents of police attention to the Chicago gay community during the week ending July 7, 1981. Although thirty persons were detained on charges ranging from prostitution to underage drinking, police officials stated that this did not represent a general increase in anti-gay action.

1540. "Owner, Patrons Arrested in Boston Bar Raid." THE ADVOCATE, 326 (17 September, 1981), 15.

A news report on a July 26, 1981 raid on a Boston bar in which the proprietor and manager, as well as thirty patrons, were arrested. Charges have been preferred of unlicensed showing films on Sunday, keeping a "house of ill fame" and dissemination of obscene material.

1541. "Vice Activity on Rise in New Zealand." THE ADVOCATE, 327 (1 October, 1981), 8.

A news report published in *Pink Triangle*, New Zealand's gay and lesbian newspaper profiling statistics of reported cases of "indecency between males" for 1980. Assembled by the Lesbian and Gay Media Collective, a sharp increase in police activity is noted, with 69% of all reports coming from Auckland. Information on section 146 of the Crimes Act, permitting prosecution for "keeping a place of resort for homosexual acts" is also provided. The section has been applied recently in New Zealand cases.

1542. "Police Recruits Like Gay Education." THE ADVOCATE, 330 (12 November, 1981), 54.

Recruits at the Chicago Police Training Academy were asked to rate the fifty-minute orientation sessions on the gay community presented on August 17-19, 1981 by representatives of Gay Horizons and the Illinois Gay and Lesbian Task Force. More than 94% responded favorably. Sessions have included periods of open questions from the floor.

1543. "U.S. Rights Commission Urges Control of Cops." THE ADVOCATE, 332 (10 December, 1981), 11.

> A summary of the contents of a report by the U.S. Commission on Civil Rights entitled "Who Is Guarding the Guardians?" Based upon nationwide hearings, it concludes that minorities are most frequently the victims of police misconduct and that, while ten thousand complaints of police abuse are received each year by the Justice Department, only fifty to one hundred are actually prosecuted. Increased representation of minorities on police forces is called for.

1544. "Twin Cities Cops Can't Say 'Faggot', Chief Rules." THE ADVOCATE, 337 (4 March, 1982), 11.

> Police Chief Anthony Bouza of Minneapolis has issued a directive stating that homophobic, racist or sexist language use by officers will not be tolerated. Bouza's political opposition is profiled.

1545. Califia, Pat. "Ex-S.F. Gay Cop Tells of Harassment During Training." THE ADVOCATE, 338 (18 March, 1982), 14.

> An interview with former San Francisco police officer P. Thomas Cady, who has filed a complaint against the force charging poor evaluation and harassment during training, resulting in "resignation under duress." Police homophobic behavior and attitudes are vividly described.

1546. "Houston Cops Get Training on Gays." THE ADVOCATE, 339 (1 April, 1982), 15-16.

> A profile of a five-part program on the gay community scheduled to begin March 22, 1982 at the Houston Police Academy. Sections include a four-hour course for new cadets, an in-depth curriculum on aspects of the gay lifestyle, field training, courses for officers presently serving on the force and presentations by community leaders. The program was constructed over one and one-half years of negotiation between the police force and the Houston Gay Political Caucus.

1547. "Houston Police Renege on Gay Rookie Training." THE ADVOCATE, 340 (15 April, 1982), 16.

The Houston, Texas Police Academy has cancelled plans to hire gay teachers to implement a program on gay affairs for police trainees. Instructors will now be chosen from within existing staff. Excessive publicity was blamed for the failure of the proposed curriculum.

1548. "NGTF Surveys Hiring on City Police Forces." THE ADVOCATE, 344 (10 June, 1982), 11.

The National Gay Task Force has sent letters of inquiry to police chiefs in the fifty largest cities in America to determine the status of hiring openly gay and lesbian officers. The planned publication of the survey will emphasize "those cities with effective programs."

1549. "Toronto Cops Accused of Torturing Suspects." THE ADVOCATE, 344 (10 June, 1982), 13.

The police department of Toronto is under investigation for alleged abuse of gays and lesbians during questioning. A suit filed with the Ontario attorney general by the Citizens Independent Review of Police Activities group cites twenty cases of torture. Tactics are said to include racist and sexual assaults, beating handcuffed subjects and placing plastic bags over their heads. Amnesty International has stated its support for the case. Community groups are scheduled to meet with the Toronto city council to discuss the matter.

1550. "Chicago's Top Cop Issues 'Positive' Bulletin on Gays." THE ADVOCATE, 344 (10 June, 1982), 14-15.

On April 13, 1982, Chicago Police Superintendent Richard Brzczek issued a two-page training bulletin to all officers. Entitled "The Gays and the Police," the text describes the gay subculture in general terms and condemns "queer bashing." The Illinois Gay and Lesbian Task Force rated the statement as a positive step in relations. Training classes involving gay representatives will continue.

1551. "Police Gay Task Force Gets Official L.A. Status." THE ADVOCATE, 344 (10 June, 1982), 15.

The Gay and Lesbian Police Advisory Task Force of Los Angeles, formed in October, 1981, has been granted official recognition by the city police commission.

1552   Baker, Joe. "Dallas Gays Protest Treatment by Cops." THE ADVOCATE, 345 (24 June, 1982), 11.

A news report on current efforts by the Dallas Gay Alliance to eliminate harassment by police and educate the city council on gay community concerns. Political details on this issue are summarized.

1553.   "Dallas Police Make Some Concessions to Gay Demands." THE ADVOCATE, 346 (8 July, 1982), 11-12.

A summary of the contents of a letter sent to the president of the Dallas Gay Alliance by Levi Davis, assistant city manager, detailing planned steps for improving police-gay relations. This action followed protests sponsored by the DGA over police behavior in the city's Oak Lawn section. Specific provisions include regular dialogue with community leaders, limiting the use of paddy wagons and informing members of the force of the agreement.

1554.   "ACLU Lawsuit--Against S.F. Police." THE ADVOCATE, 349 (19 August, 1982), 19-20.

Profile of a lawsuit brought by the American Civil Liberties Union against the police department of San Francisco. At issue is the alleged use of a California law against obstructing the sidewalk to arrest "people who could not otherwise be punished by legal means." Statistics for the period 1981-1982 are provided.

1555.   "D.C. Police Outlaw Antigay Cop Actions." THE ADVOCATE, 351 (16 September, 1982), 13.

A revised police conduct rule has been issued by the Washington, D.C. police department barring discrimination against gays in "the enforcement of the law or the provision of police services." Comments by Capt. Gary Albrecht, police-community liaison and Chief Maurice Turner are included.

1556. "New Orleans Must Pay Damages to Gays." THE ADVOCATE, 351 (16 September, 1982), 13-14.

A report on the decision by a federal court in New Orleans against the city police department following an incident in a bar raid where the owner was handcuffed, beaten and dragged away. All patrons were searched on the charge of a lost gun.

1557. "Police-Gay Relations in L.A. Worsen." THE ADVOCATE, 354 (28 October, 1982), 12.

Summaries of four recent developments in the relationship between the Los Angeles gay community and the city police. They include homophobic remarks by Chief Daryl Gates and transfer of popular liaison officer Commander Ken Hickman to an administrative job.

1558. Hardy, Robin. "Tracking Down Police Repression." THE ADVOCATE, 354 (28 October, 1982), 44-45.

A report on the filming of the Canadian documentary *Track Two* covering the February 5, 1982 police raid on a Toronto bathhouse and subsequent political militancy within the city's gay community.

1559. "400 New Yorkers Protest Brutal Bar Raid." THE ADVOCATE, 356 (25 November, 1982), 10.

A report on a massive demonstration in the Times Square area of New York City held on October 15, 1982 protesting police abuse and tactics used in a September 29th bar raid. Photographs of the rally are included.

1560. "San Jose Committee Fights 'Entrapment' in Adult Bookstore Arrests." THE ADVOCATE, 359 (6 January, 1983), 16, 63.

A news report covering the formation of the Committee for Fair Police Practices in San Jose, California as a consequence of increased police entrapment tactics in that city's adult book stores. Victims are being charged under section 647a of the California Code and forced to register as sex offenders. A defense fund has been created and possibilities of a class-action suit explored. An interview with David Treadwell, one of the founders of the committee, completes the article.

1561. "L.A. Activists Welcome First Breakthrough in Gay-Police Relations." THE ADVOCATE, 363 (17 January, 1983), 13.

Stephen Yslas, president of the Los Angeles police commission, has drafted statements in reply to a five-point request submitted to the commission by the Gay and Lesbian Police Advisory Task Force in September, 1982. These were unanimously adopted at a February 1, 1983 meeting, with several exceptions. Those endorsed were the placement of police recruiting literature in gay and lesbian publications and dispatch of police recruiting vans to gay social events. Other requests not addressed called for the repetition of a non-discriminatory code of hiring at roll calls and liaison with local divisions.

1562. "British Gays Worry About Bill to Expand Police Powers." THE ADVOCATE, 364 (31 March, 1983), 10.

A profile of a bill introduced into Parliament by the Conservative party vastly expanding the power and authorities of the British police, with particular attention to the areas of search, arrest and detention. The Campaign for Homosexual Equality and other groups representing minorities have mounted opposition to the legislation and probable passage of the bill. Of special concern to gays is a clause enabling police officers to arrest persons for actions which could "affront the public decency."

1563. Young, Perry Deane. "Officer Almstead: On the Force and Openly Gay." THE ADVOCATE, 370 (23 June, 1983), 30-35.

An historic profile and interview with Robert Almstead, an openly gay member of the police force of Washington, D.C. Prejudices encountered and coping strategies are discussed.

1564. "Capitol Report." THE ADVOCATE, 385 (10 January, 1984), 14-15.

On November 28, 1983, Kevin Berrill, director of the National Gay and Lesbian Task Force's Violence Project

and James Creedle of Black and White Men together
testified before a congressional subcommittee chaired
by Rep. John Conyers on police harassment of gay
people. Five recommendations were made involving
regular liaison and police education.

1565. "New Briefs." THE ADVOCATE, 388 (21 February, 1984), 11.

A news story filed from Cincinnati, Ohio on the formation of a special police task force to deal with sex in
public washrooms. One of the forty-five persons
arrested in a recent sweep was an assistant city prosecutor. A brief summary of relations between the
Cincinnati gay community and the police is provided as
background.

1566. Heim, Chris. "Chicago Police Chief Names Liaison to Gay
Community." THE ADVOCATE, 389 (6 March, 1984), 13, 17.

On January 27, 1984, a meeting was held in Chicago
between Al Wardell, co-chair of the Illinois Gay and
Lesbian Task Force, and superintendent of police Fred
Rice. Topics addressed included AIDS education of
officers and recruits, job-protection policy, gay and
lesbian officers and the appointment of a liaison
between the police and the Chicago gay community. Rice
has appointed his administrative assistant, Raymond
Risley, to the latter post.

1567. "ACLU Suit Seeks Data About FBI Spying on Gays Since
1950." THE ADVOCATE, 389 (6 March, 1984), 16.

A news report on the filing of a suit under the provisions of the Freedom of Information Act by Activist Dan
Siminowski and the ACLU requesting the release of any
documentation relating to domestic surveillance of gay
and lesbian groups and organizations by the FBI. Prior
research on this issue is summarized.

1568. Maves, Carl. "San Francisco Police Officer Paul Seidler
Bridges An Historically Wide Gap." THE ADVOCATE, 396 (12
June, 1984), 23-25.

A lengthy interview with Paul Seidler, the gay community liaison officer in the community relations unit of
the San Francisco Police Department. Reactions of both

individuals to his initiatives within the city and gay community are discussed, with the bulk of the evidence favorable.

1569. "San Diego, Calif. Grand Jury Supports Sheriff's Ban Against Gay Deputies." THE ADVOCATE, 397 (26 June, 1984), 28.

A four-page interim report by the San Diego County Grand Jury has supported the policy of the city sheriff not to hire gay deputies. Full particulars of the political situation this issue has occasioned in San Diego are provided, including an interview with Mayor Roger Hedgecock.

1570. "Police Group Rejects Gay Cops, Loses Official City Recognition." THE ADVOCATE, 400 (7 August, 1984), 19.

New York City's Police Brotherhood-In-Action, a coalition of eighteen police organizations created in 1971 to deal with ethnic and racial stresses within the force, has voted to exclude the Gay Officers Action League from membership. The city police commissioner stated that departmental recognition would be withdrawn from the coalition unless the G.O.A.L. were admitted, as the department would then be in violation of an executive order prohibiting city agencies from discriminating against gay people.

1571. "Kiss Brings Hassle for S.F. Policemen." THE ADVOCATE, 402 (4 September, 1984), 10.

A news report on a complaint filed against openly gay officer Paul Seidler by other members of the San Francisco police department for embracing and kissing a participant in that city's 1984 Gay Pride Parade.

1572. Freiberg, Peter. "Summer Protest Stops Antigay Harassment by Police in Downtown Area of Indianapolis." THE ADVOCATE, 405 (16 October, 1984), 16.

Following weekly protests capped by a mass rally in the heart of Indianapolis, Mayor William Hudnet ordered the city's police chief to meet with representatives of Justice, the statewide umbrella group for twenty-five gay and lesbian organizations. Protests were begun against perceived harassment by police in a traffic circle of central Indianapolis.

1573. Cori, Joan. "FBI Releases 6,000 Pages of Gay Files." THE ADVOCATE, 406 (30 October, 1984), 26.

In response to a lawsuit filed in federal district court in Los Angeles in October, 1983 by the American Civil Liberties Union of Southern California, the FBI has released some six thousand pages of documents revealing substantial surveillance of gay and lesbian groups in San Francisco, Los Angeles, San Diego, Denver, Chicago, Boston, New Haven and Washington, D.C. beginning in the 1950s. Contents include reprints of literature and pamphlets as well as internal FBI memoranda.

1574. "N.Y. Police Reach Out to Gay Recruits." THE ADVOCATE, 407 (13 November, 1984), 13.

A recruitment meeting was held in New York City on September 22, 1984 under the aegis of the Gay Officers Action League to assist the New York Police Department in its efforts to increase the number of minority officers. Present membership in the G.O.A.L. stands at seventy-four.

1575. Balter, Michael. "Decades of FBI Surveillance Unveiled." THE ADVOCATE, 409/410 (11 December, 1984), 25-26.

A lengthy news analysis of the mass of FBI documentation illustrating domestic surveillance of gay and lesbian groups begun in 1953 by J. Edgar Hoover and recently released to activist Dan Siminowski with the assistance of the American Civil Liberties Union under the Freedom of Information Act.

1576. Walter, Dave. "Police Raid Atlanta Baths." THE ADVOCATE, 416 (19 March, 1985), 8-9.

A news report on recent arrests by Metro Atlanta police at two bathhouses three days after the filing of civil suits citing both establishments "for spreading AIDS and being public nuisances." Background on the police-gay community relationship in Atlanta is provided, as

412

are profiles of current litigation on the bathhouse issue nationwide.

1577. Freiberg, Peter. "Gays and Police: Old Problems, New Hope." THE ADVOCATE, 422 (11 June, 1985), 10-11, 19.

A survey article on the state of relations between police forces and local gay communities in the United States as they existed in 1985. Cities profiled are Chicago, Philadelphia, Oklahoma City, Portland, Maine, Indianapolis, Dallas, New York City, New Orleans, Seattle and San Francisco. Topics addressed include strategies for effective recruit education on gay subjects and coming out professionally.

1578. "NYC Police Bias Unit Expanded." THE ADVOCATE, 430 (1 October, 1985), 15.

Following negotiation with corporate counsel for the New York City Commission on Human Rights, the New York Police Department on July 30, 1985 agreed to expand the jurisdiction of its special Bias Incident Investigative Unit to include "crimes motivated by antigay prejudice." Statistics will now be kept on such incidents by the twelve-member unit. The move was taken because failure to do so would have been in violation of Mayor Koch's executive order banning discrimination against gays by city agencies.

1579. Bernstein, Mark. "Arizona Sodomy Law Challenged by Gay Cop." THE ADVOCATE, 432 (29 October, 1985), 17.

A profile of a lawsuit filed in federal court questioning the constitutionality of an Arizona law classifying homosexual acts as a class 3 misdemeanor by narcotics officer Steve Horn. Despite a perfect record in his term of service for the city of Mesa, Horn was fired in December, 1980 following revelation of his homosexuality. Litigation has been under way at the state level since 1981, with an appellate court upholding Horn's dismissal in July, 1984.

1580. Freiberg, Peter. "Policing Rest-Stop Sex: Invasion of Privacy Or Necessary Control?" THE ADVOCATE, 449 (24 June, 1986), 10-11, 22-23.

On March 18, 1986, forty-two men were arrested in the Lansing, Michigan area on the basis of evidence via police videotaping and recording of license plate numbers at a rest stop near that city. Legal action by the defense seeks to suppress this evidence on constitutional grounds of violation of privacy and the inapplicability of Michigan's "gross indecency" statute. The position of civil liberties groups nationwide on such electronic surveillance is surveyed.

1581.   "Canadian Official Says He Would Ban Gay Police." THE ADVOCATE, 455 (19 September, 1986), 16.

Nova Scotia Attorney General Ron Giffin has stated that his province would "opt out" of the protections extended to gay persons by Canada's new constitution rather than let homosexuals serve as police officers. Condemnation of this position has been almost universal, including the premier of Nova Scotia, and calls for Giffin to resign are mounting. Opponents state that he can no longer be credibly seen as a defender of minority rights for any minority group in Canada.

1582.   "News Briefs--Farmingdale, N.Y." THE ADVOCATE, 458 (28 October, 1986), 27.

A news report on the decision by Suffolk County Police Commissioner DeWitt Treder to begin discussions with representatives of the Gay and Lesbian Action Coalition of Long Island. Reports of harassment have been filed by several local gay bars.

1583.   "New Briefs--Georgia." THE ADVOCATE, 461 (9 December, 1986), 26.

On October 28, 1986, the board of trustees of the Fraternal Order of Police of Georgia unanimously approved a resolution calling upon that state's legislators "to pass laws barring the hiring of gays by police departments." A similar resolution was passed in September, 1986 by Georgia's largest organization of law enforcement officials. Both actions are seen as reactions to an August 31 announcement by the Atlanta police chief that openly gay officers would be accepted on the force.

Index

Alberts, Rev. William - 971, 975, 977, 981
Alexander Hamilton Veterans Organization - 385
Alioto, Joseph - 495, 1409, 1452
All in the Family - 774
Almstead, Robert - 1563
American Armed Forces Association - 254
American Association for the Advancement of Science - 729
American Baptist Convention - 907
American Booksellers Association - 804, 809
American Broadcasting Company - 433
American Civil Liberties Union - 55, 109, 153, 194, 197, 205,
    219, 222, 240, 243, 259, 293, 319, 334-35, 353, 358, 372,
    387, 409, 418, 456, 459, 478, 488, 490, 518, 541, 545, 552,
    564, 613, 658, 715, 826, 837, 846, 1276, 1321, 1329, 1347,
    1440, 1456, 1461, 1495, 1496-98, 1502, 1554, 1567, 1573,
    1575
American Federation of Teachers - 685
American Friends Service Committee - 680, 1129, 1267
American Gay Atheists - 1253
American Jewish Congress - 1179
American Legion - 385
American Library Association - 449, 470, 482, 523, 551, 572, 782,
    814, 846
American Medical Association - 1317
American Newspaper Guild - 580
American Nurses Association - 566
American Orthodox Church - 916, 1223
American Pentecostal Movement - 1194
American Psychological Association - 89, 251, 589
Amnesty International - 571
Anaya, Gov. Tony - 756
Anderson, Betty - 361
Anglican Church (see Church of England)
Anonymous v. Macy - 426
Antigay Violence - 1476, 1503, 1506, 1522, 1531, 1533, 1536,
    1550, 1564, 1572, 1578
Antiochian Orthodox Church - 1015
Archives - 838
Arizona - 28, 112, 715, 718, 736, 786, 789, 1182, 1579
Arizona State University - 786, 789
Arrests (see also Mass Arrests) - 152, 1276-77, 1284-87, 1292-93,
    1295, 1305-06, 1309, 1315, 1360-63, 1365, 1370-72, 1421,
    1459, 1482-83, 1489, 1535, 1539, 1562
Ashland, Oregon - 810
Asner, Edward - 335
Aspin, Rep. Les - 216
Assembly of the Disciples of Christ - 1110
Association of Chicago Priests - 598
Atheism - 1165, 1253

Scott, Bruce - 408, 412

Scott v. Macy (1965) - 450

Seattle, Washington - 49-50, 64, 69, 79, 481, 534, 540, 591, 630, 634, 676, 1239, 1258, 1382, 1461, 1483, 1493, 1533, 1577

Security Clearances - 154, 161, 173, 327, 340, 354, 361, 402, 413, 420, 427, 431, 435, 474, 487, 496, 509, 520, 538, 548, 552, 568, 573, 595, 617, 683, 740

Security Risks - 148, 150, 402, 417

Seidler, Paul - 1568, 1571

Selective Service - 175, 183, 186-87, 234

Self Defense Groups - 1475

Seminaries - 883, 1142, 1145, 1159

Seventh Day Adventists - 1182

"Sex Offender" Law and Legislation - 403, 1303, 1362, 1369, 1378, 1464, 1477, 1481, 1493-94, 1560, 1580

The Sexual Outlaw - 797

Shanley, Fr. Paul - 1000, 1109

Shapp, Gov. Milton J. - 602, 605, 624, 626

Sherwood, Zalmon - 1254, 1271

Shilts, Randy - 75, 79, 1086, 1126

Siefkes, Rev. Jim - 1006

Silverstein, Michael - 465

Sindt, Rev. David - 9-10, 953, 1042, 1069

Singer v. United States Civil Service Commission (1976) — 629, 634, 649, 666, 681

Singer, John - 629, 634, 649, 670, 681

Single Parents - 24

Sirico, Rev. Robert - 534, 1483

Slater, Don - 158, 175

Smith v. Liberty Mutual Insurance Co. - 638

Smith, Arlene - 54

So Many Voices - 1054

Socarides, Dr. Charles - 1317

Social Responsibilities Round Table (American Library Association) - 782

Social Work - 6, 9-10, 530

Society for Individual Rights - 188, 198, 437, 466, 614, 1335, 1337, 1339, 1390, 1399, 1446

Society for Individual Rights and Heckerson v. Hampton (1973) - 614

Society of Anubis - 1344, 1349, 1357

Society of the Divine Savior - 987, 1001

Society of Friends - 861-63, 919, 925, 952, 990, 993, 1064, 1094, 1129, 1191

Sociology - 176, 190, 992, 1413, 1420, 1501

Sode, Marie - 299

Sons - 86, 96-97, 99, 109, 113, 121, 123, 130

Southern Baptist Church - 1248

Soviet Union - 569, 571, 798, 852, 854

Spaht, Jane A. - 1167